GLOBALISATION

Historical Materialism Book Series

More than ten years after the collapse of the Berlin Wall and the disappearance of Marxism as a (supposed) state ideology, a need for a serious and long-term Marxist book publishing program has risen. Subjected to the whims of fashion, most contemporary publishers have abandoned any of the systematic production of Marxist theoretical work that they may have indulged in during the 1970s and early 1980s. The Historical Materialism book series addresses this great gap with original monographs, translated texts and reprints of "classics."

Haymarket Books is proud to be working with Brill Academic Publishers (http://www.brill.nl) and the journal *Historical Materialism* to republish the Historical Materialism book series in paperback editions. Current series titles include:

Alasdair MacIntyre's Engagement with Marxism: Selected Writings 1953–1974
Edited by Paul Blackledge and Neil Davidson

Althusser: The Detour of Theory, Gregory Elliott

Between Equal Rights: A Marxist Theory of International Law, China Miéville

The Capitalist Cycle, Pavel V. Maksakovsky, Translated with introduction and commentary by Richard B. Day

The Clash of Globalisations: Neo-Liberalism, the Third Way, and Anti-globalisation, Ray Kiely

Critical Companion to Contemporary Marxism, Edited by Jacques Bidet and Stathis Kouvelakis

Criticism of Heaven: On Marxism and Theology, Roland Boer

Exploring Marx's Capital: Philosophical, Economic, and Political Dimensions, Jacques Bidet

Following Marx: Method, Critique, and Crisis, Michael Lebowitz

The German Revolution: 1917–1923, Pierre Broué

Globalisation: A Systematic Marxian Account, Tony Smith

Impersonal Power: History and Theory of the Bourgeois State,
Heide Gerstenberger, translated by David Fernbach

Lenin Rediscovered: What Is to Be Done? In Context, Lars T. Lih

Making History: Agency, Structure, and Change in Social Theory, Alex Callinicos

Marxism and Ecological Economics: Toward a Red and Green Political Economy, Paul Burkett

A Marxist Philosophy of Language, Jean-Jacques Lecercle and Gregory Elliott

The Theory of Revolution in the Young Marx, Michael Löwy

Utopia Ltd.: Ideologies of Social Dreaming in England 1870–1900, Matthew Beaumont

Western Marxism and the Soviet Union: A Survey of Critical Theories and Debates Since 1917
Marcel van der Linden

GLOBALISATION
A SYSTEMATIC MARXIAN ACCOUNT

TONY SMITH

Haymarket Books
Chicago, Illinois

First published in 2005 by Brill Academic Publishers, The Netherlands
© 2006 Koninklijke Brill NV, Leiden, The Netherlands

Published in paperback in 2009 by
Haymarket Books
P.O. Box 180165
Chicago, IL 60618
773-583-7884
www.haymarketbooks.org
ISBN: 978-1-608460-23-6

Trade distribution:
In the U.S., Consortium Book Sales, www.cbsd.com
In the UK, Turnaround Publisher Services, www.turnaround-psl.com
In Australia, Palgrave Macmillan, www.palgravemacmillan.com.au
In all other countries, Publishers Group Worldwide, www.pgw.com

Cover design by Ragina Johnson. Cover image by Natalia Goncharova, 1913.

This book was published with the generous support of
the Wallace Global Fund and the Lannan Foundation.

Library of Congress Cataloging-in-Publication Data is available.

Contents

Acknowledgements and Dedication

Over the last decade and a half it has been my good fortune to participate in the annual International Symposium on Marxian Theory, founded by Fred Moseley. I would like to thank him and the other participants, Chris Arthur, Riccardo Bellofiore, Martha Campbell, Mino Carchedi, Roberto Fineschi, Mike Lebowitz, Paul Mattick, Jr., Patrick Murray, Geert Reuten, and Nicky Taylor. I have learned an immense amount from each. I would also like to thank Sebastian Budgen, Bertell Ollman, Robert Went, and my colleagues at Iowa State for the encouragement and feedback they have provided on this project.

Chapter 4 is a revised version of 'Globalisation and Capitalist Property Relations: A Critical Assessment of Held's Cosmopolitan Theory', *Historical Materialism*, 11, 2, 2003: 3–35.

Section 6 of Chapter 5 incorporates material from 'Surplus Profits from Innovation: A Missing Level in Volume III?', in *The Culmination of* Capital: *Essays on Volume III*, Martha Campbell and Geert Reuten (eds.), New York: Palgrave/Macmillan, 2002: 67–94.

Material from 'Systematic and Historical Dialectics: Towards a Marxian Theory of Globalization', *New Dialectics and Political Economy*, Rob Albritton and John Simoulidis (eds.), New York: Palgrave/Macmillan, 2003: 24–41 has been included in Chapter 6.

Portions of Chapter 7 are based on 'Towards a Marxian Theory of World Money', *Marx's Theory of Money: Modern Appraisals*, Fred Moseley (ed.), New York: Palgrave/Macmillan, 2005: 222–33.

This book is dedicated to my mother, Alice McBurney Smith, and to Rebecca, Bridgit, and Conor, all of whom are reminders that the story begun in the last paragraph of Part Seven, *Capital*, Volume I has yet to conclude.[1]

---

[1] Marx 1976, p. 870.

Introduction

'Globalisation' is a deeply contested concept. Is it a mythical term, like 'unicorn' or 'devil', circulating in social discourse with material effects without referring to anything at all? Does it refer to the last few decades of human history? Should it be dated from the world plunder and trade that arose in the sixteenth century? Or perhaps from the first migration of *homo sapiens* from Africa? What benefits, if any, does it bring? To whom, and at what costs? What alternative forms might it take?

These sorts of questions can be explored in a variety of ways within a vast number of theoretical frameworks.[1] In any particular investigation, some topics must come to the foreground while others recede. The more concrete and specific the study, the less terrain can be covered; the more comprehensive the overview, the less room for details. There is no one correct way to make such trade-offs. The proper level of abstraction in a particular case depends upon the author, the projected audience, and the theoretical and practical interests motivating the inquiry.[2]

In social philosophy, my own area of specialisation, two main questions dominate discussion. What normative principles should be employed when

---

[1] The most comprehensive survey of the various debates is Held et al. 1999.
[2] The various levels of generality relevant to social theory are discussed in Ollman 1993.

assessing social institutions and practices? And what set of institutions and practices best embodies these principles? Discussion of the former takes place on a relatively high level of abstraction, while the latter ranges from concrete assessments of particular social practices (such as Nike's wage policies in overseas plants, or Nestle's marketing strategies in Africa) to evaluations of abstract models of entire socio-political orders. The present work is devoted primarily to the last project.

In the history of social theory, there is a long and distinguished tradition of inquiry into models of socio-political frameworks. In Aristotle's *Politics* the dominant political systems of his day (democracy, oligarchy, aristocracy, monarchy) were contrasted and evaluated. Two thousand years later, the German philosopher G.W.F. Hegel described and defended what he took to be the essential institutional forms of the modern epoch. The main line of argument in *Capital* falls on a similar level of abstraction, although Marx's masterwork incorporates a vast amount of concrete empirical material as well. The most discussed work of twentieth century social philosophy, John Rawls's *A Theory of Justice*, provides a more recent example. Rawls's chief object of investigation is the 'basic structure' of a society, defined as 'the way in which the major social institutions distribute fundamental rights and duties and determine the division of advantages from social cooperation'.[3]

Aristotle, Hegel, Marx and Rawls are all less concerned with the concrete details of particular social formations than with the general properties distinguishing one sort of institutional framework from another. In Aristotle's view, for example, it is possible to construct a general model of oligarchy, and to derive a set of structural tendencies that necessarily arise from its essential features. This derivation does not rule out social agency. Individuals and groups living in oligarchies have the capacity to modify the operation of these tendencies, and even replace that institutional order entirely. Aristotle does not deny that the concrete historical paths of different oligarchical city-states can diverge wildly, due to countless contingencies. But not all possibilities are equally likely in a given social order. The essential determinations of a social framework make some patterns of events far more probable than others. To put the point in the form of a slogan: Social forms matter![4]

---

[3] Rawls 1971, p. 7.
[4] The relationship between structure and agency is an immensely complicated and

The present work operates on a similar level of generality. The dominant social forms of our own historical epoch include the family, a predominantly capitalist organisation of production and distribution, the state, interstate relations, and the so-called 'regime of global governance'. What is the precise nature of these forms? How do they fit together? What structural tendencies do they generate? Different positions in the globalisation debate comprehend these matters in different ways. These views can be articulated in alternative models of globalisation.

The first major aim of the present work is to present an overview of the most significant positions in the globalisation debate, expressed in what I shall term the 'social-state', 'neoliberal', 'catalytic-state', 'democratic-cosmopolitan', and 'Marxian' models of globalisation.[5] Each of these models has been asserted to capture the essential features of the contemporary global order.[6] The second central goal of this book is to provide a theoretical and practical assessment of these five competing positions. Concrete empirical matters will be introduced insofar as they contribute to constructing, comparing, and evaluating these frameworks.

Critical assessments are always based on some set of standards. What standards ought to be employed here? Fortunately, there is considerable

---

contentious issue. The term 'tendency' refers to a middle ground between the complete structural determination of agents' behaviour and a complete indeterminacy of actions. Every institutional framework necessarily encourages certain courses of action rather than others. But no institutional framework eliminates the 'political moment' in which social agents modify the structures within which their activity occurs and takes shape. This complex dynamic is explored in Bensaïd 2002. The category 'tendency' will be discussed in more detail in Chapter 6.

[5] These are, of course, ideal types. No institutional framework of the past or present has ever embodied any of these models in anything like a pure form. Similarly, most theorists eclectically combine elements from different frameworks at various points in their writings.

[6] The term 'contemporary' is extremely ambiguous. For defenders of the social state, it refers to the post-World-War-Two era of the welfare state, a period which in their view has not yet ended, despite rhetoric of neoliberals to the contrary. For proponents of neoliberalism, the catalytic state, and democratic cosmopolitanism, the contemporary 'globalisation age' began with the rise of Eurodollar markets and the end of the Bretton Woods agreements in the 1970s. From Marx's perspective, our age continues to be the epoch of capitalism, which has operated on the level of the world market for centuries. From this point of view, 'globalisation' is not a recent development, whatever unique features it may take today (see Clarke 2001). This ambiguity does not need to be resolved at this point.

agreement in the relevant literature regarding the proper criteria for theoretical assessments. All of the theorists considered in this work implicitly or explicitly agree that one position can be deemed theoretically superior to another if it possesses greater comprehensiveness or empirical relevance. In other sorts of enquiry, it may be completely legitimate to investigate closely this or that feature of the family, the economy, the state, interstate relations, or international organisations, while abstracting from other dimensions of the social order. But, if one wishes to examine the 'basic structure' of society adequately, one must do so in a comprehensive fashion. Further, an acceptable model of globalisation must be broadly consistent with relevant empirical data, however complex and mediated the relationship between the model and that data might be.

There is also a general consensus that any acceptable model of globalisation must be feasible; it must tend to function over time in a reasonably efficient manner. Needless to say, 'reasonably efficient' is more than a bit vague. Here, as elsewhere, the devil is in the details. To work out these details, we must first make explicit the general structural tendencies implicit in a given model, that is, the patterns of events that necessarily tend to arise, given its essential features. We can then ask whether the operation of these tendencies would lead to a reasonably stable reproduction of the model over time. Here, too, the example of Aristotle can be invoked. The long-term stability of various constitutional forms is a crucial factor in his comparative assessment of these forms.

Assessments of competing models also include a normative component, and here too standards must be selected. Investigating the strengths and weaknesses of competing normative standards adequately would require countless volumes. To make things more manageable, from the start I shall simply rule out two candidates. Theorists in the 'realist' school of international relations hold that a global order should be evaluated according to the extent to which it enables the interests of a particular nation – their nation – to flourish. Others hold that institutional orders and sets of social practices are to be evaluated according to the extent to which they are compatible with the (allegedly) traditional modes of life of a given culture. Nationalism and traditionalism continue to have many adherents, and writers accepting these principles have made significant contributions to debates about globalisation. But these authors do not provide reasons for anyone outside the given nationalist or traditionalist communities to accept their judgments, apart from the dogmatic assertion that this is simply how things are and should be.[7]

In very general terms, proponents of all of the positions examined in the present work agree that a model of globalisation is normatively attractive if and only if it necessarily tends to function such that the interests of particular individuals and groups are reconciled with the interests of other individuals and groups, including those from different nations and traditions. This agreement is not insignificant. But it does not provide a determinate normative principle (or set of principles) to add to the criteria of comprehensiveness, consistency, empirical richness, and feasibility/efficiency. The assertion that the interests of individuals and groups within the global order ought to be reconciled is ridiculously vague, and disputes regarding how to unpack this idea are bitter and apparently irresolvable. Leading adherents of the social-state, neoliberal, catalytic-state, democratic-cosmopolitan, and Marxian theories of globalisation have quite different notions of the sorts of interests and rights that can be legitimately claimed by groups and individuals. There are also profound disagreements regarding the conception of the general social good, and its relationship to the good of particular individuals and groups. Some theorists deny that the notion of 'the general social good' is even meaningful. Given these disagreements, it is hardly surprising that normative assessments of institutions and social practices diverge so wildly.

One way to proceed at this point – the most familiar way – would be to select one or another set of normative principles, argue for it as cogently and vehemently as possible, and then employ it in assessments of competing models of globalisation. As familiar as it is, however, there is something vaguely unsatisfying about this method. What if the selection of principles ultimately rested on a dogmatic prejudice? If a different set of principles had been selected, would not a quite different set of conclusions likely follow? And is it not all too easy to criticise positions from an external standpoint, that is, from the perspective defined by a set of standards different from those accepted by the position's leading defenders?

---

[7] A philosophically sophisticated critique of realism is found in Buchanan 2004, 29–38. See also Held 2004, pp. 146–7.

These sorts of questions have led many to regard normative assessments as merely rhetorical exercises, persuasive or not depending on the skills of the assessor and the receptivity of the audience. Normative social theory would then be counted as one of the minor branches of marketing. In my view, accepting this perspective would be more than vaguely unsatisfying. If a promising alternative can be found, it should be embraced. There is, I believe, a more promising methodological framework: *dialectical social theory.*[8] This approach is not usually taken in discussions of globalisation, and so a few remarks on the different sorts of dialectical social theories and their relevance to the present study are in order.

The goal of *historical dialectics* is to rationally reconstruct of a pattern of development underlying the contingent twists and turns of empirical history. Hegel's lectures on the philosophy of history, tracing an alleged sequence from the Oriental World, through the Greek and Roman Worlds, to the Modern World, provides one example.[9] Marxian theories in which modes of production rise and fall in a non-arbitrary order provide others.[10] Habermas's theory of social evolution, based on a supposed logic of development of cognitive and moral-practical structures of consciousness, also counts as an example of historical dialectics.[11]

When we ask whether globalisation refers to some new stage in the historical evolution of capitalism, or in human history as a whole, we are investigating the dialectics of history, whether we choose to use that term or not. If we enquire whether the present stage of development of global capitalism points beyond itself to a new historical epoch, this too is a question of historical dialectics. Insofar as the present study is concerned with such questions, it illustrates this first type of dialectical social theory.

The standard objection to historical dialectics is that it assumes a determinist and teleological view of history. Human agency appears to become all but

---

[8] While dialectical theorising goes back at least as far as Ancient Greece, it is most associated today with Hegel and those influenced by him. I believe that Marx was quite correct to insist that there is a 'rational core' to Hegel's admittedly idiosyncratic and confusing dialectical method. I have attempted to explicate this core elsewhere, and shall not repeat those discussions in detail here. See Smith 1990, 1993, 1999, 2000b, 2003a.
[9] Hegel 1956.
[10] See Levine and Wright 1980.
[11] Habermas 1979.

irrelevant, as one historical stage inexorably gives way to the next.[12] Joseph McCarney has argued persuasively that this is a caricature of Hegel's position, while Daniel Bensaïd has established that, for Marx, history is an open-ended process in which human agency is the absolutely crucial factor.[13] Habermas, too, has vehemently denied that standard objections to teleological theories of history apply to his account of social evolution.[14] There is no need to pursue these controversies here. The historical-dialectical questions posed in the present work will be formulated in ways that do not call into question the contingency and path dependency of history, or the transformative power of human agency. Even more importantly, the ordering of positions in the globalisation debate that makes up the heart of this work is not a historical ordering. The type of dialectics of main concern here is *systematic dialectics*.

Two distinct forms of systematic dialectics can be distinguished in social theory. The first takes a particular historical epoch as given, and attempts to reconstruct in thought its essential determinations in a systematic fashion, beginning with its most abstract and simple social forms, and then proceeding step-by-step to ever-more concrete and complex categories.[15] Hegel's *Philosophy of Right* is a classic instance of this sort of theory. The categories in the systematic progression making up this book are historically specific in that they are meant to refer to the essential social forms of modernity.[16] But the ordering of these categories is *not* historical; early categories did not necessarily appear first in history, and later categories do not necessarily map more recent developments.[17] While the three volumes of *Capital* include numerous extended examinations of historical processes, systematic dialectics provides the unifying thread to Marx's *magnum opus* as well. His goal is the reconstruction in thought

---

[12] Popper 1950.
[13] McCarney 2000; Bensaïd 2002.
[14] Habermas 1979.
[15] The distinction between historical dialectics and this form of systematic dialectics is examined at length in the works cited in footnote 8. See also Arthur 1997, and Reuten and Williams 1989. The relationship between systematic and historical dialectics is discussed further in Chapter 6 below.
[16] 'Whatever happens, every individual is a child of his time; so philosophy too is its own time apprehended in thoughts'. Hegel 1967, p. 11.
[17] 'What we acquire . . . is a series of thoughts and another series of existent shapes of experience; to which I may add that the time order in which the latter actually appear is other than the logical order'. Hegel 1967, p. 233.

of a given totality, the capitalist mode of production, beginning with its most abstract and simple determinations ('the commodity-form', 'the money-form') and proceeding step-by-step to ever-more complex and concrete social forms (such as 'banking capital' and 'ground rent'). Marx, like Hegel, insisted that the systematic ordering of these forms must follow a distinct path from the order in which they appeared in history.[18]

Most of the authors discussed in the following chapters do not have the least interest in systematic dialectics (or any other type of dialectical thinking, for that matter). Nonetheless, they all claim to comprehend the contemporary global system in a comprehensive and coherent fashion. They all also attempt to articulate the essential relationships holding among the defining institutions and social practices of this system (for example, the relationship between the state and the world market). These considerations suggest that the various positions in the globalisation debate could be presented as instances of this first sort of systematic dialectics without significant distortion. We would simply need to present the social forms considered in a particular model of globalisation in a specific order, moving from the simplest and most abstract level of determinations to progressively more complex and concrete levels. I shall adopt this method of presentation here, taking Hegel's *Philosophy of Right* as a rough template.

The second sort of systematic dialectics takes as its theoretical goal the systematic ordering of a *plurality* of distinct theoretical positions, as opposed to the ordering of different social forms within a *single* framework. The goal here is to develop a rational reconstruction in which less adequate frameworks give way to progressively more adequate ones. This progression may or may not echo the historical sequence in which they arose. The paradigmatic instance of this sort of dialectical theory is Hegel's *Phenomenology of Spirit*. Portions of Marx's *Grundrisse, Theories of Surplus Value*, and *Capital* illustrate this approach as well.

In Part One of this work, I shall trace a systematic progression from the social-state model of globalisation, through the neoliberal and catalytic-state models, to the democratic-cosmopolitan framework. I shall show that

---

[18] As Marx wrote in the *Grundrisse*, 'It would be unfeasible and wrong to let the economic categories follow one another in the same sequence as that in which they were historically decisive'. Marx 1973, p. 107.

each model in this progression necessarily tends to function in a manner contradicting essential claims made by its leading advocates (such as John Rawls, Friedrich Hayek, John Gray, and David Held respectively). In Hegelian jargon, an 'immanent contradiction' justifies a 'determinate negation'.[19] The contradiction in a given position provides a theoretical warrant for moving to a new model, in which the implicit shortcoming besetting the previous framework is explicitly addressed.

The immanent contradictions afflicting the democratic-cosmopolitan position justify a transition to a Marxian model of capitalist globalisation, where the irresolvable contradictions and social antagonisms of the contemporary global order are explicitly recognised. The first three chapters of Part Two are devoted to this model. Marxian theory certainly stands in need of further development, and there are areas where it needs to be revised or rejected. But its defenders do not make claims regarding the efficiency and normative attractiveness of the Marxian model of capitalist globalisation that are undermined by its essential features. And so this position is not afflicted with immanent contradictions that force us to 'negate' it. In this sense, the model brings the systematic dialectic of globalisation to a conclusion.

In another sense, however, the systematic dialectic remains incomplete. Theorists holding a Marxian position avoid an immanent contradiction between their model of capitalist globalisation and the claims they assert of it only by making explicit the immanent contradictions in the model itself. What might a determinate negation of these contradictions look like? If such an alternative global framework could be built upon the positive features of capitalist globalisation, then it could be said to 'sublate' capitalism, incorporating its strengths while going beyond it.[20] This is exactly the relationship of each succeeding stage in a systematic dialectic to its predecessor. Suppose, finally,

---

[19] This 'immanentist' approach to the relationships among the different positions in the globalisation debate is perfectly consistent with – and must be supplemented by – an 'externalist' account connecting these positions with material interests. For example, whatever the proper place of neoliberalism in a systematic dialectic of globalisation might be, it remains true that neoliberalism expresses the material interests of financial capital. See Duménil and Lévy 2004, Part III.

[20] The term 'sublation' refers to the way each succeeding stage in a systematic-dialectical ordering includes the essential determinations of the previous stage, while adding new determinations that explicitly address the structural shortcomings of the earlier position.

that essential clues to the construction of this alternative order were implicit in the systematic dialectic traced previously. This, too, would provide a reason to proceed, since a systematic dialectic should continue forward as long as there is some essential implicit matter to be made explicit.

These considerations suggest that we must ask whether there is a model of a possible form of globalisation that would institutionalise a qualitatively higher level of efficiency and normative attractiveness than any possible form of global capitalism. If such a model could be constructed, there is a sense it would count as a radical break with the ordering of positions considered thus far. In an equally valid sense, however, it would count as the culmination of the systematic dialectic of globalisation. The final chapter of this work is devoted to this alternative.

The ordering of positions just described is a rational reconstruction of the globalisation debate. Like all rational reconstructions, it is revisable. Perhaps I have left out some crucial dimension of a position that would justify a quite different assessment from that provided here. Perhaps there are variants of a given position that do not fit the account given below. Perhaps both the Marxian model of capitalist globalisation and the socialist model presented in the final chapter suffer from internal contradictions no less serious than those afflicting other positions. If any of these things were the case, a compelling argument for a different ordering of positions might be made. There might also be positions do not fit neatly under any of the headings I have employed, and perhaps they would have pushed the dialectical progression in entirely different directions. Worst of all, perhaps the manner in which the different positions construct different objects of investigations (and are thus incommensurable) is, when all is said and done, far more profound than the way they investigate the same global order (and are thus commensurable, at least to a certain degree). If that were the case, the entire project would have to be abandoned.

No doubt this list of potentially fatal problems could be extended indefinitely. In the present intellectual and political climate, where few accept either the cogency of dialectical method or the promise of socialism, many readers may have already decided that the main project of this book cannot possibly be carried through successfully.

Defending a systematic-dialectical ordering is not like proclaiming a transcendental truth. It is an invitation to dialogue. Dialecticians, no less than other theorists, must be prepared to abandon their claims if convincing counter-arguments are forthcoming. In the meantime, as Hegel rightly insisted, it is impossible to justify a systematic-dialectical theory prior to working through the sequence of determinations making it up; the only justification of its results is the path by which they are attained. Only the course of the work as a whole can establish – or fail to establish – that the particular ordering traced here adequately illuminates the immanent relationships holding among the main positions in the globalisation debate.

Finally, besides historical dialectics and the two forms of systematic dialectics there is a fourth type of dialectical endeavour in social theory, surely the most important of all.[21] This is the dialectic of theory and practice. It, too, is relevant to the present work.

If it can be established that a given model of globalisation suffers from an immanent contradiction, this provides a theoretical motivation to move to a new position. But this theoretical claim also provides a good reason to reject the political project of institutionalising the model in question. If the systematic ordering of positions in the globalisation debate points towards a feasible and normatively attractive alternative global order, this has a practical implication as well: there is a good reason to embrace the political project of furthering this alternative. A systematic dialectic of globalisation provides no guarantees that social agents with the interests and capacities to engage effectively in this project will emerge. Nonetheless, it still may claim a role in the dialectic of theory and practice.

---

[21] Other sorts of dialectical theories are found outside social theory. For example, there is the systematic ordering of pure thought and being, as in Hegel's *Science of Logic*. Left Darwinians have also interpreted evolutionary biology as a dialectical theory that parallels the historical dialectics of historical materialism in many striking respects. See Levins and Lewontin 1985. For illustrations of various forms of dialectical inquiries within a Marxian framework, see Ollman and Smith 1998.

.

Part One

A Systematic Reconstruction of
the Globalisation Debate

Chapter One
The Social-State Model of Globalisation

The first crucial question for any work in systematic dialectics is where to begin. It is impossible to give a fully adequate justification for the starting point at the beginning of a systematic dialectic. That can come only come at its conclusion, when the relevant alternatives have been explicitly considered. Still, some beginning point must be selected, and some preliminary justification for that selection provided.

Both Hegel and Marx considered this question at great length, and they both characterised the appropriate starting point in the same general terms: a systematic ordering must begin with the most abstract and simple determination of the realm being investigated. The category 'being' begins the systematic progression of ontological categories making up Hegel's *Science of Logic* because it defines the most abstract and simplest ontological structure possible. The category 'possession' falls at the beginning of Hegel's *The Philosophy of Right* because, in Hegel's view, it defines the simplest and most abstract structure of the modern socio-political realm. And Marx settled on 'the commodity' as the proper starting point for *Capital* due to the fact that the simplest and most abstract categorisation of the capitalist mode of production is that it is a system of generalised commodity exchange.

What position conceptualises the contemporary global order in a simpler and more abstract fashion than any relevant alternative? I believe that the appropriate place to begin is with a conceptualisation of the global order as an aggregate of more-or-less independent states and national economies, externally connected to each other in ways that do not substantively affect domestic structures and practices. A more minimalist categorisation of the global order cannot be conceived, making this the appropriate place to inaugurate a systematic ordering of positions in the globalisation debate.[1]

A number of distinct theoretical frameworks conceptualise the global order in this minimalist fashion. In contemporary social theory, two quite different schools of thought are most pertinent. The above notion of globalisation has been the standard paradigm in international relations theory, especially the 'realist school' mentioned in the introduction. For theorists in this tradition, globalisation is primarily a matter of co-operation among externally related states when their self-interests coincide, and conflict when they do not. As mentioned in the Introduction, however, I regard realism as a non-starter from the standpoint of normative social theory.[2] And, so, the systematic dialectic of globalisation will begin with the other option, the 'social-state' (also termed the 'Keynesian-state', 'social-democratic state', or 'liberal-state') perspective. Like realists, advocates of this position accept a general framework in which states and national economies are externally related to each other. Their normative views, however, are far more worthy of consideration.

Strictly speaking, there is no single 'social-state model of globalisation'. There are a wide variety of different frameworks presented by various theorists, loosely bound together by certain family resemblances.[3] In many theoretical and practical contexts, the differences within this family would be far more important than the resemblances. But on the relatively high level of abstraction of a systematic reconstruction of the globalisation debate, I believe the

---

[1] Many theorists would deny that this conceptualisation refers to a form of globalisation at all, preferring the term 'internationalisation' for the case at hand. I have chosen instead to treat 'globalisation' as a more universal concept, with 'internationalisation' its simplest form. As far as I can tell, this is a purely semantic matter that does not affect any substantive analysis.

[2] See Buchanan 2004, pp. 29–38.

[3] This point holds for the positions considered in subsequent chapters as well.

resemblances are more worthy of emphasis, although this too can only be a provisional assumption at this point.

The social-state model could be constructed from a range of particular examples, or one example could be taken as representative. In the present chapter, I shall take the latter option and focus on the model of globalisation developed by John Rawls, the most discussed political philosopher of the twentieth century. In Rawls's writings, foreign trade, international relations among states, and international agencies are explicitly acknowledged. But, in principle at least, these phenomena do not substantively affect domestic structures and practices. In this sense, Rawls presents a 'ground-zero' account of globalisation.

An essential element of the social-state position is the normative defence of a (suitably regulated) capitalist market society. I shall argue that these markets necessarily tend to function in a manner that undermines the ability of the social state to fulfil the tasks assigned to it by Rawls and other leading proponents of the social state. This contradiction between the claims made for the model, and the way the model necessarily tends to function over time, will provide the systematic warrant for a transition to the second stage in the systematic dialectic of globalisation.

1. Rawls, the social state, and the global order

In his masterwork, *A Theory of Justice*, Rawls begins his normative social theory by carefully designing a thought experiment in which imaginary individuals are to select a set of abstract principles of justice to govern the basic structure of their society. Rawls proposes various ideal conditions to ensure that this agreement is fair and rational. To ensure fairness Rawls asks us to imagine individuals under a 'veil of ignorance' preventing them from knowing their age, race, gender, class, talents, or conceptions of the good life. To ensure rationality, we are to suppose that the individuals in this hypothetical 'original position':

- have knowledge of the general facts of social life;
- are not susceptible to envy;
- comprehend that access to primary social goods (wealth and income, powers and opportunities, rights and liberties, and the social bases of self-respect) generally enhances their ability to carry out their life plans;

- are capable of adhering to the decision rule appropriate to the original position, the maximin rule;[4] and
- have an equal opportunity to participate in debates regarding the strengths and weaknesses of various proposed principles.

Rawls argues that in an 'original position' where rational individuals debate principles of justice behind a veil of ignorance and adhere to the maximin rule the following principles would be selected:

First Principle
Each person is to have an equal right to the most extensive total system of equal basic liberties compatible with a similar system of liberty for all.

Second Principle
Social and economic inequalities are to be arranged so that they are both:
a) to the greatest benefit of the least advantaged, consistent with the just savings principle,[5] and
b) attached to offices and positions open to all under conditions of fair equality of opportunity.[6]

Rawls's methodological framework and the substantive content of the above normative principles have both been subjected to extensive critical discussion. In the present context, however, our foremost concern is with the institutional implication of these principles. What sort of social framework would embody these principles of justice to the greatest feasible degree?

---

[4] In other words, these individuals are to select principles of justice that 'maximise the minimum' such that the worst-off representative person in a social system based on the selected principles would be better-off than the worst-off representative person in social systems based on any alternative set of principles. The goal is to ensure that if you turn out to be a member of the worst-off group when the veil of ignorance is lifted, you will still find yourself in an acceptable position.

[5] The first part of this clause is termed 'the difference principle'. The just savings principle refers to the imperative to avoid a level of consumption that condemns the next generation to a level of material deprivation that individuals behind a veil of ignorance (who do not know whether they are young, middle-aged, or old) would find unacceptable.

[6] Rawls 1971, p. 302. The complete list of Rawls's principles also includes the first priority rule (liberty can only be restricted for the sake of liberty), and a second priority rule (the second principle has priority over efficiency considerations, and within the second principle fair equality of opportunity has priority over the difference principle).

Rawls's own discussion of institutions is scattered throughout *A Theory of Justice* and other writings. Taken together, these texts define a model of globalisation whose constitutive parts are the household, civil society (the national economy), the social state, the interstate system, and international agencies.[7]

Susan Moller Okin is surely correct that the structures and social practices of the modern family fall within the scope of Rawls's theory of justice.[8] She is also correct to insist that an adequate normative assessment of contemporary family structures is missing from *A Theory of Justice*. She argues persuasively that any family structure normatively acceptable on Rawlsian principles would have to be egalitarian, including in particular a fair sharing of the burdens of domestic labour (or, if that is not possible, acknowledgement that a partner performing most of the child-rearing work is entitled to an equal share of the income earned by a partner working outside the house).

Rawls has come to express sympathy with this view.[9] He would also insist that, throughout his writings, he has recognised that the family is an essential institution in the contemporary social order, and that the good of the household as a whole can, in principle, be reconciled with the interests of its individual members.[10] As Martha Nussbaum points out, however, it remains unclear whether Rawls categorises the family as a voluntary association or as an intrinsic element of the basic social structure alongside the economy or the state. It matters which option is taken, for reasons that will be mentioned below in the discussion of the responsibilities of the social state.[11]

---

[7] This ordering parallels that found in the culminating section of Hegel's *Philosophy of Right*, *Sittlichkeit* ('Ethical Life'): family, civil society, the state, international law. Throughout Part One, I shall use this section as a rough template. Rawls does not present his account of institutional forms in a similar systematic fashion. But his scattered remarks can be presented in this order without distortion.

[8] Okin 1989. See also Nussbaum 2001, Chapter 4.

[9] 'The equal rights of women and the basic rights of their children as future citizens are inalienable and protect them wherever they are. Gender distinctions limiting those rights and liberties are excluded. . . . If the so-called private sphere [of the family T.S.] is alleged to be a space exempt from justice, then there is no such thing'. Rawls 1997, p. 599. See also Rawls 1999, pp. 160, 162.

[10] It is worth noting in passing that the household need not take the form of the traditional family: '[N]o particular form of the family (monogamous, heterosexual, or otherwise) is required by a political conception of justice so long as the family is arranged to fulfill these tasks effectively and doesn't run afoul of other political values'. The tasks Rawls has in mind are 'the nurturing and development of such citizens in appropriate numbers to maintain an enduring society'. Rawls 1999, p. 157.

[11] See note 23 below.

I shall also refer later in this chapter to Rawls's claim that poverty in the global order is partially explained by the range of opportunities offered to women in particular national economies. Whether these opportunities are extensive or not depends in good measure on the practices defining family life.

While the family plays an absolutely essential role in Rawls's account of social life, he is well aware that, in modern societies, the household is not capable of providing the material preconditions for its own reproduction. Nor does the household offer an adequate arena for the development and exercise of individual autonomy. For this, we must turn to the realm of civil society, where the particularity of individual subjects comes to the fore.

In a free society, a wide variety of voluntary associations dedicated to the pursuit of shared interests will be found in civil society. In the present context, however, I shall focus primarily on the production and distribution of goods and services. The Rawlsian justification for this decision is that the economy is fundamental to the basic structure of the social order, while particular churches, universities, and other voluntary associations are not. The rules defining economic life are pervasive and affect the life chances of every member of society in a way that sets them apart from the rules of particular associations in civil society.

For Rawls, the freedom of particular persons to make decisions for themselves regarding their occupations and wants is of crucial importance. He believes that a market society institutionalises this form of autonomy far better than any feasible alternative:

> A further and more significant advantage of a market system is that, given the requisite background institutions, it is consistent with equal liberties and fair equality of opportunity. Citizens have a free choice of careers and occupations. There is no reason at all for the forced and central direction of labor. Indeed, in the absence of some differences in earnings as these arise in a competitive scheme, it is hard to see how, under ordinary circumstances anyway, certain aspects of a command society inconsistent with liberty can be avoided.[12]

---

[12] Rawls 1971, p. 272.

Rawls mentions in passing that it is possible in principle for a democratic form of market socialism to be compatible with his two principles of justice.[13] But the most cursory exploration of his writings confirms that his main project is to provide a normative defence of a suitably regulated form of market capitalism. This is the project of social-state theorists as a group, and, in the present context, Rawls is of interest only insofar as his work is representative of this group.[14]

The reference to 'earnings' in the above passage is a reminder that money is a crucial element of capitalist market societies. While Rawls does not devote attention to the topic, we may assume that he accepts the familiar functions of money as a unit of account, means of circulation, store of value, and so on. We may also assume that, in a global order divided into distinct national economies, various national currencies will operate, even if these currencies are in principle based upon a single form of money.[15]

The passage just quoted also reflects Rawls's acceptance of wage-labour as a social form. He does not devote special attention to this topic either, apart from the contrast between free choice and forced labour. For a more detailed philosophical legitimation of wage-labour we must look to Hegel, who explicitly develops views Rawls takes for granted. Since the other positions considered in Part One of this book take some version of Hegel's argument for granted as well, a brief digression is in order.

In an early section of *The Philosophy of Right*, Hegel defines ownership as a right to the complete use of a thing.[16] In slavery systems, slaves are owned by their masters, who have full use of them. Such ownership is obviously incompatible with a mutual recognition of the autonomy of co-subjects. Feudalism is also incompatible with a reciprocal acknowledgement of freedom, for, in feudalism, the serf is in effect 'owned' by a particular estate, embodied

---

[13] Rawls 1973, p. 280.

[14] I shall return to the question of markets and socialism in Chapter 8 below.

[15] When *A Theory of Justice* was published, the gold exchange standard had not yet been abandoned.

[16] '[M]y full use or employment of a thing is the thing in its entirety, so that if I have the full use of the thing I am its owner. . . . My merely partial or temporary use of a thing, like my partial or temporary possession of it (a possession which itself is simply the partial or temporary possibility of using it) is therefore to be distinguished from ownership of the thing itself'. Hegel 1967, p. 50, # 61–2. At later stages of the theory, this right is modified by various political regulations.

by a lord. In contrast, Hegel insists, the system of wage-labour institutionalises the principle of autonomy. His argument rests on the crucial distinction between the person as a whole and particular periods of a person's activity. After the wage contract has been completed, the purchaser does not own the wage-labourer, since the purchaser lacks the right to use the wage-labourer over the complete course of her life. The wage contract merely grants use of the wage-labourer's activity for a restricted period of time. The wage contract thus presupposes that the wage-labourer is a person who cannot be owned. I may legitimately sell to another 'the use of my abilities for a restricted period, because, on the strength of this restriction, my abilities acquire an external relation to the totality and universality of my being'. In contrast,

> [B]y alienating the whole of my time, as crystallized in my work, and everything I produced, I would be making into another's property the substance of my being, my universal activity and actuality, my personality.[17]

By ruling out such complete alienation, the wage contract implicitly acknowledges the 'universal activity', 'actuality', and 'personality' of the wage-labourer. In this manner, wage-labour institutionalises the mutual acknowledgement of the personality and autonomy of the contracting parties.

We can approach the point from a slightly different angle. To recognise the autonomy of others is to grant that they possess certain inalienable characteristics that are not legitimate objects of commodity exchange: 'Such characteristics are my personality as such, my universal freedom of will, my ethical life, my religion'.[18] But 'single products of my particular physical and mental skill and of my power to act' do not fit under this heading.[19] They can thus be exchanged without calling into question my status as a co-subject whose autonomy is worthy of respect.

Turning back to Rawls, he, like Hegel, justifies commodity exchange, money, and wage-labour primarily in terms of the manner in which they institutionalise liberty and the mutual recognition of autonomy. Both also give qualified assent to Adam Smith's 'invisible hand' thesis, according to which the pursuit of self-interest by individuals in markets necessarily tends to further the

---

[17] Hegel 1967, p. 54, # 67.
[18] Hegel 1967, p. 53, # 66.
[19] Hegel 1967, p. 54, # 66.

general social good. The logic of market competition systematically rewards those who contribute to the satisfaction of the wants and needs of others in an efficient manner, while imposing penalties on those who do not.[20]

In a passage quoted earlier, Rawls wrote that 'A[n] . . . advantage of a market system is that, given the requisite background institutions, it is consistent with equal liberties and fair equality of opportunity'. Rawls echoes Hobbes, Locke, Hegel and many others when he asserts that these background conditions include a coercive state apparatus to protect against force and fraud. And he is firmly in Hegel's camp when he insists, against Hobbes and Locke, that a just state must go far beyond that minimal agenda. One reason for this is the fact that the invisible hand of the market breaks down when public goods or public bads are involved. Markets do not automatically tend to provide public goods and avoid public bads to the greatest feasible degree.[21] An efficient social order requires an institution capable of correcting the market failures that necessarily tend to arise 'once goods [and bads, T.S.] are indivisible over large numbers of individuals'. This institution is, of course, the state:

> It is evident, then, that the indivisibility and publicness of certain essential goods, and the externalities and temptations to which they give rise, necessitate collective agreements organized and enforced by the state. That political rule is founded solely on men's propensity to self-interest and injustice is a superficial view. For even among just men, once goods are indivisible over large numbers of individuals, their actions decided upon in isolation from one another will not lead to the general good. Some collective arrangement is necessary and everyone wants assurance that it will be adhered to if he is willing to do his part.[22]

When state policies are implemented to provide public goods and avoid public bads, this furthers the normative attractiveness of the social order no less than its efficiency.

---

[20] Rawls 1971, pp. 271–2, 529.

[21] The only way to avoid this conclusion is to abstract from essential features of 'the real world': 'Under certain conditions competitive prices select the goods to be produced and allocate resources to their production in such a manner that there is no way to improve upon with their choice of production methods by firms, or the distribution of goods that arises form the purchases of households'. As Rawls immediately goes on to note, 'the requisite conditions are highly special ones and they are seldom if ever fully satisfied in the real world'. Rawls 1971, pp. 271–2.

[22] Rawls 1971, p. 268.

The state also furthers its normative attractiveness when it provides the 'requisite background institutions' for liberty and equality of opportunity in economic life.[23] The rights of citizens are not limited to 'formal' or 'negative' rights, such as freedom from interference with speech, association, or property. Citizens may rightfully claim 'substantial' or 'positive' entitlements to the satisfaction of basic needs for nutrition, housing, health care, income security, employment opportunities, and so on. This requires political regulation of markets in order to further the proper allocation of economic resources, the stabilisation of socio-economic life, acceptable standards of living for all citizens, and limitations on the extreme inequalities that undermine political equality.

It is striking that, in a six hundred-page work, fewer than ten pages of *A Theory of Justice* are devoted to the political institutions required to provide the 'requisite background' for a capitalist economy to function in a normatively acceptable manner.[24] Precious little is said on this issue in Rawls's subsequent writings either. But these few pages are more than sufficient to establish Rawls as a defender of 'the social state'. Besides a constitution, elected governments, and a judicial apparatus securing equal civil and political liberties for all citizens, Rawls insists that a just socio-political order must include four branches of government or their functional equivalents.[25]

The *allocation branch* has the task of 'keep[ing] the price system workably competitive and [preventing] the formation of unreasonable market power'.[26] It also must correct matters when market prices fail to reflect social benefits and costs accurately. Rawls suggests that this can be accomplished 'by suitable

---

[23] If the family is categorised as an essential element of the basic structure, the state must similarly take steps to construct family forms that further the fair value of liberties and fair equality of opportunities. If, in contrast, the family is categorised as a private association, interference with traditional decision-making patterns would be much more difficult to justify on Rawlsian grounds. This contrast is discussed at length in Nussbaum 2001, 270–83. Nussbaum argues persuasively that Rawls mistakenly inclines towards the latter.

[24] Rawls 1973, pp. 274–80.

[25] From the standpoint of Rawls's first principle, the principle of liberty, constitutional democracy is the only fully legitimate state form. In *The Law of Peoples*, Rawls argues that non-democratic ('associationist') social orders should be tolerated by liberal peoples as long as they are 'decent' and 'well-ordered' institutional frameworks (these terms will be defined below). Calling for toleration, however, is far short of affirming that they are justified from a normative point of view. Rawls 1999, pp. 72–3.

[26] Rawls 1971, p. 276.

taxes and subsidies and by changes in the definition of property rights'.[27] The *stabilisation branch* 'strives to bring about reasonably full employment in the sense that those who want work can find it and the free choice of occupation and the deployment of finance are supported by strong effective demand'.[28] The third branch of government, the *transfer branch*, ensures that all citizens and their dependents attain a certain minimal level of well-being. Finally, the *distribution branch* imposes tax schemes and adjustments in property rights in order 'gradually and continually to correct the distribution of wealth and to prevent concentrations of power detrimental to the fair value of political liberty and the fair equality of opportunity'.[29] The distribution branch must also collect the revenues required for the public goods and transfer payments provided by other branches.

It is often thought that the strong egalitarian component of Rawls's theory rests on the difference principle ('social and economic inequalities are to be arranged so that they are to the greatest benefit of the least advantaged'). But this principle allows indefinitely large increases in relative economic inequality, so long as the absolute position of the least advantaged group is improved in the least degree. The strongest egalitarian thrust in Rawls's position stems instead from the principles of the fair value of political liberties and fair equality of opportunity. These principles imply that, past a certain point, *relative* inequalities undermine the justice of the social order. Besides equality under the law, all citizens must have a fair opportunity to participate in the process of democratic will formation in the public sphere, the ultimate basis of legitimate public policy. The distribution branch of the state is explicitly assigned the task of ensuring that economic inequalities do not grow to the point where they undermine the fair value of political liberties, or the fair equality of opportunity to hold political (and other) offices. Maintaining fair equality of opportunity is a crucial task of the allocation branch as well.[30]

Many passages in *A Theory of Justice* suggest that, when all is said and done, Rawls agrees with classical liberals who see the state as an instrument enabling

---

[27] Ibid.

[28] Ibid.

[29] Rawls 1971, p. 277.

[30] Numerous defenders of the social state do not accept the difference principle. One reason Rawls's framework can be used to illustrate the general social-state model of globalisation is because so few of its most important features rest on this controversial principle.

individuals and groups to pursue their interests more effectively. Alongside these texts, however, there are others where Rawls echoes the Hegelian theme that membership in a political community is an intrinsic part of our identity. The just state is not an alien thing over and above us. The state embodies principles whose acceptance constitutes a significant part of who we are. For Rawls, as for Hegel, we see ourselves in the just state.[31] From this perspective, the constitutional-democratic republic of Rawls counts as a 'concrete universal' in Hegel's sense of the term; it is the site where the particular interests of individuals and groups are reconciled with the 'substantive unity' of the community as a whole.[32]

As Rawls himself notes, the discussion thus far has employed a simplifying assumption, 'the notion of a self-contained national community'.[33] He now drops this assumption, taking into account the fact that states stand in relationships to other states. This acknowledgement requires a further development of the theory of justice, since the normative principles considered above do not characterise 'the justice of the law of nations and of relations between states'.[34] At this point, Rawls re-activates his methodological apparatus, asking his readers to undertake another thought experiment. We are now to imagine an original position, in which representatives of different (just) nations attempt to come to an agreement regarding principles governing relations among states.[35] We are to imagine further that these representatives are under

---

[31] Membership in the political community does not define a citizen's entire identity for either theorist. Hegel explicitly acknowledges how membership in a family and particular associations in civil society (such as religious communities) are also intrinsic components of our personal identity. In Rawls's account, our identity is partially constituted by our conception of the good, which will typically be formed through participation in a particular community with a comprehensive worldview. In all multicultural societies there is a plurality of different communities with distinct comprehensive worldviews. In a liberal multicultural society, however, there is also an overlapping consensus regarding the political principles that are appropriate when differences in comprehensive worldviews can be expected to persist. The political values expressed in these principles are (partially) constitutive of a citizen's identity. For Rawls too, then, individuals recognise themselves in the just state. See Rawls 1985.
[32] In Hegel's inimitable style: 'The principle of modern states has prodigious strength and depth because it allows the principle of subjectivity to progress to its culmination in the extreme of self-subsistent personal particularity, and yet at the same time brings it back to the substantive unity and so maintains this unity in the principle of subjectivity itself'. Hegel 1967, p. 161, # 260.
[33] Rawls 1971, p. 557.
[34] Rawls 1971, pp. 7–8.
[35] Rawls 1971, p. 286.

a modified veil of ignorance. Each knows that the state she represents has specific interests, but does not know what those interests are, or the particular circumstances that have generated them, such as the state's 'power and strength in comparison with other nations'.[36] Rawls asserts that the principles that would be agreed to in such an ideal hypothetical situation include many of the traditional principles of international law, including rights to self-determination and self-defence, the principles of non-intervention and adherence to treaties, as well as the precepts to wage only just wars and to maintain just conduct in those wars.[37]

Towards the end of his life, Rawls complicated matters by distinguishing two thought experiments on the level of interstate relations. The first considers an original position in which representatives of liberal régimes debate the principles that ought to govern relations among states of this sort. In the second, representatives of non-liberal but 'well-ordered' régimes face the same task. Non-liberal well-ordered régimes are those in which one particular comprehensive doctrine has official state sanction, but the powers of the state are not used to coerce those with different worldviews, either within or beyond national borders. These régimes also provide settings in which the opinions of their subjects are regularly consulted, even if many of the citizenship rights enjoyed in liberal democracies are absent. Finally, non-liberal well-ordered régimes honour the basic rights of their subjects to subsistence, security, liberty, personal property, equal treatment under the law, emigration, and so on.

Rawls insists that the results of both thought experiments would be identical; a social contract affirming principles of international justice similar to those derived in *A Theory of Justice*, now termed 'the law of peoples':

1. Peoples (as organized by their governments) are free and independent, and their freedom and independence is to be respected by other peoples.
2. Peoples are equal and parties to their own agreements.
3. Peoples have the right of self-defense but no right to war.
4. Peoples are to observe a duty of nonintervention.
5. Peoples are to observe treaties and undertakings.

---

[36] Rawls 1971, p. 378.
[37] Rawls 1971, pp. 378–9.

6. Peoples are to observe certain specified restrictions on the conduct of war (assumed to be in self-defense).

7. Peoples are to honor human rights.[38]

For our purposes, it is important to note that the treaties referred to here include those setting the terms of cross-border trade and investment.

The theory of international justice also requires principles governing the relations between well-ordered and non-well-ordered régimes. Tyrannical and dictatorial régimes must not be tolerated, in Rawls's view, and the same holds for otherwise acceptable states dedicated to imposing their particular comprehensive worldview on others by force. The pressure of world public opinion should be brought against such régimes, and they should not be materially supported. In some cases, more active forms of encouraging régime change, such as economic sanctions or humanitarian military interventions, may be justified, depending on the severity of rights violations and whether such actions are likely to be effective in the particular circumstances.[39]

Régimes in which the material preconditions for a well-ordered society are lacking must also be characterised as 'non-well-ordered'. Rawls holds that more privileged peoples have a duty to assist these societies, based on the imperative to help a disadvantaged people become 'a full and self-standing member of the societies of peoples, and capable of taking charge of their political life and maintaining decent political and social institutions'.[40] This duty, however, is limited, given Rawls's account of 'the causes of the wealth of a people':

> I believe that the causes of the wealth of a people and the forms it takes lie in their political culture and in the religious, philosophical, and moral traditions that support the basic structure of their political and social institutions, as well as in the industriousness and cooperative talents of its members, all supported by their political virtues.[41]

Rawls concludes that the most fundamental causes of poverty in the global order are political corruption and oppressive cultural practices, especially those regarding women:

---

[38] Rawls 1993, p. 540; see Rawls 1999, p. 37.
[39] Rawls 1993, p. 562; see Rawls 1999, pp. 89–93.
[40] Rawls 1993, p. 559; see also Rawls 1999, pp. 105–13.
[41] Rawls 1999, p. 108.

The great social evils in poorer societies are likely to be oppressive government and corrupt elites; the subjection of women abetted by unreasonable religion, with the resulting overpopulation relative to what the society can decently sustain.[42]

Overcoming these afflictions is a task that ultimately can only be accomplished by the members of the afflicted societies themselves. These theses imply that liberal principles of distributive justice are fairly irrelevant in this context. While Rawls does insist that there is a duty to assist those in dire need in the global economy, he also explicitly rules out the sort of continuous redistribution of economic resources that a just national order demands, in his view.

Following Kant's vehement rejection of the project of instituting a world government, in Rawls's framework there is no sovereign power capable of legislating, applying, and enforcing international law. But Rawls does refer to a series of international agencies that are necessary for a proper 'regime of global governance'. The United Nations provides a crucial forum for discussions uniting representatives of the various peoples of the globe. It enables, for instance, complaints against 'outlaw regimes' to be brought before the court of international public opinion. Another sort of international agency, loosely modelled on the World Trade Organisation, is required to ensure that the rules of trade are fair to all peoples.[43] A global co-operative bank is also required to ensure that any well-ordered régime wishing to spur economic growth in its national economy is able to borrow the requisite capital.[44]

It is important to note that the powers of these international agencies are ultimately derived from states. While Rawls supplements his account of the state with a discussion of interstate relations and international agencies, in

[42] Rawls 1993, p. 559.

[43] 'Consider fair trade: suppose that liberal peoples assume that, when suitably regulated by a fair background framework, a free competitive-market trading scheme is to everyone's mutual advantage, at least in the longer run. A further assumption here is that the larger nations with the wealthier economies will not attempt to monopolize the market, or to conspire to form a cartel, or to act as an oligopoly. With these assumptions, and supposing as before that the veil of ignorance holds, so that no people knows whether its economy is large or small, all would agree to fair standards of trade to keep the market free and competitive (when such standards can be specified, followed, and enforced). Should these cooperative organisations have unjustified distributive effects between peoples, these would have to be corrected, and taken into account by the duty of assistance'. Rawls 1999, p. 43.

[44] Rawls 1999, p. 42.

his framework, the social state remains the central institution of the global order. Social states have both the ultimate responsibility for instituting a just and efficient global order and (burdened societies apart) the capacities to fulfill this responsibility.

The institutional framework Rawls defends can be interpreted as a model of globalisation in that it explicitly includes foreign trade, relations among states, and international agencies.[45] But the impact of foreign trade, interstate relations, and international agencies on the domestic order is held to be minimal. None of these things replaces or lessens the responsibilities of the state; none undermines its essential capacities. Just as for Hegel, the state is the 'concrete universal' attaining the highest-order reconciliation of universal and particular possible in the socio-political realm, for Rawls, the state is the primary site of justice. For both, the state is conceptualised as the central institution of social life, with the national community taken to be the primary 'community of fate' that social agents share with their fellow citizens. Foreign trade, international relations, and the rulings of international agencies may complicate the state's tasks. But they do not change the fact that the state has primary responsibility for establishing and maintaining the preconditions for human happiness and human flourishing.[46]

Needless to say, there always have been – and always will be – numerous states that fail to meet their challenges. Accounting for these failures is an important task for historians and policymakers. Theorists such as Rawls, however, operate on a far more abstract level. To use some more Hegelian jargon, their goal is to articulate a set of social forms capturing the 'actuality' of the present social order. Since this point is absolutely crucial for understanding the level of abstraction of a systematic dialectic of globalisation, another brief digression is in order.

One of the most notorious statements in the history of social theory is surely Hegel's claim that 'what is rational is actual and what is actual is rational'.[47] At first glance, this remark from the *Philosophy of Right* seems to assert that whatever exists is rational simply because it exists, a hyper-conservativism

---

[45] See note 1 above.
[46] As Beitz noticed, for Rawls, the main motivation of agents in an original position considering principles of international justice 'is in providing conditions in which just domestic social orders might flourish'. Beitz 1985, p. 288.
[47] Hegel 1967, p. 10.

that would have made Edmund Burke blush. Even more than other philosophers, however, Hegel does not always use ordinary language in an ordinary way. Throughout his writings, he makes a sharp distinction between 'actuality' and 'existence', and this distinction enables him to assert the rationality of what is 'actual' without affirming each and every feature of existing social orders.

In Hegel's social theory, distinguishing the 'actual' from mere 'existence' today requires comprehension of the normative principles appropriate to our historical epoch. In his unequivocally Eurocentric view, the relevant principles were first introduced into world history by Christianity in its stories of the incarnation and the presence of the Holy Spirit in the religious community. In Hegel's reading, both stories convey the same truth: the divine is not 'out there' in some region beyond the skies, but here on earth, in the universal spirit uniting particular groups and individual subjects together.[48] Christianity thus expresses, in the form of picture thinking, the philosophical truth that social orders are to be evaluated according to the extent to which they enable a true reconciliation of universality with particularity and individuality:

> The right of individuals to be subjectively destined to freedom is fulfilled when they belong to an actual ethical order, because their conviction of their freedom finds its truth in such an objective order, and it is in an ethical order that they are actually in possession of their own essence or their own inner universality.[49]

It has taken humanity thousands of years to institute such an 'actual ethical order'. In the modern period, Hegel thinks, this world-historical task has finally been accomplished, at least in principle. In Hegel's view, the ultimate goal of political philosophy is not the articulation and defence of abstract normative principles, or a meticulous examination of the logic of normative statements. Its purpose is, instead, to discover the rationality of our social order, those features of the contemporary social world that adequately embody the highest principles attained in human history. These features, and these alone, are 'actual', in his sense of the term. Social forms are rational precisely

---

[48] Hegel, 1977, Chapter VII: Hegel 1988, pp. 481–9. The notions of an immortal soul and an afterlife in heaven are conspicuously absent in Hegel's philosophy of religion.
[49] Hegel 1967, p. 109, # 153.

to the degree to which they attain (and reproduce over time) a true reconciliation between the community as a whole and the particular groups and individuals within it. This is why not everything that exists in the social world can be affirmed as rational. Only what is actual is rational.

Rawls, writing for a far more secular and multicultural audience than Hegel's, introduces and defends his principles of justice without reference to their relationship to religious traditions.[50] But these principles also articulate the normative claim that universality (the social good) and particularity and individuality (the fundamental interests of groups and individuals) must be united, however distinct they may remain. Like Hegel, Rawls does not hold that every feature of contingent existence is normatively acceptable from this perspective:

> The Law of Peoples does not presuppose the existence of actual decent hierarchical peoples any more than it presupposes the existence of actual reasonably just constitutional democratic peoples. If we set the standards very high, neither exists. In the case of democratic peoples, the most we can say is that some are closer than others to a reasonably just constitutional regime.[51]

However, Rawls in effect distinguishes 'actuality', in Hegel's sense of the term, from mere existence. His project too is to reconcile us with our social world by convincing us that its essential determinations, its 'deep tendencies and inclinations', embody in principle a normatively attractive global order:

> While realization is, of course, not unimportant, I believe that the very possibility of such a social order can itself reconcile us to the social word. The possibility is not a mere logical possibility, but one that connects with the deep tendencies and inclinations of the social world.[52]

This completes the presentation of the social-state model of globalisation. It provides an appropriate beginning for a rational reconstruction of the globalisation debate due to the relatively minimal role it grants to foreign trade, interstate relations, and the 'régime of global governance'. While Rawls

---

[50] See Rawls 1985.
[51] Rawls 1999, p. 75.
[52] Rawls 1999, p. 128.

is but one of numerous social theorists who have described and defended a variant of this model, for the purposes of this book, his version can be taken as representative of the position.[53]

The two crucial notions in the methodological framework of systematic dialectics are 'immanent contradiction' and 'determinate negation'. If the essential determinations of a given position contradict fundamental claims associated with it, this 'immanent contradiction' justifies a 'determinate negation' of that position, that is, a transition to a new position in the systematic ordering explicitly addressing the contradiction implicit in the previous position. Are there internal tensions in the model of globalisation defended by Rawls and others? More specifically, would the essential determinations of the social-state model of globalisation necessarily tend to generate systematic tendencies that undermined its feasibility and normative attractiveness, as measured by the principles of the model's leading adherents? The systematic reconstruction of positions in the globalisation debate attempted here can only proceed if the answers to these questions is yes.

---

[53] After World War Two, political élites in the West, influenced by Keynes, attempted to construct a social and political order revolving around three sets of social policies (see Drache 1996, p. 36; Boyer 1996, p. 87). The first was the establishment of social programmes providing basic levels of nutrition, housing, health care, and income security to all citizens. For these theorists and policymakers, the rights of citizens included 'substantial' or 'positive' entitlements, not just 'formal' or 'negative' rights (such as freedom of speech, association, property, and so on). They also held that these entitlements were fully compatible with the second goal of Keynesian social policy, macro-economic management. Unemployment insurance, social security, welfare, health care, housing subsidies, and so on, were all thought to smoothe out the cycles of a capitalist economy by preventing extreme declines in the overall level of effective demand. The state regulation of money and credit aimed at the same end. Deficit spending and increases in the money supply were seen as further tools that could prevent an economic slowdown from degenerating into an extended recession or depression. The third set of public policies of the Keynesian state, designed to further 'Fordist' relations between capital and labour, complemented the first two. Legislation officially acknowledging workers' rights to organise collectively was intended to ensure that real wages grew in tandem with productivity, contributing to a stable economy with rising living standards. These three features clearly aimed the same objectives as the branches of government discussed by Rawls. Rawls's political philosophy can be seen as an attempt to articulate and defend normative principles legitimating the Keynesian state, principles that could also measure the limitations of existing governments.

2. The immanent contradictions of the social-state model of globalisation

In the social-state model of globalisation, foreign trade and interstate relations are explicitly acknowledged. 'The notion of a self-contained national community' is a simplifying initial assumption, abandoned as the model is fleshed out. Even after this assumption has been dropped, however, the global economy is still conceived primarily as a set of relatively independent national economies, subordinate to the states that regulate them and bound together through external relations. These external relations (foreign trade and investment) are assumed either to be without substantive effects on the domestic economy, or to have effects that can be controlled by the state with relative ease. In brief, the 'basic structure' that is the focus of Rawls's position is supposedly contained within national borders. This essential feature of the model is implicitly called into question by other determinations that are no less essential to it.[54]

(i) *The world market*

Rawls and other defenders of the social state defend generalised commodity exchange on the grounds that it institutionalises the principles of autonomy and efficiency. Individuals and groups are granted a *prima facie* right to make economic choices based on their own assessment of how best to pursue their interests. These choices are both exercises of liberty and means of securing the greatest feasible satisfaction of wants and needs in society as a whole. *Neither the principle of autonomy nor the invisible hand thesis is defined in a territorially restricted fashion.* Their scope does not end at a nation's borders. The notion of liberty to which social-state theorists appeal implies that, in principle at least, consumers should be as free to purchase imports as they are to purchase goods and services produced nationally. Workers should be as free to labour for foreign companies as they are to seek employment from nationally-based firms. And investors should be as free to invest in other regions of the world as they are to invest within domestic borders. Similarly, the notion of efficiency to which social-state theorists appeal implies that in principle, at least, cross-border transactions are governed by the 'invisible

---

[54] See Beitz 1979, and 1985; Pogge 1989, and 2002, pp. 104–8; Barry 1998; Buchanan 2004, pp. 209–16.

hand' in precisely the same ways and precisely the same extent as transactions within a particular set of borders.[55]

Of course, the mere fact that economic agents might choose to exercise their autonomy and pursue their self-interests in a certain fashion does not imply that they will in fact behave in this manner to a significant extent. To reach that conclusion, we need to add a further premise to the effect that there are systematic tendencies in the social-state model of globalisation making it progressively easier for social agents to choose to engage in cross-border economic activities furthering their interests. The technological dynamism of capitalism generates these tendencies.

A general drive to seek innovations in communication and transportation technologies, and to institute these innovations when this search is successful, can be derived from the economic relations incorporated in the social-state model of globalisation. These innovations necessarily tend to lead to reductions in the prices of shipping raw materials, machinery, partially finished goods, and finished goods. They are also strongly associated with reductions in the transaction costs associated with portfolio investments. We may assume that these technologies will necessarily tend to be employed in cross-border transactions whenever doing so furthers the interests of economic agents.

Recent illustrations abound. Advances in information technology now enable production chains to be organised across borders to an unprecedented degree. Global computer networks allow engineers from across the globe to cooperate simultaneously in product design ('concurrent engineering'). Computer-aided-design and computer-aided-manufacturing (CAD/CAM) software let engineers working in one region program computerised numerically controlled machine tools on the other side of the planet. Electronic Data Interface (EDI) allows managers in corporate headquarters to track processes of production and distribution spread across the globe involving hundreds of subsidiaries and subcontractors, while the internet allows the same tasks to be fulfilled in a simpler, less expensive, fashion. Information

---

[55] Throughout *The Law of Peoples*, Rawls refers to 'the benefits of trade' (for example, Rawls 1999, pp. 46, 52, and 69). I believe that Rawls has Ricardo's principle of comparative advantage in mind here, according to which mutual benefits from international trade can be won even when one trading partner has lower levels of productive efficiency than the other in all relevant sectors. (The principle of comparative advantage will be critically examined in Chapter 2.)

technologies also enable a continuous monitoring in real time of various inputs and outputs as they are transported from one part of the globe to another. These same technologies also permit investments in currencies, bonds, equities, and a mind-numbing array of derivatives, to flow across borders with a magnitude, speed and complexity far exceeding the capacity of finite minds to comprehend.

As a corollary to this argument, we may note that advances in communications technologies also allow information regarding the cultural practices of different regions (and changes in those practices) to be transmitted on an unprecedented scale and with unprecedented velocity. In systems of generalised commodity exchange, cultural changes are typically embodied in new commodities, with advertising agencies spurring the rapid diffusion of cultural fads through media technologies. In the social-state model, then, consumers across the globe tend to become increasingly aware of commodities produced throughout the globe, which, in turn, tends to lead to increased demand for imports.

The social-state model of globalisation grants economic agents the liberty to engage in economic transactions. The same sort of mutual benefits that provides the motivation to undertake trade and investment within national borders also provides the motivation to participate in economic transactions extending across borders. And the technological dynamism that is also an essential feature of the model necessarily tends to make such transactions easier, less costly, and more likely to be demanded. We may conclude that extensive webs of economic connections across borders necessarily tend to arise in the social-state model of globalisation. At some point, 'quantity becomes quality', to invoke the famous dialectical slogan. The greater the cross-border connections, the weaker the case for seeing national economies as more-or-less independent entities, and the more overpowering the case for conceptualising them as 'moments' of a larger whole, the world market.[56] The precise point at which this line is crossed may be indeterminate. But that there is such a point, and that it will tend to be crossed in the social-state model, is not.

---

[56] In the dialectical tradition, the term 'moments' is used to describe the internally related elements of a self-organising whole, as opposed to the 'parts' of a mechanical system or the separate things that in aggregate make up a heap. See Ollman 1976.

One reason, perhaps, why Rawls fails to appreciate the force of the tendency for cross-border economic transactions to occur – and the way this tendency undermines his conceptual framework of the contemporary global order – is suggested by his rather odd reference to an old idea of John Stuart Mill, 'the stationary state':

> [S]avings may stop once just (or decent) basic institutions have been established. At this point real saving (that is, net additions to real capital of all kinds) may fall to zero; and existing stock only needs to be maintained, or replaced, and nonrewable resources carefully husbanded for future use as appropriate. Thus, the savings rate as a constraint on current consumption is to be expressed in terms of aggregate capital accumulated, resource use forgone, and technology developed to conserve and regenerate the capacity of the natural world to sustain its human population. With these and other essential elements tallied in, a society may, of course, continue to save after this point, but it is no longer a duty of justice to do so.[57]

Rawls comments in a footnote that 'The thought that real saving and economic growth are to go on indefinitely, upwards and onwards, with no specified goal in sight, is the idea of the business class of a capitalist society', implying that some other idea of some other group could trump this view within a model of globalisation incorporating capitalist markets. Since 'economic growth . . . go[ing] on indefinitely, upwards and onwards, with no specified goal in sight' surely eventually tends to involve a proliferation of cross-border transactions, if the former is put out of play perhaps the latter can be ignored as well. We are to imagine, I suppose, that, somehow, at some point and in some manner, the drive to economic growth will be curtailed in a sufficient number of regions well before the notion of more or less independent national economies loses all plausibility.

Unfortunately for the coherence of the social-state position, in a capitalist society, the commitment to indefinite growth 'with no specified goal in sight' is not an option to be selected or discarded at whim. The logic of competition in capitalist markets, an explicit feature of the social-state model of globalisation, is necessarily expressed in an expansionary dynamic. Expansion often promises

---

[57] Rawls 1999, p. 107.

lowers unit costs, allowing lower prices and greater market share. Whenever such economies of scale can be won from expanded production, a firm that does not take advantage of this necessarily tends to be undercut by competitors who do. Further, benefits can be won from expansion even without economies of scale in production. Suppose expansion allows a firm to double the mass of its profits, while its rate of profit remains the same. Rational investors would probably punish a firm that did not take this option. Managers, wishing to increase the amount of retained earnings under their control, have an incentive to select this option as well. Expansion might also enable the firm to attain economies of scale in areas outside the realm of production, such as marketing. Finally, in many cases, expansion improves the bargaining position of a firm in negotiations with suppliers, distributors, creditors, and so on.

It is time to summarise the argument. In the social-state model of globalisation, the global economy is conceptualised as a set of distinct and externally related national economies. These national economies are organised on capitalist principles, which necessarily generate both an expansionary drive and a tendency to lower transportation and communications costs through technological change. When combined with the liberties and interests of economic agents, the result is a necessary tendency for extensive foreign trade and cross-border capital flows to occur. As economic circuits within and across national borders become thoroughly intertwined, a single world market arises, with emergent properties quite distinct from the aggregate of national economies taken separately. No set of protectionist measures consistent with the liberty rights granted to economic agents in the model is capable of preventing or reversing this state of affairs. *The essential determinations of the social-state model of globalisation thus generate structural tendencies that are inconsistent with the manner in which the global economy is conceptualised in this model.* This immanent contradiction provides an initial justification for a transition to a new position in the systematic dialectic of globalisation.

The addition of the world market as a new level of determinations does not necessarily call into question other fundamental claims asserted by advocates of the social-state model of globalisation. Everything depends on the emergent properties arising on this level and the manner in which they affect the model as a whole. In the case at hand, the tendencies that arise on the level of the world market call into question the utterly essential claim that the social state is capable of fulfilling the tasks assigned to it by its proponents.

The limits of the social state

In Rawls's version of the social state, the stabilisation branch of government has the responsibility to maintain full employment in the national economy. But once extensive webs of cross-border transactions have arisen, the effectiveness of government spending to stimulate the economy and eliminate unemployment necessarily tends to be quite limited. As these webs expand, a significant portion of the economic stimulus provided by government spending is diverted to expenditures on imports, weakening the spur to domestic production and job creation.[58]

Suppose further that those who make investment decisions believe – as they generally do – that full employment policies encourage wages to increase faster than productivity advances, setting off an inflationary spiral. Industrial and financial investments tend to flow to areas where inflationary expectations are low, everything else being equal.[59] And, so, the more effective the stabilisation branch is at eliminating unemployment in the national economy, the greater the danger that capital investment will flow elsewhere, generating unemployment in the national economy. The policies of the stabilisation branch thus appear to be self-defeating; the more they fulfil their objectives in the short-term, the more likely they are to undermine those same objectives in the medium-to-long term.

---

[58] Paul Davidson, perhaps the leading post-Keynesian economist, has developed this criticism of the 'Keynesian' state Rawls defends: 'Any nation foolish enough to attempt, on its own, to engage in Keynesian fiscal (and/or monetary) policies aimed at deliberately stimulating internal effective demand to lift its industries out of a recessionary or slow growth mode will become enmeshed in a balance of payments problem as imports rise relative to exports. Simultaneously, any resulting stronger domestic markets that significantly reduce unemployment might encourage inflationary wage and profit demands by domestic workers and firms'. Davidson 2002, p. 217.

[59] It is important not to overstate the extent to which capital is 'footloose' in the global economy. Industrial capital in particular remains bound to particular regions by previous investments in fixed capital, the need to be close to state-of-the-art research facilities, the need for quick delivery to consumer markets, the availability of managers and workers with the requisite skills, and so on (Storper and Walker 1989). But the technological dynamism of capitalism tends to result in a faster rate of 'moral depreciation' of investment in fixed capital, enhancing the medium-term mobility of industrial capital. The fact that industrial investment capital is not completely 'footloose' does not in itself rule out the thesis that the exit options of industrial and financial capital call into question the internal coherence of the social-state model of globalisation.

The danger of outflows of financial capital can be reduced by raising interest rates on government and corporate borrowings. But higher rates are generally correlated with lower overall investment and levels of job creation. The policy best designed to defend the stabilisation branch simultaneously tends to undermine its capacity to attain its objectives.

Maintaining a full employment economy may also require deficit spending for extended periods. This is widely thought by investors to crowd out private investment, thereby undercutting economic growth. It is also widely thought to increase the danger of inflation, since governments will be tempted to repay holders of government debts by printing excess money. To the extent these beliefs are widely shared, capital investment will tend to flow out of regions with high government deficits, increasing unemployment. Higher interest rates can counteract such flows. But, once again, higher interest rates themselves undercut full employment policies.

These considerations do not imply that government employment programmes are always and everywhere ineffectual. But they do entail that the more aggressively and effectively the social state pursues the goal of full employment, the less likely it is that private investment flows will provide the necessary material preconditions for attaining this goal. 'Immanent contradiction' is the appropriate term to describe this state of affairs.

Analogous arguments can be developed regarding the transfer and distribution branches. These branches are to redistribute income to ensure that the least advantaged groups benefit from economic inequality, and that fair equality of opportunity and the fair value of political liberties are preserved.[60] Rawls and other proponents of the social state explicitly acknowledge that capitalist markets necessarily tend to generate inequalities pushing strongly in the opposite direction, and so the redistribution that must be undertaken by the transfer and distribution branches is considerable, requiring extensive state revenues. But cross-border flows of trade and investment grant exit options to the owners and controllers of great concentrations of wealth, allowing them to implement effective tax-minimising strategies. Is this compatible with strong redistributive programmes?

---

[60] The discussion in the main text does not depend on the specifics of Rawls's difference principle. See note 30 above.

One example should suffice to illustrate the problem. The leading units of capital in the contemporary global order are organised in form of multinational corporations. As Paul Davidson and many others have pointed out:

> The transfer price recorded in the multinational corporation's accounting books need not be a market price. Rather, it can reflect a valuation picked by the multinational's comptroller. Transfer prices can be arbitrarily set to avoid national tax liabilities in a nation.[61]

A company with various subsidiaries in different nations can set up a 'daisy-chain' of transfer prices in response to a high rate of corporate taxation in some country A. The company can first transfer a commodity to a subsidiary in a nation B with negligible corporate profit taxes, at a price that shows a loss. The subsidiary in B can then ship the product at a high price to a subsidiary in nation C, another high-tax region. The chain is completed when the subsidiary in C sells the product for a loss in C. The profits from production and distribution have been entirely transferred to the subsidiary in the tax-haven nation. The 'losses' inflicted on the subsidiaries in A and C can then be used to offset profits on their strictly domestic operations, enabling them to avoid tax liabilities. The commodity can even be shipped directly from A to C without ever physically being in B, with the subsidiary in B taking legal title while the commodity is in international waters.[62] Any social order organised on capitalist lines will include vast armies of financial experts competing to find ingenious strategies to minimise the tax burden of corporations and wealthy individuals.[63]

This does not mean that all forms of progressive taxation are impossible, or that government revenues can never be used to reduce inequality and alleviate poverty. However, the costs associated with the transfer and

---

[61] Davidson 2002, p. 141.

[62] Davidson 2002, pp. 148–9. According to *The Economist*, 'An extraordinary 60% of international trade is within these multinationals, ie, firms trading with themselves. . . . Of course, transfer pricing is open to manipulation. A report by America's Senate in 2001 claims that multinationals evaded up to $45 billion in American taxes in 2000'. *Economist* 2004a, p. 72. The IMF concurs: 'Globalization may be expected increasingly to constrain governments' choice of tax structures. . . . Internationally mobile factors of production . . . can more easily avoid taxes levied in particular countries'. International Monetary Fund 1997, p. 70.

[63] An illuminating discussion of the vast opportunities to evade regulations and taxes provided by derivatives is found in Neftci 2002.

distribution branches tend to fall the so-called 'middle class' and ordinary workers, as opposed to the corporations and individuals who enjoy both the greatest wealth and the greatest number of effective exit options from the domestic economy. The more the transfer and distribution branches fulfill the ambitious tasks assigned to them by Rawls and other defenders of the social state, the greater the tax burden placed on the 'middle class' and lower-income workers.[64] In certain circumstances – general prosperity, relative ethnic and cultural homogeneity – this may be sustainable for an extended period. However, in other circumstances – a 'middle class' and national workforce feeling increasing economic strain and insecurity, persistent racial and ethnic divisions – this will *not* be the case.[65] In such circumstances, the more the transfer and distribution branches successfully attain their objectives, the more politically unsustainable this result becomes.

I conclude that the dominant tendency in the social-state model of globalisation is for the social programmes that endure to be far less ambitious than what justice requires in the view of the model's leading proponents. While some forms of absolute deprivation may be addressed, relative inequality sufficient to rule out the fair value of political liberties and fair equality of opportunity necessarily tends to remain in place. The Rawlsian claim that the social-state model of globalisation can in principle institutionalise these normative principles thus directly conflicts with the dominant structural tendencies implicit in this model.

A similar immanent contradiction besets the allocation branch as well. In certain circumstances, and to a certain extent, a functioning social state might be able to devise 'suitable taxes and subsidies and . . . changes in the definition of property rights' to correct market prices failing to reflect social benefits and costs accurately. But, here too, we must recall that the social-state model of globalisation implicitly grants significant exit options to the individuals and enterprises faced with new taxes or a redefinition of their property rights.

---

[64] In this context, it may be relevant to note that the big welfare states of Europe are less redistributive than commonly thought. They tax habits to which a relatively high proportion of the income of non-élites is devoted far more than luxuries, and suppliers of capital far less than labourers. See Lindert 2004.

[65] Ethnic and racial diversity is strongly correlated with low government spending on poverty programmes throughout the world, even after adjusting for differences in average income (Alesina and Glaeser 2004).

The more effectively the allocation branch fulfills its tasks, the more likely it is that these exit options will be taken. And the more they are taken, the less the allocation branch can be fulfil these tasks effectively. Rawls's claim that this branch is able to correct market prices to the degree necessary to maintain the justice of the social order (as he defines it) also does not appear to be grounded in the basic determinations of the model he defends.

The other task of the allocation branch is to prevent 'unreasonable concentrations of market power'. What counts as 'unreasonable'? From one point of view, the term refers to concentrations of market power inconsistent with economic efficiency.[66] From another, an 'unreasonable' concentration of economic power in the social-state framework is one that threatens the fair value of political liberties and fair equality of opportunity. Once the implicit tendencies for a world market to emerge are acknowledged, what is 'reasonable' from one point of view fundamentally diverges from what is 'reasonable' from the other.

Many theorists and policymakers insist that the traditional anti-trust concerns expressed by Rawls must be rethought in light of trade and investment flows across borders. An increase in corporate size need not imply any decline in competition; if giant foreign firms enter domestic markets competitive pressures can increase. Economic efficiency ('competitiveness') then may demand that domestic firms increase in size more or less in tandem with foreign competitors. But there is absolutely no reason to suppose such increases in size are compatible with the fair value of political liberties and fair equality of opportunity, as advocates of the social state define these terms. Past a certain point, at least, concentrations of economic power are inconsistent with the broad dispersal of political power and a roughly equal chance of making one's voice heard.[67]

How should state officials in the allocation branch respond when this tension arises between the two notions of 'reasonable'? Sacrificing the fair value of political liberties and fair equality of opportunity would appear to be ruled

---

[66] '[U]nreasonable market power ... does not exist as long as markets cannot be made more competitive consistent with the requirements of efficiency and the facts of geography and the preferences of households'. Rawls 1971, p. 276.

[67] There is no good reason to think that the public funding of elections would eliminate this difficulty. It is the only reform Rawls suggests for setting public deliberation 'free from the curse of money'. Rawls 1999, p. 139.

out by the priority given to these principles in Rawls's framework. But, if this condemns the national economy to uncompetitiveness in the world market as domestic firms are not allowed to grow as much as foreign competitors, the social state will not be able to appropriate the revenues it requires to fulfill its functions. Once again, an immanent contradiction can be perceived at the very heart of the social-state position.

The goal of this section has not been to present a comprehensive analysis of the social-state model of globalisation. In the present context, all that is required is to establish an irresolvable tension between the most significant claims asserted by the model's leading defenders and essential features of the model. I have shown that a global framework centring on social states implicitly includes determinations that necessarily tend to undermine the claims of feasibility and normative attractiveness made by the framework's foremost proponents. These claims rest on the social state's capacity to thoroughly shape the workings of domestic markets. The cross-border transactions and exit options of enterprises and individuals, however, necessarily tend to undermine precisely this capacity. While it is possible to imagine the social state imposing protectionist measures that restrict those transactions and options, measures strong enough to grant the power to thoroughly shape the workings of domestic markets are clearly inconsistent with the liberty rights granted to economic agents in the model. In other words, one sort of immanent contradiction can be avoided only at the cost of falling into another.

Many other criticisms of the social-state model could be proposed and defended.[68] But those that have been presented here are sufficient to justify

---

[68] Another line of criticism is suggested by the following striking passage: 'given the great shortcomings of actual, allegedly constitutional democratic regimes, it is no surprise that they should often intervene in weaker countries, including those exhibiting some aspects of a democracy, or even that they should engage in war for expansionist reasons. As for the first situation, the United States overturned the democracies of Allende in Chile, Arbenz in Guatemala, Mossadegh in Iran, and, some would add, the Sandinistas in Nicaragua. Whatever the merits of these regimes, covert operations against them were carried out by a government prompted by monopolistic and oligarchic interests without the knowledge or criticism of the public'. Rawls 1999, p. 53. Rawls clearly holds that the pernicious influence of 'monopolistic and oligarchic interests' is a merely contingent matter that has nothing to do with what he terms 'the deep tendencies and inclinations of the social world' today. If he is mistaken about the ability of the social state to check the rise of 'monopolistic and oligarchic interests', then his assessment of the dominant geopolitical tendencies in the capitalist

a transition to a new position in the systematic dialectic of globalisation. The essential determinations of social-state model of globalisation necessarily tend to generate forms of behaviour that undermine its feasibility and normative attractiveness, as measured by principles accepted by the model's leading adherents. According to the methodological framework of systematic dialectics, the next position must explicitly address the immanent contradictions implicit in the social-state model. If a number of models meet this criterion, the one we seek must be simpler and more abstract than any relevant alternative. This is the *neoliberal model of globalisation*.

---

global order is mistaken as well. A disproportionate influence of these interests on government policy would be the normal state of affairs, with pernicious results going far beyond periodic covert interventions.

Chapter Two

The Neoliberal Model of Globalisation

In this chapter, I shall argue that neoliberalism explicitly incorporates features of the contemporary global order merely implicit in the social-state framework. In this sense, the neoliberal model of globalisation is an advance in complexity and concreteness over the social-state model, and so forms the appropriate next stage in a systematic dialectic of globalisation. I shall then investigate whether this second framework would tend to be reproduced over time in an efficient and normatively acceptable fashion, as measured by the standards of its leading supporters. If this is the case, the systematic ordering of positions in the globalisation debate concludes. If it is not the case, the neoliberal model of globalisation is itself afflicted with immanent contradictions pushing the dialectic forward.

A vast number of contributions to social theory and public policy fit under the heading of neoliberalism.[1] There are many profound differences among them, differences that in countless other contexts would be crucial. In the present context, however, the family resemblances are more significant, although I shall distinguish two main variants of

---

[1] For example, elements of classical political economy, neoclassical economics, Austrian alternatives to neoclassical economics (Hayek, Schumpeter, and so on) can be found in the writings of contemporary neoliberals.

neoliberalism in Section 2 below. A model of globalisation capturing the family resemblances could be constructed from the work of a representative neoliberal theorist, or from a variety of authors. In contrast to the previous chapter, I have chosen the latter option here.

1. The neoliberal model (1): households, national economies, and the world market

In some respects, at least, the normative principles defining neoliberalism are not so different from those defended by advocates of the social state. Neoliberals, no less than Rawls, hold that all individuals have a basic right to autonomy and a fundamental interest in material well-being. The most profound disagreements between the two positions regard the institutional framework that furthers this right and interest the most effectively.

We may once again begin with the household. Official neoliberal doctrine grants central importance to the autonomy of the individual. Neoliberal theorists sharply rebuke traditional patriarchal views regarding gender relations in heterosexual households, according to which women's activities are properly limited to the domestic sphere. They instead adopt the 'liberal-feminist' view that women should be granted equal formal rights to education, employment opportunities, access to credit, participation in political processes, etc.[2]

So far, at least, this position is fairly close to that of Rawls and other social-state theorists.[3] Suppose, however, that the established division of labour is 'gendered', in the sense that the husband in a heterosexual household is likely to have significantly greater opportunities to obtain better paid and higher status positions than a comparably talented wife. Given this state of affairs, household decisions granting priority to the husband's career are most likely to maximise total household income, a self-evident imperative for neoliberals.[4]

---

[2] For a thorough comparison of liberal feminism with other variants, see Jagger's classic study, Jagger 1988.

[3] Many neoliberals also agree with Rawls that gender oppression explains the persistence of poverty in the global economy to a considerable extent. In this causal chain, oppressive cultural practices against women lead to overpopulation relative to economic resources, that is, to low per capita income. See Wolf 2004, p. 165.

[4] See Becker 1981. Gary Becker won a Nobel Prize in economics for employing the methodological precepts and ontological assumptions of neoclassical economics to the study of everyday life, including the family. Within this framework, the decisions taken by family heads are directed towards the maximisation of the utility of the

In this manner, neoliberalism can, in effect, function as a belief system legitimating the systematic reproduction of traditional gender relations, however vehemently patriarchal worldviews are officially decried.[5] Whatever other problems may have beset Rawls's position on the household, it did not suffer from this sort of immanent contradiction quite so blatantly.

The effects of neoliberal institutions and policies on households will be discussed below. For now, two points introduced in the previous chapter must be recalled. In modern societies, families cannot provide for their own material reproduction. And the family does not provide an institutional setting for the full development of individual autonomy. Within the neoliberal framework, as in the social-state perspective, these considerations justify a shift from a narrow focus on the family to a wider perspective explicitly taking into account the social context within which the family is embedded. The first element of this wider context is civil society.

At first glance, at least, neoliberals and social-state theorists broadly agree on the sorts of entities and structures found in civil society. These include a wide variety of voluntary associations dedicated to the pursuit of shared interests. In the neoliberal position, as in the social-state model, the organisation of production and distribution is given special attention.

Neoliberals insist that a capitalist market society provides individuals with opportunities to develop and exercise their autonomy more than any feasible alternative economic framework. They also invoke Adam Smith's invisible hand thesis: the pursuit of private self-interest in the market generally tends to further the interests of others. And they acknowledge the technological dynamism of capitalist market societies.[6] All of this is broadly compatible with the views of Rawls and other proponents of the social state. As we saw in the previous chapter, however, many of the implications of these assertions remain merely implicit in the social-state framework. These implications are explicitly affirmed in neoliberalism.

---

family as a whole. A critical assessment of Becker's work is found in Nussbaum 2001, Chapter 4.

[5] See Kessler-Harris 2002.

[6] This acknowledgement is more consistent with some variants of neoliberalism than others. It fits far better with Schumpeter's analysis than with neoclassical economics, which generally treats technological change as exogenous to capitalist markets. See Smith 1997a and 2004.

Neoliberal theorists happily acknowledge that advances in transportation and communication technologies tend to encourage cross-border economic transactions. The compass, steamships, railroads, telegraphs and telephones have all had this effect in the past.[7] Consumers today can log onto the internet and purchase commodities from anywhere on the planet. Information technologies significantly heighten the ability of industrial capitals to shift parts of the production chain across borders through foreign direct investment and subcontracting arrangements. Financial investments in a nation's currency and bonds, or in the bonds and equity of a nation's enterprises, can be shifted across the planet with a few keystrokes. Neoliberal theorists stress how the rational self-interest of economic agents ensures that these exit options will be pursued regularly in capitalist market societies.

This certainly does not imply that it is illegitimate to refer to 'national economies'. But attempts to impose a sharp distinction between the 'inside' and 'outside' of a national economy today are quixotic. The ratio of imports and exports to gross national product necessarily tends to be high enough to rule out categorising the global economy as a set of more-or-less independent national economies externally related through trade and investment.[8] If national economies significantly depend upon investment and consumption decisions made outside their borders, then national economies must be categorised as moments of a bigger whole, a world market with emergent properties distinct from the aggregate of properties of national economies taken separately.

This thesis can be elaborated in terms of the notions of absolute and comparative advantage. For Adam Smith, David Ricardo, and the subsequent generations of economists influenced by them, foreign trade provides mutual benefits to the trading nations.[9] To take the standard example, suppose England produces textiles more efficiently than Portugal, while Portugal enjoys higher levels of productivity in the wine sector. If each nation specialises in the sector

---

[7] O'Rourke and Williamson 2000.

[8] The trend in the global economy is clearly for this ratio to increase. In the early 1960s, for example, 4% of U.S. domestic production was subject to international competition. This figure jumped to 70% by the early 1990s. Hoogvelt 2001, p. 133. And this ratio understates the increasing integration of national economies in the world market. It does not capture the impact of the mere threat of losing market share to imports.

[9] Landreth 1976, pp. 102–6.

where it has an absolute productivity advantage, more total textiles and more wine will be produced in the world market as a whole than will be the case if each nation tries to be self-sufficient in both commodities. Specialisation and foreign trade therefore allow more of the wants and needs of the citizens of each nation to be met.

It is not intuitively obvious that the same conclusion holds if one nation enjoys an absolute advantage in both sectors. Ricardo, however, argues that this is in fact the case whenever 'opportunity costs' in the two regions differ. Suppose Portugal enjoys an absolute advantage in the production of both wine and textiles, but it must give up more units of wine to produce an extra unit of textiles than England would. While England lacks an absolute productivity advantage in the production of textiles, it still enjoys a 'comparative advantage' in this sector, where its opportunity costs are lower than Portugal's. If each nation specialises in the sector where it has a comparative advantage, greater output of each commodity will be produced in the world market as a whole. Once again, specialisation and foreign trade make it possible for more of the wants and needs of the citizens of each nation to be met.

In the social-state model, the essential determinations of generalised commodity production are located on the level of the national economy. Given these determinations, however, there is a dominant tendency for sectors in a national economy to produce for export markets whenever they enjoy a comparative advantage in the world market. The other side of the coin is a strong tendency for a significant proportion of wants and needs in any given nation to be met through imports. The more such cross-border flows occur, the less plausible it is to conceive of the world as a set of more or less independent national economies standing in external relations to each other. The neoliberal perspective makes explicit the fact that any discussion of generalised commodity production prior to an account of the world market will necessarily be radically incomplete and provisional.

This major contrast with the social-state framework immediately demands another. The manner in which the state is categorised must be rethought as well. The state can no longer be seen as an overarching institution whose territorial limits contain the boundaries of the economy. Instead of standing over capitalist markets, the state occupies a middle position between the not-at-all self-sufficient national economy and global markets. The implications of this far reaching shift must now be explored.

2. The neoliberal model (2): the state

There are a great many versions of neoliberalism, just as there are many variants of the social-state position. The differences between what I shall term the 'pure' and the 'moderate' versions of neoliberalism are great enough to warrant separate examination here. These differences largely centre on the state. First, however, some significant points of agreement are worth emphasising.

Any adequate model of the contemporary global order demands explicit recognition of the world market as a distinct region with its own emergent properties. All neoliberals hold that developments in the realms of finance, industry, and culture necessarily tend to restrict the range of feasible state policies, excluding in particular those most closely associated with the social state. Given the principle that 'ought implies can', it follows that we ought not attempt to institute the social state.

The social state is a redistributive state, appropriating considerable income from corporations and wealthy individuals and transferring this income to less successful members of society. It should go without saying that corporate executives and other wealthy individuals will generally judge that strong redistribution is not in their best interests.[10] The technological dynamism of capitalism necessarily tends to increase the exit options of precisely these groups, making it easier for corporations to shift production and other investments across borders, and for wealthy investors to minimise what they take to be onerous tax burdens. These economic agents can be expected to make plausible threats to employ their exit options, and to carry out these threats whenever their perceived self-interest is significantly threatened. State officials must adjust to these realities, or suffer a long-term loss of the investment capital that creates productivity advances and improved living standards.[11] The project of constructing a confiscatory social state must thus be ruled out. This result, merely implicit in the social-state model of globalisation, is explicitly acknowledged within the neoliberal framework.

---

[10] It should also go without saying that they will learn how to draw this conclusion in good conscience, convincing themselves that excessive redistribution creates a 'culture of poverty' harming the poor themselves.

[11] In Part Two, this assumption of the creative powers of capital will be called into question. An internal critique of neoliberalism requires that this crucial assumption be provisionally granted.

Attracting mobile capital investment also requires imposing a minimum of burdensome regulatory requirements on corporations, while encouraging maximum flexibility in the work force. The social-state model discussed in the previous chapter pushes in the opposite direction, tending towards maximising regulatory burdens on corporations while minimising the flexibility of the work force. Here too it is ultimately incompatible with the realities of technological dynamism and global markets.

There is nothing especially new about consumers wishing to purchase imports. But technological change in capitalism includes the development of communications technologies, leading to a tremendous diffusion of information regarding products available from overseas markets. Advances in transportation technologies lower the costs of distributing these products across borders. Consumer demand for commodities produced outside their home region accordingly tends to grow in economic importance over time. Any government attempting to restrict the flow of commodities across its borders under these circumstances is likely to feel the wrath of its citizens sooner rather than later, even when developments such as e-commerce do not condemn such endeavours to futility from the start.[12] This state of affairs also drastically limits the state's ability to maintain full employment through government spending. The greater the role of imports in the national economy, the less a given amount of state spending stimulates the domestic economy, and the more the benefits are appropriated by foreign exporters. The burdens of this government spending, in contrast, must eventually be borne by the domestic economy. Advocates of all variants of neoliberalism conclude that the full-employment policies of the social state are not politically sustainable for these reasons.

Turning again to the financial sector, it is remarkable that the international dimension of money is ignored in Rawls's *The Law of Peoples*, despite the fact that this work is devoted to international relations and was written well after the rise of global currency markets in the wake of the collapse of the Bretton Woods fixed exchange-rate system. Currency exchange is implicitly treated as just another form of foreign trade. But currency markets have a unique feature setting them apart: they provide direct and continuous oversight of

---

[12] Friedman 2000.

governments. As William Wriston, the world's most powerful banker during his tenure as chair and CEO of Citicorp/Citibank, noted:

> What annoys governments about stateless money is that it functions as a plebiscite on your policy. There are 300,000 screens out there, lit up with all the news traders need to make value judgements on how well you're running your economy. Before the Euro-market and floating exchange rates, the president could go into the Rose Garden and make a statement about the dollar, and the world would quietly listen. Today, if the president goes into the Rose Garden and says something dumb, the cross rate of the dollar will change within 60 seconds.[13]

The scale of currency circulating through the circuits of global finance capital has all but eliminated the ability of governments to protect the value of their currency against speculative runs. As Wristen poetically explains:

> When I first went into banking, the Federal Reserve could call up Citibank or Morgan and say, 'We want you to buy $10 million to support the currency'. Back then we controlled 20 percent of the foreign exchange market, so that would stabilize it – boom! Now, the Fed could tell us to buy $100 million, and this would be pooping down a well.[14]

It is easy enough to understand what 'pooping down a well' signifies. But what does it mean to 'say something dumb' in this context? According to prevailing views among participants in global capital markets, there is a natural rate of unemployment that cannot be lowered without setting off inflation. And there is a point beyond which government deficit spending may crowd out credit in the private sector, causing interest rates to rise. Government policies that attempt to lower unemployment below what market sentiment considers the natural rate of unemployment, and deficit spending foreseen to crowd out the private sector, are thus 'dumb'. Rational state officials will realise that global capital markets tend to punish states pursuing such policies, making this pursuit worse than ineffective.

It should be clear that the case for the normative model of institutions discussed by Rawls and other defenders of the social state rests upon the

---

[13] Wriston 1996, p. 201.
[14] Ibid.

unstated assumption that capital mobility is severely restricted. Without extremely harsh protectionist measures, governments cannot carry out the tasks assigned to them by supporters of this model. But the combination of technological changes, the interests that necessarily tend to arise within capitalist markets, and the power to pursue those interests granted money holders by the property relations of capitalism, necessarily tends to rule out such measures. This same combination of factors simultaneously tends to restrict the range of feasible state policies, excluding those most intimately associated with the social state.

If the strong redistributive and regulatory agenda of the social state cannot be adequately actualised in practice, and if 'ought implies can', then it follows immediately that we ought not affirm the social-state model of globalisation. While this argument may be sufficient to establish the inadequacy of the social state, it does not establish the normative attractiveness of a neoliberal state. Neoliberal theorists have developed three main arguments to ground this positive claim.

Neoliberals trace their intellectual roots to the classical liberalism of Hobbes and Locke, who understood that the mutual gains from trade and specialisation cannot be securely enjoyed without a coercive apparatus protecting individuals from force and fraud.[15] Generalised commodity production and exchange therefore requires some form of government. The rise of global markets does not lessen this requirement one iota. Nor does it call into question the thesis that no world government is likely to fulfil this requirement as effectively as states. Regions with states capable of establishing and maintaining the rule of law tend to prosper in the global order, while those that fail in this regard necessarily tend to stagnate or decline.

Second, even if the social state could pass the 'ought implies can' test, it would still have to impose illegitimate restrictions on economic agents. It could only function if most of the choices made by investors and consumers were restricted to opportunities offered within national borders. From the standpoint of this second position in the systematic dialectic of globalisation, any attempt by the state to enforce such restrictions must be categorised as

---

[15] The classical liberalism of Hobbes and Locke is quite distinct from the egalitarian liberalism of Rawls and other defenders of the social state. 'Liberalism', like other central categories in social theory, is an ambiguous and bitterly contested term.

an arbitrary and morally illegitimate check on the fundamental rights of liberty and property. The neoliberal state contributes to a just global order simply by refusing to impose such illegitimate restrictions.

Friedrich Hayek presents a particularly powerful and influential version of this argument. In premodern tribes, the interests of individual members were thoroughly subordinated to the interests of the collective. In complex modern societies, in contrast, there are no general agreements regarding conceptions of the good life. Governments cannot impose a particular conception of the good on individual citizens without massive violations of liberty rights.[16] In a just social order the state must concentrate instead on establishing and maintaining 'the rule of just conduct', which allows social agents to act freely as long as doing so does not interfere with the liberty of others. This will best enable its members to accumulate the resources required to pursue their own conceptions of the good. States limited to this task contribute to the formation of an 'Open Society of free men' on the global level:

> It is only by extending the rule of just conduct to the relations with all other men, and at the same time depriving of their obligatory character those rules which cannot be universally applied, that we can approach a universal order of peace which might integrate all mankind into a single society. While in the tribal society the condition of internal peace is the devotion of all members to some common visible purposes, and therefore to the will of somebody who can decide what at any moment these purposes are to be and how they are to be achieved, the Open Society of free men becomes possible only when the individuals are constrained only to obey the abstract rules that demarcate the domain of the means that each is allowed to use for his purposes.[17]

Hayek supplements this rights-based argument with a consequentialist justification of the neoliberal state. Market prices convey relevant information for decision making in a decentralised fashion, providing each individual with feedback regarding the extent to which her decisions fit together with

---

[16] If individuals voluntarily join an association with others sharing the same values and goals, that is a different matter. In that case the behaviour of individuals can be coordinated *ex ante* in a non-oppressive fashion.

[17] Hayek 1976, p. 144.

the decisions of others. No other way of effectively processing the immense amount of information regarding economic activities relevant to modern life can be conceived. Capitalist markets thus enable individuals to co-ordinate their economic behaviour more efficiently than any feasible alternative. Neoliberal states that protect the freedom of economic agents engaging in cross-border transactions do not simply respect liberty and property rights. They also further the positive consequences that result when agents separated by borders co-operate for mutual benefit. In this manner, the neoliberal state furthers the fundamental interest of all individuals in material well-being.

A third normative consideration rests on an appeal to democratic values. On the level of individual states, ordinary citizens lack the time, the inclination, and the monetary resources to monitor state actions effectively. Long intervals between elections also limit the extent to which state officials are accountable even in formally democratic régimes. Participants in global capital markets, in contrast, have the temporal and monetary resources, and the incentive, to subject state officials to continuous oversight. From the neoliberal perspective, the instantaneous plebiscites of financial markets do more than just rule out the social-state model of globalisation. They have a positive dimension as well. They provide the most effective form of 'economic democracy' ever known in world history:

> [B]y the end of the day, the market will have conducted a referendum reflecting the collective wisdom of people all around the world on what they think of our economic policies. . . . This is the first time in the history of the world that every major country has a flat currency that is not based on gold or silver or some other commodity. Today, the value of money is hooked to nothing other than the information that flows through it. If your currency becomes worthless, the world knows about it very quickly. If your economic policies are lousy, the market will punish you instantly. I'm in favor this kind of economic democracy. There's nothing you can do to change it, except do it right.[18]

Both 'pure' and 'moderate' neoliberals agree that the world market must be placed at the centre of any adequate model of the global order, with the state occupying a space between a porous national economy and global markets.

---

[18] Wriston 1996, pp. 202–4. See also Friedman 2000, p. 137, and Wolf 2004, p. 273.

There is also a general consensus among neoliberals that global markets rule out the social state, selecting out a state form that renounces strong redistributive policies and restrictions on trade and investment. Both camps agree that liberty rights, efficiency, and democratic values legitimate this type of state. These considerations, however, still leave the precise form and function of the neoliberal state fairly indeterminate.

Defenders of pure neoliberalism accept the libertarian thesis that the only normatively acceptable state is a minimal state, restricted to protecting citizens from fraud and force (the 'rule of law').[19] There are three main arguments for this thesis. First, there is the claim that the operation of global markets necessarily tends to restrict the state to these tasks. In other words, in their view, pure neoliberalism results from simply pushing the criticisms of the social state based upon the 'ought implies can' principle to their logical conclusions. A number of these criticisms were based on the technological dynamism of capitalism, and the exit options this provides. Innovations tend to enable consumers and investors to shield their activities from effective tax assessment and government oversight. With strong encryption programs, for example, governments cannot even know about international transactions routed through off-shore banking facilities. The inability to monitor, let alone regulate, economic transactions effectively, and the restricted tax revenues that result, necessarily tend to reduce states to an absolute minimum of functions.[20] For pure neoliberals, only the 'minimal state' is 'actual', in Hegel's sense of the term. While more-than-minimal states exist now, and will surely continue to exist in the foreseeable future, the dominant tendencies in the social world undermine the capacity of such states to reproduce themselves stably over time.

Another argument for the pure (libertarian) version of neoliberalism presents moderate neoliberals with a great intellectual and political challenge, since they unequivocally affirm its main premises. Human nature is not magically transformed the instant someone assumes a position in the state apparatus; state officials, like everyone else, are primarily motivated by self-interest. But, in market societies, there is a profound difference between the institutional

---

[19] Nozick 1974 remains the classic philosophical defence of libertarianism.
[20] An interesting overview of the politics and culture of 'technolibertarianism' is found in Borsook 2000.

context in which state officials pursue their private self-interest and the context in which the rest of us do so. In the market, the 'invisible hand' is in place; market competition ensures that the pursuit of private self-interest necessarily tends to result in mutual benefits. State officials do not confront this check.

It would be pleasant to think that the mechanisms of political democracy guarantee that decisions made by state officials necessarily tend to coincide with the social good. But only the terminally naïve could spout such rhetoric. For one thing, most state officials hold appointed positions, and are not accountable to the general populace in any direct manner at all. For another, according to Hayek and other pure neoliberals, there simply is not any general social good for state officials to further, even were they disposed to do so. Various individuals and groups inevitably have different and often incompatible conceptions of the good life. It would be a terrible mistake to define the policies contingently accepted by state officials, or by a majority of voters at a given time, as 'the social good'.[21] Democratic mechanisms also break down completely when public policies result in concentrated benefits and dispersed costs. If the benefits of proposed policies can be appropriated by relatively small special interest groups, those groups have a strong incentive to forge alliances with state agencies to institute them, using all the legal, quasi-legal, and outright illegal means at their disposal.[22] When the costs of those public policies are widely dispersed, individual citizens have very weak incentives to devote the time, energy, and money that effective oversight of state officials requires. Similarly serious problems arise in cases of dispersed benefits and concentrated costs.

Pure neoliberals conclude that all more than minimal states are afflicted with a systematic tendency to 'crony capitalism'. State officials and their cronies will always and everywhere attempt to use their political positions and influence to appropriate rents from the productive sectors of society. And if the majority can enjoy benefits from policies that concentrate costs upon a few (such as the wealthy), they will be disposed to elect representatives to institute such policies. In both cases the liberty and well-being of those from whom rent is appropriated, and the overall efficiency of the economy, are undermined. The continuous plebiscites of global capital markets may lessen

---

[21] Hayek 1976, p. 111.
[22] Cigler and Loomis 1998.

these difficulties in some policy areas, but only a minimal state eliminates them entirely.

A third argument in favour of the libertarian variant of neoliberalism is based upon the so-called 'Fundamental Theorem' of welfare economics, which asserts in part that competitive markets yield 'Pareto optimal equilibria'. The idea underlying this assertion is intuitive enough; it is yet another formulation of the invisible hand thesis. Freely undertaken trades provide mutual benefits, otherwise they would not be freely undertaken. Such trades will continue as long as further mutual benefits can be won. And, so, the market automatically tends to a 'Pareto optimal' result, in which no one can be made better-off without someone else becoming worse-off. A corollary of this argument is that market economies automatically tend to operate at full capacity. It follows that economic efficiency requires free markets in all goods and services. Competition in global markets will consequently tend to select for minimal states that do not interfere in these markets. In the long term, such competition will also do more to improve the material well-being of the least advantaged groups than any feasible alternative.

Moderate neoliberals agree with many of the above assertions. Nonetheless, they do not accept the conclusion that the only normatively acceptable state is a minimal state. Nor do they agree that the minimal state is somehow privileged in the age of globalisation.

Regarding the first argument, the vast majority of neoliberals reject the technological-determinist justification for asserting the inevitable triumph of libertarianism. There may be a tendency for information technologies to develop that enable cross-border economic transactions to avoid certain forms of detection. But the same technological developments may make it possible to *extend* the state's capacity to monitor international money flows. Further, coalitions of leading states retain the capacity to restrict access to tax havens, as legislation directed against the laundering of drug money shows. Additional restrictions could be imposed whenever access to tax havens undermines the ability of states to appropriate sufficient revenues for tasks deemed necessary. Finally, not all forms of taxation are threatened by capital mobility across borders. State revenues can be appropriated from consumption taxes collected at the point of sale. Further, corporate headquarters, offices, warehouses, factories, and homes all continue to be located in geographically specific places. They are relatively immobile, and thus remain subject to various forms of effective state taxation.[23] Moderate neoliberals agree that there are systematic tendencies in the global economy undermining the ability of governments to appropriate the massive revenues required for the strong redistributive schemes of the social state. But this does not imply that the minimal state of pure neoliberalism is the only feasible alternative.

In contrast to their dismissal of the first argument, moderate neoliberals concede the power of the second. All more-than-minimal states are threatened by rent-seeking behaviour and crony capitalism. But a closer consideration of the third argument reveals why the conclusions libertarians draw from the second should be rejected.

Whatever their other disagreements, critics of libertarianism across the political spectrum share one belief in common: while libertarians may talk about the virtues of markets *ad nauseam*, they do not understand the ABC's of the way markets actually work. The 'Fundamental Theorem' that was the basis of the third argument for the minimal neoliberal state presupposes perfect competition, an economy that always remains in equilibrium, and an absence of positive and negative externalities.[24] Not a single one of these conditions has ever held in any capitalist market society, and none ever will. While moderate neoliberals themselves appeal to the 'Fundamental Theorem' when arguing for the superiority of markets over other ways of organising production and distribution, they recognise that the conditions under which it holds are so restrictive that it does *not* provide an adequate foundation for a theory of the state.[25] Each of the three conditions is worth discussing briefly.

---

[23] Wolf 2004, pp. 269–70.

[24] Graaf 1957. See also Chapter 1, note 21.

[25] Advocates of other positions considered in this work have a much harsher assessment of the theorem. While simplifying assumptions must always be invoked when constructing theoretical models, assumptions should not be employed that fundamentally distort essential features of the realm under investigation. The 'Fundamental Theorem' does precisely that. For example, proofs for the 'Fundamental Theorem' also presuppose that consumer tastes are innate, another wildly implausible assumption given the social factors shaping consumer desires. These proofs also assume that all market participants possess perfect information regarding all past, present and future markets, and that transaction costs do not arise in the course of production and exchange. For opponents of pure neoliberalism these are all distorting – rather than merely simplifying – assumptions. Critics of neoliberalism also note that the very notion of Pareto optimality is deeply flawed from a normative standpoint with respect to distributional issues. A society in which a small handful of individuals appropriates almost all the income and wealth of a society, leaving the vast majority in hopeless poverty, can count as 'optimal' according to this notion.

In capitalist markets, firms necessarily tend to do whatever they can to *escape* pure competition. If a firm makes a widget more or less indistinguishable from those produced by numerous other firms, competition can be expected to reduce its profits to the vanishing point. But, if a firm innovates and introduces a new sort of widget that meets consumer wants and needs in a new manner, or that creates new wants or needs, then it enjoys a temporary monopoly. During the period it takes other firms in the sector to imitate the innovation successfully (or to leapfrog over it with a new generation of products) a higher price can be charged, and greater profits appropriated. This dynamic is at the root of the technological dynamism so crucial to so many neoliberal arguments in favour of market capitalism.[26]

The technological dynamism of capitalist markets also undermines the assumption that the economy naturally tends towards equilibrium. Tendencies to equilibrium undoubtedly exist in capitalist markets. But they exist alongside tendencies to disequilibrium; innovations by definition upset established ways of combining inputs and outputs.

Further reflection on the innovation process reveals the pervasiveness of externalities in capitalist markets. The mere fact that an innovation has been made has positive spillover effects on other market participants, informing them that a particular sort of innovation is possible. Usually the positive externalities from successful investments in research and development are far more extensive than this.[27] Investments in infrastructure, education, and training typically have high levels of positive spillover effects as well. The more extensive these effects, the greater the danger of market failure according to standard neoliberal theory. If innovators are unable to appropriate a significant portion of foreseeable benefits, the level of investment in innovation in the economy as a whole necessarily tends to be less than what is socially optimal. And, so, successful innovations typically require public investments in research and development, infrastructure, and education and training, all of which transcend the limits of the minimal state.

Libertarians have answers to this set of problems. Adjustments can be made allowing innovators to appropriate a greater portion of the benefits from their investments, thereby encouraging greater private expenditures. The intellectual

---

[26] See, especially, Schumpeter 1934.
[27] Mansfield et al. 1967.

property rights régime can be revised to extend the scope of an innovator's monopoly right and the period in which it is enjoyed. Tolls can be charged for the use of new infrastructure. Employees can be made to sign agreements to repay investments in their education and training if they decide to leave the employer who made these investments.

All of these adjustments come at a very high cost. Extending the temporary monopolies granted by intellectual property rights would further undermine the assumption of pure competition, an absolutely essential assumption in the argument for the Pareto efficiency of markets. Further, the more this measure is effective, the slower the diffusion of innovations. Past a certain point, at least, delays in diffusion undermine the argument that markets automatically function in a maximally efficient manner. Finally, removing positive externalities from the innovation process would slow that process to a crawl. Regions characterised by high rates of innovation necessarily tend to be 'technological milieus' in which extensive positive spillover effects are generated within networks of informal communication among workers, engineers, managers, venture capitalists, and end-users.[28]

Market failures also arise from negative externalities, such as environmental harms. Market competition forces firms to attempt to minimise their costs of production (factories, transportation, labour, raw materials, etc.). Everything else being equal, a firm with lower production costs wins higher profits. These internal costs are not equivalent to the total social costs of production. If someone downwind from a plant gets cancer as a result of its pollution, this too counts as a cost. In the short-to-medium term, at least, addressing negative externalities such as environmental harms often requires a higher level of outlay to develop and introduce new production technologies. Market competition discourages such expenditures, since higher costs are generally correlated with higher prices, declining market share, and lower profits.

Once again, pure neoliberals have a response at hand. A minimal state can pass 'polluter pays' legislation, granting those harmed by pollution the right to compensation for harm to their property. Polluters are then forced to internalise the costs of pollution. At that point, market competition provides a rational incentive for them to search for ways to minimise these costs.[29]

---

[28] Storper and Walker 1989.
[29] Anderson and Leal 1991.

This reply assumes that causal chains are relatively easy to establish, that victims of negative externalities always have sufficient legal resources to pursue offenders, and that all harms can be compensated. It is not reasonable to assume any of these things, and so it is not reasonable to assume that 'polluter pays' legislation forces polluting firms to internalise all pollution costs.[30] Moderate neoliberals accept that more intrusive government actions will be required. In some contexts, for instance, state officials should set an overall level of pollution emission, grant private property rights to pollute up to that level, and establish new markets in which such emission rights can be traded. In cases of extreme and well-documented harms, outright government bans of certain production technologies may be preferable.

Moderate neoliberals are adamant that the state adopt measures interfering with the functioning of markets as little as possible. But they do not deny that there is a need for public policies designed to minimise the market failures associated with both positive and negative externalities, policies ruled out by pure neoliberals. Extensive cross-border flows of trade and investment do not eliminate positive and negative externalities, or the need for state interventions in response to them. In fact, a compelling case can be made that an increasing scale and velocity of these flows intensifies the need for the development of effective state capacities to reverse market failures. The easier it is for investments to flow across borders, the stronger the imperative to attract capital investment. A state effectively addressing market failures furthers this end; the minimal state of pure neoliberalism does not.

If the empirical relevance of the 'Fundamental Theorem' is called into question, the thesis that a pure neoliberal order will do more to improve the material well-being of least advantaged groups than any feasible alternative must also be reconsidered. Moderate neoliberals understand that globalisation generates losers as well as winners, especially among the ranks of the unskilled. Within the moderate neoliberal framework income supplements, housing and medical benefits, and other forms of social protection, are legitimate means of helping the most vulnerable sectors of society adjust to the social disruptions imposed by globalisation.

Turning back to the second argument for pure neoliberalism, libertarians see the state as a necessary evil, a mere means to enable individuals and

---

[30] Smith 1995.

groups to further their private ends without falling into a war of all against all. In their estimation, few things threaten the justice and efficiency of society more than the rent-seeking activities of state officials and their cronies in the private sector. The pure neoliberal state minimises this problem by minimising the scope of state activities. This 'solution' addresses one problem at the cost of creating another far worse, the dismantling of the state's capacity to address systematic tendencies to market failure. Moderate neoliberals insist that many public policies vehemently condemned by pure neoliberals are necessary, legitimate, and feasible. They too decry rent-seeking, and favour legislation and statecraft designed to reduce it significantly.[31] In this imperfect world more cannot be hoped.

Addressing market failures adequately requires revenues. I have already mentioned some reasons to think that extensive cross-border flows do not eliminate the state's ability to appropriate the needed revenues. There are also good reasons to hold that the appropriations required by the neoliberal state are politically sustainable, unlike the tax policies of the social state. In the social state, the very individuals and corporations whose wealth is most confiscated benefit least from its programmes, while enjoying the largest number of exit options. This is a highly volatile combination. In contrast, corporations and wealthy individuals can be generally expected to support moderate neoliberal programmes funding infrastructure, research and development, education and training, and so on. These programmes are congruent with their interests, as well as those of their fellow citizens, and the burdens of supporting them can be widely dispersed. Turning to social welfare programmes, these can be as generous as citizens wish, so long as they are willing to make the inevitable trade-offs. The citizens of a society offering relatively generous welfare programmes must accept higher taxes and lower wages than would otherwise be the case.[32] There are obvious limits to this acceptance. Political realism dictates that the strong redistributive agenda of the social state give way to state policies addressing social needs primarily through measures stimulating economic growth. State programmes targeting disadvantaged groups will tend to be designed to encourage

---

[31] See Dam 2001, Chapters 1–2.
[32] Burtless, et al. 1998, Chapter 7; Wolf 2004, pp. 271–2.

beneficiaries to seek the job experiences and training that develop new skills.[33] But social programmes need not be eliminated in the neoliberal state.

The arguments in favour of the moderate neoliberal view are compelling. Nonetheless, the points of agreement between pure and moderate neoliberals regarding the state are as telling as the divergences. Both hold that the world market, constituted through capital mobility and international trade, forms a distinct region of social ontology above and beyond national economies and states. Both agree that states hoping to prosper in the contemporary global order must abandon any pretence of implementing public policies that undercut international competitiveness. Specifically, both acknowledge that the ceaseless plebiscite of government policies undertaken daily by investors rules out the normative model of institutions advocated by Rawls and other advocates of the welfare state. Global markets force the state to wear what Thomas Friedman calls the 'Golden Straightjacket:

> To fit the Golden Straitjacket a country must either adopt, or be seen as moving toward, the following golden rules: making the private sector the primary engine of its economic growth, maintaining a low rate of inflation and price stability, shrinking the size of its state bureaucracy, maintaining as close to a balanced budget as possible, if not a surplus, eliminating and lowering tariffs on imported goods, removing restrictions on foreign investment, getting rid of quotas and domestic monopolies, increasing exports, privatizing state-owned industries and utilities, deregulating capital markets, making its currency convertible, opening its industries, stock and bond markets to direct foreign ownership and investment, deregulating its economy to promote as much domestic competition as possible, eliminating government corruption, subsidies and kickbacks as much as possible, opening its banking and telecommunications systems to private ownership and competition and allowing its citizens to choose from an array of competing

---

[33] Thomas Friedman, the leading populariser of neoliberalism in the United States, calls for a 'Rapid Change Opportunities Act' designed to minimise the social costs imposed by global markets on national communities. Specific policies include government-funded retraining of unemployed workers, tax breaks to companies providing generous severance packages to discharged workers, measures allowing workers to retain health benefits while they search for new jobs, a right to flex time, greater public subsidies for child care, and so on. Friedman 2000, pp. 447 ff.

> pension options and foreign-run pension and mutual funds. When you stitch
> all of these pieces together you have the Golden Straightjacket.[34]

While the Golden Straightjacket is forced upon states that wish to be successful
in the contemporary global order, by a fortunate coincidence, this arrangement
is normatively justified as well, according to neoliberal theorists. The normative
legitimation of the neoliberal state can be derived from the general principle
of autonomy, combined with the thesis (taken as self-evident) that government
restrictions on cross-border flows infringe the autonomy of investors and
consumers. It follows as well from the principle that those exercising political
authority ought to be accountable, combined with the thesis, which neoliberal
theorists again take as self-evident, that deregulated global capital markets
further the accountability of state officials. States willing to accept the Golden
Straightjacket also foster the material well-being of individuals and groups
by enabling global markets to function as uniquely effective mechanisms for
transmitting relevant information regarding wants and needs, on the one
hand, and productive capacities, on the other. Individuals and firms are able
to co-ordinate their behaviour efficiently across vast geographical and cultural
differences. With specialisation and trade, a higher level of satisfaction of
wants and needs can then be attained in the global order as a whole (the
principle of comparative advantage).[35]

Having to put on the Golden Straightjacket is hardly equivalent to the
death of the state. Nor is it inconsistent with the state performing many of
the tasks assigned by defenders of the social state. But it does mean that the
heart of the neoliberal model of globalisation lies elsewhere, on the level of
the world market.

3. The neoliberal model (3): the determinations of the world market and the régime of global governance

The above passage on the Golden Straightjacket alludes to a number of features
of global markets in the neoliberal model. Tariff and non-tariff barriers to
trade are reduced to a great extent, if not eliminated entirely, as are restrictions
on foreign direct investments. 'Financial repression', that is, government

---

[34] Friedman 2000, p. 105.
[35] Kenen 1994, Chapter 2.

policies preventing or significantly restricting global flows of portfolio investment, is also ruled out. What structural tendencies emerge on the level of a world market with these sorts of features? Two technical terms must be defined before this question can be addressed.

The *current account* measures in monetary terms the balance between claims to foreigners and debits to foreigners in four areas: (i) merchandise exports relative to merchandise imports (the balance of trade in a narrow sense); (ii) exports of services relative to imports of services; (iii) investment incomes on foreign assets owned by nationals relative to income payments to foreigners owning national assets, and (iv) unilateral transfers (gifts, remittances, etc.) to agents in the domestic economy relative to unilateral transfers to those residing elsewhere. If we subtract the second term of each pair from the first, and then add the results, the current account is said to be in balance if the sum is zero. A positive number reflects a current account surplus, while a negative reveals a current account deficit.

The *capital account* refers initially to the balance (or lack thereof) between credits (claims on foreigners) and debits (debts to foreigners) in two areas: (i) short-term credit from foreigners relative to short-term credit granted to foreigners; and (ii) long-term investment of foreigners in the domestic economy relative to long-term investment by nationals abroad. If we subtract the monetary measure of the second term in each pair from that of the first, combine the results, and then add (or subtract) any change in the amount of foreign reserves held domestically, the final sum tells us whether the capital account of a particular nation is in balance, surplus, or deficit.

By definition, the current account and the capital account must balance. If the current account is in deficit, for example, then the capital account must be in surplus. In other words, the current account imbalance must be financed by some combination of short-term credits from foreigners, direct investments by foreigners purchasing domestic assets, and the sale of foreign reserves held domestically.

We are now in a position to state one of the most significant emergent properties on the level of the world market asserted by leading neoliberals. In their view, there is a general tendency for trade to be balanced over time, everything else being equal. While misguided government policies can upset this balance, mechanisms operate in the world market that tend to re-establish equilibrium.

Neoliberal theorists hold that if governments allow excess money to circulate in the domestic economy, inflation will result. Inflation upsets the balance of trade. Economic agents in the inflationary country, feeling themselves wealthier, tend to increase their purchases of imports at a faster rate than agents in a trading partner increase theirs. A trade deficit results. But this trade deficit reduces the stock of money in the economy whose imports increased, leading to a lowering of the prices of its domestically produced goods relative to imports, causing imports to decline in the future. The trade imbalance simultaneously increases the stock of money in a country enjoying a trade surplus, raising the relative prices of its domestically produced commodities vis-à-vis imports from the deficit nation. The deficit nation's exports to this country thus tend to increase. The net result of these developments is a systematic tendency for trade balance to be restored.

David Hume provided the classic account of this mechanism in the epoch of the gold standard. H.J. Johnson has developed a contemporary version of Hume's argument:

> [All] balance of payments deficits or surpluses are by their nature *transient and self correcting*, requiring no deliberate policy to correct them. . . . The reason is simply that deficits reduce money stocks whose excessive size underlies the deficit, and surpluses build up the money stocks whose deficiency underlies the surplus.[36]

These price adjustments take time to work. What if the deficit nation runs out of international reserves (gold or hard currencies) before the expansion of exports and reduction of imports restore the balance of trade? Fortunately, neoliberals assert, this danger can be avoided by simply devaluing its currency.[37] This raises the cost of imports relative to domestically produced commodities, while lowering the cost of its exports relative to commodities produced in the trade-surplus nation (thereby encouraging that nation to increase imports). A systematic tendency for a return to equilibrium automatically kicks in.

Turning to the capital account, we may distinguish two main types of cross-border capital flows. Foreign direct investment (FDI) refers to cross-border

---

[36] Johnson 1976, p. 16, quoted in Davidson 2002, p. 152 (emphasis added).
[37] Friedman 1953; Melamed 1988.

investments resulting in significant ownership of production facilities. Neo-liberal theorists hold that such flows are the single most effective mechanism for transferring technologies, advanced organisational practices, and labour skills across borders. Considerable empirical evidence also confirms that foreign manufacturing firms tend to pay wages higher than those prevailing in the domestic economy.[38]

Portfolio investment, the other category of capital flows, includes both loans and investments in financial assets (foreign currencies, bonds, equities). While individuals and firms investing financial capital certainly commit mistakes, those who consistently err are soon eliminated from the markets. Neoliberals conclude that participants in financial markets collectively gather, process, and transmit relevant information regarding the real counterparts of financial assets more efficiently than any feasible alternative.[39] When these markets operate freely, capital necessarily tends to be allocated to the areas in the global economy with the most productive potential. No set of government officials can exceed the collective wisdom of markets, and so government intervention in financial markets necessarily tends to lower efficiency.

Matters become more complex when we consider trade flows and capital flows simultaneously. The thesis that trade flows tend to balance in the world market was subject to the crucial 'everything else being equal' qualification. If there are areas of capital abundance in the global economy, and other regions of capital scarcity, then everything else is *not* equal. It is a fundamental axiom of neoliberal theory that factors of production tend to be rewarded in proportion to their relative scarcity or abundance. Just as rewards to labour tend to be higher in regions where there is a scarcity of labour, and lower in regions of labour abundance, rewards to capital tend to be greater in regions where capital is scarce. On the level of the world market, this implies that financial capital tends to flow from developed countries to emerging economies. As capital flows to regions of capital scarcity, deficits will arise in their capital accounts. Agents in emerging economies will, for instance, borrow more from

---

[38] An exceptionally clear presentation of this thesis is found in Wolf 2004, Chapter 11.

[39] More technically, asset prices in global financial markets 'gravitate toward the means of normal probability distribution of the present values of their net revenue streams'. Eatwell 1996, p. 10. (This is not Eatwell's own view of how markets for financial assets work.) A forceful defence of the thesis is found in McKinnon 1973.

agents in developed countries than they lend to them. Since the overall current account and capital account must balance, countries with a capital account deficit must enjoy a trade surplus. In brief, the tendency to trade balance in the global economy is put out of play until emerging economies join the rank of developed economies.

These considerations bring us to the very heart of the normative defence of the neoliberal model of globalisation. Throughout human history, most of humanity has lived in poverty, lacking access to the material preconditions necessary to develop their capacities and exercise their autonomy. The present epoch thankfully brings this tragic period of human history to a close. With global capital markets, any region anywhere is able to attain access to the funds required for industrial development and economic growth, which bring rapid gains in per capita income and living standards. As long as investments flow to the sectors where the region in question enjoys a comparative advantage, its exports will increase, providing the revenues required to pay the principle and interest on foreign loans, the interest on bonds due to foreign bondholders, and the dividends owed to foreign investors in equities. In other words, capital account deficits tend to be self-liquidating, assuming the allocation of capital inflows is not distorted by government policies.

Global justice unquestionably demands the eradication of extreme material deprivation and the provision of the material preconditions for autonomous action. An institutional framework that accomplishes this far better than any feasible alternative must be judged normatively superior. According to its exponents, the neoliberal model of globalisation, with free trade and free capital movements at its core, is this framework. Neoliberals insist that they, not their critics, have the best claim to speak in the name of global justice. From this perspective, the critics of neoliberalism are thoroughly muddled and/or thoroughly duplicitous, unable to acknowledge that the extension of global markets in recent decades has enabled previously poor regions to enjoy the fastest gains in per capita income and living standards in human history:

> Indeed, for all the churning that global capitalism brings to a society, the spread of capitalism has raised living standards higher, faster and for more people than at any time in history. It has also brought more poor people into the middle classes more quickly that at any time in human history. . . . According to the 1997 United Nations Human development report, poverty has fallen more in the past fifty years than in the previous five hundred.

Developing countries have progressed as fast in the past thirty years as the industrialized world did in the previous century. Since 1960, infant mortality rates, malnutrition and illiteracy are all significantly down, while access to safe water is way up. In relatively short periods of time, countries that have been the most open to globalization, like Taiwan, Singapore, Israel, Chile and Sweden, have achieved standards of living comparable to those in America and Japan, while the ranks of the middle class in countries like Thailand, Brazil, India and Korea have swelled, due partly to globalization.[40]

The state is not the culmination of the neoliberal model of globalisation, however necessary and significant its role might be. The world market holds that distinction:

> What the successful countries all share is a move towards the market economy, one in which private property rights, free enterprise and competition increasingly took the place of state ownership, planning and protection. They chose, however haltingly, the path of economic liberalization and international integration. This is the heart of the matter. All else is commentary.[41]

To operate properly, however, the world market requires more than neoliberal states wearing the Golden Straightjacket. The neoliberal model of globalisation also incorporates interstate relations and a so-called 'régime of global governance'.

In the standard neoliberal view, the high scale and velocity of cross-border flows of commodities, portfolio capital, foreign direct investment, and so on, demand fairly extensive interstate agreements regarding the rules governing these flows. An array of global institutions is also required to articulate these general rules and apply them in specific cases. Few neoliberals applaud every feature of global institutions such as the World Trade Organisation (WTO), the International Monetary Fund (IMF), or the World Bank (WB), let alone every policy these agencies have ever pursued. But even fewer deny that global institutions of this sort are needed if global markets are to reproduce themselves over time in an efficient and normatively attractive manner.[42]

---

[40] Friedman 2000, p. 350. See also Wolf 2004, pp. 141, 160.
[41] Wolf 2004, pp. 143–4.
[42] Theorists defending what I have termed 'pure' neoliberalism do deny this. Since

The resources required by these institutions for both their day-to-day operations and the enforcement of their decrees are granted by states at their discretion. As opposed to states, which ordinarily have the capacity to enforce their laws on individual citizens, international agencies lack independent coercive powers to enforce their dictates. However, this does not imply that international relations are reducible to power relations among states, as realist theorists of international relations assert.

The realist position is based on a comparison of individuals in a 'state of nature' and interstate relations. They hold that, in a state of nature, particular disputes among individuals would inevitably result in a 'war of all against all', threatening everyone's survival. The sovereign state, with coercive powers standing above conflicting parties, has been established to prevent this outcome. In sharp contrast, there is no world government standing above individual states. Realists conclude that the danger of war haunts the interstate system whenever disputes arise. From the neoliberal perspective, this account downplays the most crucial matter, the mutual benefits generated by free-trade and free-capital flows. These benefits ensure that it is in the rational interests of individual states to come to binding agreements regarding flows of commodities and investments across borders. It is also in the rational interests of states to establish international agencies with the mandate to apply these rules in complex and controversial cases, and to assign appropriate penalties when a state refuses to comply with their rulings. The general benefits resulting from trade and cross-border capital flows are so extensive that it is even in the rational interests of states to comply with unfavourable rulings in particular cases.

This conclusion is reinforced if we consider a striking disanalogy between antagonistic individuals in a 'state of nature' and state conflicts, such as a trade disputes regarding a specific sector.[43] There are likely to be many sectors in both countries that are unaffected by the dispute. In fact, it is likely that there will be a number of sectors in both states that would benefit if the dispute were resolved in favour of the opposing state. A ruling by an

---

compelling reasons for rejecting pure neoliberalism have already been presented, there is no need to examine this point of view further in the present context.

[43] This paragraph is loosely based on Dam 2001, which provides an excellent insider's account of the theoretical presuppositions of neoliberal policymaking.

international agency going against a nation's exporters will often aid its importers; a ruling against government policies protecting steel producers from foreign competition, for example, will benefit car manufactures importing steel. The reverse may hold as well; a ruling in favour of a particular state's claim on behalf of a sector may harm other firms in other sectors of the national economy. Unlike conflicts among individuals in the familiar state of nature narrative, a ruling in an interstate trade dispute going against a particular state does not profoundly threaten its very existence. This point holds as well for other instances of global governance by international agencies.

A fundamental tendency for a war of all against all thus does *not* necessarily tend to emerge on the level of interstate relations, given a world market generating mutual benefits across borders through trade and investments. From this standpoint, interstate wars are exogenous to the neoliberal framework, rooted in political contingencies rather than the essential determinations of the contemporary global order.[44] For neoliberals, a true 'régime of global governance' necessarily tends to emerge instead.[45] This régime has the power to reconcile the autonomy of individuals and particular groups with that of other individuals and groups on the level of the world community. *Neoliberalism is a form of moral cosmopolitanism.*

Consider an institution with responsibility for defining the rules of international trade, applying these rules in controversial cases, and deciding appropriate penalties for infractions. Lacking sovereign coercive powers of its own, it must rely on the states favoured by its rulings to impose effective sanctions on other states. This arrangement can endure nonetheless. The mutual benefits resulting from an established set of rules and a reasonably neutral institution to apply them far outweigh any benefits that might come to individual states from dissolving the system of global governance as soon as a particular ruling goes against them. Whether or not the World Trade Organisation persists in its present form, some international agency of this sort is inherent in the neoliberal model of globalisation.

---

[44] A number of authors in Kaul et al. 1999 argue that it is in the mutual interests of states to co-operate to provide 'global public goods', basing their arguments on neoliberal principles. This does not imply, of course, that a global régime responsible for providing these goods arises automatically, or that is equally easy to provide global public goods in all areas of concern. All the contingencies connected with the exercise of 'statecraft' come into play.

[45] Reinecke 1998.

The International Monetary Fund provides a second illustration. The neoliberal account of the necessary tendency of global financial markets to allocate capital in a rational and efficient fashion does not rule out financial crises stemming from external shocks or the policy errors and rent-seeking of state officials. A government may engage in excessive spending, with excessive borrowing from global capital markets following close behind. State policies may encourage inefficient rigidities in the labour market, or enable local borrowers with personal ties to state officials to hide their true level of debt from global investors. Other forms of 'crony capitalism' are all too familiar as well, ranging from small subsidies to connected firms to the most extreme forms of kleptocracy. Or the state may simply attempt to maintain a fixed peg between its currency and a hard currency even as it becomes increasingly obvious that devaluation is all but inevitable. The list of misguided state policies capable of distorting flows of global capital is practically endless.

Economic growth is the only effective way of raising living standards in the global economy, and capital investment is required for economic growth. Elementary morality thus dictates that capital-scarce regions of the global economy should have access to global capital markets. When misguided government policies lead to financial disturbances, global capital markets need assurance that these policies will be reversed. An international agency that lends to afflicted regions on the condition that governments reverse excessive state deficits, increase transparency, dismantle crony capitalism, increase flexibility in labour markets, undertake revaluations of the currency when circumstances demand, and so on, can provide this assurance. Such an institution is in the interest of creditor states, for it minimises the danger that their investors will see their investments squandered by perverse government policies. Such an institution is in the interest of debtor states as well, since attracting new inflows of needed capital is the only alternative to extended economic stagnation or decline in the neoliberal view. In the present global order, the International Monetary Fund plays this role.[46] While few neoliberal theorists are happy with all aspects of the IMF, few deny that if it did not exist, something like it would have to be invented. Here, too, it is in the

---

[46] Hale 1998.

rational interest of states to co-operate in order to establish an international institution of this sort as part of the régime of global governance.[47]

This completes the presentation of the neoliberal model of globalisation. Systematic tendencies towards the formation of a world market above states and national economies were implicit in the social-state model of globalisation. The force of these tendencies, the reconceptualisation of the state that they demand, and the emergent properties that arise on the level of the world market, the interstate system, and the régime of global governance, are all made explicit in the neoliberal framework. From this perspective, the neoliberal model of globalisation counts as an advance in complexity and concreteness over the social-state model. In the jargon of dialectics, the immanent contradictions of the social-state position lead to its determinate negation by neoliberalism.

The contingencies of world history are not about to disappear. Wars will continue to break out, treaties will continue to be broken. Nonetheless, neoliberals insist, the continuing eruptions of interstate conflicts should not blind us to the fact that, for the first time in world history, a just global order has emerged and can be discerned in what Rawls calls 'the deep tendencies and inclinations of the social world'.

Is the systematic dialectic now completed? Or is the neoliberal model of globalisation itself plagued by immanent contradictions forcing a transition to some third position?

4. The immanent contradictions of the neoliberal model of globalisation

The neoliberal framework has been subjected to numerous criticisms. A closer examination of the principle of comparative advantage, the claim that trade flows tend to balance, the neoliberal account of the financial sector, and various factors effecting economic growth, shows that the neoliberal model of globalisation suffers from serious internal tensions. Two other immanent contradictions will be considered at the beginning of the following chapter.

---

[47] A very useful and comprehensive survey of the issues here is found in Tirole 2002.

(i) *Comparative advantage*

As we have seen, Ricardo insisted that specialisation and trade can bring mutual benefits to two trading nations, even when one has an absolute productivity advantage in every relevant sector. All that is required is that the other nation holds a comparative advantage in at least one sector. Appeals to this principle continue to be at the heart of arguments in favour of the neoliberal model of globalisation today.[48] Any neoliberal theorist defending the principle of comparative advantage, however, is faced at once with the following difficulty: *the principle is only relevant when money capital does not move across borders, and capital mobility is one of the essential determinations of the neoliberal model of globalisation.*

Ricardo explicitly notes that, if investment capital were mobile and one nation enjoyed an absolute productivity advantage over another in all relevant sectors, capital would necessarily tend to flow to it from the second nation, even if the latter possessed a comparative advantage in one or more sectors. Ricardo's argument thus assumes a global order in which investors in a country lacking an absolute advantage in relevant sectors will not 'seek a more advantageous employment of their wealth in foreign nations':

> Experience, however, shows, that the fancied or real insecurity of capital, when not under the immediate control of its owner, together with the natural disinclination which every man has to quit the country of his birth and connexions, and intrust himself with all his habits fixed, to a strange government and new laws, check the emigration of capital. These feelings, which I should be sorry to see weakened, induce most men of property to be satisfied with a low rate of profits in their country, rather than seek a more advantageous employment of their wealth in foreign nations.[49]

This assumption, however, is not one that can be made without contradicting the basic determinations of the neoliberal model of globalisation. This model explicitly emphasises the tendency towards the 'emigration of capital' and affirms this tendency on both normative and efficiency grounds. It is not coherent for proponents of this model to dismiss their critics with a haughty invocation of the principle of comparative advantage, when this principle

---

[48] Irwin 2002; Dam 2001, Chapter 4; Bhagwati 2004.
[49] Ricardo 1970, pp. 136–7, quoted in Cobb and Daly 1997, p. 214.

holds if and only if the emigration of capital is continually 'checked', contradicting a basic element of the neoliberal order.[50]

This leads immediately to a second difficulty. The comparative advantage argument for neoliberalism rests on the claim that specialisation and trade lead to a Pareto optimal situation; trade and specialisation leave some (many) social agents better off without others being made worse off. No one denies that specialisation and trade will bring about 'losers' as well as 'winners' in any given national economy. And, so, if the result is truly to be Pareto-optimal, the latter must adequately compensate the former. Neoliberal theorists insist that the gains from specialisation and trade are sufficient to allow this to happen in principle.[51] I have just given a reason to doubt that this will always be the case. But, even when it is, the normative force of the comparative advantage argument requires that there be a necessary tendency for the compensation to actually occur. The same argument that neoliberals use against the redistributive agenda of the social state now come into play against their own position. Why should the 'winners' compensate the 'losers' enough to bring them up to their status quo ante position if they do not have to, especially given the way neoliberal ideology absolves them of responsibility for the failures of others? Given the essential determinations defining the neoliberal model, which grant significant exit options to corporations and wealthy individuals, the most likely results are inadequately funded job programmes and income supplements that do not bring globalisation's victims back to the status quo ante baseline. It is thus incoherent for neoliberals simultaneously to assert that the comparative advantage argument has normative force and to affirm the exit options enjoyed by corporations and wealthy investors.

---

[50] Ricardo's theory of comparative advantage rests upon a number of other assumptions whose applicability to the contemporary global economy is also highly doubtful. See Cobb and Daly 1997, Chapter 11, and Went 2002, Chapter 2 for more complete accounts. Wolf attempts to prove the continuing relevance of the doctrine of comparative advantage in a world of capital mobility. All he establishes, however, is the abiding importance of regional specialisation in establishing and maintaining *absolute* advantages in the global economy. This is true, but irrelevant to the point he is trying to make. See Wolf 2004, pp. 260–5.

[51] Burtless et al. 1998.

(ii) *Trade balances*

A crucial premise in the argument for the efficiency and normative attractiveness of the neoliberal model of globalisation is the claim that there is a systematic tendency for balanced trade on the level of global markets, at least among nations on roughly comparable levels of development. This thesis does not rule out trade imbalances. But it does imply that, when they arise, economic agents necessarily tend to act in a manner that quickly and harmoniously re-establishes equilibrium. Given the essential features of the neoliberal framework, however, neoliberal theorists cannot assert this tendency without falling into another immanent contradiction.

Consider again Johnson's conclusion that trade imbalances are temporary phenomena, soon eliminated when the market is allowed to operate in an unfettered fashion. His argument rests on the thesis that small movements in relative price levels between trading partners necessarily tend to eliminate trade imbalances. In other words, small increases in the prices of imports in the trade-deficit nation supposedly lead imports to fall, while small decreases in the prices of imports into the trade-surplus region cause these imports to rise.[52] This claim rests, in turn, on what Paul Davidson terms 'the classical gross substitution axiom': both national economies produce (or could easily produce) commodities that are more or less identical substitutes for imports. But, within the neoliberal framework, this assumption cannot be coherently made. According to the principle of comparative advantage, different regions of the global economy will tend, over time, to specialise in the production of *different* sorts of goods and services. The specialisation thesis and the gross substitution axiom are equally indispensable to the neoliberal position, while being fundamentally incompatible with each other.

Within the neoliberal framework we can expect numerous cases to arise in which the domestic economy does *not* produce a more or less identical substitute for an import. Consumers and businesses who have met their wants and needs through the purchase of imports without close domestic substitutes

---

[52] For the sake of the argument, I am granting Johnson's underlying assumption that fluctuations in the money supply of the two nations are directly reflected in price changes, despite the fact that the quantity theory of money is deeply suspect.

will not necessarily change their behaviour as a result of small movements in the relative prices of imports and exports.[53] The claim that trade imbalances are automatically eliminated by fairly small relative price movements thus does *not* necessarily tend to hold in the neoliberal model.

A parallel consideration undermines the argument that trade imbalances can be quickly and harmoniously reversed in the neoliberal framework through a devaluation of the deficit country's currency. If the need for certain imports (oil, food) is sufficiently great in a deficit country, a devaluation may not change even the physical volume of these imports significantly. In the extreme case, where the price elasticity of demand is zero, the result of devaluation will be that the price of the imports rises by the full amount of the devaluation, worsening the deficit by that full amount. In less extreme cases, devaluation may reduce the *physical volume* of imports, and increase that of exports, without reversing the international payments deficit, since that falls only if the *monetary value* of exports rises relative to that of imports. If no adequate domestic substitutes are available, in brief, the major impact of devaluation may simply be a rise in the prices of imports in high demand.[54] Consequently, there is no warrant for assuming that devaluations automatically restore trade equilibrium, at least not when they are relatively small, as they would have to be for trade balance to be re-established in a reasonably smooth and harmonious fashion. Reversing this imbalance can require a massive change in the relative prices of imports and exports, that is, a devaluation (or series of devaluations) imposing a very significant decline of the income of agents in the deficit region.[55]

To summarise, neoliberal economists are able to argue that trade balances can be re-established through devaluation without drastic affects on real

---

[53] Davidson 2002, p. 152.

[54] More technically: 'This aggregate change in the monetary value of exports minus imports is determined by the magnitude of the absolute sum of the price elasticity of demand for imports plus the price elasticity of demand for exports. Assuming no change in aggregate income, when the exchange rate for nation A's money declines if, *and only if*, the sum of these price elasticities exceeds unity (the Marshall-Lerner condition), then the total monetary value of nation A's imports will decline relative to the total market value of A's exports; nation A's balance of payments position will improve. If the sum of these price elasticities is less than unity, then a fall in the exchange rate worsens the nation's payment imbalance'. Davidson 2002, p. 153.

[55] Davidson 2002, p. 154. Neoliberal economists acknowledge that an exchange-rate depreciation is likely to worsen the balance of payments for a period of time. But they believe that the payments imbalance after devaluation will follow a J-curve, in which the downward slope representing a worsening of the imbalance is soon reversed. This

income only because they assume the classical gross substitution axiom. If the axiom is accepted, the conclusion follows; a very small change in exchange rates would be sufficient to change the monetary value of imports and exports significantly. But neoliberals cannot accept this axiom without falling into an immanent contradiction. The axiom loses its relevance as national economies become more open and specialised, and the tendencies for economies to become more open and more specialised over time are two of the most essential attributes of the neoliberal model of globalisation.

(iii) *Instability in the financial sector*

The free flow of financial capital across borders is another defining feature of the neoliberal model of globalisation. This feature is justified by the claim that global financial markets necessarily tend to allocate capital in an efficient and rational manner. This claim is plagued by major difficulties, pointing to another immanent contradiction in the neoliberal position.

The rational efficiency thesis rests on the assumption that participants in financial markets collectively price the value of financial assets correctly so that prices 'gravitate toward the means of normal probability distribution of the present values of their net revenue streams'.[56] But neoliberal theorists also hold that capitalist markets exhibit a historically unprecedented level of technological dynamism. *This dynamism rules out in principle even a probabilistic knowledge of net revenue streams in the future.*

To a limited extent, incremental innovations can be foreseen in the immediate future. The vague outlines of more radical forms of innovation may sometimes be discerned by especially perceptive futurists. But the technological dynamism of capitalism includes truly radical innovations that cannot be anticipated decades (or even years) before their emergence even in principle. These radical innovations then usher in a series of incremental innovations, many of which surprise contemporary observers. The technological dynamism at the heart

---

too is no more than an assumption for which no plausible arguments are provided. As Davidson notes, 'Of course, this short-run worsening in the payments balance, can force another devaluation. A new J-curve will be encountered with a further immediate decline in the value of net exports. In a series of short runs it is possible that devaluation provokes continued devaluation, and an improved trade balance is never achieved'. Davidson 2002, p. 155.

[56] Eatwell 1996, p. 10.

of the neoliberal model thus implies that that the financial sector does not simply operate with risks, that is, unknown outcomes to which a probability number can be assigned. Financial decisions are made, instead, in a world of radical uncertainty.[57]

Given the technological dynamism intrinsic to the neoliberal model, financial markets resemble the sort of beauty contest described by Keynes. In this peculiar contest, judges do not themselves proclaim which individual contestant they regard as the most beautiful. They instead attempt to guess which contestant a majority of other judges will favour. A theory of mass psychology is more relevant here than either the mathematics of general equilibrium theory or neoliberal notions of rationality and efficiency. In financial markets, vast fortunes can be won and lost by anticipating short-term shifts in the average perception of investors, and so great efforts are devoted to developing a sense of when such shifts are likely to occur.

These anticipations easily become self-fulfilling prophecies. Suppose, for example, it becomes widely known that a few leading investors in capital markets have judged that average investors will soon believe that a particular currency or set of equities is overvalued. A critical mass of other investors, hoping to profit from the soon-to-emerge trend, might then sell the currency and equities short, thereby bringing about the very reversal in value that was anticipated. There may be investors in the financial assets in question who believe that a rational assessment of their long-term prospects does not warrant such a reversal. They will suffer considerable losses in the short-to-medium term if they do not join the stampede, and, so, they are likely to do just that.

---

[57] Critics of neoliberalism often complain that the liberalisation of global capital markets creates a 'global casino'. But, in a casino, the probabilities of all possible results can be calculated. This is *not* the case in liberalised capital markets. It should also be noted that technological change is obviously not the only source of radical uncertainty. There have been countless cases in which shifting geopolitical alliances and wars profoundly affected financial markets and the pricing of financial assets. Very few of these cases were rationally foreseeable – let alone foreseen – by investors years or even months before (Kindleberger 1993). Neoliberal theorists dismiss such geopolitical factors as exogenous contingencies, rather than intrinsic features of the neoliberal model of institutions. This is a very questionable move (see Wood 2003). Be that as it may, no plausible argument can be possibly be given for defining technological change as exogenous to a capitalist global order (Smith 1997a). If technological change necessarily rules out essential neoliberal assumptions regarding global capital markets, this counts as a profound immanent contradiction in the position.

If they go under, it will be small consolation to be proven correct later. This shows that financial markets in the neoliberal framework do not necessarily fluctuate narrowly in the region of an equilibrium point defined by 'fundamentals'. In George Soros's striking image, they regularly operate like immense wrecking balls, oscillating wildly and inflicting horrific damage on everything in their way.[58] It is not possible to assert simultaneously that capitalist markets are characterised by unprecedented technological dynamism and that the financial sector tends to function in an efficient and rational manner (as those terms are defined by neoliberal theorists) without falling into incoherence. The neoliberal position, however, includes both assertions.

(iv) *Depressionary bias*

Further incoherence stems from the way the financial sector of the neoliberal global order undermines the long-term economic growth that neoliberal theorists claim is a defining feature of that very order. Long-term investments in productive capacity involve considerable risks in the best of cases; if consumer demand for the commodities produced with that capacity slows or declines, or if the facilities in question become technologically outdated, the rate of return on the investment may fall drastically. These risks hold for both domestic investments for export markets and cross-border fixed investments. If currency exchange rates fluctuate unpredictably, as they can with capital liberalisation, a high degree of currency risk is added to these already serious risks. Liquidity risks also increase when investments in productive capacity are funded from foreign borrowings. Long-term borrowers must worry that investors may stampede out of their country, making it all but impossible for them to roll over their loans. Volatility in the financial sector, and recurrent and unpredictable financial crises, hardly encourage the long-term fixed investments so crucial to long-term economic growth.[59] There is, thus, a depressionary bias in the neoliberal global order.

---

[58] Soros 1998. As a leading proponent of neoliberalism is forced to admit, 'Between 1945 and 1971, in what might be called the "age of financial repression," there had been only thirty-eight [financial] crises in all, with just seven twin crises. Emerging market economies experienced no banking crises, sixteen currency crises and just one twin crisis in this period. Then, between 1973 and 1997, there were 139 crises. The age of financial liberalization has, in short, been an age of financial crises'. Wolf 2004, p. 280. See also note 21 in the following chapter.

[59] Eatwell 1996.

Governments, hoping to avoid stampedes of capital outflows, necessarily tend to reinforce this depressionary bias. Real interest rates tend to be relatively high, while government programmes to stimulate the economy tend to be small, given the manner in which governments are 'accountable' to global capital markets.[60] These states of affairs are generally correlated with lower growth and higher unemployment.

Empirical evidence corroborates the thesis that there is a depressionary bias in the neoliberal model of globalisation. Between 1980 and 2000 – a period characterised by greater global integration along neoliberal lines – growth rates in all categories of countries declined in comparison to the previous twenty year period. For the poorest countries (based on per capita income), the decline was from 19% a year to -0.5%. The second poorest quintile declined from 2% to 0.75%, and the third from 3.5% to 0.9%. The rate fell in the second richest quintile from 3.4% to 1.1%, and in the top group from 2.5% to 1.75%.[61]

The testimony of Joseph Stiglitz is very noteworthy in this context. Stiglitz has been chair of the President's Council of Advisors in the US, a senior vice president and chief economist of the World Bank, and a recipient of the Nobel Prize in economics. It is a remarkable development indeed when an economist of Stiglitz's stature proclaims that, in many respects, the critics of neoliberalism have a deeper understanding of the global economy than élite academics and policymakers: 'Globalization today is not working for many of the world's poor. It is not working for much of the environment. It is not working for the stability of the global economy'.[62]

Stiglitz's analysis echoes Thorstein Veblen's at the beginning of the twentieth century. For Veblen, the most significant social division in capitalism is between producers (including both industrialist entrepreneurs and the workers they employ) and financial speculators. While the actions of the former bring about

---

[60] The benefits to financial investors from high real interest rates are obvious. Government stimulus programmes are thought to crowd out private capital and generate inflationary dangers, both of which tend to go against the perceived self-interest of agents in the financial sector.

[61] Weisbrot et al. 2002. It is interesting that Wolf, one of the world's most prominent and influential neoliberals, comes close to admitting this in the course of trying to reassure his readers that the top hundred corporations in the global economy are not doing all that well: 'Overall corporate profits in US GDP rose from a low level in the 1990s, but its average for that decade was no higher than that for the past half-century. It has never since reached the peaks of the 1960s'. Wolf 2004, p. 223.

[62] Stiglitz 2002, p. 214.

long-term technological progress, the latter are primarily concerned with short-term profits from trades in financial assets. The more power and prestige claimed by financiers relative to producers, the less likely it is that society will undertake the long-term investments in fixed capital necessary for social dynamism. In this sense, actions that appear rational from the standpoint of the holders of financial capital necessarily come into conflict with what is rational from the standpoint of society as a whole. Veblen calls for institutional reforms to ensure that the operations of financial capital are strictly subordinate to industrial development. In a parallel fashion, Stiglitz argues that neoliberal policies further the interests of financial capital to the detriment of the overall social rationality of the global economy:

> [T]rade liberalization *accompanied by high interest rates* is an almost certain recipe for job destruction and unemployment creation – at the expense of the poor. Financial market liberalization *unaccompanied by an appropriate regulatory structure* is an almost certain recipe for economic instability – and may well lead to higher, not lower, interest rates, making it harder for poor farmers to buy the seeds and fertilizer that can raise them above subsistence. Privatization, *unaccompanied by competition policies and oversight to ensure that monopoly powers are not abused*, can lead to higher, not lower, prices for consumers. Fiscal austerity, *pursued blindly*, in the wrong circumstances, can lead to high unemployment and a shredding of the social contract.[63]

Stiglitz also complains that the distortions imposed by financial markets are exacerbated by the neoliberal régime of global governance. He presents an exhaustive account of the operation of the International Monetary Fund in East Asia and Eastern Europe as evidence. Appealing to orthodox neoliberal doctrine, the Fund encouraged the premature deregulation of capital markets in these regions, which led to stampedes of speculative capital into already overheated stock and real estate markets. When the all but inevitable crashes and reverse stampedes of capital outflows occurred, the Fund then imposed severe austerity programmes.[64] Governments were forced to restrict credit and spending, despite the fact that downswings are precisely the time when access to credit and government spending are most needed. Motivated by

---

[63] Stiglitz 2002, p. 84.
[64] Stiglitz 2002, pp. 98 ff.

the fear that currency devaluation would raise the cost of imports and lead to inflation, the IMF also provided funds to troubled economies to help them maintain the given exchange rate. As Stiglitz notes, these funds in effect bailed out international investors, allowing them and local élites time to protect their financial assets through capital flight to dollars on an immense scale.[65] Soon enough, the exchange rates were devalued anyway. The subsequent burden of paying back these IMF loans – a much more difficult task, after the devaluation of the local currency – fell on the very group that benefited least from them, working men and women.[66]

The four immanent contradictions discussed in this section do not concern peripheral matters. They involve the very heart of the neoliberal model of globalisation. If there are systematic tendencies in the framework that make the theory of comparative advantage irrelevant, prevent trade imbalances from automatically correcting, lead to financial crises, and impose a depressionary bias on the global economy, then there is an immanent tension between the normative claims made by the model's main defenders and the essential determinations of the model. This is more than sufficient to justify a transition to a new position in the systematic dialectic of globalisation. As of yet, however, we do not have many clues regarding the shape of this new position. The two immanent contradictions derived at the beginning of the next chapter will supply more.

---

[65] Stiglitz 2002, p. 95.

[66] As Stiglitz also points out, many ex-IMF and US Treasury Department officials have been appointed to absurdly lucrative positions in the very financial firms that profited greatly from IMF and Treasury Department policies. One would have to be naïve indeed, he implies, to think that this 'revolving door' between government and Wall Street has absolutely no effects on policymaking. To my knowledge no 'insider' has ever come closer than Stiglitz to conceding the grain of truth in Marx's dictum that the state is the executive committee of the ruling class. Stiglitz extends this insight to international agencies: '[M]any of its [the IMF's] key personnel came from the financial community, and many of its key personnel, having served these interests well, left to well-paying jobs in the financial community. Stan Fischer, the deputy managing director who played such a role in the episodes described in this book, went directly from the IMF to become a vice chairman at Citigroup, the vast financial firm that includes Citibank. A chairman of Citigroup (chairman of the Executive Committee) was Robert Rubin, who, as secretary of Treasury, had had a central role in IMF policies. One could only ask, 'Was Fischer being richly rewarded for having faithfully executed what he was told to do?'. Stiglitz 2002, p. 208.

Chapter Three

The Catalytic-State Model of Globalisation

The neoliberal model of globalisation explicitly incorporates essential characteristics of the contemporary global order merely implicit in the social-state model. These aspects of globalisation – primarily the formation of a world market incorporating national economies, and the limits on state capacities resulting from this – undermine any tendency for the social-state framework to be reproduced over time in an efficient and normatively attractive manner, as measured by the principles of its leading proponents. This provides sufficient justification for a transition to neoliberalism, the second stage in the systematic dialectic of globalisation.

If the neoliberal global order necessarily tended to be reproduced over time in an efficient and normatively acceptable manner (as measured by the theoretical and practical commitments of *its* leading adherents), the systematic dialectic would conclude. But this is not the case. The social forms most vehemently defended by neoliberal theorists tend to operate in a manner that rules out their most vehemently defended claims. Their main intellectual weapon in globalisation debates, the theory of comparative advantage, is based on assumptions that blatantly contradict their own descriptive and prescriptive contentions regarding capital mobility. Their insistence that trade imbalances automatically tend to correct themselves through relatively minor price changes or currency devaluations rests on an axiom that patently contradicts the theory of comparative advantage (the 'gross substitution axiom'). The technological dynamism so crucial to the neoliberal case against the social state thoroughly undermines neoliberal claims regarding deregulated financial markets; in a world of uncertainty, there are no guarantees these markets will automatically tend to allocate capital 'rationally' and 'efficiently'. And the claim that the neoliberal model fosters economic growth more effectively than any feasible alternative breaks down in the face of the depressionary bias built-into the model.

The first two sections of the present chapter continue the presentation of immanent contradictions in the neoliberal standpoint. These sections have been placed here because they do more than simply strengthen the justification for a transition to a new position in the systematic dialectic. They also directly point towards a third model of globalisation, including the elements of truth in neoliberalism while explicitly addressing its structural shortcomings.

The terms 'social state' and 'neoliberalism' are quite familiar in contemporary social theory. Unfortunately, there is no generally accepted term for the next stage in the progression. Borrowing a designation from Linda Weiss, I shall refer to the *catalytic state* model of globalisation'.[1] According to defenders of this perspective, the neoliberal state is a weak state. It is not necessarily weak in a military sense, at least not in the short-to-medium-term. But the more any particular state formation adopts neoliberal policies, the less it is able to provide the necessary preconditions for successful participation in the global economy. To invoke Hegel's distinction once again, this or that aspect of the neoliberal state may 'exist' in the contemporary historical epoch.[2] But, for proponents of this third position, the form of state that is 'actual', the one

---

[1] Weiss 1998, pp. 209–12. Once again, as always, the initial justification for assigning a position a place in a systematic dialectic can only be provisional. The claim that the catalytic-state model of globalisation provides the simplest and most immediate alternative to the neoliberal framework can only be fully justified at the conclusion of the reconstruction, after the relevant alternatives have been considered.

[2] No state has ever perfectly embodied the ideal type 'neoliberal state', and no state ever will. On the level of concrete existence, all institutional frameworks are complex and contingent combinations of various elements with distinct histories and features. The gap between the abstract model of neoliberalism and alleged concrete instances is especially great, however. See note 7 below.

connected to 'the deep tendencies and inclinations of the social world', is a *catalytic* state, actively aiming to establish the preconditions for a region's flourishing in the global order.

John Gray's *False Dawn: The Delusions of Global Capitalism* contains perhaps the most forceful defence of the catalytic-state model of globalisation. This work will serve as the main point of reference for this chapter. As we shall see below, Gray appeals to communitarian values. These values are fundamentally incompatible with the libertarian claim that the only matters of importance in the moral universe are the liberty and property rights of individuals. But advocates of the social-state model of globalisation, and defenders of moderate neoliberalism, insist on the importance of flourishing and reasonably stable communities no less than communitarians. And Gray and other communitarians grant that flourishing and reasonably stable communities are important because they are necessary conditions of the possibility of flourishing individuals. It would be absurd to conflate the normative principles of, say, Rawls, Hayek, and Gray. But, from the perspective of a systematic dialectic of globalisation disagreements on the level of abstract principles are relatively secondary matters in comparison to disagreements regarding the institutional framework that best embodies widely shared normative values.

I. From the neoliberal state to the catalytic state (1): technology policy

In the neoliberal state, there is a systematic tendency for corporations and wealthy individuals to be taxed at the lowest feasible rates. There is also a propensity to reduce business regulations, tariff and non-tariff barriers to trade, and so-called 'financial repression' to the greatest feasible degree. Needless to say, 'feasible' is a quite mushy term. Moderate neoliberals call for higher rates of taxation, greater business regulation, and a more gradual dismantling of barriers to cross-border trade and capital investment, than pure neoliberals. Nonetheless, moderate neoliberals too call for a 'weak' state in the sense of a state that imposes the lowest tax rates, the least business regulations, and the least interference with cross-border trade and investment practicable in the given context.

The previous chapter established the superiority of moderate neoliberalism over pure neoliberalism. I shall now argue that the same considerations favouring moderate neoliberalism over libertarianism also favour the catalytic-state model of globalisation over *any* version of neoliberalism. Moderate neoliberals cannot coherently affirm these considerations in the former context and deny them in the latter. Technological change once again provides a key point of entry to the issues.

Suppose a firm is considering a major investment in a long-term research project. Will the research successfully expand scientific-technical knowledge? Will it ever result in commercialisable commodities? Will future effective demand for these commodities be sufficient to ensure a high rate of return? The uncertainty with which these questions must always be answered is exacerbated tremendously if the investment in question aims to push the frontier of scientific-technical knowledge forward. This hyper-uncertainty is generally accompanied by hyper-financial risk as well; significantly pushing the scientific-technical frontier ahead generally requires an immense investment of funds. This combination of extremely uncertain reward and enormous financial risk implies a systematic tendency for underinvestment in these sorts of projects. But the long-term prospects for economic growth crucially depend on undertaking precisely these sorts of projects.[3]

There may be some occasions when the potential rewards, as uncertain as they are, are estimated by private investors to be sufficiently high to compensate for the risks. Even on these relatively rare occasions, however, another problem immediately arises to discourage them from risking their own capital. Suppose that extensive investments pushing the scientific-technical frontier are made, and commercialisable products for which there is ample market demand result. What prevents competitors from free-riding on this advance, appropriating a considerable portion of the economic benefits of the innovation? This danger further undercuts the motivation for a given unit of capital to undertake uncertain-reward/high-risk investments.

These considerations are completely generalisable; they hold for each and every sector of the economy. The result is a general tendency to underinvest in scientific-technical development in the economy as a whole relative to what

---

[3] Mansfield et al. 1967.

is socially optimal. This is no small matter for neoliberal theorists, since technological dynamism is an absolutely crucial element of their critique of the social state and defence of the neoliberal model of globalisation.

As I observed in the last chapter, pure neoliberals call for adjustments to the intellectual property rights system in response to this difficulty. If private investors were able to appropriate more of the returns on successful innovations, they would have a greater incentive to undertake long-term investments with high financial risks. Extending the intellectual property rights régime does indeed affect investment patterns. But there is absolutely no reason to believe that it would ever come close to eliminating the tendency to underinvest in long-term projects with great scientific-technical uncertainty and financial risk. And extending the intellectual property rights régime profoundly hampers technological development in other ways. It encourages secrecy, either indefinitely (in the case of trade secrets) or for a considerable period of time (in the case of patents). Innovative activities are discouraged whenever they might infringe on enforceable patent rights held by others, and the more complex a technological system, the more likely it is that infringement problems will arise.[4] Further, intellectual property rights are as much rights to *not* develop innovations as they are rights to enjoy a quasi-monopoly when they are utilised. Firms typically investigate many potential paths of innovation simultaneously. Given financial restrictions and the limits of their 'core competencies', they will concentrate on a subset of possible paths. But they are not indifferent to the prospect of others pursuing a potentially profitable path they themselves have forsaken. If another enterprise successfully commercialises an innovation, the competitive threat it poses could significantly increase in the future. The logic of capitalist competition therefore provides an incentive for corporations to claim intellectual property rights even if they do not intend to commercialise the innovation themselves, simply to ensure that competing firms do not claim these rights. In some cases, this may stop further technological developments in the field completely. In other cases, the patent-holding enterprises may be happy to license research results that they themselves do not intend to pursue, or to enter into cross-licensing agreements. Other units of capital may be willing to pay these fees or enter

---

[4] Even a publication as sympathetic to neoliberalism as *The Economist* has expressed the worry that the extension of intellectual property rights is significantly hampering innovation in the computer sector. *The Economist* 2002.

into these agreements in order to attain access to scientific-technological knowledge. But there are no guarantees that the firms most able to pay licensing fees or enter cross-licensing agreements are the most innovative firms. A recent article in *The Economist* suggests that this is generally *not* the case; they are merely the wealthiest firms in the sector.[5]

The sort of technological dynamism pure neoliberal theorists themselves call for requires a rejection of the libertarian myth that all problems in the innovation process would disappear if only intellectual property rights were extended sufficiently. Given the systematic tendencies to market failure, many forms of scientific-technical knowledge must be treated as public goods, and governments must allocate public funds to provide them.

Research and development is but one example of a public good necessary for technological dynamism. Infrastructure, education, training, and so on raise the same concerns. Suppose, for example, that a corporation is considering extensive investment in training its work force. It is likely to hold back if the payoff is uncertain, or if there is a chance employees will leave for other firms that then appropriate the economic benefits of the training. Here, too, a market failure necessarily tends to arise, that is, a tendency for a level of investment below what is socially optimal. And so here, too, there is a need for the government to correct this market failure.

So far, the discussion has merely gone over ground covered in the previous chapter. It is now time to introduce a new point: while most neoliberal theorists and policymakers reject libertarianism, even moderate neoliberals limit the scope and scale of government intervention in processes of scientific-technological development. The default setting of *all* variants of the neoliberal state is to minimise state funding of research and development, infrastructure, education, and training. The difference between pure and moderate neoliberals simply regards where the minimally acceptable point lies.

Ample private investment funds can generally be relied upon for immediate product development, and all but the most deluded libertarians agree that extensive government support of basic research is necessary to correct systematic market failures. But what of the so-called 'valley of death' falling between basic research and innovations that are commercialisable in the short-to-medium-term?[6] Given the logic of the neoliberal position, with its strong

5 *The Economist* 2002.
6 See Wessner 2001.

faith in the 'magic of the marketplace', the default setting of the neoliberal state is to minimise government support for R&D in the 'valley of death'. As a result, the more the neoliberal state is institutionalised in a given region, the greater the danger that units of capital in that region will suffer in international competition against units from regions where more extensive state support is provided for R&D. The latter will tend to enjoy greater capacities for innovation, everything else being equal. Technological innovation is a crucial weapon of competition in capitalist markets. And, so, the more the neoliberal state has been institutionalised, the more likely it is that leading units of capital operating within its territory will organise effectively to replace it with a state form more compatible with their essential interests. In brief, the more thoroughly the neoliberal model is institutionalised, the closer we are to its demise. Parallel arguments can be developed for other crucial preconditions for success in international competition – investments in infrastructure, the education and training of the workforce, and so on – strengthening the case that an irresolvable immanent contradiction lies at the heart of the neoliberal model of globalisation.

The point can be extended further. State officials require revenues to carry out their various agendas. The revenues a state is able to appropriate are generally a function of the rate of capital accumulation within its borders, even if the rate of direct taxes on corporations is low. The structural tendency for units of capital under the jurisdiction of the neoliberal state to fail in technological competition (and thus in the competition for the accumulation of capital) has direct and severe negative effects on state revenues. Consequently, the more the neoliberal state has been institutionalised, the more likely it is that leading agents in the state apparatus and other political élites will organise effectively to replace it with a state form more compatible with their essential interests. The social relations of capitalism demand a state that furthers capital accumulation, and this requires government policies addressing market failure in scientific-technical development more consistently and aggressively than any version of the neoliberal state allows. The social relations of capitalism demand a catalytic state.[7]

---

[7] The rhetoric of neoliberalism can be retained only at the cost of institutionalised hypocrisy, as when government subsidies for advanced scientific-technological development take the form of military expenditures, while state official vehemently

This argument is general, holding for all states in the global system. But the argument holds with special force if the national economies in question are attempting to catch up in the world market. In the previous chapter I quoted two long passages from Thomas Friedman's influential defence of neoliberalism, *The Lexus and the Olive Tree*. The first described the 'Golden Straightjacket' imposed on the neoliberal state by global markets. The second asserted what is perhaps the strongest normative claim in favour of the neoliberal model of globalisation, the claim that its institutionalisation – however inconsistent and incomplete – has lifted more people out of poverty at a faster rate than ever before in world history. When these two points are simultaneously affirmed – as they are by virtually all neoliberal theorists and policymakers – the following difficulty arises: *the states that are the supposed success stories of neoliberal globalisation did not in fact put on the 'Golden Straightjacket' defining the neoliberal state.* They were catalytic states.

When Friedman and other neoliberal theorists discuss the successes of neoliberal globalisation, they primarily have the so-called 'East-Asian miracle' in mind. In recent decades, industrial development, exports, economic growth, and per capita income have increased in countries such as Korea, Taiwan, and now China at an even faster rate than Japan after World War Two. Each of these countries has developed along a unique path, and more concrete historical investigations would have to devote great attention to differences in their cultural traditions, organisational structures, policy choices, mass social movements, and so on. In the present context, however, it is legitimate to construct an ideal type out of elements found in a broad range of these social formations. This ideal type is termed 'the developmental state'.[8]

In the developmental state, high levels of domestic savings are accumulated within the domestic economy and mediated through the banking system. Government officials charged with the formulation and implementation of industrial policy preside over negotiations between banks and industrial concerns. Select industrial corporations (and networks of corporations) are

---

proclaim their hostility to industrial policy. See Markusen and Yudken 1992. In the US, to take a not entirely random example, 'Federal support has constituted about 70% of total university research funding in computer science and engineering since 1976', most of which has been provided by the US Department of Defense's Defense Advanced Research Projects Agency. OECD 2000, p. 83.

[8] See Wade 1990, Rodrik 2001, and Chang 2002.

granted credit at extremely low rates relative to those offered in global capital markets. If they use these funds effectively and begin to develop the productive capacities required to compete successfully in export markets, low-cost financing for further expansion will be generously provided. In the meantime, these industrial corporations are protected by tariff and non-tariff restrictions on trade (with these restrictions loosened for imports required for industrial development). Foreign direct investment is also restrained and subject to strict requirements regarding technology transfer, linkages with local producers, employment levels, and so on. Finally, inflows of financial capital are strictly regulated (if not excluded altogether) in order to maintain local control of leading banks and industrial firms.

The developmental state is designed to attain economic growth through competing successfully in export markets. In this respect, the model incorporates the fundamental neoliberal thesis that national economies are moments of a higher-level totality, the world market, rather than more or less independent entities externally related to each other. Proponents of this state form agree with neoliberals that autarchy is neither feasible nor normatively attractive. The development state, however, is thoroughly incompatible with the state form found in the neoliberal model of globalisation. Once the 'Golden Straightjacket' defining the neoliberal state has been put on, 'the private sector [is] the primary engine of . . . economic growth' and there is a 'shrinking [of the] the size of . . . state bureaucracy'.[9] In the developmental-state framework, in contrast, the private sector on its own is *not* an adequate 'engine of economic growth'; it can play this role if and only if it is effectively guided and supported by an extensive array of state agencies. Friedman holds that states wearing the 'Golden Straightjacket' must 'eliminate and lower tariffs on imported goods [and] . . . get rid of quotas and domestic monopolies'. This rules out policies designed to protect local manufactures from destruction at the hands of technologically advanced foreign firms before they had a chance to catch up or surpass them. But the greatest success stories in the global economy have made extensive use of such policies. The neoliberal state also 'remov[es] restrictions on foreign investment . . . deregulat[es] capital markets, mak[es] its currency convertible, [and] open[s] its industries, stock and bond markets

---

[9] Friedman 2000, p. 105.

to direct foreign ownership and investment'. These policies eliminate the ability to mobilise national savings within the domestic banking system. They also rule out prioritising the expansion of domestic productive capacities over other forms of investment in credit allocations. Finally, the 'Golden Straight-jacket' imposed on the state within the neoliberal framework encourages the foreign takeover of leading banks and industrial corporations by foreign investors, who necessarily tend to be more concerned with profits in the short-to-medium term than with the long-term industrial development of the domestic economy.

Neoliberal theory predicts that regions where the state has accepted the 'Golden Straightjacket' will tend to enjoy higher rates of growth than regions where the developmental-state model has been adopted. The empirical data do not corroborate this prediction. As both Dani Rodrik and John Eatwell have argued, the transition from the developmental-state model to the neoliberal model that took place in the last decades of the twentieth century in many regions of the global economy is correlated with *lower* rates of growth.[10]

One cannot coherently argue for the advantages of the neoliberal model of globalisation by appealing to the successes of the developmental state, when the former systematically rules out the latter. Yet defenders of neoliberalism fall into this immanent contradiction when they claim that the model of globalisation they defend 'has raised living standards higher, faster and for more people than at any time in history'.[11] The sort of global order that enables

---

[10] Rodrik 2001; Eatwell 1996; see also the text associated with note 61 of the previous chapter.

[11] Friedman 2000, p. 350; similar statements are found in Wolf 2004, pp. 141, 160. More clearly than Friedman, Wolf recognises that 'the creation of indigenous technological capacities has demanded special efforts by developing countries', and admits it is legitimate to ask if WTO rules designed to dismantle the developmental state 'impose unreasonable constraints on [the] policy discretion' of developing countries. Wolf 2004, p. 204. But Wolf also applauds the elimination of 'the most damaging non-tariff barriers and the highest tariffs'. Wolf 2004, p. 204. And he insists that 'Inward direct investment must be liberalized. Investors must also believe that they will be able to repatriate their capital and remit earnings (which requires convertibility on the current account). To function well . . . foreign financial companies will also need access to global financial markets . . . for all these reasons, a symbiosis exists between both current and capital account liberalization and the contribution made by the presence of foreign financial enterprises in the economy'. Wolf 2004, p. 286. In other words, Wolf ends up falling into the same immanent contradiction as Friedman; he, too, defends neoliberalism by appealing to the successes of the developmental state, while simultaneously advocating policies fundamentally incompatible with that state form.

living standards to be raised in poor regions pivots around catalytic states, which pursue industrial and technology policies far more consistently and aggressively than is compatible with any variant of the neoliberal state.[12]

In dialectical theories, an immanent contradiction justifies a determinate negation, that is, a transition from a given position to a new stage in the systematic ordering. In the present context, the new position must explicitly acknowledge the need for a form of state that can provide the preconditions for success in global markets more consistently and aggressively than the neoliberal state. In the systematic dialectic of globalisation, the neoliberal model of globalisation must give way to the catalytic-state model.

2. From the neoliberal state to the catalytic state (2): the Polanyi thesis

Karl Polanyi's masterwork, *The Great Transformation*, serves as a reminder that contemporary neoliberalism is by no means the first attempt to liberate capitalist markets from social controls. A similar experiment was undertaken in England in the nineteenth century. In Polanyi's account, the failure of this experiment was due primarily to its internal dynamic rather than extrinsic factors. Freed from effective social regulations, capitalist markets in England generated massive social disruptions and pathologies, leading to generalised economic anxiety. Enormous social movements arose in response, effectively demanding that the government abandon the experiment with unregulated markets.[13]

Polanyi's contemporary disciples argue that attempts to institute neoliberalism are doomed to the same fate. If global markets are not subjected to effective social regulations by states, they necessarily tend to generate gigantic social disruptions, social pathologies, and generalised economic anxiety. Social discontent inevitably leads to the emergence of social movements demanding

---

[12] The region of the global economy where neoliberalism is now pushed the most forcefully – the United States – did not itself become an industrialised power by submitting to the dictates of the Golden Straightjacket. The US government protected its infant industries throughout the extended historical period in which 'free trade' would have led to their eradication by more advanced European manufacturers. See Chang 2002.

[13] Polanyi 1944.

that governments abandon neoliberal experiments with so-called 'free' markets. Governments must eventually respond to this social pressure and 're-embed' markets within society. From this perspective too, then, the more thoroughly neoliberal policies are pursued, the sooner their demise. The project of institutionalising free markets is thus inherently self-contradictory, whether pursued on the level of the national economy or the global economy.

Why does neoliberalism necessarily tend towards generalised economic anxiety? Only a few considerations can be mentioned here. We may begin with deregulated ('flexible') labour markets, a central goal of the neoliberal policy agenda. They necessarily tend to lead to a higher rate of lay-offs during economic slowdowns than feasible alternative arrangements. They also are correlated with massive lay-offs, even when corporations are profitable and the economy is enjoying a boom period.[14] The more neoliberal policies successfully further the 'flexibility' of labour markets, the greater the proportion of part-time and temporary workers in the economy. Policies that deregulate the labour market are also closely associated with a tendency for the work hours of full-time employees to increase.[15] The net effect of these developments is a tendency for economic insecurity and stress to increase throughout the workforce.

There is also a tendency for inequality to increase significantly over time in regions of the global economy adopting neoliberal policies. On the theoretical level, it is difficult for neoliberals to deny this, given the neoclassical theory of 'factor price equalisation'. According to this view, trade between high-wage regions and low-wage regions (including trade resulting from foreign direct investment in low-wage regions) necessarily tends to lead to an equalisation of wages. Since there are far more workers in low-waged regions of the global economy, the elementary laws of supply and demand so beloved by neoliberals dictate that high wages tend to decline far more than low wages tend to rise. In contrast, the income and wealth of capitalist investors are not subject to an analogous constraint in the neoliberal model of globalisation. Their rewards should tend to increase when they are allowed to shift investments freely from less to more profitable regions, sectors, and

---

[14] The rate at which waves of lay-offs occurred in profitable companies in the US in the 1990s was historically unprecedented for an expansionary period.

[15] Schor 1993; Fraser 2001.

firms. And, so, the gap in income and wealth between will necessarily tend to widen, given the abstract principles of neoliberal economics.[16]

Despite this theoretical consideration, however, neoliberal theorists typically deny that inequality has increased in the global economy as a result of imports from (and capital flight to) regions where wages are low. After all, most foreign direct investment in the global economy does not flow to low-wage regions, but to areas where wages are relatively high.[17] When inequality has increased, de-unionisation and technological dynamism, not global free trade, are the true culprits, in their view.[18] But 'de-unionisation' is, to a large extent, the direct result of neoliberal state policies seeking a more 'flexible work force', policies neoliberals hold are forced upon the state by the pressures of global competition. Thus it hardly refutes the thesis that the neoliberal model of globalisation necessarily tends to exacerbate inequality. Regarding technological change, the obvious point to make is that no technological artefact has itself ever caused job insecurity and stagnant/declining wages. If particular technological artefacts are associated with particular patterns of employment and distribution, the explanation is not to be found in those artefacts. It is to be discovered, instead, in the set of social relations in place at the particular place and time. In the case at hand, the adoption of neoliberal policies determines the social consequences associated with technological changes, enabling firms to employ technologies in a manner that heightens job insecurity and exacerbates economic inequalities. Technological artefacts are not to blame for this social fact.

---

[16] Cobb and Daly 1994; Kapstein 1999.

[17] So-called 'developed countries' received 61.2% of world FDI between 1993–9, with only 35.3% flowing to developing countries. In 1999–2001, the share of the developed countries increased to 68.4% (UNCTAD 2002, p. 5). A mere 2% of the FDI inflows into developing countries went to the 49 least developed nations (UNCTAD 2002, p. 9). These empirical facts do not cohere with the neoclassical assumption that capital tends to flow to capital-scarce regions, a crucial claim in the standard normative defence of the neoliberal model of globalisation. Neoliberal theorists cannot have it both ways. Either capital investment tends to flow to areas of capital scarcity, in which case heightened economic anxiety among workers in wealthier regions is fully justified. Or capital investment does not tend to flow in this manner, in which case an essential element of the claim that neoliberal policies further global justice must be abandoned. (In the latter case, heightened economic anxiety among workers in wealthier regions can still be fully warranted; jobs lost to other high-wage regions are no less lost.)

[18] Wolf 2004, pp. 169–70.

We must also note that threats can be effective even when they are not carried out. Foreign direct investment predominantly takes the form of flows of investment capital from one wealthy region of the global economy to another, and foreign trade also occurs mostly between regions with relatively high wages. Does this mean that a workforce told it must accept increased job insecurity, longer work hours, and lower wages in order to prevent its employer from relocating to a low-wage region does not have to take this threat seriously? Hardly.[19]

Further, we need to be wary of extrapolating trends into the indefinite future. Certain categories of workers have been able to maintain and even increase their wage levels during an extended historical period in which neoliberal policies have encouraged free global flows of commodities and investment capital. This does not imply that they will continue to be able to do so in the foreseeable future. There are strong reasons to think that the continued implementation of neoliberal policies eventually heightens economic insecurity among groups of workers initially able to avoid this.[20]

Another source of generalised economic insecurity generated by the neoliberal model concerns the financial sector. Is it an accident that financial crises have occurred in the global economy at a historically unprecedented frequency after neoliberal policies of financial liberalisation were implemented?[21] A myriad of contingent factors are needed to explain why a given financial crisis broke out at a particular place and a particular time, and misguided government policies will almost always deserve a place on this list. But is it really plausible to assert that there has been a sudden and inexplicable increase in the stupidity and corruption of government officials in recent decades? If not, some other explanation for the more frequent occurrence of financial crises must be proposed. By far the most plausible thesis is that the neoliberal

---

[19] A survey of US firms revealed that, between 1993 and 1995, 50% of all firms – and 65% of the manufacturing firms unions attempted to organise – threatened to relocate if unions were formed. Bronfenbrenner 2001; see also Bronfenbrenner 1996.

[20] At the time of writing, for example, the business press in the US has begun to note the high numbers of professional jobs in the computer sector being shifted overseas.

[21] In the last two decades of the twentieth century, more than 125 countries experienced one or more serious cases of banking problems. In more than half of these cases, a developing country's entire banking system was basically insolvent. And, in over a dozen of these cases, it cost a tenth or more of the annual national income to 'resolve' the crisis. Council of Foreign Relations Task Force 1999.

policy of deregulating these markets necessarily tends to lead to periodic outbreaks of financial crises, as investors stampede in and out of economies at unprecedented scale and velocity.[22]

John Gray's study, *False Dawn: The Delusions of Global Capitalism*, is, to my knowledge, the most important and influential account of globalisation presented from what may be termed a 'neo-Polanyian' perspective. Gray agrees that, if markets are not effectively regulated, they necessarily tend to generate extreme levels of economic insecurity.[23] He also argues that the neoliberal project of extending global free markets to the greatest extent possible leads to profound social pathologies, including:

- the disintegration of family life;[24]
- an erosion of the material foundations of particular communities;[25]
- an erosion of 'intermediate institutions' between the individual and the state, institutions that are absolutely essential for social stability, such as trade unions, professional associations, and so on;[26]
- the eradication of many bourgeois values, such as those associated with a career;[27]
- the formation of an 'underclass', a 'neoliberal dependency culture';[28]
- levels of inequality incompatible with social cohesion;[29] and
- socially destructive levels of crime and incarceration.[30]

According to Gray, the worst instances of these social pathologies are found in precisely those regions where the neoliberal agenda has been implemented to the greatest extent.

---

[22] Argentina provides an especially sobering reminder of the social costs inflicted financial crises. As of January 2003, at least 60% of the nation's 37 million people lived in poverty, double the number at the end of 2001. Between December 2001 and the end of 2003, the economy shrunk by 12% and unemployment hovered around 25%. Avoidable deaths and illnesses greatly increased, while hunger became rampant in this nation with more cattle than people (Rohter 2003, A1; see also Smith 2003b).

[23] Gray 1998, pp. 71–2.

[24] Gray 1998, pp. 29–30; 72.

[25] Gray 1998, p. 112.

[26] Gray 1998, p. 26.

[27] Gray 1998, p. 217.

[28] Gray 1998, pp. 30; 42.

[29] Gray 1998, pp. 32; 48; 107; see also Phillips 2002.

[30] Gray 1998, pp. 32; 113; 116–18.

If Polanyi and Gray are correct, we must add yet another item to the ever-growing list of immanent contradictions afflicting the neoliberal position. Theorists operating within the neoliberal paradigm insist that free markets automatically tend to function in an efficient manner, furthering the good of individuals to the greatest feasible extent. Adam Smith's invisible hand argument, Ricardo's principle of comparative advantage, Hayek's discussion of markets as efficient mechanisms for transmitting information, are three examples of this quintessential neoliberal claim. This is a consequentialist argument, and neoliberals who wish to employ it cannot coherently reject the principle that *all* relevant consequences need to be considered when institutional frameworks and social policies are compared and evaluated. But their theories contradict this principle. The only consequences neoliberals seriously consider are levels of individual consumption and returns to investment.[31] For Polanyi and Gray, social stability and cohesiveness are absolutely essential considerations. The very identity of individuals is shaped in the process of socialisation within a community. If neoliberal policies undermine community stability and cohesiveness, an increase in consumption levels or returns on investment will not compensate for such a profound loss.[32]

In the methodological framework adopted in this study, the fact that neoliberals fail to carry through a sufficiently rigorous cost/benefit analysis due to their neglect of communitarian values is not the essential matter. In a systematic dialectic of globalisation, the crucial consideration is whether the institutional framework defended by neoliberals includes structural tendencies undermining the claim that it would reproduce itself in an efficient and normatively acceptable fashion, as they themselves define these terms. Gray argues that the massive social disruptions inflicted by global free markets will necessarily tend to lead to politically effective demands to escape this chaos, forcing states to abandon the neoliberal agenda. Gray echoes Polanyi's conclusion: the more thoroughly the neoliberal model of globalisation has been institutionalised, the closer it is to being dismantled. If anything counts as an immanent contradiction, it is surely this. Insofar as this course of events expresses structural tendencies built into the neoliberal model of globalisation,

---

[31] This limitation is admitted without apparent embarrassment in Dam 2001, Chapter 1.

[32] Sennett 1998; Miller 2000.

rather than mere contingencies, the already strong case for a transition to a new stage in the systematic dialectic of globalisation becomes even more compelling.[33]

---

[33] Providing a satisfactory justification for the systematic transition from the social-state position to neoliberalism did not require a comprehensive critique of the former. Similarly, the need to go beyond neoliberalism in the systematic dialectic can be established without an examination of all of its structural shortcomings. However, I would like to note in passing a further shortcoming of particular importance: even moderate neoliberalism necessarily tends to generate an excessive level of environmental harms in the global order. The presumption shared by all neoliberals that governments should regulate business activity to the minimum feasible extent allows paths of development to be selected before the medium-to-long-term environmental risks associated with these paths are adequately understood. The presumption that free trade should be fostered to the greatest feasible extent results in many environmental concerns being categorised as pernicious 'non-tariff trade barriers', that is, as disguised forms of protectionism (see Dam 2001, Chapter 13). And too much of the development of environmentally sustainable technologies will be left to a too indifferent private sector. Other difficulties arise from the fact that neoliberals generally hold that environmental regulations are justified if and only if their (monetary) benefits clearly outweigh their (monetary) costs. This apparently neutral methodology is inherently biased. Corporations systematically overestimate their costs of complying with proposed environmental regulations (Kuttner 1997, Chapter 8). Further, most environmental benefits do not take the form of commodities with price tags attached, and methods of imposing a price value on them are fraught with controversy. Estimating the monetary values of future environmental benefits is especially arbitrary, with estimations fluctuating wildly, depending on the discount rate employed to reduce future monetary values to present ones. ('By deflating future earnings into current dollars, cost-benefit analysis devalues the benefit of saving workers from injury and disease over an entire lifetime. During the 1980s, OMB [the US Office of Management and Budget, T.S.] used a relatively high discount rate of 10 percent. This means that a regulation that would produce a million dollars' worth of benefits in fifty years is discounted to a value of less than ten thousand dollars today. Cost, however, are incurred in current dollars. So benefits are systematically discounted against costs'. Kuttner 1996, p. 302.) Questions of environmental justice are inevitably generated within this framework as well, since the monetary value of avoiding a given level of environmental harms will necessarily tend to be higher in wealthy regions. Neoliberals categorise this state of affairs as a positive expression of local autonomy: 'Difference in incomes, preferences, and geography could quite reasonably give different localities, or countries, entirely different environmental standards for local environmental spillovers. If polluting industries were then to migrate from high-standard regions or countries to low-standard regions or countries, the world would be unambiguously better off. The high-standard regions or countries would be able to consume the products of polluting activities without having to host them, and the low-standard regions or countries would have more economic activity, in return for pollution to which they are, relatively speaking, indifferent'. Wolf 2004, 91. In many cases, however, the low standards were implemented by local élites without the consent of the populace. In others, the environmental harms are 'accepted' only because the poor region is bereft of even minimally acceptable alternatives. Either way, the only people who are 'unambiguously better off' are those who profit from the sale and use of commodities while displacing the environmental costs of producing those commodities to others. We may conclude that environmental

In the previous section, we saw that the next model in the systematic progression must centre on catalytic states committed to an aggressive industrial policy. We can now formulate a second dimension of this state form: it subjects markets to social controls designed to ensure that the functioning of these markets is consistent with healthy and reasonably stable communities. In this manner, it explicitly addresses the immanent contradictions of the neoliberal model of globalisation.

While the catalytic state forms the heart of the catalytic-state model of globalisation, there are other elements too. It is now time to outline the model as whole.

3. The catalytic-state model of globalisation

The catalytic-state model of globalisation includes the same regions of social life considered in the previous chapters: the family, civil society (especially the national economy), the state, the world market, the interstate system and the régime of global governance. Its distinctive features are found in the particular determinations defining these regions, along with the relative weight given to each region within the framework as a whole.

On the level of the family, supporters of this position agree on three central points. First, the priority given to the individual's pursuit of private self-interest in neoliberalism fails to account adequately for the role of trust and care in family life. Second, the extreme social instability and stress generated by deregulated markets is fundamentally incompatible with healthy households.[34] Third, families lack the capacities required to address the

---

regulations within a neoliberal framework are not likely to be adequate to the scope of the problems. No less seriously, the neoliberal agenda of tax reductions necessarily tends to result in understaffed agencies lacking the ability to enforce the environmental regulations that do exist effectively. Even the moderate neoliberal state is systematically prone to allow excessively high levels of environmental risks and harms to be imposed on communities. This, too, counts as immanent contradiction between the structural tendencies of the neoliberal model of globalisation and the claims to efficiency and normative attractiveness made by its leading proponents.

[34] In the United States, for example, after two decades of neoliberal policies 'Family finances have grown much more insecure. Although insecurity dropped in the booms of the late 1980's and late 1990's, the long-term trend is sharply upward. In fact, the instability of family income was roughly five times greater at its peak in the 1990's than in 1972. . . . [E]ven as wages have become more unstable, the financial effects of losing a job have worsened, and the cost of things families need, from housing to education, has ballooned'. Hacker 2004, p. 15.

structural problems afflicting them. They are embedded within larger systems of institutions and social practices, and these problems must ultimately be addressed within those larger systems.

On the level of civil society, advocates of the catalytic state do not propose an alternative to capitalist markets. They insist, however, that these markets are 'inseparable from other areas of social activity'.[35] There is nothing whatsoever 'natural' in the view that 'the exercise of personal choice is more important than social cohesion, the control of economic risk, or any other collective good'.[36] The neoliberal appeal to the absolute moral primacy of liberty and property rights is illegitimate, an ideological tactic employed 'to shield the workings of the free market from public scrutiny and political challenge'.[37] Neoliberals also assume that free markets arise spontaneously whenever they are not repressed by extraneous political power. This too is completely mistaken: 'Encumbered markets are the norm in every society, whereas free markets are a product of artifice, design, and political coercion'.[38] In brief, the affirmation of 'market economies' must be combined with a vehement rejection of the 'market societies' of neoliberalism:

> A basic shift in economic philosophy is needed. The freedoms of the market are not ends in themselves. They are expedients, devices contrived by human beings for human purposes. Markets are made to serve man, not man the market. In the global free market the instruments of economic life have become dangerously emancipated from social control and political governance.[39]

The more global markets invade civil society in a direct and unmediated fashion, the more the social bonds holding together corporations, networks of corporations, and other private voluntary associations together are broken. Only a 'catalytic state' can enable these social bonds to flourish in the contemporary global order, because only an activist state can protect civil society from these incursions. The importance of global markets, the interstate system, and international institutions cannot be denied. But, for defenders of

---

[35] Gray 1998, p. 12.
[36] Gray 1998, p. 108.
[37] Gray 1998, p. 109.
[38] Gray 1998, p. 17. This dimension of Gray's position can also be traced back to Polanyi.
[39] Gray 1998, p. 234.

this third position in the systematic dialectic, the manner in which the state mediates the impact of global markets on the family, local associations, and the national economy is the most crucial dimension of the global order.

Why not simply call the catalytic state a variant of the social state? Supporters of the social state also deny that globalisation makes weak states inevitable, and that only weak states are normatively justified. They hold that globalisation has been, and will continue to be, a state project, pursued by central banks, departments of the treasury, and other sections of the state apparatus in alliance with financial capital and significant factions of manufacturing capital. For them, the concept of 'globalisation' has been an important ideological weapon in the political project of deregulation, privatisation, and the liberalisation of markets, deployed to persuade the public that all alternatives to neoliberalism are eliminated by irresistible technological and economic developments. If the political will were present to pursue full employment and reduced inequality, these theorists conclude, the social state project could be effectively revived.[40] Is not the pursuit of flourishing and reasonably stable communities a vital part of this same agenda? Is not the catalytic state merely a variant of the social state?

John Gray and other leading defenders of the catalytic state vehemently reject this line of thought. From their standpoint, neoliberals are completely correct to insist that the social-state model of globalisation fails the 'ought implies can' test. In capitalist economies, there is a systematic tendency for extensive trade and capital flows across borders. Once trade and capital mobility extend past a certain (admittedly indeterminate) point, the strong redistributive and regulatory policies characteristic of the social state are simply not feasible. In his discussion of the Keynesian welfare state, Gray lists five specific factors behind its demise:

(i) The pressures of competitive deregulation force nations to attract capital investment, and lowering regulations on capital is an effective way of attracting capital.[41]

(ii) Similar pressures force a lowering of corporate taxes, since 'worldwide mobility of production allows enterprises to locate where regulatory and tax burdens are least onerous'.[42]

---

[40] Palley 2000.
[41] Gray, 1998, p. 98.
[42] Gray 1998, p. 213.

(iii) Workforces in regions where social democracy holds sway are increasingly in competition with highly educated, low-wage workforces from other areas of the globe, a competition sure to intensify.[43]

(iv) Governments are now more dependent on international capital markets, and the global bond market has a 'chronic allergy' to job creation through public borrowing and to all forms of counter-cyclical policies perceived to be excessively expansionary.[44]

(v) In the medium-to-long term, the social-state model of capitalism may enjoy significant advantages over the neoliberal model. It may well tend to foster superior education and skill levels, higher investment in infrastructure and other public goods and services, and superior social cohesion, while attaining comparable levels of efficiency.[45] All of this is quite irrelevant. Short-term economic pressures prevent variants of capitalism with long-term advantages from competing successfully with variants enjoying lower labour, regulatory, or tax costs in the short-to-medium term.[46] These pressure 'drive down social provision and raise the taxes on labour'.[47]

'Social democracy', Gray concludes, 'belongs to a world that cannot be revived'.[48]

In systematic-dialectical terms, these considerations establish that the proper response to the immanent contradictions of neoliberalism is a transition to a new stage, rather than a regression to the social-state model, the first position in the systematic ordering. Empirical history is beset by countless contingencies,

---

[43] Gray 1998, p. 98.

[44] Gray 1998, pp. 34; 98.

[45] For proponents of the catalytic state, the high levels of economic insecurity and inequality associated with the neoliberal model tend to lead to lower levels of labour productivity over time: '[E]xtreme inequalities finally do more harm than good *vis-à-vis* market efficiency; they foster poor commitment and loyalty, insecurity, threats to private property and personal security. . . . These ideas especially apply to the contemporary labour market. If unfairly treated, wage-earners will reply with poor productivity, low quality, high absenteeism and growth in social conflict. By contrast, a more equitable income distribution can enhance private and global efficiency. Similarly, labour markets are not self-adjusting as typical goods markets because workers have definite feelings about the unfairness of wage cuts which would destroy group solidarity'. Boyer 1996, p. 107.

[46] Gray 1998, p. 80.

[47] Gray 1998, p. 88.

[48] Gray 1998, p. 204.

and Gray is surely mistaken to rule out any and all revivals of social democracy *a priori*. In a specific historical context, the immanent contradictions emerging in the course of an attempt to institute neoliberalism might lead to a revival of social-democratic parties and policies. But matters are different in a systematic dialectic. The contradictions in some position A justifying a transition to another position B do not disappear when we discover that B too is beset by contradictions. If the immanent contradictions of B are used to justify a return to A, we have what Hegel termed a 'bad infinite', an endless repetition without systematic advance.[49] Empirical history may take this shape for extended periods. But, in systematic-dialectical theories, once a stage has been superseded there is no turning back. The task at this juncture of the study is to go beyond the neoliberal position, while incorporating the elements of truth within it. These elements rule out a return to the social-state model of globalisation.

Gray insists that 'the replacement of global *laissez-faire* by a managed régime for the world economy is, at present, nearly as Utopian a project as a universal free market'.[50] This leaves only one possibility. The state must occupy the central place in the global order, as it did in the social-state model. But a new sort of state must emerge, capable of maintaining social cohesion and avoiding social pathologies in a world where cross-border flows of trade and investment rule out even semi-autonomous national economies. What is required, in brief, is a state capable of implementing 'policies which harness markets to the satisfaction of human needs'.[51]

Gray does not presume to dictate in detail what these policies should be. But he does make some general observations. First, the rise of a global economy does not tend to result in the homogenisation of either cultures or economies. Different traditions and cultural values remain in place, and the most effective public policies will be appropriate to the unique culture and history of a particular political community. The traditions and cultural values of the United States and England, for example, are quite different from those of Germany or the Netherlands, let alone China or Japan. Catalytic states must creatively forge national variants of capitalism appropriate to their unique conditions:

---

[49] Hegel 1975, pp. 137–8, #94.
[50] Gray 1998, p. 200.
[51] Gray 1998, p. 92.

[R]ecognition of the state's economic role in preserving and fostering cohesion in society [is required today]. The policies dictated by this responsibility cannot be deduced from the supposed universal truths of economic theory. They will vary, according to the cultural traditions of different peoples and the kinds of capitalism they practise.[52]

State structures and policies must also be appropriate to the particular stage of development that has been attained in the community, evolving as the community evolves. The developmental state, for example, is a form of catalytic state appropriate to poorer regions of the global economy. After a certain point of development, another form of catalytic state will be preferable.

Despite these divergences, the various sorts of catalytic states all face the same general tasks. The labour market must be effectively regulated in order to foster employment and good jobs.[53] Best-practice business regulations must also be encouraged through public policies. Social-welfare programmes must ensure that the material preconditions for effective participation in social, political, and cultural life are provided, and that families, voluntary associations, and communities are protected from disruptions caused by economic changes beyond their control. National innovation systems must be established to foster technological dynamism in a manner appropriate to a particular political community.[54] The state must accept its proper responsibilities in the national innovation system, which include tracking new technologies and markets,

---

[52] Gray 1998, p. 203.

[53] 'The challenge is to find effective measures that put employment creation rather than the restless pursuit of export markets at the centre of the public agenda. Governments everywhere want to promote a high-wage, high quality and high-value-added economy. This requires harnessing trade to ensure that when industries restructure, good jobs are the result. Wages and employment structure have to be tied to productivity growth. This involves discouraging companies from competing on age and low employment standards'. Drache 1996, p. 56.

[54] 'The twenty-first century will probably experience a genuine social and political engagement of markets with networks, associations and local communities along with renewed state intervention. It is the task of governments to set political priorities; they cannot simply be replaced by any other mechanisms, especially not markets which usually are quite myopic and generally unable to deal with strategic complementarities which are so crucial in modern economies. The domain for state intervention is, therefore, large indeed, and comprises education and training, the access and financing of healthcare and last, but not least, the production of knowledge, i.e. innovations which are at the core of economic growth'. Boyer 1996, p. 86. The critical importance of national innovation systems in the global economy is discussed in Dosi et al. 1988, Part V and Nelson 1993.

promoting new infant industries, maintaining long-term programmes for investment in mature industries, helping to regain ground lost in strategic industries, and assisting an orderly retreat for industries in decline.[55] The catalytic state, in short, provides public goods to correct the most significant forms of market failures in a more consistent and comprehensive fashion than can occur within a neoliberal framework:

> Countries who think that powerful trends of internationalization and interdependence have eroded the basis of national sovereignty *tout court* are mistaken. Despite all the claims to the contrary, it is premature to announce the death of the nation-state. Countries still remain in charge of the essential part of their national sovereignty: law-making and jurisprudence; macroeconomic policy, including money, finance and taxation. National governments are as much responsible today as ever for the environment, education, training, labour-market policy, industrial relations and economic restructuring; pensions, family law and well-being, health and safety; police and security; social policy, science and technology; transportation and communication; forestry, agriculture, fishing, mining and water.[56]

These objectives were also essential elements of the social-state agenda. In the social-state model of globalisation, however, it was simply assumed that the state could fulfil these tasks. This assumption rested upon (a) a conceptualisation of the global economy as an aggregate of more-or-less independent national economies connected externally by trade and investment, and (b) the belief that this independence could be fairly easily maintained through various forms of protectionism. As neoliberals realise, national economies cannot even provisionally be conceived as separate entities without fundamentally distorting the contemporary social world. National economies can be distinguished, but only as moments of a greater whole, the world market. No normatively acceptable level of protectionism can reverse this state of affairs. The catalytic-state model incorporates ('sublates', to use the Hegelian jargon) this element of truth in the neoliberal model.[57] The challenge

---

[55] Weiss 1998.
[56] Drache 1996, p. 54.
[57] See Introduction, note 20.

for the catalytic state is to attain its objectives without falling back on the traditional protectionism associated with the social state:

> Today, a return to traditional protectionism is not on the cards for any country. Thus, all states require an alternative. They need to have strong policy instruments that will let them plan and finance their strategic goals including job creation, science and technology policy, R&D, environmental policy, affirmative action programmes and the like. This re-tooling of state regulatory policy does not require governments to choose between free trade or protectionism, but between the diminishing prospect for free trade and expanding the conditions for managed trade.[58]

The operation of the catalytic state implies that the essential determinations of the world market, the interstate system, and the régime of global governance in the catalytic-state model of globalisation will be quite different from those found in the neoliberal framework. If states are to protect their citizens from the social pathologies that global free markets would otherwise inflict, some controls on cross-border economic transactions are required. A 'framework of global regulation – of currencies, capital movements, trade and environmental conservation' is necessary in order to create the political space for effective state policies.[59]

The only part of this framework explicitly discussed by Gray is a 'Tobin tax' on short-term (speculative) capital inflows, named after the Nobel prize-winning economist to first suggest this way of minimising the dangers of financial instability.[60] He is certainly aware of the extent to which this proposal breaks with the neoliberal perspective dominating policy debates today. But there is considerable empirical evidence that states can, in principle, impose effective restrictions on global capital flows. The international capital adequacy standards for banks, developed initially in the 1988 Basle accord and since updated, provide one example. The international accounting standards imposed by a coalition of states (led by the US) to monitor cross-border flows of drug money, provide another.[61] If these sorts of measures can be effectively implemented, other restrictions can be as well.

---

[58] Drache 1996, pp. 34–5.
[59] Gray 1998, p. 199.
[60] Gray 1998, p. 200.
[61] Helleiner 1996; 2002.

Joseph Stiglitz agrees with the need for exit taxes to protect countries against 'the ravages of speculators'.[62] He adds a number of other proposals for reforms of the régime of global governance, all of which are intended to limit the harm global markets and international agencies can inflict on domestic economies.[63] His suggestions include:

- standstills on debt repayment when financial crises occur, giving otherwise healthy firms an opportunity to recover from financial crises;[64]
- special bankruptcy provisions that kick in when exceptional macroeconomic disturbances break out, providing management a chance to restructure ailing companies;[65]
- greater reluctance by the IMF to lend billions in bail-out packages;[66]
- granting more seats at the IMF to countries from poor regions in the global economy;[67]
- more open discourse at the IMF, the World Trade Organisation, and other international agencies;
- a narrowing of focus at the IMF to managing crises, leaving policies of development and transition to other institutions such as the World Bank;
- loans from developed countries and international financial institutions enabling developing countries to buy insurance against fluctuations in the international capital markets; and
- debt relief and a more balanced trade agenda.

In Stiglitz's view, a set of international agreements instituting these practices would solidify a global order within which catalytic states in general, and developmental states in particular, can flourish.

---

[62] Stiglitz 2002, p. 205.
[63] See Stiglitz 2002, pp. 208–10; 236–43, *passim*.
[64] Stiglitz 2002, p. 130.
[65] Ibid.
[66] The IMF is the 'preferred creditor', which means that when an economy is in trouble it gets paid back before foreign creditors. This leads private investors to insist on higher interest rates to cover their higher risk of not being paid back. The greater the bail-out package, the higher the perceived risk to private investors, and the higher the interests rates they charge. The higher the interest rates, the more industrial development is hampered.
[67] Stiglitz would prefer that countries in Africa and elsewhere receive more voting rights at the IMF. He recognises, however, that this is not likely to occur in the present period.

Later stages in a systematic dialectic incorporate the essential elements of truth in earlier positions, while making explicit what had been merely implicit. In the catalytic-state model of globalisation, the need for the state to provide the background conditions enabling markets to function in an efficient and normatively acceptable manner is acknowledged. This is the element of truth in the social-state model. But national economies are thoroughly intertwined, and the formation of a world market with distinct emergent properties has profound implications for how the state must be conceptualised. These are the main elements of truth in the neoliberal perspective, and they too are incorporated in the catalytic-state model. Finally, the neoliberal framework is plagued by various irresolvable tensions between the core claims asserted by leading neoliberal theorists and the dominant structural tendencies of a neoliberal global order. These immanent contradictions are explicitly addressed in the catalytic-state model. Its proponents do not renounce industrial policy and place their faith in 'free' trade and global capital flows. They explicitly acknowledge that the adequate provision of public goods and avoidance of public bads requires more extensive state intervention than is consistent with neoliberal principles. Defenders of this position also realise that markets must be 'embedded', that is, subject to effective social regulation, if profound social disruptions and pathologies are to be avoided. These considerations justify ordering the catalytic-state model of globalisation after the social-state and neoliberal models in a systematic dialectic of globalisation.

Is the rational reconstruction of positions in the globalisation debate now complete? Does the catalytic-state model of globalisation necessarily tend to reproduce itself over time in an efficient and normatively acceptable fashion, as evaluated by the principles of its leading proponents? Or does it, too, suffer from immanent contradictions that justify moving to a yet further stage in the systematic dialectic?

4. A critical assessment of the catalytic-state model

The catalytic state must fulfil two main functions. It must address market failures, especially those connected with technological change, more comprehensively and aggressively than is consistent with any form of neoliberal state. And it must subject markets to social control in order to further communitarian values, protecting communities from the social disruptions and social pathologies that necessarily tend to be generated by 'disembedded' markets.

Regarding the former, matters seem clear enough, at least in principle. In the contemporary global order, successful states have been and will always be catalytic states, actively pursuing industrial policies designed to correct market failures. State officials and other élites may proclaim allegiance to neoliberal ideology. But no state that hopes to succeed in the global market will ever actually leave scientific-technical development to the 'magic of the marketplace', whatever the rhetoric of its ruling groups.

What about the second task, the fostering of healthy and reasonably stable communities? Before turning to this question, I would like to review briefly the five factors John Gray believes condemn the social state to irrelevance. They are the pressures of competitive deregulation, the pressures to lower corporate taxes, the role of educated, low-wage workforces in global labour markets, the 'chronic allergy' of the global bond market to job creation through public borrowing and 'excessively' expansionary counter-cyclical policies, and the irrelevance of long-term advantages in a global economy in the face of unrelenting short-term competitive pressures. In Gray's view, these factors remove the breathing room required by the social state. Would a catalytic state dedicated to protecting communities from social disruptions and pathologies require significantly less breathing room? If the measures proposed by advocates of the catalytic state cannot revive social democracy, can we simply assume that they are sufficient to allow the catalytic state to attain its objectives?

The only reform of the global order Gray himself mentions, a Tobin tax, leaves the first four factors completely untouched. At the most, it might make certain sorts of competitive pressures a bit less unrelenting in a fairly narrow range of circumstances. But, as Paul Davidson has convincingly argued, a Tobin tax would come woefully short of adequately attaining even the objective it tackles most directly, control of short-term speculative inflows of portfolio capital. A Tobin tax is, in effect, a transaction tax, and transactions will continue even when transaction taxes are in place as long as the anticipated profits are sufficiently high. The potential rewards from participating in speculative bubbles in financial assets are such that a transaction tax at the levels discussed by Tobin and others would likely be ineffectual in precisely the cases that matter most.[68]

A closer look at Gray's discussion of Germany and Japan, his two main empirical examples of catalytic states, illustrates the problem of implementing communitarian values in the contemporary global economy. Regarding Germany, Gray concedes that 'at some point, social relations among stakeholders will become more marginal in the life of German firms', as global competition for equity leads companies to give increasing weight to share values at the cost of 'weaken[ing] the company's commitment to other stakeholders'.[69] The irreversibility of this development is an essential premise for Gray's conclusion that social democracy in Germany is doomed. Gray insists, however, that Germany is not about to evolve towards the neoliberal model, in which shareholder interests trump all other social concerns. He argues that 'the complex system of cross-holdings in Germany together with the institutions of co-determination will prevent this. These restraints on corporate policy will counterbalance the increasing power of shareholder interests'.[70] Let us consider each of these restraints in turn.

Gray himself invokes the ever-increasing force of the 'global competition for equity' in his argument against social democrats.[71] This feature of the world market is incorporated in the catalytic-state model of globalisation. But this implies that there are essential structural tendencies in that model to dismantle a 'complex system of cross-holdings' like that found in Germany.

---

[68] '[I]f the magnitude of the Tobin tax is 0.5 per cent, then the expected future spot price must increase only by more than 1.1 per cent more than it would have had to increase in the absence of the tax to induce a bullish sentiment. In other words, even though the negative annual rate of return on a one-day round trip is 365 per cent when there is a 0.5 per cent Tobin tax, any increase in the spot price of more than an additional 1.1 per cent compared to the no tax situation can still spawn significant speculative flows. Consequently, the imposition of a Tobin Tax *per se* will not significantly stifle even very short-run speculation if there is any whiff of a weak currency in the market. . . . All that is required to set off speculative flows is an expected change in the exchange rate that is $(1+x)/(1-x)$ greater than what would set off speculation regarding the exchange rate in the absence of the Tobin tax. . . . Almost by definition during a speculative run on a currency, one expects significantly large changes in the exchange rate over a very short period of time. For example, the Mexican peso fell by approximately 60 per cent in the winter of 1994–95'. Davidson 2002, p. 207.
[69] Gray 1998, p. 96.
[70] Gray 1998, p. 97.
[71] Gray 1998, p. 34.

An ever-greater percentage of equity in German corporations is in fact held today by foreign investors rather than German banks. This move away from a system in which flows of equity capital are 'intermediated' by banks is not a contingent or easily reversible feature of economic globalisation. As the scale of capital accumulation increases over time, there is a general tendency towards 'disintermediation', that is, for direct relations between firms and investors, without banks mediating between them.

This extremely important dimension of the world market does not concern only equity markets. The same tendency can be seen in the credit market, where the sale of corporate bonds to international investors is also becoming increasingly important in comparison to bank lending (and where the bank loans that are made are almost immediately 'securitised', that is, repackaged in various ways and sold in global markets for capital assets). A general tendency towards disintermediation can be derived from a number of features of global capitalism:[72]

- As information technologies continue their advance, investors in distant regions are potentially able to acquire more and more relevant information regarding possible objects of investment directly for themselves, without the intermediation of banks.
- This potential tends to be actualised, due to the fact that the managers of leading firms have a number of incentives to provide information to capital markets.[73] Once they have grown past a certain size, at least, they generally prefer reliance on impersonal markets to the much more intrusive oversight that tends to develop when they are dependent on a specific bank.
- Also, the one-to-one interaction of relationship banking may not be as advantageous to the interests of the largest corporations as the many-to-one relations established when they tap global capital markets. The more investors there are competing to provide investment funds, the better the rate firms can hope to pay on their debt, everything else being equal.[74]

---

[72] See Guttmann 1994.

[73] Of course, firms also have an incentive to engage in systematic deception on a massive scale, as the recent dot.com bubble shows clearly enough (Mulford and Comiskey 2002). I expect that the investor class will prove sufficiently strong politically to establish regulations that allow at least minimal standards of accuracy to be generally met.

[74] In the global economy as a whole, borrowers in general have *not* enjoyed the

Further, in periods of rapid growth of asset values, corporations can acquire funds from selling equity to investors without having to pay either high dividends or interest payments in return.[75] This, too, tends to obviate the need to turn to banks.

- By bundling loans of different risk together, securitisation allows the overall risk from any given unit of investment to be lower. It also allows a dispersion of risk among numerous investors, as opposed to a concentration of risk in a few banks. Both tend to lower the capital costs of firms. Banks themselves favour developments that displace risks to others, while lower borrowing rates encourage firms to break from relationships they have had with investment banks.[76]

- In periods of rapid innovation banks have an even greater interest in being freed from long-term ties to corporations. Even the most successful firms regularly have difficulty adjusting to rapidly changing technological and economic environments.[77] If they decline, banks do not want to share their fate.[78]

- Finally, large-scale depositors can regularly expect better rates of return from international capital markets than from deposits in national savings systems.

In the light of all this, anyone believing that the 'system of cross-holdings in Germany' can serve as a basis for an alternative to neoliberalism in the twenty-first century has an extremely difficult case to make.

---

lower real interest rates that neoliberals promised would result from free capital flows (Eatwell 1996). This does not prevent the politically most influential borrowers from supporting and benefiting from disintermediation.

[75] Toporowski 2000.

[76] This does not rule out an increase in the level of risk in the financial system as a whole. In fact, there are good reasons to think that such risks worsen as disintermediation proceeds (*The Economist* 2003). See note 78.

[77] Christensen 1997.

[78] 'The most dramatic development, however, has been the rise of credit derivatives, especially credit-default swaps (insurance against the risk of default), which have been bought overwhelmingly by big banks. . . . The effect of all this has been to soften the effect of corporate defaults. . . . When companies defaulted on their bonds, or when bond prices were marked sharply downwards, it was all bondholders who suffered, meaning hedge funds, pension funds and insurers as well as banks. When companies defaulted on loans, the costs were spread through syndicates or passed on to the sellers of credit-default swaps, not dumped on the lending banks'. *The Economist* 2004b, p. 9. In this manner individual banks are able to retain profitable fees from loans, while displacing risks to others. Under such circumstances, a rise of credit risk in the economy as a whole is all but inevitable.

What of the German system of co-determination, in which labour unions are granted rights to board seats and consultation? Gray himself provides an illustration of how this system tends to work in the age of globalisation. In 1997, Osram communicated to IG Metall, the engineering union, that it was considering setting up a new production line in Italy, where labour costs are forty per cent lower. IG Metall kept the jobs in Germany by signing an agreement that increased management flexibility in assigning shifts lengthening the workweek. This example does indeed point to a specifically German form of capitalism. Most firms in the US would have simply implemented a unilateral management decision to move, or unilaterally imposed a longer workweek. But this should not blind us to the fact that the actual results are not all that different. The consultation process in Germany resulted in a significant worker concession that did not lessen job insecurity, even in the short-to-medium term. More threats to leave Germany followed, eliciting yet more concessions. It is accurate enough to insist that national variations of social relations persist in the age of globalisation, and that some institutionalise labour rights to consultation that are not part of the neoliberal model. This does not make it less doubtful whether 'policies that harness markets to the satisfaction of human needs' can be adequately implemented by the catalytic state in the face of effective threats of capital flight.[79]

Gray's discussion of the Japanese variant of capitalism raises similar difficulties, as his speculation on the likely evolution of the Japanese economy reveals. Globalisation is now forcing Japan to abandon the institutional forms within which its market was embedded in the decades following World War Two:

---

[79] It is worth noting in this context that German firms now have the third largest holdings of foreign direct investment stocks in the world. Held 2004, p. 43. '[S]izable German manufacturers have been moving production to Eastern Europe or Asia for years. ... [U]nion reps say the pressure is unrelenting. "It's a declared Siemens program," said Wolfgang Müller, a member of Siemens' supervisory board who represents employees. "They tell us: 'If you're not cheaper, we'll move overseas'." While insisting it doesn't plan massive exports of jobs Siemens has been warning workers at the local level they must make concessions to avoid layoffs ... even that won't guarantee their jobs for more than a few years. ... "Today it's Hungary, tomorrow it will be Lithuania and Estonia. We're not going to be able to keep up with every low-wage country," says Heinz Cholewa, a representative of the IG Metall union in Bocholt'. Ewing 2004, p. 51; see also Ganssmann 2004.

> Japan's social contract for job security may not survive in its present form.
> The guarantee of lifetime employment in one firm is no longer credible. . . . The
> question is whether Japan can preserve its *culture* of full employment while
> moving away from the post-war guarantee of lifetime job security with a
> single firm.[80]

For the sake of the argument, we may overlook the fact that lifetime job
security was offered to a relatively small fraction of Japan's labour force, and
that it is a bit difficult to imagine what a 'culture' of full employment might
mean in the absence of the material practice of full employment.[81] This leaves
the problem that the Japanese variant of capitalism was premised on high
growth rates, rates that cannot be (and have not been) sustained indefinitely.
Gray responds to this state of affairs with the following question:

> Can Japan achieve something akin to the 'stationary-state economy' advocated
> by John Stuart Mill, in which technological progress is used to enhance the
> quality of life rather than merely to expand the quantity of production?
> Elsewhere in the world the vision of a no-growth economy has proved a
> chimera. Perhaps in Japan's uniquely mature industrial society the collapse
> of economic growth could be an opportunity to reconsider the desirability
> of restarting it. But that would involve defying the central imperative of the
> Washington consensus, which dictates that social betterment is impossible
> without unending economic growth.[82]

But the growth imperative is hardly the imposition of neoliberals in Washington!
As noted in Chapter 1, this imperative is built-into the ways capitalist markets
work. Units of capital that do not grow have fewer resources to invest in the
battle for market share; they necessarily tend to disappear or be taken over
by other units of capital. Within the rules of the capitalist game, there is
simply no escaping the 'grow or die' imperative.

Gray is caught in a trap. He insists that the German and Japanese variants
of capitalism can provide social cohesion and job security in a way consistent
with their respective traditions and cultural values.[83] But, in his critique of

---

[80] Gray 1998, p. 174.
[81] These themes are discussed extensively in Smith 2000a.
[82] Gray 1998, p. 175.
[83] Gray 1998, p. 230.

the social state, he acknowledges that the global economy necessarily tends to erode essential features of these variants. And his proposals for modifying the global order stop well short of anything capable of reversing this erosion.

We arrive again at the fundamental dilemma. Gray and other adherents of the catalytic-state model of globalisation could take the pressures of global markets as given, and simply accept the social disruptions and pathologies that follow as a price that must be paid. They could still emphasise that the response to these disruptions and pathologies will take different forms in different national settings, and that most states should be able to compensate for harms inflicted by global markets to a certain extent. But they would then have to give up the idea that states are capable of formulating and implementing effective 'policies which harness markets to the satisfaction of human needs'. Or they could continue to insist on the necessity of precisely such policies, and demand a more profound transformation of the neoliberal order than anything yet considered. Neither option can be accepted without abandoning essential tenets of their position. The former option pushes them towards the neoliberal camp. The latter pushes them towards a model of globalisation in which the state is displaced from the central place it enjoys in the catalytic-state model. Unwilling to embrace either alternative, defenders of the catalytic state are left in the incoherent position of accepting certain features of the neoliberal global order more or less intact, while denying their inevitable consequences, despite the fact that they themselves emphasise these very consequences in their critique of the social state.

This immanent contradiction in the third model of globalisation becomes even more apparent when we shift our attention from countries like Germany and Japan, two quite privileged regions of the global economy, to poorer regions. For defenders of the catalytic state, the historically unprecedented rates of economic growth and increases in per capita income attained in a number of East-Asian countries in recent decades are profoundly important developments. The 'East-Asian miracle', based on the ability of industries in this region to compete successfully in global export markets, justifies the claim that, in principle, all poor countries can enjoy success in the world market, if only states follow intelligent policies. The successes of the developmental state, a species of the catalytic state, do not rebound to the glory of neoliberals, perversely committed to dismantling all forms of 'strong states'. Advocates of the catalytic state believe that all would be well, and rapid economic development could recommence in East Asia and elsewhere, if only neoliberal policy élites in Wall Street, the US Treasury Department, and the IMF could be politically neutralised.

Joseph Stiglitz realises that, without a more profound break from the neoliberal framework than the imposition of a Tobin tax, the prospects for the developmental state are entirely bleak. He calls for standstills on debt repayment when financial crises occur, special bankruptcy provisions that kick in when exceptional macro-economic disturbances break out, greater reluctance by the IMF to lend, more seats at the IMF to be given to poor countries, debt relief, and similar reforms of the so-called 'international financial architecture'. The goal of these reforms is to enable developing states to follow a proper sequence of policies. In the absence of adequate laws enforcing competition, privatisation will result in oligopolies and monopolies that harm the interests of consumers. Therefore, privatisation should only occur after effective antitrust laws have been put into place. The unemployment that inevitably follows the dismantling of protectionist trade barriers will generate immense social suffering if adequate safety nets and job creation programmes have not been established. And, so, openness to trade should only be instituted after an apparatus addressing the social costs of free trade has been established. While wealthy economies can handle stampedes of capital inflows and outflows, these stampedes will wreak havoc on smaller developing economies. Thus, states must develop the capacity to impose short-term capital controls, and these controls should only be dismantled after a national economy has attained a critical mass. Effective state regulation of the financial sector, including, for example, restrictions on speculative real estate lending by banks, must also be instituted.

There is no question that these measures would improve the prospects of states and economic agents in less developed regions of the global economy. But standstills on debt repayments, special bankruptcy provisions, more IMF seats for poor countries, debt relief, and similar reforms would not lessen the pressures of competitive deregulation, the pressures to lower corporate taxes, the drive by corporations to make use of educated, low-wage workforces, the 'chronic allergy' of the global bond market to job creation through public borrowing and 'excessively' expansionary counter-cyclical policies, or the irrelevance of long-term advantages in a global economy when short-term competitive pressures are unrelenting. Even if we imagine that all of Stiglitz's proposed reforms are implemented, states in poor regions would still not have the breathing room to attain the level of efficiency and normative attractiveness that advocates of the catalytic-state model of globalisation seek.

Two other problems with this version of the catalytic state need to be mentioned as well. The first concerns its extent to which it can be duplicated, the second the extent to which it is stable over time.

It is certainly true that, at some points in time, some developing countries have enjoyed success in some export markets. It does not follow, however, that all developing countries can in principle do so at any time, as Stiglitz and others presuppose. There is an immanent contradiction between this claim, an essential element of the catalytic-state position, and an equally essential determination of the catalytic-state model of globalisation, the recognition of the importance of technological dynamism in the global order. The latter necessarily generates a tendency to the systematic reproduction of *uneven development* in the global economy, contradicting the assumption that the policies of the development state can in principle bring about a global convergence of development.

The heart of inter-capital competition is the drive to appropriate surplus profits through temporary monopolies from product or process innovations.[84] The research and development process is obviously a crucial element in process and product innovations. Units of capital with access to advanced (publicly or privately funded) R&D are best positioned to win this form of surplus profits. Even more importantly, they are also best positioned to establish a virtuous circle in which surplus profits enable a high level of R&D funding in the future, which provides the most important precondition for the appropriation of future surplus profits.[85] In contrast, units of capital without initial access to advanced R&D tend to be trapped in a vicious circle. Their inability to introduce significant innovations prevents an appropriation of surplus profits, which tends to limit their ability to participate in advanced R&D in the succeeding period. This, in turn, limits future innovations and future profit opportunities.

This fundamental dynamic of capitalist property relations has profound implications for our comprehension of the world market. Units of capital

---

[84] See Schumpeter 1934; Mandel 1975, Chapter 3; Storper and Walker 1989; and Smith 1997a, 2002, 2004.
[85] Etro 2004.

with the greatest access to advanced R&D almost by definition tend to be clustered in wealthy regions of the global economy. Units without such access tend to be clustered in poorer regions.[86] The former are in a far better position to establish and maintain the virtuous circle described above, while the latter have immense difficulty avoiding the vicious circle. When units of capital in poorer regions engage in economic transactions with units of capital enjoying temporary monopolies due to innovations, the former necessarily tend to suffer disadvantageous terms of trade. When a handful of giant First-World oligopolies operating at or near the frontier of scientific-technical knowledge sells inputs to, and purchases the outputs of, small-scale Third-World producers far from that frontier, the prices these producers must pay for their inputs tend to rise, while the prices they receive for outputs tend to stagnate or decline over time. In this manner, the oligopolies tend to appropriate a disproportionate share of the value produced in the production and distribution chain. As a direct result, the pressure on work conditions, wage levels, and worker communities in poorer regions remains unrelenting, a pressure quickly transferred to working men and women and their communities in the so-called North. In this manner, the drive to appropriate surplus profits through technological innovation – an essential feature of capitalist property relations and production – systematically tends to reproduce both uneven development in the world market over time and generalised economic insecurity. Yes, in some historical contexts, a handful of developmental states have been able to put this tendency out of play to a certain extent for a certain period. This hardly establishes the irrelevance of the tendency to uneven development in the world market as a whole.[87]

---

[86] At present, 95% of research and development is located in the so-called 'First World', and 97% of all patents today are granted to entities based in the First World. Friedman 2000, p. 319. The push to extend the definition and enforcement of intellectual property rights – an absolutely central element of US foreign policy under both Democratic and Republican administrations – obviously reinforces the dialectical unity of virtuous and vicious circles in the global economy.

[87] The great number of contingencies associated with the East-Asian 'miracle' also call into question the extent to which it provides empirical support for the catalytic state model of globalisation. The success of East-Asian economies has been at least partially premised on increasing exports to the United States. These exports have been absorbed thanks to a historically unprecedented rate of credit expansion. The limits of this credit expansion reveal the limits of the ability of US markets to absorb exports from East Asia at continually increasing rates. Further, many of the most striking successes of the developmental state rested on contingent geopolitical considerations

In those regions in which the development-state model is successful, there are good reasons to believe that it is not stable over time. The main problem stems from the transition away from bank-centred financial systems discussed above, which necessarily tends to occur in both developed states and states in the so-called developing world. This transition is supported by leading sections of both industrial and financial capital in almost all regions of the world market, quite apart from the machinations of US and IMF policymakers. Wealthy depositors throughout the global economy now seek better rates of return from international capital markets than they can attain from deposits in national savings systems. The biggest corporations prefer reliance on impersonal markets – and the hope of lower rates – to the much more intrusive oversight that arises when they are dependent on local banks for credit. The biggest banks in the global economy wish to be freed from long-term ties to corporations, in order to avoid being brought down when those corporations have difficulty adjusting to rapidly changing technological and economic environments. The tendency for the number and scope of cross-border production chains and cross-border mergers and acquisitions to increase also tends to make the developmental-state model less feasible in the global economy.[88]

This line of reasoning can be summarised in the thesis that the system of property relations incorporated in the developmental-state model of globalisation necessarily tends to undermine its ability to reproduce itself indefinitely over time in a normatively acceptable manner. The greater its successes, more its banks and industrial firms expand. The more its banks and industrial firms expand, the stronger the pressures for disintermediation, that is, the dismantling of the 'relationship banking' lying at the heart of the developmental state (as well as the catalytic state in general). When a model

---

that do not generally hold. The Cold War motivated the US government to accept high levels of exports from East-Asian countries despite the fact that they greatly restricted both imports from US manufacturers and portfolio capital investments from the US. With the end of the Cold War, this arrangement ceased being acceptable to US political and economic élites. See Gowan 1999. For a comprehensive critical assessment of the so-called East Asian miracle, see Burkett and Hart-Landsberg 2000, 2001. I shall return to the issue of uneven development in Section 4 of the following chapter, and in Chapter 7 below.

[88] 'Between 1993 and 1995 the foreign assets of the fifty largest MNCs based in developing countries increased by some 280 per cent'. Held 2004, p. 44.

of globalisation necessarily tends to undermine its own institutional pre-conditions, it suffers from an immanent contradiction. In the methodological framework of systematic dialectics, an immanent contradiction of this magnitude justifies a determinate negation, that is, a transition to a new position in the systematic ordering of positions in the globalisation debate.

5. Conclusion

In the view of supporters of the catalytic-state model of globalisation, the proper response to the fundamental flaws of neoliberalism is a return to the primacy of the state. They assert that only an activist state pursuing industrial and social policies with an aggressiveness and comprehensiveness beyond any form of neoliberal state can correct market failures and ensure social stability. Proponents of the catalytic-state model also call for managed trade and regulation of the financial sector in order to prevent stampedes of speculative capital inflows and outflows operating like wrecking balls on political communities. And they call for reforms of the régime of global governance in order prevent international institutions such as the IMF from exacerbating the suffering of communities when financial difficulties do arise.

These are not insignificant matters. But neither are they sufficient to reverse many of the essential determinations of the neoliberal model of globalisation. They do not reverse the dominant tendency for corporations and wealthy investors to have increased exit options as capitalist development proceeds. They do not reverse the tendency for units of capital to be able to play one sector of the global work force off against another through plausible threats of capital flight. These reforms do not remove the continuous plebiscites on governmental policies conducted by global capital markets that Walter Wriston spoke of. They do not reverse the tendency to uneven development. Nor do they prevent the erosion of relationship banking, which profoundly restricts the capacities of the catalytic state in general, and the developmental-state variant in particular.

The central conclusion of this chapter follows at once: the catalytic state necessarily tends to take the form of a 'competitive state', rather than a communitarian state.[89] Already-advantaged catalytic states will be able to

---

[89] Jessop 1997, p. 576.

help units of capital operating in their regions to prosper, thereby reproducing their advantages. If a series of contingent conditions are met, catalytic states in previously disadvantageous regions will be able to help domestic units of capital prosper as well. But a model of globalisation with catalytic states at its centre will not tend towards a global order in which the material preconditions for human flourishing are established in all communities. And the exit options and plebiscites referred to above ensure that the social protections instituted by all variants of the catalytic state will necessarily tend to be far more partial and precarious than is compatible with the communitarian values of its leading defenders. The more effectively the catalytic state attains one of its objectives, the technological competitiveness of units of capital operating within its territories, the more it fails to attain a second objective, a global order in which the vast majority of humanity are not condemned to radical economic insecurity. The essential determinations of the catalytic-state model of globalisation, in brief, do not cohere with the most significant claims of its leading proponents.

The contingencies of empirical history do not rule out a repeating loop in which the immanent contradictions of neoliberalism lead to the rise of catalytic states, whose structural shortcomings, in turn, provoke a return to neoliberalism, only to have the first set of contradictions arise once again. A systematic-dialectical progression, however, is linear in a way that empirical history can never be; the need to avoid a 'bad infinity' is a fundamental methodological precept. If a given position is beset by immanent contradictions, if it is defined by an institutional framework incapable of reproducing itself in a stable and normatively attractive manner (as measured by its advocates), there are only two possibilities. The systematic ordering must either be abandoned, or it must go forward. Going backward is not an option.

In the case at hand, the dialectical progression can go forward if, and only if, there is a position explicitly taking into account the immanent contradictions afflicting the catalytic-state model of globalisation. Some of the features such a new model of globalisation would have to possess are clear. If it is impossible to address adequately the social disruptions and pathologies inflicted by global markets primarily on the level of the state, then a transition must be made to a framework in which these issues are rigorously addressed on a global level. If it is impossible to address global inequality and material deprivation adequately through the developmental state, this too justifies a transition to a framework beyond the state. A new sort of 'régime of global governance' is required, capable of subjecting flows of global capital to far more effective social controls than those recommended by proponents of the catalytic state. We require a new form of cosmopolitanism.

Chapter Four
The Democratic-Cosmopolitan Model of Globalisation

A pattern has emerged in the course of the systematic dialectic thus far. We began with the social-state model of globalisation, centring on states with the responsibility to ensure economic efficiency and social justice. The cross-border flows of trade and investment that necessarily tend to occur within this framework undermine this state form. The neoliberal model of globalisation explicitly acknowledges the external constraints on states imposed by the world market. All would be well if global markets automatically tended towards economic efficiency and social justice in the absence of distorting government interference. Unfortunately, however, the essential determinations of the neoliberal framework necessarily tend to constrain growth, generate financial crises, hamper technological innovation, and inflict massive social disruptions and pathologies on communities, all of which are in fundamental tension with the core claims of its proponents. When this implicit immanent contradiction is made explicit, the systematic progression is pushed forward to a third position, according to which catalytic states must protect communities from the ravages of global markets while simultaneously providing the background conditions for economic dynamism.

The pattern in this progression is clear enough. A model of globalisation revolving around states gives way to one centring on determinations emerging on the cosmopolitan level; the limits of the latter then force a return to a model in which the state once again has primary responsibility for institutionalising economic efficiency and social justice. Given the structural limitations of the catalytic state explored at the end of the previous chapter, we can expect the next stage in the systematic ordering to be a return to a model of globalisation centring on determinations arising on the global level, above the state. Since neoliberalism must be left behind if an endlessly repeating loop (a 'bad infinity') is to be avoided, a quite different sort of cosmopolitanism is called for. Instead of a régime of global governance designed to enable the world market to function 'naturally', that is, without distorting political interventions, a régime of global governance is required that subjects the world market to effective social regulation. What is required, in brief, is a democratic form of cosmopolitanism.

A number of important contemporary social theorists defend this fourth position in the globalisation debate. A partial list of members of what this 'global justice school' includes Jürgen Habermas, Charles Beitz, Thomas Pogge, Brian Barry, Alan Buchanan, and Martha Nussbaum.[1] I believe that the most comprehensive and powerful defence of this perspective is found in David Held's work, especially *Democracy and the Global Order*. The present chapter is devoted to a critical examination of the transformations in the global economy called for by Held and other defenders of 'cosmopolitan democratic law'.

The normative foundation of Held's cosmopolitanism lies in the principle of autonomy:

> [P]ersons should enjoy equal rights and, accordingly, equal obligations in
> the specification of the political framework which generates and limits the
> opportunities available to them; that is, they should be free and equal in
> the determination of the conditions of their own lives, so long as they do
> not deploy this framework to negate the rights of others.[2]

---

[1] Helpful surveys of the global justice school are found in Jones 1999 and Pogge 2001. Habermas, Beitz 1979, Pogge 1989 and 2002, Barry 1998, Buchanan 2004, and Nussbaum 2001 are representative works. Another major contribution to this position, Davidson 2004, will be discussed in detail in Chapter 7 below.

[2] Held 1995, p. 147. See also Held 2004, p. 56.

Held notes seven dimensions of human life in which autonomy may be exercised and developed (or stifled by the exercise of power): *the body* ('the way in which physical and emotional well-being is organized through distinctive networks and institutional milieux, informal and formal, across intersecting social spaces from the local to the international'), *welfare* ('the organization of the domain of goods and services that aids the transition of the citizen from the private person to full membership of the community'), *cultural life* ('those realms of social activity where matters of public interest and identity can be discussed, where differences of opinion can be explored and where local custom and dogma can be examined'), *civic associations* ('areas of social life – the domestic world, social activities, economic interchange and political interaction – which are organized by private or voluntary arrangements between individuals and groups outside of the direct control of the state'), *the economy* ('the collective organization of the production, distribution, exchange and consumption of goods and services'), *the organisation of violence and coercive relations* (the 'concentrated physical force [that] can function of behalf of a community, acting for its preservation or defence, or against it, eroding security and undermining pre-established regulatory mechanisms'), and, finally, *the state as independent corporation*, in other words, 'the sphere of regulatory and legal institutions . . . made up of an ensemble of organizations coordinated by a determinate political authority'.[3] Held then deduces the seven clusters of rights that must be in place if autonomy is to flourish in these seven realms: health rights, welfare rights, cultural rights, civic rights, economic rights, pacific rights, and political rights.[4] This set of rights incorporates the social-democratic values invoked by defenders of the social state, the importance of 'the rule of law' emphasised by neoliberals, and the communitarian values underlying the catalytic state. Cosmopolitan democracy can be seen as an attempt to institutionalise these normative principles on the assumption that they cannot be adequately institutionalised on the national level alone.

In a different theoretical and practical context, it would be important to contrast Held's principle of autonomy and the seven clusters of rights with alternative abstract normative principles. However, the methodological

---

[3] Held 1995, pp. 176–85.
[4] Held 1995, pp. 191 ff.

framework of systematic dialectics allows us to place disputes about abstract ethical precepts to the side. The normative principles of cosmopolitan democrats are, accordingly, taken as given here, just as those of social democracy, neoliberalism, and communitarianism were in previous chapters. Three other questions will occupy us instead. What institutional framework best embodies the principle of autonomy and the seven clusters of rights derived from it? Does this framework explicitly address the immanent contradictions of the model of globalisation that preceded it in the systematic ordering? And, finally, does democratic cosmopolitanism fall into immanent contradictions of its own?

1. The democratic-cosmopolitan model of globalisation

Held's list of the sites of power does not directly correspond to the regions of social life discussed in previous chapters (family, civil society, state, world market, interstate system, régime of global governance). Nonetheless, it is possible to present the institutional framework of cosmopolitan democracy in a parallel fashion to earlier discussions without affecting any substantive issues.

Held, following feminist theorists, emphasises how the ability to exercise autonomy in other realms of social life crucially depends on the organisation of the domestic realm. Regarding the right to control over fertility, for instance, he writes,

> [C]ontrol over fertility, creating the possibility of freedom of choice with respect to biological reproduction, parenthood and child-rearing, is a further important determinant of the nature and range of participative possibilities faced by citizens and, particularly, female citizens. Its common absence . . . can be linked directly to inequalities between men and women with respect to political participation.[5]

---

[5] Held 1995, p. 195. Gender inequality, of course, is hardly limited to political participation: 'Seventy per cent of the 1.2 billion people living on less than a dollar a day are women; the increase in the number of people in poverty in rural areas is 17 per cent higher for women than for men over a two-decade period; and twice as many women as men are among the world's 900 million illiterates'. Held 2004, p. 37.

Held notes that rights to childcare and education are 'critical conditions for the establishment of equal opportunities for women to enter non-domestic work and the broader framework of civic associations and political life'.[6] He also calls for rights to 'community (or social) services – those organizations and institutions which provide crisis management in the event of a severe disruption of household, family and social life'.[7]

These remarks echo themes expressed by supporters of the social state and the catalytic state. In particular, Held and other cosmopolitan democrats share Gray's concern that unregulated global markets impose an unacceptable level of costs on households. The main distinguishing features of the democratic-cosmopolitan model of globalisation do not lie here.

Nor are they found in the general categorisation of civil society and the national economy. Held does call for the 'enhancement of non-state, non-market solutions in the organization of civil society', advocating a 'pluralization of patterns of ownership and possession' that includes 'strict limits to private ownership of key "public-shaping" institutions: media, information, and so on'.[8] But proponents of the social-state and catalytic-state models of globalisation could consistently argue for these objectives as well. And, at the heart of Held's framework, we find the same acceptance of capitalist property relations encountered in all of the models of globalisation considered thus far:

> Capitalism, in the context of democratic constitutional societies, has strengths as well as weaknesses – *strengths that need to be recognized and defended as well as extended and developed.* Accordingly, if the implications of the arguments about the tensions between democracy and capitalism are to be pursued, it needs to be on terms which break from the simple and crude juxtaposition of capitalism with planning, or capitalism with systems of collective ownership and control, and in terms which are more cautious and experimental.[9]

In light of the italicised portion of this passage, Held's 'cautious and experimental' project would appear to be the reformation of capitalism in light of the normative imperatives of cosmopolitan democracy. This supposition

---

[6] Held 1995, p. 195.
[7] Held 1995, p. 195.
[8] Held 1995, p. 280.
[9] Held 1995, p. 249; italics added.

is confirmed elsewhere: 'The corporate capitalist system requires constraint and regulation to compensate for the biases generated by the pursuit of the "private good"'.[10] Providing 'compensation' is, obviously, far different from rejecting the corporate capitalist system.

This compensation is required for all the familiar reasons. Market failures tend to arise in capitalism with respect to the provision of public goods and avoidance of public bads. There is a general tendency in capitalist markets for systematic underinvestment when positive externalities arise, and systematic overinvestment when negative externalities occur. Capitalist markets also necessarily tend to undermine substantive (as opposed to merely formal) autonomy. These themes are explored by social democrats, advocates of the catalytic state, and even by moderate neoliberals to a certain extent. The distinguishing features of the cosmopolitan-democratic position do not lie in recognition of these issues. They are found, instead, in the account of the 'constraint and regulation [required] to compensate for the biases generated by the pursuit of the "private good"'.

Defenders of the social state regard national economies as more or less independent entities, while in the neoliberal and catalytic-state models of globalisation, they are conceptualised as moments within the world market as a whole. But, for adherents of all three viewpoints, the state alone is in a position to compensate for the limits of markets, for only the state exercises sovereign power within its borders. For Held, in contrast,

> [S]overeignty can be stripped away from the idea of fixed borders and
> territories and thought of as, in principle, malleable time-space clusters.
> *Sovereignty is an attribute of the basic democratic law, but it could be entrenched*
> *and drawn upon in diverse self-regulating associations, from states to cities and*
> *corporations.*[11]

Problems ought to be addressed on the level in which they primarily arise. States must deal with collective problems that 'stretch to, but no further than, their frontiers. But issues that primarily affect people at local, workplace or city levels ought to be addressed at those levels'.[12] And, so, difficulties arising

---

[10] Held 1995, p. 251.
[11] Held 1995, p. 234; see Held 2004, Chapter 5.
[12] Held 1995, p. 235.

on the global level ought to be addressed at *that* level. If national markets are not self-contained separate entities, but components of regional and world markets, the effective social regulation of markets requires governance on regional and global levels. Given the manner in which decisions by agents operating outside national borders can profoundly affect the lives of those within them, democratisation requires far more than the democratisation of the national state and local forms of government. A democratic political régime on the global level is required if those exercising decision-making power are to be accountable to those over whom that power is exercised:

> [D]emocratic law can prevail only if it is established both within the power domains of particular political communities and within those which cut across them. Sites of power can be national, transnational and international. Accordingly, democratic public law within a political community requires democratic law in the international sphere.[13]

If national economies are ultimately intertwined as moments of a single world market, market failures can, ultimately, only be adequately addressed on the level of the régime of global governance. This thesis is implicit in the immanent contradictions besetting the catalytic-state model of globalisation. Insofar as the democratic-cosmopolitan model explicitly addresses these contradictions and explicitly affirms this thesis, Held's position 'sublates' the catalytic-state position. The democratic-cosmopolitan model simultaneously incorporates and transcends the catalytic state.

Held advocates a global 'Charter of Rights and Obligations' affirming the general right to autonomy and the seven clusters of rights derived from it. A system of international courts is required to which appeal can be made when particular agents – including state officials – fail to adhere to these precepts of cosmopolitan-democratic law.[14] He also calls for regional parliaments on the continental level, general referenda cutting across national borders, elected supervisory boards for international organisations, and an 'authoritarian assembly of all democratic states and agencies'. Finally, Held does not shirk from demanding a permanent independent military force under the control of this global assembly. It is needed both to enforce laws on the regional and

---

[13] Held 1995, pp. 226–7.
[14] Held 1995, p. 272; see Held 2004, pp. 110 ff.

global levels and to provide a 'general check on the right of states to go to war'.[15]

Most debates regarding the institutional implications of cosmopolitanism have concerned the feasibility and normative attractiveness (or lack thereof) of these proposed political institutions.[16] In present context, however, I shall focus on Held's proposals to reform the global economy. The relationship between global markets and states has been the main source of the immanent contradictions that have pushed the systematic dialectic of globalisation forward up until the present point. And, as Held himself unequivocally recognises,

> if the rule of law does not involve a central concern with distributional questions and matters of social justice, it cannot be satisfactorily entrenched, and the principle of democratic accountability cannot be realized adequately.[17]

Held insists that the global Charter of Rights and Obligations must guarantee two fundamental economic rights and two forms of economic policy. Each of the four proposals is designed to provide a necessary condition for substantive (as opposed to merely formal) autonomy throughout the global economy. They are:

(i) the right to a basic income;

(ii) the right to ' "access avenues to the decision-making apparatus of productive and financial property; that is, to the creation of participative opportunities in firms and in other types of economic organization" ';[18]

(iii) increased social control of global investment through 'management of interest rates to induce capital to invest in certain areas' and through the pooling and allocation of democratically-controlled social investment funds;[19] and

(iv) controls on short-term capital flows.

These proposals form the core of 'a new "Bretton Woods" agreement – an agreement which would tie investment, production and trade to the conditions

---

[15] Held 1995, pp. 272–6.
[16] See, for example, the texts collected in Archibugi, Held and Koehler 1998.
[17] Held 1995, p. 248.
[18] Held 1995, p. 253.
[19] Held 1995, p. 259.

and processes of democracy'. Corporations and states would then be subject to democratic audits measuring their compliance with cosmopolitan law. If an audit reveals that they have disregarded the precepts of the global social charter, sanctions would follow:

> Restrictions could be imposed on the provision of capital for investment; for instance, the release of funds – whether public or private – to companies or governments could be linked directly to the latter respecting and satisfying the conditions of democratic autonomy.[20]

These bans would be 'enforced by agencies which would monitor not just the rules of sound finance and market transaction, but also the rules which specified the possibility of mutual respect for autonomy and self-determination'.[21]

The goal of cosmopolitan law is to ensure that the material preconditions for effective exercises of autonomy are provided throughout the global economy. It is important to recall once again that these proposals do not call for a break from global capitalist markets, merely the effective social regulation of these markets. Consider Held's comment regarding rights to participation in workplace decision-making:

> Such opportunities do not translate straightforwardly into a right to social or collective ownership. For what is centrally at issue is an opportunity for involvement in the determination of the regulative rules of work organizations, the broad allocation of resources within them, and the relations of economic enterprises to other sites of power. . . . At stake is a balance between the requirements of participation in management and those of economic effectiveness, that is, a balance between the discipline of democracy and the discipline of the market. *The question of the particular forms of property right is not itself the primary consideration.*[22]

There are, of course, no past or present empirical examples of a fully institutionalised democratic-cosmopolitan model. But the tasks of social theory are not exhausted by empirical analysis of existing social formations. There

---

[20] Held 1995, p. 255.
[21] Held 1995, p. 256.
[22] Held 1995, pp. 253–4 (italics added).

is also a place in social theory for inquiry into what is 'actual', in Hegel's sense of the term, that is, into a general institutional framework that is a) normatively attractive and feasible in principle, in other words, capable of reproducing itself more or less stably over time if it were fully established; and b) rooted in what Rawls referred to as 'the deep tendencies and inclinations of the social world'.[23] The latter condition requires that there are social agents with the capacity and interests to further these 'deep tendencies and inclinations'.

The social-state model of globalisation, the neoliberal model of globalisation, and the catalytic-state model of globalisation fall on the same level of abstraction as the democratic-cosmopolitan model. While empirical illustrations of this or that feature of each model are readily available, there has never been a period in which any of these models exclusively claimed the world stage for itself in anything like its pure form. There may be fewer empirical illustrations of features of the democratic-cosmopolitan model. But this could be merely a difference of degree, not of kind; the 'actuality' of a model cannot be determined by counting up the number of times some feature or other has been illustrated. If a compelling case could be made that the model captures the deepest structural tendencies of the contemporary global order, while adequately resolving the immanent contradictions of the previous positions in the globalisation debate, then the 'actuality' of that framework could be affirmed plausibly, however many concrete contingencies fail to conform to it.

Defenders of the catalytic state are correct to insist that national differences of culture and political traditions can be expected to persist. But there is every reason to believe that forms of transnational identities will become increasingly salient, even as more localised identities remain in place:

> The contemporary phase of globalization is transforming the foundations of world order, leading away from a world based exclusively on state politics to a new and more complex form of global politics and multilayered governance. At the beginning of the twenty-first century there are good reasons for believing that the traditional international order of states cannot be restored and that the deep drivers of globalization are unlikely to be

[23] Rawls 1999, p. 128.

halted. Accordingly, a fundamental change in political orientation is unavoidable.[24]

The case for the 'actuality', of the cosmopolitan model of globalisation rests on the emergence of a 'global civil society' consisting to agents with both the motivation and the capacity to institute democratic-cosmopolitan law:

> A coalition of political groupings could develop to push the agenda of global social democracy further. It could comprise European countries with strong liberal and social democratic traditions; liberal groups in the US which support multilateralism and the rule of law in international affairs; developing counties struggling for freer and fairer trade rules in the world economic system; non-governmental organizations, from Amnesty International to Oxfam, campaigning for a more just, democratic and equitable world order; transitional social movements contesting the nature and form of contemporary globalization; and those economic forces that desire a more stable and managed global economy.[25]

Given the contingencies of social existence, there are no guarantees that this emerging global civil society will be allowed to mature. But, Held would undoubtedly aver, the most fundamental structural tendencies in the global order point towards its medium-to-long-term growth, whatever short-term reverses it may experience. '[A]ccordingly, it can be argued, a political basis exists upon which to build a more systematic democratic future'.[26] For the sake of the argument – and because it is required for an immanent critique – I shall grant this assumption.

Would the model of globalisation proposed by cosmopolitan democrats adequately institutionalise the normative principles they accept in a reasonably stable fashion? The main thesis of this chapter is that 'the question of the

---

[24] Held 2004, p. 162. See also Sassen 1998; Jameson 2000; Held 2004, pp. 56–7.

[25] Held 2004, p. 166. For a general assessment of 'new social movement' theories of this sort, see Wood 1986. A critical assessment of the concept of 'global civil society' is found in Colas 2001, Chapter 5. Colas argues that international civil society long predates contemporary globalisation, that many agents of international civil society are neither accountable nor democratic, and that democratic politics today remains essentially connected to the sovereign state. Held, I think, would grant all three points. But he fails to acknowledge fully the difficulties they raise for his account of the agency underlying the future institutionalisation of cosmopolitan-democratic law.

[26] Held 1995, p. 237.

particular forms of property right' cannot be dismissed quite as quickly as Held and other cosmopolitan theorists proclaim. Capitalist property and production relations are ultimately incompatible with the democratic values Held seeks to advance, as an examination of each of the four main proposals introduced above will establish. The cosmopolitan model of globalisation, no less than the social-state, neoliberal, and catalytic-state models, suffers from immanent contradictions pushing the systematic dialectic of globalisation further.

2. The basic income proposal

Those who enjoy basic income guarantees have a greater ability to make choices in consumer markets than they would otherwise enjoy. The ability to make such choices counts as a form of economic autonomy, one that sets capitalism apart from earlier social systems.[27] Instituting a basic income guarantee would thus count as an extension of autonomy in itself. If the basic income were set at a sufficiently high level, autonomy would also be furthered in that the economic coercion forcing workers to take low pay, low status, and dangerous jobs would be significantly lowered, if not abolished.[28]

Is the provision of a reasonably high basic income consistent with capitalist property relations? The fact that some social-democratic régimes have provided relatively generous basic income guarantees appears to offer conclusive empirical proof for an affirmative answer. This is not the place to examine the history and limits of social democracy in different national contexts, for Held's project is the reform of the global capitalist economy.[29] But this is a

---

[27] Surprisingly, perhaps, this point is emphasised by Karl Marx too (Marx 1973, p. 287). It is one reason why the model of socialism defended in Chapter 8 includes consumer markets.

[28] 'A commitment to a basic income is a commitment to the conditions for each employee's economic independence; that is, the conditions which are commensurate with an individual's need for material security and the independence of mind which follows from it. Without a resource base of this kind, people remain highly vulnerable, dependent on others and unable to exercise fully their capacity to pursue different courses of action'. Held 1995, pp. 252–3. Given the forcefulness of this assertion, one must wonder why all references to the basic income proposal have been expunged from Held 2004, which otherwise covers the same ground as *Democracy and the Global Order* in a more informal and popular fashion.

[29] The reader interested in the fate of social democracy on the national level should consult Therborn 1995.

place to worry about the fallacy of composition. From the fact that *some* regions with capitalist property relations have provided somewhat high levels of basic income in *certain* historical contexts, it does not follow that *all* regions with those property relations in place can do so in *all* contexts.

The most basic social relation in capitalism is the capital/wage-labour relation. If democratic-cosmopolitan law is to cohere with the capitalist world market, the provision of basic income must be compatible with the continued reproduction of this relation. This cannot occur unless those without access to capital continue to regard entering wage contracts as their best available option. In circumstances where wage levels and workplace satisfaction are low, this implies that social assistance must be quite limited if capitalist property relations are to be reproduced. Few would choose to sell their labour-power in such conditions if acceptable alternatives were available.[30] The limited level of basic income compatible with capitalist property relations in these circumstances is unlikely to provide the material conditions for effective exercises of autonomy, at least not to the extent required by the precepts of cosmopolitan-democratic theory.

A corollary of this point is worth stressing. The lower the wages and the worse the work conditions in a particular region of the global economy, the lower the basic income must be if the reproduction of the capital/wage-labour relation is not to be undermined. The basic income proposal considered by itself would reproduce, rather than transform, the profound disparities characterising the contemporary global order.

It would be very unfair to place too much weight on this first proposal in isolation. It is but one of a set of reforms intended to function together. Other aspects of democratic-cosmopolitan law seek to ensure that levels of wages and work satisfaction are relatively high throughout the global economy. If these objectives were attained, Held might reply, the level of basic income could be set relatively high without undermining the capital/wage-labour relation.

Criticisms of Held's other proposals will be developed below. For the moment, I shall simply assume for the sake of the argument that they are capable of instituting a global economy with low unemployment and high

---

[30] de Brunhoff 1978.

levels of real wages and work satisfaction. I shall also assume that, under these conditions, basic income guarantees could indeed be set at a level high enough to provide essential material conditions for the effective exercise of autonomy without undermining the attractiveness of wage contracts. If these (highly doubtful) points are granted, the question then becomes whether such a 'golden age' could persist indefinitely.

This question brings us to the complex and contentious question of crisis tendencies within capitalism. In previous chapters, I have referred to the tendency for financial crises to erupt frequently in the neoliberal model of globalisation, and the inability of the catalytic-state model to address this tendency adequately. Held's remarks on financial crises in the global economy will be considered below. What of crisis tendencies in non-financial sectors? If the root cause of general economic downswings were underconsumption, that is, an insufficiency of consumer demand, it would be plausible to assert that instituting a right to a basic income could help avoid them indefinitely. This would provide higher levels of income to precisely those economic agents with the greatest propensity to consume.[31] Matters look rather different, however, from the perspective of other, more convincing, theories of economic crisis.

Geert Reuten and Robert Brenner have argued persuasively that a systematic tendency to overaccumulation crises can be derived from the property relations defining capitalism.[32] Their account begins by noting that the drive to appropriate surplus profits necessarily tends to lead to more efficient plants and firms entering a given sector. Established firms and plants do not all automatically withdraw when this occurs. Their fixed capital costs are already sunk, and so those still able to receive at least the average rate of profit on their circulating capital may be happy to do so. These units of capital may have also established relations with suppliers and customers impossible (or prohibitively expensive) to duplicate elsewhere in any relevant time frame. Further, their management and labour force may have industry-specific skills. And governments may provide subsidies for training, infrastructure, or R&D that would not be available if they were to shift sectors. When a sufficient

---

[31] I believe that this assumption lies behind Rawls's discussion of the stabilisation and transfer branches of the social state.
[32] Reuten 1991; Brenner 1998; see also Smith 2000b.

number of firms and plants do not withdraw as a result of these sorts of factors, the result is an overaccumulation of capital, manifested in excess capacity and declining rates of profit. When this dynamic unfolds simultaneously in leading sectors, an economy-wide fall in profit rates for an extended historical period results.[33]

When overaccumulation crises break out, those who control capital mobilise their vast economic, political, and ideological weapons in the attempt to shift as many of the costs of the downturn as possible onto wage-labourers, through increased unemployment, lower wages, and worsened work conditions. Each unit of capital, each network of capitals, and governments of each region, will attempt to shift the costs of devaluing excess fixed capital onto other units, networks, and regions.

I have already argued against both Rawls and John Gray that the notion of 'steady-state capitalism' is an oxymoron. The 'grow or die' imperative is an inherent feature of the global capitalist order. While firms tend to be relatively small when new sectors arise, and new small firms may arise in established sectors, units of capital that survive necessarily tend to expand in scale. As this expansion proceeds in the course of capitalist development overaccumulation, difficulties necessarily tend to emerge on an ever-more massive scale, demanding ever-more massive devaluations. Global turbulence and generalised economic insecurity increasingly become the normal state of affairs.[34] It may not be logically impossible for a high level of basic income guarantees to be maintained across the global economy in such circumstances. But this will necessarily tend to not be the case.

---

[33] The theory of overaccumulation crisis is discussed further in Part Two.

[34] Brenner has provided considerable empirical evidence that the lower rates of growth that afflicted the world economy after the so-called 'golden age' ended in the late 1960s and early 1970s were due primarily to excess capacity in the leading sectors of the global economy (Brenner 1998, and 2002). See also Smith 2000a, Chapter 5. We should observe that the systematic tendencies to overaccumulation crises in global capitalist markets provide a further reason to reject the claim that the catalytic-state model of globalisation can attain the objectives sought by its adherents. When overaccumulation crises break out and previous investments in fixed capital must be devalued on a massive scale, the generalised economic insecurity and social disruptions that tend to accompany the world market in the best of circumstances are greatly exacerbated. As long as the systematic tendency to overaccumulation crises is in place, catalytic states will not be able to protect communities from social disruptions and pathologies, which undermine the communitarian values to which proponents of the catalytic state appeal. Parallel arguments can easily be constructed regarding the social-state and neoliberal models of globalisation.

To summarise, if we assume that the other facets of cosmopolitan law fulfil their objectives, a case could be made that a high level of basic income is initially compatible with the continued reproduction of the capital/wage-labour relation in the global economy. But this compatibility is unlikely to be maintained over time, given the structural tendency to overaccumulation crises. Held's first proposal thus does not appear to be generally compatible with capitalist property relations, even if an exceedingly favourable (and, as we shall see below, quite implausible) assumption is made for the sake of the argument.

One final comment is in order before turning to Held's other proposals. Setting a baseline of income below which people are not allowed to fall does not, in itself, remove economic inequality. Providing such a baseline is fully compatible with a significant *increase* in the relative inequality of the distribution of income and wealth. This is a profound problem for Held, since he explicitly grants that large economic disparities tend to be translated into disparities in social power great enough to constrict the effective exercise of autonomy by disadvantaged individuals and groups.[35]

3. Access avenues

The second feature of cosmopolitan-democratic law relevant to the global economy is the precept granting labourers, local communities, consumers, and investment fund holders access to the sites of industrial and financial decision-making. Held insists that this access must go beyond mere 'conversation or consultation'. Management must negotiate with representatives of these groups 'to create decision frameworks on matters as diverse as employment prospects, work methods, investment opportunities, and income and dividend levels'.[36] The German system of co-determination, a social-democratic reform reserving just under half of all board of director seats in large firms for representatives of labour, offers an example of this on the

---

[35] '[S]ome of the main threats to autonomy in the contemporary world can be related not to demands for equality or the ambitions of the majority to level social difference, as thinkers from Tocqueville to Hayek have feared, but to inequality, inequality of such magnitude as to create significant violations of political liberty and democratic politics'. Held 1995, p. 246.
[36] Held 1995, p. 253.

national level. Here, too, one can question whether Held's objectives are compatible with the property and production relations underlying the capitalist world market.[37]

A first point to note is that, even if 'access avenues' were somehow established and functioning smoothly, the external pressures imposed on units of capital by the imperative to increase profits would remain in force. When sufficient profits are not appropriated by a given unit of capital – whether due to product or process innovations successfully introduced by competitors, a general economic slowdown, or any other cause – the workers employed by that unit of capital necessarily tend to suffer unemployment, lower wages, job speed-ups, and so on. The communities in which they live also tend to suffer significant material losses. Under capitalist social relations, then, a tendency would arise for workers enjoying 'access avenues' to seek to deflect the social costs of innovation and crises onto other units of capital, other workforces, other communities. Implementing the proposal would thus appear to have the foreseeable consequence of strengthening the bonds between workers in particular enterprises and the managers and owners of those enterprises, at the cost of exacerbating divisions among the workforce as a whole. When these divisions are exacerbated, the balance of power between capital and labour shifts in favour of the former.[38] In this manner, rights to negotiation may improve the situation of particular sectors of the workforce at the cost of worsening the situation of the labour force as a whole.[39] It can surely be questioned whether this should count as furthering the institutionalisation of autonomy of the labour force as a whole, Held's major objective here.

Held might reply that a high degree of worker solidarity and organisation could put any tendency to exacerbate differences among workers out of play. The ease with which capitalist property relations allow 'divide and conquer' strategies to be implemented suggests that such a high level of solidarity and

---

[37] I shall examine 'access avenues' to investment decisions in the following section. The implications of the access avenues proposal for community groups, consumers, and so on, will not be discussed here, although many of the following arguments regarding wage-labourers could be extended to these other 'stakeholders'.

[38] Lebowitz 1992.

[39] This dynamic has been a feature of 'enterprise unionism' in post-World-War-Two Japan (Smith 2000a, Chapter Three). Held's global social charter would, in effect, extend enterprise unionism to the global economy.

organisation is extremely difficult to attain and maintain over time. Nonetheless, I grant that attaining this level of solidarity and organisation is not merely possible; it is the most important political project of the twenty-first century. But this merely shifts the problem. Once a sufficiently high level of solidarity and organisation has been attained, would not a unified global workforce begin at once to consider ways to remove capital's future ability to implement divide and conquer strategies? And would not this inevitably lead to capitalist property relations being called into question? A consideration of the so-called 'principal/agent problem' provides further reasons for thinking this would be the case.

In the business literature, the principal/agent problem is usually defined in terms of the relationship between investors and managers, with the former taken as the 'principals' and the latter as their 'agents'.[40] The problem arises from the fact that managers can be expected to pursue their own interests, which may not always coincide with those of investors. Recent accounting scandals in the United States have revealed just how wide this divergence can become.[41] When such conflicts arise, however, there are a series of mechanisms within capitalism that tend to re-align the interests of investors and managers closer together. Ultimate power to appoint, reward, and remove managers lies with investors and their representatives, and those who do not effectively operate as the agents of investors can be sued under due diligence legislation. Such mechanisms provide strong incentives for most managers to further their interests in a manner that is broadly congruent with the interests of investors over time.

Held's proposal to institute fora for negotiation between management and the workforce can be seen as an attempt to view the management/labour relation in terms of the principal/agent problem. These fora are meant to provide an institutional mechanism ensuring that managers will further their own interests in a manner generally consistent with the interests of wage-labourers. But what of cases where the perceived self-interest of investors and labourers are in essential conflict? Which group would management then consider itself the agent of? To answer this question we must ask a series of

---

[40] Stiglitz 1994.
[41] Mulford and Comiskey 2002.

others. Under Held's proposal, are the workforce or its representatives granted the power to appoint management? No. Are the workforce or its representatives granted the power to change management? No. Are the workforce or its representatives granted the power to fix the reward of management? No. Does Held's proposal grant workers legal rights to sue if managers do not exhibit due diligence in the pursuit of workers' interests? No. The system of capitalist property rights continues to grant these (and many other) social powers to private owners. Cosmopolitan law grants workers the much weaker right to 'negotiate'. Is it really plausible that in the controversial cases – that is, the cases that matter most – this will be sufficient to ensure a systematic tendency for management to act in a manner consistent with the interests of the workforce rather than private capital?[42]

The third and final point to consider in this context concerns the institutional settings in which the access avenue proposal would be implemented. Some forms of relationship between financial capital and industrial capital are, surely, far more compatible with providing opportunities for worker participation in decision-making than others. In the previous chapter, I argued that bank-centred systems appear to be most compatible with the catalytic-state model of globalisation. A (significantly modified) bank-centred system is the only financial order compatible with the 'stakeholder capitalism' of Held's model of globalisation.

To see why this is the case, we need to review quickly two main features of bank-centred systems: national savings are 'intermediated', that is, deposited in the banking system, and formal and informal negotiations between banks, state agencies, and industrial corporations determine the general direction of credit flows from these banks to non-financial sectors of the economy. No system of relationship banking in the history of capitalism has actually institutionalised anything remotely approaching the sort of democratic 'access avenues' called for by Held. But, insofar as the determination of the general

---

[42] What of the social investment funds to be considered below? The principal/agent problem discussed in the main text does not arise in this context, since these are not private funds. But social investment funds are meant to complement, not replace, private capital investment. As long as capitalist property relations remain dominant in the global economy, social investment funds will play a relatively secondary role, leaving the principal/agent problems discussed in the main text in place at the heart of the social order.

direction of financial flows is already a matter for negotiation among various social groups in relationship banking, an institutional space is established within which representation could in principle be extended to wage-labourers and other 'stakeholders' of corporations. And explicit government commitments enable banks to take a long-term perspective on their investments in non-financial corporations. They are, thus, somewhat capable, at least in principle, of resisting pressure to sacrifice the medium-to-long term interests of other stakeholders for the sake of short-term benefits to private shareholders.

Matters would be greatly complicated for supporters of democratic cosmopolitanism if there were a tendency in global capitalism towards 'disintermediation', that is, for relatively direct relations between firms and investors, without the extensive mediation of banks between them. Such a development would remove the most favourable institutional space for 'stakeholder capitalism'. I have already argued in the last chapter that a general tendency to disintermediation is, in fact, necessarily generated by capitalist property relations, and there is no need to repeat the case again.[43] If it is true that, as capitalism evolves, we can derive a systematic tendency for relationship banking to give way to impersonal capital markets, and if it is true that the 'stakeholder' ideal of capitalism requires the latter, then we have a reason to doubt whether Held's embrace of this ideal fits easily with his acceptance of capitalist property relations. At a certain stage of development, capitalist property relations tend to lead to financial systems that make the effective implementation of 'stakeholder' capitalism increasingly unlikely. Insofar as the cosmopolitan model of globalisation incorporates capitalist property relations, it is beset by a profound internal tension here.

This line of thought reinforces the conclusion of the above discussion of the principal/agent problem. As the tendency for 'disintermediation' in global capital markets unfolds, investors tend to acquire more and more 'exit options' relative to those possessed under relationship banking. If they choose to exercise these options, managers lose access to external sources of capital.

---

[43] See Guttmann 1994 and Gowan 1999, Chapter 2. Gowan rightly emphasises the extent to which disintermediation has been a strategic objective of the US government, pursued in order to maintain the hegemonic position of US financial capital in the world market. But there are strong tendencies towards disintermediation apart from this, as Gowan notes as well.

The threat of this occurring reinforces the systematic tendency for managers to act as the agents of private investors whenever the perceived self-interest of investors conflicts with that of other 'stakeholders'. Disintermediation thus provides a further reason to hold that forums for negotiation will not be sufficient to ensure that managers serve as effective agents of these other stakeholders. The property and production relations of capital rule out in principle negotiations meeting the standards of impartiality Held accepts, that is, negotiations resulting in decisions 'that would be defensible in relation to all parties if they had participated as equal partners in public debate'.[44]

Held's proposals for cosmopolitan law form a package. Might it be the case that increased social control of investments in the global capitalist economy would greatly alleviate the difficulties discussed thus far?

4. Social control of investment

Held and other defenders of cosmopolitan democracy agree with defenders of the catalytic state that the 'free' global markets of neoliberalism necessarily tend to generate economic disparities and disruptions incompatible with economic efficiency and social justice. If flows of investment funds in the global economy are left to capital markets, individuals and groups in many regions will inevitably lack the material conditions necessary for effective exercises of autonomy and the maintenance of healthy communities. The solutions proposed by proponents of the catalytic-state model of globalisation, however, are inadequate for reasons presented in the previous chapter. The problems of global poverty and inequality cannot be adequately addressed on the level of individual states, with relatively minor reforms of the neoliberal régime of global governance

The justification for ordering the democratic-cosmopolitan model of globalisation after the catalytic-state model in the systematic dialectic is the manner in which the essential determinations of the former explicitly address the shortcomings of the latter. Attaining the goals of the catalytic state requires a more thorough reform of the régime of global governance than its advocates propose. More specifically, Held calls for 'a new coordinating economic agency,

---

[44] Held 2004, p. 110.

working at both global and regional levels . . . capable of deliberation about the broad balance of public investment priorities, expenditure patterns and emergency economic situations'.[45] One of this agency's tasks would be to direct flows of investment funds to disadvantaged regions through the use of interest-rate differentials. It would also oversee the collection of social investment funds and their allocation to community banks in regions of the world with the most pressing social needs. These funds would be expanded by taxing corporate profits at an increasing rate as profits rise. Held also calls for greater democratic control of pension funds, suggesting that a percentage of the dividends paid out by enterprises should be set aside for allocation by their workforces. He clearly assumes that worker-controlled investment funds would tend to flow in the same general directions as those allocated by the 'new coordinating economic agency'.

Before commenting on these proposals separately, I would first like to present what I take to be a general problem. They are all designed to complement, not replace, flows of private capital. Held explicitly states that his goal is to 'work wherever possible, "with the grain of private property rather than against it"'.[46] This implies that if global flows of private investment capital result in a certain pattern of development, there is no reason to assume *a priori* that Held's proposals would reverse it, working 'with the grain of private property' as they do. In the previous chapter, I argued that one of the essential determinations of the world market is an inherent tendency to uneven development, in which units of capital from regions at the 'centre' of the global system (the 'North') systematically reproduce and expand their

---

[45] Held 1995, pp. 259–60. Other 'global-Keynesian' proposals are formulated in Guttmann 1994, Eatwell and Taylor 2000, and Davidson 2002. (Davidson's position is discussed in Chapter 7 below.)

[46] 'It is essential, therefore, that strategies of economic democratization, if they are to be feasible strategies, work wherever possible, "with the grain of private property rather than against it." Examples of such strategies include, for instance, the formulation of a general incomes policy, which allows profits to rise while using increased taxation on a percentage of these to create social investment funds on a local, national or regional basis; and/or the creation of special representative bodies at local, national and regional levels to control the investment of pension funds; and/or the alteration of company dividend policy to allow a proportion of profits to be set aside as shares or income for the collective control and future benefit of employees. Individually or together, such proposals would increase the possibility of the social determination of investment by creating further "access avenues" to productive and financial resources'. Held 1995, p. 261.

advantages over economic agents at the 'periphery' (the 'South'). There is no reason to assume *a priori* that social investment funds designed to work 'with the grain of private property rather than against it' would reverse this tendency.

The proposals to manipulate interest rates and to set aside a pool of social investment funds targeted to poor regions of the global economy address two underlying factors in uneven development, fixed capital formation and foreign direct investment. In the contemporary global economy, most fixed capital formation remains within national borders.[47] This enables areas that, for one reason or another, have enjoyed a higher level of capitalist development to reproduce their advantages through the replacement of previous investments in fixed capital, and through the introduction of new technological artefacts complementing the fixed assets already in place. It is also the case that most foreign direct investment flows from wealthy regions of the global economy to other wealthy regions.[48] Investments in productive facilities tend to flow towards regions where consumer markets are the biggest, labour and managerial skills are the most advanced, infrastructure minimising transportation, communications, and transactions costs is in place, and so on. Since already wealthy regions tend to possess such advantages, flows of foreign direct investment tend to reproduce their superior position in the world market over time.

Neoliberals insist that the 'rules of the game' are nonetheless fair, for it is always possible for poor regions to break out of their position.[49] All they need are effective states capable of instituting the rule of law (especially regarding the protection of investors' rights) and implementing intelligent government policies encouraging foreign investment. They will then be able to tap global capital markets, gaining access to investment funds for development. This facile optimism is unequivocally rejected by democratic-cosmopolitan theorists. No less vehemently than defenders of the catalytic-state model, they hold that the weight of theoretical arguments and empirical evidence points in a quite different direction. The liberalisation of global capital markets necessarily

---

[47] '[A]bout 95% of all fixed capital formation is national, as opposed to overseas'. Moody 1997, p. 57.

[48] See footnote 17 of the previous chapter.

[49] But recall that, if neoliberals concede that there is overwhelming empirical evidence that global flows of investment do *not* tend to go to regions of the greatest capital scarcity, this undercuts an essential element of the normative defence of their framework.

tends to lead many regions of the global economy to suffer stampedes of capital inflows, speculative bubbles in currency, real-estate, stock, and bond markets, the inevitable bursting of those bubbles, stampedes of outflows, and crippling levels of international debt. When levels of debt exceed what can be repaid, borrowers must return to the global capital markets, borrowing (at higher rates) to repay the debt of the initial loans. The various mechanisms of uneven development tend to prevent these loans from being self-liquidating. When they are not, a 'debt trap' looms: further loans must be taken out to meet the interest due on the loans taken out to meet the interest due on the initial borrowing, and so on and on.[50] This debt trap is invariably accompanied by structural adjustment programmes imposed by international lenders and the global institutions representing their interests.[51] As Stiglitz has pointed out, these programmes exacerbate, rather than lessen, the systematic tendencies to uneven development. They also further the dismantling of the developmental state, which, for all its limitations, has been the only institutional framework with any success at checking the tendencies underlying uneven development.

Where are the funds for industrial development in poor regions to come from if they are not provided in sufficient or stable quantities from either private industrial investments or global capital markets? Defenders of the catalytic-state model of globalisation propose that states mobilise domestic savings towards this objective. But, once again, there is an immanent contradiction between this proposal and the acceptance of capitalist property relations, which tend to augment the exit options of individual investors and corporations as their holdings increase. The use of interest-rate differentials, and the pooling of social investment funds targeted to the poorest regions of the global economy, are designed to accomplish what the normal flows of foreign direct investment, global financial capital, and domestic savings cannot: access to the funds necessary for the industrial development for poor regions throughout the global economy. If interest-rate differentials and global social investment funds can generate economic growth and higher per capita living standards in disadvantaged regions, a plausible case can be made that this model of globalisation reverses the tendency to uneven development.

[50] See Chapter 7 below.
[51] Jagger 2002.

Before drawing this conclusion, however, we must consider other important factors generating uneven development that Held's proposals do *not* address. They include the repatriation of profits from the South to the North, capital flight by élites in the South attempting to avoid currency risks (or possible future demands for restitution), the effective implementation by Northern multinationals of 'divide and conquer' strategies in their dealings with subcontractors (and their workforces) in the South, and the transfer of value from the South to the North through the manipulation of transfer prices in intra-firm trade.[52] The fact that, in some historical contexts, a handful of developmental states have been able to put these mechanisms out of play, to a certain extent for a certain period, hardly establishes their irrelevance to the world market as a whole. Most importantly, Held does not adequately take into account the dynamic introduced in the discussion of uneven development in the previous chapter. The heart of inter-capital competition is the drive to appropriate surplus profits through temporary monopolies from product or process innovations.[53] Units of capital with access to advanced (publicly or privately funded) R&D are best positioned to establish a virtuous circle in which surplus profits enable a high level of R&D funding in the future, which provides the most important precondition for the appropriation of future surplus profits.[54] In contrast, the inability of units of capital without initial access to advanced R&D to introduce significant innovations prevents an appropriation of surplus profits, which tends to limit their ability to participate in advanced R&D in the succeeding period. This, in turn, limits future innovations and future profit opportunities, trapping them in a vicious circle. Units of capital with the greatest access to advanced R&D, almost by definition, tend to be clustered in wealthy regions of the global economy. Units without such access tend to be clustered in poorer regions. When units of capital in poorer regions engage in economic transactions with units of capital enjoying temporary monopolies due to innovations, the former

---

[52] These topics are discussed at length in Moody 1997, Toussaint 1999, and Went 2000, 2002. Regarding transfer pricing it should be recalled that 'An extraordinary 60% of international trade is within . . . multinationals, i.e., firms trading with themselves'. *The Economist* 2004a, p. 72.

[53] See Schumpeter 1934; Mandel 1975, Chapter 3; Storper and Walker 1989; and Smith 1997, 2002, 2004.

[54] Etro 2004.

necessarily tend to suffer disadvantageous terms of trade. When a handful of giant First-World oligopolies operating at or near the frontier of scientific-technical knowledge sells inputs to, and purchases the outputs of, small-scale Third-World producers far from that frontier, the prices these producers must pay for their inputs tend to rise, while the prices they receive for outputs tend to stagnate or decline over time. In this manner, the oligopolies tend to appropriate a disproportionate share of the value produced in the production and distribution chain. As a direct result, the pressure on work conditions, wage levels, and worker communities in poorer regions remains unrelenting, a pressure quickly transferred to working men and women and their communities in the so-called North. Thus, the drive to appropriate surplus profits through technological innovation – an essential feature of capitalist property relations and production – systematically tends to reproduce uneven development in the world market over time.[55]

It would be a vast oversimplification to divide the world up in a rigid centre/periphery dualism. A number of national economies fall between the two poles, forming a 'semi-periphery'.[56] The centre/semi-periphery/periphery distinctions are also fluid to a certain extent. Hegemonic firms and regions in the 'centre' may lose their leading position over time, and, under certain conditions, less wealthy regions may enjoy high rates of growth and rising per capita income for extended periods. But fluidity within the general pattern of uneven development does not imply that the pattern of increasing uneven development is unstable, as even the staunchest defenders of neoliberalism admit on occasion:

> According to the 1999 UN report, the fifth of the world's people living in the highest-income countries has 86 percent of world gross domestic product, 82 percent of world export markets, 68 percent of foreign direct investments and 74 percent of world telephone lines. The bottom fifth, in the poorest

---

[55] In his recent writings, Held has called for granting developing countries 'the right to maintain short-term and more flexible systems of intellectual property protection' and for 'the creation of an international knowledge bank to help defray the costs of the use of patents, where they are already established and where particular knowledge-related inventions are vital for development purposes'. Held 2004, p. 60. Neither proposal would to eliminate the virtuous and vicious circles described in the main text.
[56] Wallerstein 1979.

countries, has about 1 percent in each of these sectors. . . . And the gap has been widening. In 1960 the 20 percent of the world's people who live in the richest countries had 30 times the income of the poorest 20 percent. By 1995, the richest 20 percent had 82 times as much income.[57]

Attempts to measure inequality and poverty in the global economy in recent decades are fraught with complicated and controversial methodological issues.[58] However, no serious argument can be made against the summary of the available evidence provided by Arrighi. Even after the industrialisation of much of the South in the 1980s and 1990s,

> [T]he division of the world between have and have-nots remained as entrenched as ever. True, China was moving rapidly from the bottom to the top of the *low-income* stratum. But the rest of the stratum registered no improvement at all, while on average the entire middle-income stratum was regressing.[59]

The centre/periphery distinction remains necessary if we are to conceptualise the capitalist world market accurately.

The general objection to Held's proposals to subject global capital flows to increased social direction can now be summarised. These proposals are explicitly designed to complement, rather than replace, the flows resulting from the decisions of those who privately own and control capital. They are designed to work 'with the grain of private property rather than against it'. But this means that the structural tendency to uneven development remains in place. The most that could reasonably be expected from the reforms associated with cosmopolitan-democratic law is that mechanisms underlying uneven development might operate with somewhat less force, improving matters at the margin. And even this vague hope may need to be qualified after a consideration of Held's specific proposals, to which I now turn.

The interest-rate differential proposal can be interpreted as an attempt to generalise a key element of the so-called 'Asian miracle'. In East Asia, certain local corporations were able to grow rapidly partly as a result of being able to borrow investment funds at quite low interest rates. Held's idea is that a

---

[57] Friedman 2000, pp. 319–20. See also Held 2004, p. 45.
[58] Contrast Pogge and Reddy 2002 and Wolf 2004, Chapter 9.
[59] Arrighi 2002, p. 82.

régime of global governance ought to include a global institution operating analogously to the 'developmental state' of East Asia, spurring economic growth in disadvantaged regions of the global economy by making credit available there at rates below those prevalent in global capital markets.

The East-Asian countries where this approach had success for a period of time enjoyed extremely high levels of domestic savings, which then flowed into the domestic banking system due to the lack of alternative outlets. Poor regions of the global economy today lack comparably high levels of domestic savings. And the rise of disintermediation (that is, the erosion of relationship banking) tends to eliminate captive pools of domestic savings. From where would the funds come that are to be lent out at low rates in the cosmopolitan model? It goes without saying that private funds from wealthier regions will not tend to flow into areas where the interest rates received for lending those funds are significantly lower than the norm in the world economy. The only alternative, it would appear, is for the global institution implementing Held's proposal to have far more power than the mere ability to set interest rates in disadvantageous regions. It must also have the power to create new credit money.[60] Given the profound economic disparities characterising the global economy today, the scale of credit money creation required for the interest-rate differential proposal to reverse uneven development would surely be colossal. For the sake of the argument, however, let us make the truly heroic assumption that this hardly insignificant difficulty can somehow be overcome, and that some form of international credit money can be instituted on an extensive scale (I shall return to this topic below in Chapter 7). There are at least five good reasons to think that interest-rate differentials are not likely to eliminate systematic disparities in the global economy even then.

First, interest-rate differentials are not likely to reduce disparities significantly during periods of economic upswings. In periods of rapid capital asset inflation, higher interest rates for borrowing do not neutralise the advantages of wealthy regions of global economy. In such boom periods, venture capital investments and returns from shares and initial public offerings provide easy access to cheap capital, so higher borrowing costs for loans may be fairly irrelevant.

---

[60] The power to appropriate already circulating money for social investment funds is distinct from the power to create money and will be considered separately below.

Second, indicative planning through interest-rate differentials is unlikely to be effective at modifying uneven global development significantly during economic downswings either. As the Japanese economy in the 1990s illustrated, corporations tend to refrain from borrowing money for expansion in periods of extended stagnation, however low interest rates may fall. Interest rates are only one factor underlying investment decisions. In situations of overproduction and weakening consumer markets, extensive investments to further industrial development will not be made, even if historically low rates are available. Also, in periods of deflation real borrowing costs can be high even as borrowing rates approach zero.

Third, the effectiveness of the proposal obviously also depends upon firms throughout the global economy requiring significant amounts of external funds. This can be assumed to hold for many small and medium firms, especially start-up companies. But, as the scale at which units of capital operate increases, more and more 'core' firms in the global economy are able to fund their investments through retained earnings.[61]

Fourth, units of capital in the South are tied to home states that generally tend to lack the revenues required for extensive public subsidies for R&D. Even if these units were able to borrow at interest rates below those holding in global capital markets they would still tend to lack access to R&D at (or close to) the frontiers of scientific-technical knowledge. And, so, they would still tend to be unable to establish a virtuous circle of innovation and surplus profits, or break out of the inverse vicious circle.

Fifth and finally, the interest-rate differential proposal rests on a fallacy of composition. The fact that it is plausible to hold that *some* countries may employ low interest rates as part of a successful developmental strategy does not imply that *all* can. To the extent the interest-rate differential proposal succeeds, the tendency to overaccumulation crises will be exacerbated in sectors where units of capital from the South are clustered.[62]

---

[61] In the 1990s, for example, the majority of corporate borrowing in the US was used to finance stock buy-backs rather than to fund new investments, which were mostly funded through retained earnings. 'During the past two years, non-financial corporations increased their debts by $900 billion, while they retired a net $460 billion of equity. The main reason for these buy-backs is that firms can pay employees in share options without depressing the share price. In effect, therefore, firms are borrowing to finance their pay bill and prop up share prices'. *The Economist* 2000, p. 21.

[62] Recent developments in East Asia exemplify this tendency. See Burkett and Hart-Lansberg 2001, p. 7.

Held hopes to modify the flow of investments in the global economy both indirectly, through interest-rate differentials, and directly, through the pooling of social investment funds. It is now time to consider the latter. He mentions three forms the pooling of social investment funds might take. First, taxes on corporations could be imposed that increase as profits rise.[63] Democratic-cosmopolitan law also enhances democratic control over the allocation of pension funds. Finally, Held suggests that a percentage of an enterprise's dividends be set aside for new investments under the control of its workers. In what direction would these funds tend to flow in the global economy?

Either these pools of investment funds would flow along similar paths as other flows of financial capital, or they would not. To the extent the relevant agents have internalised the profit imperative, the former would be the case. The proposal presently being considered would, then, not be likely to generate significant positive social effects from Held's normative point of view. For the sake of the argument, however, let us assume that the socially-controlled investment funds taken together would generally tend to flow into regions in the global economy neglected by private capital and to firms whose labour and environmental standards are higher than average at a much higher rate than other forms of portfolio investment. The returns from such investments would then either be comparable to (or higher than) those from standard capital investments, or they would be lower. If they were generally lower, over time democratically-controlled funds would eventually be stuck with the 'lemons' in the global economy.[64] It is difficult to see how this would further the cosmopolitan-democratic values Held supports.

What of the cases where comparable (or even higher) returns resulted from democratically-controlled investments? The particular areas of investment selected by the socially-controlled funds would then become increasingly attractive to private investors. Unless the social investment funds grew at a

---

[63] This suggestion leads to something of a paradox. The underlying motivation for the proposal is the fact that private investment flows lead to inequalities and material deprivations in the global economy. But increases in the fund devoted to reversing these structural flaws result from increases in the private capital accumulation that generates these problems in the first place. The proposed solution would thus seem to always lag a step (or two!) behind the defined problem.

[64] In American-English slang, the term 'lemons' refers to poor quality cars sold to unsuspecting buyers. 'Lemon socialism' refers to the nationalisation of seriously ailing firms that private capital no longer wishes to invest in.

sufficient rate to compete successfully with private investors, the most successful bits of this social sector would eventually tend to be appropriated by the private sector, once again leaving the dregs to the social sector. If the social investment funds did grow at a sufficiently rapid rate, at a certain point we would no longer be talking about 'working with the grain of private property', but about a model of globalisation that pushes private capital flows to the margins of economic life. This goes against the essential determinations of the cosmopolitan model. And, so, we may conclude that the social investment funds proposal is, in effect, a mechanism whereby the risks of initial investments in poorer regions are socialised, while most of the rewards of successful investments are eventually privatised.[65]

Why would this matter? If social investment funds push private investments down socially attractive paths, is this not precisely what is to be wished? Once again, however, the question of property relations arises. Those who own a significant amount of private capital are far more predisposed to accept a higher degree of negative externalities regarding wage levels, workplace conditions, the environment, and so on, than other categories of social agents. Such states of affairs tend to benefit them far more than other social groups, while they are able to displace many of the burdens of these externalities to others.[66] After they have been privately appropriated the firms in question will thus tend over time to lose whatever social advantages they once enjoyed.

5. Controls on short-term flows of finance capital

There is little question that rapid and massive inflows and outflows of portfolio investments generate great instability and suffering in the global economy.[67] The question here is not whether there is a need to control flows of speculative

---

[65] The recent takeover of Ben and Jerry's (a popular 'socially-conscious' US producer of ice cream) provides a cautionary example. A consortium of 'socially-responsible' investment funds was unable to come close to matching Unilever's offer. If a direct corporate takeover of a successful 'socially-responsible' firm is not possible for one reason or another, private capitals can often take over the firm's market through appropriating key technologies, key workers, etc.

[66] Roemer 1994.

[67] For accounts of the social devastation inflicted by financial crises in East Asia from quite different political standpoints, see Burkett and Hart-Landsberg 2001 and Stiglitz 2002.

financial capital. The question is instead whether this reform of the 'international financial architecture' relegates the issue of property relations in the global economy to the secondary status assigned to them by Held:

> Certain forms of ownership and control become relevant only in so far as they are obstacles to the entrenchment of the principle of autonomy and democratic legitimacy. Moreover, in the agenda of economic democratization, these obstacles, it is worth bearing in mind, may be of secondary significance in comparison to finding ways of containing the huge, destabilizing flows of the international short-term capital markets.[68]

Held is far from alone in calling for increased capital controls on short-term portfolio flows such as Tobin taxes.[69] Many more mainstream social theorists support this measure as well.[70] All leading states have made extensive use of capital controls in their history, however many rhapsodies to neoliberalism are now being sung. An international financial architecture that grants states the right to impose controls against short-term speculative inflows and outflows does not break significantly from mainstream theory and past capitalist practice. Three considerations confirm that a more radical break is required.

First, Tobin taxes set at the levels discussed by their proponents are not likely to accomplish what Held and others hope. The reason for this was presented in Chapter 3: whenever the projected gains from speculative investments are sufficiently high – as they will be whenever there is a rapid inflation of capital asset values – transaction taxes at these levels do not significantly impede capital flows or prevent speculative bubbles from expanding.[71]

Second, the attempt to minimise the social disruptions caused by short-term portfolio investments can be seen as an attempt to rationalise global

---

[68] Held 1995, pp. 264–5.

[69] If Held has other forms of capital controls in mind, he does not specific what they might be. I shall assume that his list would be more or less identical to Stiglitz's (see Chapter 3). The critique of proposals to reform the international financial architecture will be continued in Chapter 7.

[70] In contrast to Held, however, more mainstream theorists and policymakers regard such controls as temporary measures to be removed when adequate accounting and regulatory standards are put in place in 'emerging economies'. Soros 1998; Council of Foreign Relations Task Force 1999.

[71] Davidson 2002, Chapter 12.

financial flows. Even if this financial rationalisation were successful, however, many of the other crucial mechanisms generating uneven development in the global economy would still remain in place, including especially the appropriation of surplus profits through innovation. The tendency towards overaccumulation crises in industrial sectors of the world market would also remain, along with the systematic need for massive devaluations of capital in order to resolve these crises, and the profound capital/wage-labour and intra-capital conflicts that inevitably occur as attempts are made to shift the costs of devaluation to others.

Third, taxes designed to discourage short-term capital flows across borders would not remove the fundamental irrationality at the heart of the financial sector stemming from its essential role in the dynamic of overaccumulation. Flows of financial capital from across the world market tend to be centralised at a few points in the centre of the global financial order, and then allocated across borders. With credit money and fictitious capital, the provision of funds becomes a multiple of the temporarily idle profits, depreciation funds, and precautionary reserves pooled in the finance sector. Once an overaccumulation crisis commences, the rate of investment in leading industrial sectors slows significantly. An immense pool of investment capital, is then formed, seeking new sectors with a potential for high future rates of growth (that is, a potential to appropriate great amounts of future surplus-value). When such sectors are thought to be found, financial capital from throughout the world market will tend to flow in their direction.[72] If the flows of investment capital to these new sectors are high enough, capital asset inflation results. Expectations of future earnings soon become a secondary matter, as financial assets are purchased in the hope of profits from later sales of these assets. Previous (paper) gains in capital assets are then used as collateral for borrowings to fund further purchases of capital assets, setting off yet more rapid capital asset inflation.[73] 'Ponzi schemes' develop as the value of financial assets loses all connection with any rational assessment of future earnings potential. When it becomes overwhelmingly clear that the ever-increasing prices of capital assets are ever less likely to be redeemed by future profits, the speculative

---

[72] de Brunhoff 1978, p. 47.
[73] Guttmann 1994, pp. 303–4; see also Toporowski 2000.

bubble collapses and a financial crisis ensues.[74] While many wealthy firms and investors are undoubtedly hurt in these collapses, the following social law has roughly the same force in capitalism as the law of gravity in nature: groups that benefited least from an inflation of capital assets tend to bear the greatest burdens of their subsequent fall. Unemployment, declining wages, demands on women to increase their unpaid labour, household bankruptcies, and the disintegration of vulnerable communities are just the most obvious and immediate of these burdens.

The tendencies to overaccumulation crises and financial crises are intertwined. The increasing scale of the former implies that the devaluation of loans and fictitious capital following in the wake of financial crises necessarily tends to occur on an ever-more massive scale as well. The pressure on units, networks, and regions of capital to shift the costs of devaluation onto other units, networks, and regions increases. Most of all, attempts to shift as much of the cost as possible onto wage-labourers and their communities intensify. Global turbulence and generalised economic insecurity increasingly pervade the world market. The capital controls over short-term flows that Held advocates would not eradicate these perverse tendencies.

6. Conclusion

I have argued that there is a systematic incoherence between Held's acceptance of capitalist property and production relations and his claim that the democratic-cosmopolitan model of globalisation 'creates a framework for all persons to enjoy, in principle, equal freedom and equal participative opportunities'.[75] The social relations of capitalism require the reproduction of the capital/wage-labour relation. They also generate systematic tendencies to overaccumulation

---

[74] Kindleberger 1989. Needless to say, recent examples of this pattern are very close at hand. According to the IMF, the price/earnings ratio holding at the end of 1999 for the Standard and Poor 500 index of US companies implied that their real earnings growth would accelerate between 25 and 50 per cent over the rate of growth since 1995. Plender 2000, p. 20. This was always a ludicrous expectation for reasons explored in Smith 2000a, Chapter Six. In the United States alone, equity values declined by $4 trillion from the peak of the dot.com bubble to the spring 2001; the figure for the global economy as a whole was $10 trillion.

[75] Held 2004, p. 114. A similar conclusion has been reached independently in Colas 2001.

crises, financial crises, and uneven development in the world market. These features of the model are essentially incompatible with 'the idea of a global political order in which people can enjoy an equality of status with respect to the fundamental processes and institutions which govern their life expectancy and life chances'.[76] Cosmopolitan-democratic law cannot attain the substantive equality of opportunity that is its professed goal so long as its precepts are simply grafted on to a capitalist global order. As long as capitalist property and production relations persist, the vast majority of the world's population in both the centre and the periphery will be threatened by increasing inequality, economic insecurity, and erosion of the material conditions necessary for happiness and the effective exercise of autonomy.[77] The model of globalisation defended by cosmopolitan democrats, in brief, cannot reproduce itself in a stable and normatively attractive fashion, when evaluated by the normative principles cosmopolitan theorists themselves proclaim. The main conclusion of this chapter is that this immanent contradiction justifies a transition to a new position in the systematic dialectic of globalisation.

In the introduction to this chapter, I noted a pattern in the early stages of the systematic progression. Positions in which the state is assigned the central place in the global order (the social-state and catalytic-state models of globalisation) have alternated with cosmopolitan perspectives (the neoliberal and democratic-cosmopolitan models, respectively), with the limitations of the one justifying a transition to the other. This might lead to an expectation that the next position in the ordering will be another state-centric model of globalisation, revolving around a new form of capitalist state explicitly designed to address the shortcomings of democratic cosmopolitanism. But a continuing ping-pong back and forth between state-centric and cosmopolitan models would be a form of 'bad infinity', to use Hegel's astoundingly idiosyncratic term. And one of the central methodological precepts of systematic-dialectical theories is that bad infinities should be avoided. If this cannot be done in a

---

[76] Held 2004, p. 114.

[77] The presentation of the irrationalities and antagonisms of capitalism here has hardly been complete. The systematic tendencies to environmental crises in capitalism and the social-psychological effects of the most intensive, extensive, and scientifically rational system of propaganda in the history of the human species (I refer, of course, to the system of corporate advertising) are just two of the many additional topics that would need to be considered in a more comprehensive account. See Burkett 1999 and Klein 2000, respectively.

cogent fashion, the project of constructing a systematic-dialectical reconstruction has failed and must be abandoned.

In the present context, there is one and only one way of going forward: we must accept that no variant of the capitalist state, and no form of capitalist world market, can resolve the fundamental irrationality and social antagonisms at the heart of capitalist social relations. A revival of the welfare state cannot reverse this state of affairs, as adherents of the social-state model of globalisation hope. Further deregulation of global capital flows cannot reverse this state of affairs, as neoliberals maintain. New forms of nationalism and localism cannot reverse this state of affairs, whatever defenders of the catalytic state might anticipate. And attempts to institute cosmopolitan law cannot reverse this state of affairs either. The next model of globalisation in the systematic progression must be a model in which the fundamental irrationality and social antagonisms at the heart of capitalist social relations are explicitly recognised.[78] Part One of this work concludes with this result.

---

[78] This conclusion does not imply that social movements struggling for reforms of the global economy should not be joined. Reforms that improve matters on the margin may still profoundly alleviate human suffering. Transaction taxes on the volume of financial turnover in financial exchange markets, for example, may provide funds to meet the most extreme cases of need, even while failing to establish the larger objectives of cosmopolitan-democratic law. The same can be said of consumption taxes on energy use, taxes on carbon emissions, a global tax on the extraction of resources, and a tax on the GNP of countries above a certain level of development, which Held has also proposed as ways of acquiring revenues to eradicate extreme poverty and hunger. See Held 2004, pp. 65–6. Further, the attempt to bring about reforms can form part of a 'transitional programme' to a new social order. Held's proposals effectively address the level of political consciousness found within progressive groups today. The struggle to institute them is likely to contribute to a transformation of political consciousness in which it gradually – or perhaps not so gradually – comes to be recognised that an adequate institutionalisation of the values of cosmopolitan democracy eventually requires a profound rupture with capitalist property relations.

Part Two

Beyond the Capitalist Global Order: Two Marxian Models of Globalisation

Chapter Five

A Marxian Model of Capitalist Globalisation (1): The World Market

The next position to be considered in the dialectic of globalisation continues the systematic progression begun in Part One. It, too, conceptualises the systematic relations among the various dimensions of social life (the family, national economies, states, the interstate system, the so-called 'régime of global governance', the world market) in a manner explicitly addressing the immanent contradictions of the prior framework (in this case, democratic cosmopolitanism). But a rupture has occurred in the dialectical ordering. Previous transitions have moved from one 'affirmative' framework to another. This is no longer the case. The break between Part One and Part Two of this book reflects this rupture.

The theorists of globalisation considered in Part One accept Hegel's distinction between 'existence' and 'actuality', even if they do not employ this vocabulary. They all grant that existing social institutions and practices are beset by countless contingencies and irrationalities. They also insist, however, that alongside the compromises and tragedies of everyday life 'the deep tendencies and inclinations of the social world' point in a quite different direction, towards a rational core discernable at the heart of the contemporary global order.[1] Each

---

[1] Rawls 1999, p. 128.

attempts to articulate this core in a model of globalisation that is both feasible and normatively attractive. In this sense, these theorists all echo Hegel's dictum, 'what is rational is actual and what is actual is rational'. They all articulate *affirmative* social theories, theories that aim to reconcile us with the 'deep tendencies and inclinations' of our world.

Each of the four positions examined in Part One, however, is afflicted by immanent contradictions. All four models of globalisation include capitalist social relations, which systematically block any tendency of these models to function in an efficient and normatively acceptable manner, as defined by leading proponents of the various positions themselves. Capitalist property and production relations are not contingent features of the contemporary historical epoch. They are 'actual' in the sense that they determine 'the deep tendencies and inclinations of the social world'. But they are not 'rational'.

If, at the present moment in world history, what is actual is *not* rational, and what is rational is *not* (yet) actual, an adequate model of globalisation cannot be based on an affirmative theory of institutions. At this stage in the systematic dialectic, we require a position that explicitly acknowledges the immanent contradictions of the capitalist global order. This can only be done within a *critical* theory. For all the weaknesses and gaps that undoubtedly remain in Marx's unfinished project, the three volumes of *Capital* still represent the indispensable starting point for any critical theory of this sort.[2] For this reason, the next stage in the systematic progression will be a Marxian model of capitalist globalisation.[3]

The present chapter is devoted to a brief consideration of the household, followed by an extended discussion of the essential determinations of capital. These determinations hold both on the level of civil society' (capitalist national economies) and the level of the world market. As we have seen in Part One,

---

[2] This statement is yet another example of a claim that cannot be fully justified at the stage of the systematic dialectic where it is introduced, but only at the completion of the systematic progression.

[3] On the level of normative theory, Part Two of this book does *not* represent a radical rupture from Part One. I accept three theses developed at length in Callinicos 2000: (i) Marxian social theory includes a normative dimension, (ii) this dimension generally converges with the ethical principles articulated by 'liberal egalitarians' such as Rawls and Held, and (iii) and the divergences between Marxists and liberal egalitarians primarily concern the sort of institutional framework that best embodies the normative principles accepted by both camps. See also Smith 1991.

much of the globalisation debate has been concerned with the proper way to categorise the systematic relations between states and global markets. Chapter 6 addresses this question from a Marxian perspective, beginning with a sketch of a Marxian account of the state-form. World money is another crucial issue, going to the very heart of the systematic relationships connecting national economies, states, the interstate system, the régime of global governance, and the world market. Chapter 7 explores this topic through a critical assessment of proposals to reform the 'international financial architecture' in Paul Davidson's important recent work, *Financial Markets, Money, and the Real World*.

Chapters 5, 6, and 7 together provide the outline of a Marxian model of capitalist globalisation, making explicit that, in the contemporary global order, what is actual is *not* rational, and what is rational is *not* (yet) actual in the contemporary global order. What would a model of globalisation look like that would be 'rational', that is, both efficient and normatively acceptable to the greatest degree feasible in the contemporary epoch? In the final chapter of this work, I shall address this question through presenting elements of a Marxian model of *socialist* globalisation.

I. The household

Unlike Hegel, Marx never attempted to complete a comprehensive account of modern society. Marx's goal in *Capital* was the systematic presentation of the essential determinations of capital. This complicates our task, for it means that important parts of a Marxian model of globalisation are missing from *Capital*. In this work, Marx presupposes a social form within which individuals are nurtured and socialised until maturity, and this is the family or its functional equivalent. But he does not provide a separate account of the household, parallel to that found in *The Philosophy of Right*.

In Marx's view, institutions in general, and the family in particular, are not self-contained boxes. In capitalist societies, there is only one set of social relations, however complex it may be, and household relations are part of this set. It follows that very little can be said about the contemporary family in abstraction from the property and production relations of capitalism. Marx always examines family relations in this context, noting how the former are modified in the course of capitalist development. He shows, for example, how family life adjusts to variations in the proportion of women in the paid labour force, variations he explains in terms of a complex mix of technological, economic, political, and cultural factors.

Marx explicitly notes that technologies can be more or less suited to women's average strength, and more or less culturally defined in gender terms. He also explains how the rhythms of capital accumulation encourage women to join to the labour force in boom periods, while pushing them out in down-swings, all the while presupposing and reproducing a gender system in which household labour is disproportionately assigned to women. In the course of his discussion of conflicts at the workplace, he points out how pools of unemployed female workers can be mobilised by capital as strikebreakers. And his account of labour legislation illustrates how superior political organisation of male workers can result in labour legislation that simultaneously protects women from certain forms of capitalist exploitation while reinforcing patriarchal relations in both the workplace and the household.

It would be quite mistaken to assert that these scattered remarks provide anything like a satisfactory account of the role of households and domestic labour in the global economy. But it would be no less of an error, in my view, to not recognise that Marx's framework is broadly compatible with the best feminist contributions to this project.[4] Nonetheless, the defining features of a Marxian model of globalisation are not found here. Proponents of the catalytic-state and democratic-cosmopolitan models have also discussed at length the pressures placed on households by fluctuations in the world economy, calling for effective social regulation of the market in order to ensure stable and flourishing households. Marxists echo these calls. When Marxists go beyond them, it is due to divergent conceptions of the way households are integrated within the global order, and not to divergent conceptions of the household per se.

Households are integrated within a larger whole: civil society, the next level in a model of globalisation. In previous chapters, I have concentrated on one central aspect of civil society, the organisation of production and exchange in the contemporary historical era. This is the main topic of Marx's writings,

---

[4] A survey of this literature is found in Rai 2002. See also Jagger 1988 and Brenner 2000.

the key to which is the concept of capital. Marx developed this concept in the context of a critique of political economy. Accordingly, I shall begin with a brief sketch of this framework.

2. The core thesis of political economy

The most elementary act examined by political economy is the exchange of one commodity for another by two contracting parties.[5] At the starting point, the two agents have an equal right to posses the commodities they hold, and an equal liberty to exchange them, should they chose to do so. In the absence of impediments, exchanges will tend to occur whenever two agents anticipate being better able to satisfy their wants and needs afterwards. Therefore, political economists assert, generalised commodity exchange necessarily tends to lead to the greatest feasible satisfaction of wants and needs. Trades will continue as long as there are mutual benefits to be won, and producers have strong incentives to search for product and process innovations meeting human wants and needs in a more efficient manner.

If one trading partner possess a commodity another desires, while the latter does not possess anything the former wishes to obtain, an exchange will not occur. In the framework of classical political economy and its divergent offshoots, money is the solution to this 'double coincidence of wants' problem. Once money has been introduced, it is possible to sell a commodity and use the money obtained to purchase some third commodity from some third agent. The introduction of money as a means of circulation (C-M-C) greatly extends the mutual benefits that can be won from trade. The next stage in the argument is to note that an extended series of C-M-C circuits includes M-C-M circuits as well (. . . C-**M-C-M**-C . . .); economic agents will sometimes aim at a monetary return for their activities. Elementary psychology dictates that some agents at least some of the time will aim at a monetary return exceeding the amount they held at the beginning of a series of transactions, generating a M-C-M' circuit, with M'>M.

---

[5] The term 'political economy' should be taken in an extremely broad sense, including classical political economy and its many progeny (neoclassical economics, the Austrian school, Keynesianism, institutionalism, and so on).

The core thesis of political economy can now be stated: any complications arising from actions aiming at monetary returns in general, or from profit-seeking activities in specific, do not call into question the claim that generalised commodity exchange provides the material preconditions for human flourishing better than any feasible alternative. Money remains, in principle, a mere proximate goal, subordinate to the ultimate end of meeting human wants and needs.

No serious social theorist would ever dream of asserting that money functions properly in the absence of the proper background conditions. The main standpoints in normative social theory are defined by the different background conditions thought necessary. For Rawls, a defender of the social state, money flows will be subordinate to the goal of human flourishing only if the allocation, stabilisation, transfer and distribution branches of government discussed in Chapter 1 fulfill their allotted tasks.[6] In the neoliberal tradition of Hayek, the main responsibility of the state is to institutionalise the 'rule of law', protecting citizens and non-citizens alike from force and fraud. This will not abolish the uncertainties of social life. But it does allow money to serve as a reliable means for thriving in the face of contingencies:

> [I]n an uncertain world individuals must mostly aim not at some ultimate ends but at procuring means which they think will help them to satisfy those ultimate ends; and their selection of the immediate ends which are merely means for their ultimate ends, but which are all that they can definitely decide upon at a particular moment, will be determined by the opportunities known to them. The immediate purpose of a man's efforts will most often be to procure means to be used for unknown future needs – in an advanced society most frequently that generalised means, money, which will serve for the procurement of most of his particular ends.[7]

John Gray decries the neoliberal model of globalisation defended by Hayek precisely because it perverts the proper arrangement of ends and means:

> A basic shift in economic philosophy is needed. The freedoms of the market are not ends in themselves. They are expedients, devices contrived by human

---

[6] Rawls 1973, pp. 274–80.

[7] Hayek 1976, pp. 8–9. Hayek echoes Adam Smith, who wrote that 'consumption is the sole end and purpose of all production', a thesis he regarded as 'so perfectly self-evident that it would be absurd to attempt to prove it'. Smith 1976, p. 155.

beings for human purposes. Markets are made to serve man, not man the market. In the global free market the instruments of economic life have become dangerously emancipated from social control and political governance.[8]

In his view, the 'social control and political governance' of the catalytic state is required to implement 'policies which harness markets to the satisfaction of human needs'.[9] Democratic-cosmopolitan theorists, finally, believe that Gray's laudable goal of human flourishing cannot be adequately attained in the absence of a global régime of governance making human rights the basis of international law[10] Insofar as this régime is instituted, individuals and groups can be secure in their freedom to decide their ends for themselves, making use of money as a generalised means in pursuit of those ends.

Hegel's *Philosophy of Right* includes an especially comprehensive account of the foundations of political economy, one that will provide an illuminating contrast with Marx's concept of capital. I shall focus on two key relationships: that between an individual will and an owned object, and that between the shared will underlying an exchange, on the one side, and the actions of the exchanging individuals, on the other. Hegel understands both in terms of a general essence/appearance schema.[11]

For Hegel, the possession of property affirms the owner as a person, as distinct from a thing. The individual's will can be seen as an essence that comes to appearance in the use of a particular piece of property. The affirmation of personhood becomes socially objective when owners of commodities mutually recognise the rightness of each other's property claims. Of course, the owned commodity reflects the universality of a free will in a very limited way. But it does not fundamentally distort the personhood that it reflects, in Hegel's view. It reflects that personhood in the greatest conceivable fashion

---

[8] Gray 1998, p. 234.

[9] Gray 1998, p. 92.

[10] '[T]he implication of the phrase "human rights" is that there are some interests common to all persons that are of such great moral concern that the very character of our most important institutions should be such as to afford them special protection. These interests are shared by all persons because they are constitutive of a decent life; they are necessary conditions for human flourishing'. Buchanan 2004, p. 127.

[11] In the present paper, I shall use the terms 'essence', substance', and 'universal' interchangeably. While Hegel drew sharp distinctions among them in certain contexts, in others he did not. I do not believe Marx ever distinguished them sharply.

on a level of abstraction restricted to individual persons and things. In this sense, we may speak of a reconciliation of essence and appearances here.

A yet higher-level form of mutual recognition occurs in commodity exchanges. When economic agents freely agree to a contractual exchange a universal will (essence) emerges, uniting the actions of the exchanging agents (appearances) without negating the particularity of those agents. Here, too, we can talk of a (higher-level) structure of reconciliation of essence and appearance. Ultimately, of course, this form of reconciliation is limited too. This form of universal will does not have substantial power; left to itself it necessarily tends to fragment. A move to a yet higher-level structure is required. The system of generalised commodity production and exchange requires a state that both establishes an 'administration of justice' (comparable to Hayek's 'rule of law'), and concerns itself with the substantive well-being of its citizens in ways that anticipate the social state of Rawls. In particular cases, market mechanisms lead to unfortunate results for individuals and groups that no state policy can fully overcome. But it would be gravely mistaken, Hegel would insist, to expect otherwise, given the contingencies that inevitably beset social life. The rationality of the essential social forms of generalised commodity exchange must still be affirmed. No alternative manner of organising production and distribution allows the mutual recognition of participants' freedom to a higher degree, or better provides the material preconditions for human flourishing. Here, too, we may speak of a reconciliation of essence and appearances.

3. Marx's concept of capital

Marx was not a political economist; his mature works were explicitly dedicated to the *critique* of political economy. The critique begins simply enough, by pointing out that in generalised commodity exchange production is undertaken on the private initiative of producers, with no guarantees that hoped-for sales actually occur.[12] The social necessity of privately undertaken production can

---

[12] Generalised commodity exchange implies generalised commodity production. Comprehending this system thus requires taking produced commodities as the initial object of analysis, as opposed to found objects or rare commodities such as works of art.

only be established subsequently, through successful exchange. Insofar as privately undertaken labour establishes its social necessity, the product acquires an additional property besides the concrete and heterogeneous qualitative properties distinguishing it from other things in the world. The commodity now has *value*, a homogeneous property shared by all commodities that contribute to social reproduction.

The labour that has gone into the production of commodities also acquires an additional dimension besides the concrete and heterogeneous qualitative features that distinguish it from other activities in the world. It now has the homogenous property of having produced a commodity with value, a property shared in common with all other instances of labour that have proven their social necessity through exchange. Labour considered in this light may properly be termed *abstract labour*, both because abstraction is made from its concrete determinations and because it is considered insofar as it produces an abstract property of commodities, their value.[13]

In a world of sporadic barter (or regular barter at the margins of social life), products need not have any determinate exchange-value. The ratios at which they are exchanged will be almost entirely determined by contingencies. In such a world, it would not be legitimate to refer to value as an intrinsic property of these products, or to the production of value by abstract labour. But, in a world of generalised commodity exchange, the myriad contingencies that inevitably accompany exchange are accompanied by systematic features that must be elucidated in the categories of value and abstract labour. A socially objective measure of value (equivalently, a socially objective representation of abstract labour) is a necessary condition of the possibility of this sort of social world. Without some objective measure of the extent to which the direct and indirect labour that has gone into the production of commodities is in fact validated as socially necessary labour, exchange would be sporadic and contingent, rather than a generalised system capable of being reproduced over time.

---

[13] 'Abstract labour', 'value', and 'exchange-value' are not natural properties of activities and things. Nor are they merely mental constructs. They are brought into existence due to the historically unique way labour is socially organised in capitalism, and once brought into existence they have material effectivity in the social world. They are abstractions, albeit abstractions of a quite different sort from the ordinary abstractions of thought. We may refer to them accordingly as 'social abstractions' or 'real abstractions'. The classic study of these issues is Rubin 1972.

We cannot measure value in terms of the concrete use-values a commodity may possess, or the concrete wants and needs a commodity with those particular use-values might fulfill. These matters necessarily involve qualitative heterogeneity and incommensurability. The value dimension, in contrast, is homogeneous and commensurable. A measure of value must itself be a pure abstraction in order to express adequately the abstract nature of value. Only an institutionalised system of pure units has an abstractness commensurate to value and abstract labour. If abstract labour were a purely physiological matter, measuring it in terms of homogenous units of time (or, better, units of energy expended per unit of time) would be relatively straightforward in principle, however difficult it might be in practice. Time provides an intrinsic measure of labour, and temporal units have the sort of qualitative homogeneity required for measurement of the value dimension. But the time devoted to concrete labouring, the only time that can be measured by stopwatches in the labour process, will not do. Abstract labour is not a purely physiological matter. Abstract labour produces value, and value is only actually created though the social process of successful exchange. And, so, the only socially objective measure of the value of a commodity must be something for which it is exchanged, some thing external to the given commodity. If this external thing is to be a universal objective measure, it must have the property of universal exchangeability, be as homogenous as the value dimension it measures, and be able to express quantitative differences. While, in principle, any individual thing capable of being divided into homogenous units could play this role, in any given social context, one thing will tend to be singled out. That thing, whatever it is, is money. Value is represented in the exchange-value of a commodity, the ultimate form of which is its money price.[14] Whatever physical form it might take (beads, metals, paper, electronic blips), money has a social form as well: it is the form of value.

It is worth taking a moment to note how this framework already diverges from that of political economy. The naïve humanism of the latter is replaced with an emphasis on the fetishism of commodities and money. The force of

---

[14] Murray 1993, Campbell 1993. Unlike previous modes of production, capitalism is not merely a system in which money is used. It is a monetary system. General equilibrium models in which exchange-values are measured in an indefinitely expanding list of exchange ratios treat capitalism as if it were a system of generalised barter. They refer to imaginary worlds, not the capitalism of our historical epoch.

the demand that commodities be valorised, that is, that their value be realised by metamorphosis into money, calls into doubt the unquestioned assumption that attaining the material preconditions for human flourishing is the immanent end of general commodity exchange. In a world of generalised commodity exchange, agents are not self-sufficient. If commodity exchanges do not occur, that is, if the (potential) value of commodities cannot be actually transformed into the money-form, the consequences for the agents involved can be horrific. Given the enormity of the stakes, Hayek's blithe assurance that money is merely a proximate end is merely hollow rhetoric. In generalised commodity production, money forms the centre of the social universe. To be without money is to be outside society.[15]

In a number of respects, the value/money relation is analogous to Hegel's accounts of property and generalised commodity exchange. In the former case, the individual will of persons cannot be directly perceived, but can be objectively manifested in the use of owned property. In the latter, the collective will of contracting partners also cannot directly appear, but is objectively manifested in the behaviour of the exchanging agents. As many others have noted, the value/money relation fits the Hegelian motif of an essence that cannot directly appear as what it is, but must appear in the objective form of something that is its 'other'.

Yet there is a profound disanalogy. The difference does not lie in the fact that in the value/money relation appearances necessarily diverge from the underlying essence (that is, money prices diverge from values). It is always the case that the forms of appearance of an underlying essence necessarily involve countless contingencies, as Hegel well understood. Nor does the difference lie in the fact that categorising the realm of generalised commodity production in terms of the value/money relation is quite abstract and simple, and must be supplemented with more concrete and complex determinations. The same can be said of early categories in Hegel's systematic-dialectical social theory. The disanalogy is that, in Hegel's framework, essence and appearance are reconciled in the greatest conceivable fashion on the given theoretical/ontological level. In the relation between an individual's will and an external owned object, and in the relation between the general will of

---

[15] 'The individual carries his social power, as well as his bond with society, in his pocket'. Marx 1973, p. 157.

contracting parties and their individual actions, the first term is objectively manifested as what it inherently is in the second term. However much these two relations must be subsumed within higher-order relations, they remain positive structures of reconciliation to be rationally affirmed. In sharp contrast, the money price does not simply reflect the underlying essence (value). *It fundamentally distorts that essence, even as it manifests it.*

To see why this is the case we need to recall what value is. Value is an immanent property of commodities, but not one that they have as a result of their chemical make-up or their natural relationships to other things. As a property of commodities, value is conceptually and ontologically distinct from abstract social labour, which is an activity of human agents, not a property of things. But value is a social property that commodities share insofar as they have been produced by privately undertaken labour that has proven its social necessity. Value is therefore internally related to abstract social labour; value is an immanent property of commodities if and only if labour is organised in a perverse form of sociality based on the *dissociation* of private producers. Neither abstract labour nor value can even provisionally be defined apart from the other adequately. And so it is not quite accurate to say that the relevant essence/appearance relationship here is the value/money relation. Three terms are in play: abstract labour/value/money. Each term both presupposes and is presupposed by the other two. And abstract social labour and value both have a legitimate claim to be the essential matter.

Money does not reflect this ontological state of affairs to the greatest conceivable extent on the given theoretical level. Money presents matters as if the price of commodities were a natural property, rather than a social form stemming from the peculiar and perverse manner collective social labor is organised in generalised commodity production: 'the social relation of the producers to the sum total of labour' is expressed as 'a relation which exists outside the producers'.[16] In the [abstract social labor/value]/money relation the second term, money, rules out even in principle the objective manifestation of what the first (complex) term inherently is. This is a negative structure of antagonism, not reconciliation. Such a relation must be criticised, not affirmed.

After examining the elements of the concept of capital, Marx turns to what he calls 'the general formula of capital', which makes explicit the implications

---

[16] Marx 1976, p. 165.

of the special status of money in generalised commodity exchange. Capitalism is more than a complicated form of barter, and money is not a mere convenience, a generalised means, a merely proximate end. The social forms of generalised commodity exchange impose a ceaseless competitive pressure for monetary returns on all units of production. Units that systematically direct their endeavours to 'valorisation', that is, the appropriation of monetary returns exceeding initial investment, necessarily tend to grow over time in comparison to other units. The use of money to purchase goods and services to meet human wants and needs is, indeed, part of the general system of generalised commodity exchange. But it is systematically subordinated to the valorisation imperative, the accumulation of money as an end in itself.

In the general formula of capital, two levels come into play. First, there is the level in which 'value' is the principle of unity of individual circuits that begin with money, proceed to the production and circulation of commodities, and conclude with more money than initial investment:

$$\text{Value}$$
$$M - C - M'$$

Second, there is the notion of value as total social capital, the ultimate organising principle on the level of society as a whole. This notion can be unpacked by comparing the aggregate of money capital initially invested in a given period with the aggregate of money accumulated at the end of that period, after all the particular circuits of capital have been completed. *Value is an immanent property of individual commodities, if, and only if, it is simultaneously the organising principle of both individual units of production and the social order as a whole.* 'Value' now appears to be a bizarre new sort of 'entity', a higher-order 'subject', a 'self-moving substance' that maintains its identity as it takes on the forms of money and commodities in turn in its pursuit of 'self-valorisation':

> [B]oth the money and the commodity function only as different modes of existence of value itself. . . . [Value] is constantly changing from one form into the other, without becoming lost in this movement; it thus becomes transformed into an automatic subject. . . . [V]alue is here the subject of a process in which, while constantly assuming the form in turn of money and commodities, it changes its own magnitude, throws off surplus-value from itself considered as original value, and thus valorizes itself independently.

> For the movement in the course of which it adds surplus-value is its own
> movement, its valorization is therefore self-valorization. . . . [V]alue suddenly
> presents itself as a self-moving substance which passes through a process
> of its own, and for which commodities and money are both mere forms.[17]

It is almost as if a familiar nightmare of science fiction has come true: an alien
being subordinates human goals and activities to its ends, without our even
being aware of it. The fact that we are not conscious of our subordination
under this alien subject is no more relevant than is the fact that neurones
within the brain are not conscious of the subordinate role they play within
the brain as a self-organising higher-level entity with its own emergent
properties. The humanist social ontology of political economy fails to grasp
the inversion whereby humanly created social forms generate an inhuman
subject whose end ('self-valorisation') comes to have precedence over human
ends.

The relationship between value and its particular forms defines a new sort
of essence/appearance relation. At first glance, matters here appear to be
quite different from the relation between value (*qua* property of commodities)
and money examined previously. The particular moments of the circuit, M,
C, and M', are the necessary objective forms of appearance of the underlying
essence, value (*qua* organising principle of individual circuits and society as
a whole). The appearances here do not seem to distort what that essence
inherently is. This would seem to be a dynamic unity-in-difference analogous
to those Hegel affirmed in *The Philosophy of Right*. In my view, however, this
analogy misleads more than it illuminates. A problem immediately arises if
we reflect on the manner in which the notion of value as a 'self-moving
substance' is related to the notion of abstract labour as the historically specific
form taken by 'the social relation of the producers to the sum total of labour'
developed in the presentation of the elements of the concept of capital. If the
latter notion were somehow incorporated in the former, it might make some
sense to consider whether the inherent antagonism in the [abstract social
labour/value]/money relation is overcome in the higher-level essence/
appearance relation that has value as the essence pole and the moments of
its self-valorisation as the pole of appearances. But this is not the case. The

---

[17] Marx 1967, pp. 255–6.

very notion of abstract labour as the substance of value (and its claim to be the essential matter) is outside the general formula. The harmonious reconciliation of value (essence) and the moments of its self-valorisation (appearances) is not developed by *transcending* the antagonisms of generalised commodity exchange already examined, but by *abstracting* from those antagonisms.

For this reason, I believe it is a mistake to see the general formula for capital as a distinct stage in Marx's systematic dialectic. It is not itself a social form with objective material existence, considered on a high level of abstraction. It is an abstract thought construct, a Weberian ideal type, involving no claim other than being useful in certain theoretical contexts. The general formula of capital is *not* Marx's initial formulation of the concept of capital; it is not a concept of capital at all. But it is useful for the development of that concept.

Marx's concept of capital is extremely complex, and it is difficult to formulate it in a way that captures this complexity. I believe that there are four dimensions of the concept that need to be taken into account.

(i) First, there are the property and production relations defining capitalism. Explicating them requires treating a representative M-C-M' circuit as a M-C-P-C'-M' circuit, focussing especially on the social form within which abstract social labour is performed, the wage-form. In generalised commodity production, labour-power too is a commodity.[18] At the beginning of the circuit, one group owns and controls investment capital (M). Those who lack such ownership and control must sell their labour-power for a wage, to be purchased alongside other commodity inputs (C) into the production process (P).[19] Labour-power necessarily tends to be purchased by the holders of investment capital if, and only if, this purchase is foreseen to result in the production of commodity outputs (C') that can be sold monetary profits. In other words, the wages workers receive must be less than the economic value they produce in the given period. At the conclusion of the circuit, those who initially owned and controlled capital now enjoy ownership and control of M', an amount exceeding initial investment. They now decide what portion of M' will be

---

[18] 'Only where wage-labour is its basis does commodity production impose itself upon society as a whole'. Marx 1976, p. 733.

[19] I am abstracting from dependency relations within households, the so-called 'informal sector', and so on. Introducing such phenomena would complicate the analysis without leading to a revision of any of the claims made here.

devoted to their personal consumption, what portion will be re-invested in the same enterprises, sectors, and regions, and what portion will flow to different enterprises, sectors, and regions, all the while subject to unrelenting competitive pressures stemming from the fact that their future prospects depend almost entirely on the extent to which their decisions further the appropriation of surplus-value (M'-M) in the future.

For a new circuit to commence, the wages received by workers must have been sufficient to enable them to reproduce themselves materially, while *not* being sufficient to free them from the necessity of having to return to the labour market to sell their labour-power.[20] So, at the beginning of the next circuit, the individual members of the class of wage-labourers find themselves without access to either means of production or means of subsistence, forced once again to sell their labour-power as a commodity in order to obtain access.

(ii) When the property and production relations of capitalism are in place, the general formula of capital has a material basis and becomes part of the concept of capital. To comprehend capital is to grasp the force of the claim that 'capital' is a 'subject', a 'self-moving substance' of individual circuits and the organising ('totalising') principle on the level of society as a whole. Wage-labourers are subsumed under capital as a particular form that it takes in the course of its circuit, a particular type of commodity purchased as an input to the production process. At first, this subsumption is merely formal, as wage-labourers are hired and allowed to work according to their own specifications with tools under their own control. But, soon enough, this gives way to what Marx terms 'real subsumption', in which every moment of the labour process is transformed so as to better serve capital's end, its self-valorisation. At this point, workers become mere appendages to vast complexes of immense organisational and scientific-technical sophistication created by capital. While wage-labourers have special capacities other commodity inputs to production lack, once purchased the representatives of capital claim these capacities as capital's own:

---

[20] Individual capitalists can, of course, go bankrupt in the course of a circuit, and individual workers can win lotteries, save enough to start a small business, retire, or die. The statements in the text refer to the class relations that must hold on the aggregate level of total social capital if the social forms defining generalised commodity production are to be reproduced.

By the purchase of labour-power, the capitalist incorporates labour, as a living agent of fermentation, into the lifeless constituents of the product, which also belong to him. From his point of view, the labour process is nothing more than the consumption of the commodity purchased, i.e. of labour-power.[21]

From this perspective, 'capital' is a universal subject taking objective shape in the particular forms of investment capital (M), commodity capital (C), the production process (P), inventory capital (C'), and accumulated money capital (M'). From this optic, 'capital' is an essence reconciled with its appearances in a manner homologous to Hegel's categories.

(iii) There is no shortage of passages in Marx in which 'capital' is presented as an essence uniting its different moments in a harmonious whole in a process of 'creating capital out of capital'. This leads to the 'one-dimensional society' problem, the problem of how to account for opposition to capital in a world of total reification. Any 'oppositional' energies against capital that appear to arise within the structure defined by the concept of capital would seem to result from a ruse of capital itself, which immediately appropriates them as forms of its own energy. A true 'other' of capital, an other that is not a mere repetition of the same but stands in opposition to it, a real or potential counter-subject to capital, can only appear as a *deus ex machina*, introduced for reasons external to the logic of capital

Versions of this move have been made by Marxists whom I respect greatly.[22] But I believe that Marx had a different perspective. For Marx, the concept of capital is not exhausted by capital's claim to status of essence (or subject, or self-moving substance, and so forth). That is only the beginning of the story. The more important part of Marx's concept of capital is the destruction of that claim. *Capital's claim to be the essence of the valorisation process is ontologically false*: 'The secret of the self-valorization of capital resolves itself into the fact that it has at its disposal a definite quantity of the unpaid labour of other

---

[21] Marx 1976, p. 288; italics added. This is captured quite well in Arthur's striking phrase, 'labour is the negatively posited sublated ground of value'. Arthur 2003, p. 253.

[22] If I understand their positions correctly, Arthur 2003, Dussel 1997, Lebowitz 1992, and Postone 1993 in different ways all appeal to a real or potential source of opposition to capital 'outside' the concept of capital itself. Bonefeld 2004 develops an account similar to that presented here in many respects.

people'. More graphically: 'Capital is dead labour which, vampire-like, lives only by sucking living labour, and lives the more the more labour it sucks'.[23] This does not merely mean that capital would perish if it lacked a source of nourishment, something that can be said of every living thing. It means that capital is not a living thing at all in any literal sense of the term. The heart of Marx's concept of capital, I believe, is the critique of capital fetishism; ontologically, capital is a mere '*pseudo*-subject' and '*pseudo*-self-moving substance'. The process of 'creating capital out of capital' is nothing but the exploitation of wage-labour:

> If the additional capital employs the person who produced it, this producer must not only continue to valorize the value of the original capital, but must buy back the fruits of his previous labour with more labour than they cost. If we view this as a transaction between the capitalist class and the working class, it makes no difference that additional workers are employed by means of the unpaid labour of the previously employed workers. . . . In every case, the working class creates by the surplus labour of one year the capital destined to employ additional labour in the following year. *And this is what is called creating capital out of capital.*[24]

Value is a property of commodities only because social production is organised in the form of dissociated sociality, that is, privately undertaken production that may or may not prove socially necessary. Its reality is entirely dependent on that form of social organisation persisting. 'Capital' is the unifying principle of individual circuits of capital and the totalising principle of society as a whole also only because social production is organised in the form of dissociated sociality, now understood to include the class relationship in which the material preconditions of labour (means of production and means of subsistence) are owned and controlled by a different class. Capital fetishism is thus not a mere subjective error forced on ignorant masses by the deceptive propaganda of capitalist ideologues. It is materially rooted in the property and production relations of capital, which reproduce labour's lack of ownership and control of the means of production and subsistence both on the level of individual circuits and the level of society as a whole:

---

[23] Marx 1976, pp. 672, 342.
[24] Marx 1976, pp. 728–9, emphasis added.

[I]t [capital, T.S.] only produces value as the power of labour's own material conditions over labour when these are alienated from labour; only as one of the forms of wage-labour itself, as a condition of wage-labour'.[25]

Because of this, everything operates *as if* capital reigned as a true self-moving substance. But capital's claim to be the underlying essence of the social world must be unequivocally rejected, however necessarily it appears that this claim is correct. Living labour's claim to this status must be unequivocally affirmed, however necessarily it appears that labour is nothing more than a moment of capital's process of self-valorisation.[26] This is the deepest level of Marx's critique of political economists, a critique anticipated by Thomas Hodgskin:

> Since the economists identify past labour with *capital* . . . it is understandable that they, the Pindars of capital, emphasise the *objective* elements of production and overestimate their importance as against the *subjective element*, living, immediate labour. For them, labour only becomes efficacious when it becomes *capital* and confronts itself, the passive element confronting its active counterpart. The producer is therefore controlled by the product, the subject by the object, labour which is being embodied by labour embodied in an object, etc. In all these conceptions, past labour *appears* [my italics (T.S.)] not merely as an objective factor of living labour, subsumed by it, but vice versa; not as an element of the power of living labour, but as a power over this labour. The economists ascribe a false importance to the material factors of labour compared with labour itself in order to have also a *technological* justification for the *specific social form*, i.e., the *capitalist form*, in which the relationship of labour to the conditions of labour is turned upside-down, so that it is not the worker who makes use of the conditions of labour, but the conditions of labour which make use of the worker. *It is for this reason* that Hodgskin asserts on the contrary that this physical factor, that is, the

[25] Marx 1963, p. 93. I therefore cannot agree with Hardt and Negri when they write, 'The deterritorializing desire of the multitude is the motor that drives the entire process of capitalist development, and capital must constantly attempt to contain it'. Hardt and Negri 2000, p. 124. The property and production relations of capital have material effects that cannot be reduced to 'the deterritorializing desire of the multitude'.
[26] For this reason I believe it is legitimate to refer to 'capital' as acting in various ways, despite the fact that this is a very bizarre form of speech. If there is reification in the social world, any adequate social theory must employ a form of speech reflecting this.

entire material wealth, is quite unimportant compared with the living process of production and that, in fact, this wealth has no value in itself, but only insofar as it is a factor in the living production process. In doing so, he underestimates somewhat the value which the labour of the past has for the labour of the present, but in opposing economic fetishism this is quite all right.[27]

The critique of a concept of capital that grants creative powers to capital is invoked repeatedly at crucial junctures in Volume I. Consider Marx's discussion of co-operation:

> [T]he special productive power of the combined working day is, *under all circumstances*, the social productive power of labour, or the productive power of social labour. This power arises from co-operation itself. When the worker co-operates in a planned way with others, he strips off the fetters of his individuality, and develops the capabilities of his species.[28]

This is the essence of the matter from an ontological standpoint. But, once the property and production relations of generalised commodity production are in place – that is, once individual wage-labourers must sell their labour-power to a representative of a class that privately owns the means of production and subsistence – matters must necessarily appear in a way that thoroughly distorts what they essentially are:

> On entering the labour process [wage-labourers] are incorporated into capital. As co-operators, as members of a working organism, they merely form a particular mode of existence of capital. Hence the productive power developed by the worker socially is the productive power of capital [note this 'is' (T.S.)]. The socially productive power of labour develops as a free gift to capital whenever the workers are placed under certain conditions, and it is capital which places them under these conditions. Because this power costs capital nothing, while on the other hand it is not developed by the worker until his labour itself belongs to capital, it *appears as* [note how this 'appears as' rules out a literal reading of the the previous 'is' (T.S.)] a power which capital possess by its nature – a productive power inherent in capital.[29]

---

[27] Marx 1971, pp. 275–6; see also pp. 244–5, 259, 265, 273, 475–6 and Mattick 1991–2.
[28] Marx 1976, p. 447; italics added.
[29] Marx 1976, p. 451, emphasis added.

The same story holds in the period of manufacturing. From an ontological standpoint, the development of the creative powers of collective social labour is again the essential matter:

> The collective worker now possesses all the qualities necessary for production in an equal degree of excellence, and expends them in the most economical way by exclusively employing all his organs, individualized in particular workers or groups of workers, in performing their special functions. The one-sidedness and even the deficiencies of the specialized individual workers become perfections when he is part of the collective worker.[30]

But:

> In manufacture, as well as in simple co-operation, the collective working organism is a form of existence of capital. The social mechanism of production, which is made up of numerous individual specialized workers, belongs to the capitalist. Hence the productive power which results from the combination of various kinds of labour *appears as* [not 'is' (T.S.)] the productive power of capital.[31]

When machinery and large-scale industry develop, capital fetishism is yet more powerful. But, here too, collective social labour, not capital, has the better claim to be the essence of the phenomena:

> It is only after a considerable development of the science of mechanics, and an accumulation of practical experience, that the form of a machine becomes settled entirely in accordance with mechanical principles, and emancipated from the traditional form of the tool from which it has emerged.[32]

There is no entity 'capital' that discovers the laws of mechanics or undergoes practical experiences. These are expressions of the creative powers of collective social labour. But, here again, the way things necessarily appear distorts the way they essentially are:

> It is the natural property of living labour to keep old value in existence while it creates new. Hence, with the increase in efficacy, extent and value of its means of production and therefore with the accumulation which

[30] Marx 1976, p. 469.
[31] Marx 1976, p. 481, emphasis added.
[32] Marx 1976, p. 505.

186 • Chapter Five

accompanies the development of its productivity, labour maintains and perpetuates an always increasing capital-value in an ever-renewed form. This natural power of labour *appears as* [not 'is' (T.S.)] a power incorporated into capital for the latter's own self-preservation, just as the productive forces of social labour *appear as* [not 'is' (T.S.)] inherent characteristics of capital, and just as the constant appropriation of surplus labour by the capitalists *appears as* [not 'is' (T.S.)] the constant self-valorization of capital. All the powers of labour project themselves as powers of capital, just as all the value-forms of the commodity do as forms of money. [33]

Marx's concept of capital could hardly be more unlike the categories of Hegel's *Philosophy of Right*. It is nothing like an institutional framework in which individual wills are harmoniously reconciled in their freedom within a collective spirit that they both presuppose and are presupposed by (Hegel's 'the I that is We and the We that is I'). The concept of capital, instead, defines a contradictory structure that simultaneously includes a pseudo-essence that necessarily appears as a Total Subject but is, in fact, the most severe form of fetishism in the history of the human species, and a collective subject that cannot appear as what it essentially is, due to the perverse property and production relations in place at this particular period of history. This is not a reconciliation of unity and difference (essence and appearance), as in the structures whose rationality

---

[33] Marx 1976, pp. 755–6, italics added. The point is expressed even clearer in 'Results of the Immediate Process of Production', originally intended for the first volume of *Capital*:

> [M]achinery is an instance of the way in which the visible products of labour take on the appearance of its masters. The same transformation may be observed in the forces of nature and science, the products of the general development of history in its abstract quintessence. They too confront the workers as the *powers* of capital. They become separated effectively from the skill and the knowledge of the individual worker; and *even though ultimately they are themselves the products of labour* [my italics], they *appear as* [not 'are'; my italics (T.S.)] an integral part of capital wherever they intervene in the labour process. . . . [T]he science realized in the machine becomes manifest to the workers in the form of *capital*. And in fact every such application of *social labour* to science, the forces of nature and the products of labour on a large scale, *appears as* no more than the *means for the exploitation of labour*, as the means of appropriating surplus labour, and hence it *seems* [my italics] to deploy *forces* distinct from labour and integral to capital . . . . And so the development of the *social* productive forces of labour and the conditions of that development come to *appear as* [not 'are'; my italics (T.S.)] the *achievement of capital*'. Marx 1976, p. 1055. See also pp. 1005, 1020–1, 1024, 1053–4, 1056, 1058, where similar statements are found.

is affirmed in *The Philosophy of Right*. It is a structure of irreconcilable antagonism.[34]

(iv) One final dimension of Marx's concept of capital must be noted. It, too, is based on an unequivocal rejection of the notion of capital as totalising subject as anything more than a necessarily form of appearance materially grounded in the property and production relations of capitalism. The antagonism defining the concept is not limited to the inevitable and irreconcilable conflict between the ontological claims of capital as essence and collective social labour as essence. The restriction of the creative energies of collective social labour to forms compatible with valorisation are necessarily experienced as arbitrary and harmful. The not-to-be underestimated force of ideologies, the distractions of consumption, and the dull compulsion of daily routine can never fully erode this lived experience. *Resistance to capital is thus part of the concept of capital.*[35] As Marx writes in the *Results*:

> What we are confronted with here is the alienation of man from his own labour. To that extent the worker stands on a higher plane than the capitalist from the outset, since the later has his roots in the process of alienation and finds absolute satisfaction in it whereas right from the start the worker is a victim who confronts it as a rebel and experiences it as a process of enslavement.[36]

Resistance to capital does not come from 'outside' the concept of capital; it is there 'right from the start' at the core of the structure defined by that concept.

This resistance will take a variety of forms, depending on a wide variety of 'subjective' factors, including the organisational forms in which it occurs,

---

[34] Hegel's 'logic of the concept' is designed to capture the intelligibility of dynamic wholes whose different moments are harmoniously reconciled without sacrifice of their particularity. The categories of Hegel's social theory are 'homologous' with Hegel's logic of the concept; the concept of capital is not.

[35] 'As the number of co-operating workers increases, so too does their resistance to the domination of capital, and, necessarily, the pressure put on by capital to overcome this resistance. The control exercised by the capitalist is not only a special function arising from the nature of the social labour process, and peculiar to that process, but it is at the same time a function of the exploitation of a social labour process, and is consequently conditioned by *the unavoidable antagonism* between the exploiter and the raw material of exploitation'. Marx 1976, p. 449, emphasis added; see also pp. 635, 793.

[36] Marx 1976, p. 990.

the concrete strategies and tactics followed in concrete circumstances, and – last, but most assuredly not least – the particular concept of capital orienting it. A wide variety of 'objective' factors come into play as well. From the world-historical standpoint, surely the most important is the level of development of the creative powers of collective social labour. Historically, these powers have developed within the social forms of capital, which have no doubt distorted their development in countless profound ways.[37] But, if they were truly the powers of capital, socialism would be a pure fantasy, not an objective historical possibility.[38] From this standpoint too, the critique of capital fetishism forms the heart of Marx's concept of capital.

At the beginning of Marx's theory, we discovered that money is at once a mere thing and universal sociality. With the concept of capital, we discover the even more perverse fact that capital is everything and nothing, all-powerful and an insubstantiality that would dissolve instantly were the production and distribution of means of production and consumption to be democratically organised. We discover that collective social labour is nothing but a particular form of capital (in appearance), and the only source of the creative powers in the social world. The paradoxes of capital put those of quantum mechanics in the shade! Comprehending these paradoxes requires a complex concept of capital including all four dimensions developed here: (i) the property and production relations that make valorisation the immanent end of a capitalist social order, (ii) the manner in which capital's claim to be the subject of the social order is materially rooted in those social relations, (iii) the critique of this capital fetishism, and affirmation of the counter-claim that what appear

---

[37] 'The bourgeoisie . . . has accomplished wonders far surpassing Egyptian pyramids, Roman aqueducts, and Gothic cathedrals. . . . The bourgeoisie cannot exist without constantly revolutionizing the instruments of production. . . . The bourgeoisie, during its rule of scarcely one hundred years, has created more massive and more colossal productive forces than have all preceding generations together. Subjection of Nature's forces to man, machinery, application of chemistry to industry and agriculture, steam-navigation, railways, electric telegraphs, clearing of whole continents for cultivation, canalization of rivers, whole populations conjured out of the ground – what earlier century had even a presentiment that such productive forces slumbered in the lap of social labour?'. Marx 1977, pp. 224–5.

[38] The recent work of Duménil and Lévy is extremely interesting from this perspective. They present an account of capitalist development centring on a step-by-step expansion of collective social labour's capacity to manage a complex economy. Duménil and Lévy 2004.

to be powers of capital are, in fact, the creative powers of social labour in an alien form, and (iv) the assertion that class struggle is as inherent in the concept of capital as the valorisation imperative.

Theorists of cosmopolitan-democratic law fail to comprehend how the property and production relations of capitalism define a social order in which valorisation, not human flourishing, is the ultimate end of social life. They also fail to grasp the sense in which capital reigns as the totalising principle of the social order. And they lack the theoretical resources to show how the creative power of collective social labour is the revealed secret of capital, the true essence of a pseudo-essence, making class conflict in some form or other an ineluctable feature of the capitalist order. They ultimately fall into immanent contradictions because they attempt to theorise capitalism without an adequate concept of capital. This is a fatal flaw, shared by all earlier positions in the systematic dialectic of globalisation as well.

In the remainder of this chapter, I shall explore how this concept of capital can be expanded to a Marxian account of the world market.

4. Marx's concept of capital and the world market

In *Capital*, Marx reconstructs the essential determinations of the capitalist mode of production through a systematic ordering of categories, each of which defines a particular form of social relations. In this ordering, each later stage explicitly addresses immanent contradictions implicit in the previous one. At each stage, there is a contradiction between the implicit claim that a structure of social ontology defined by a particular category can account adequately for the reproduction of the capitalist mode of production, and the inability of that structure to do so. This contradiction pushes the theory forward to a new category, defining a more complex and concrete structure. Or, equivalently, the theoretical imperative to not conclude the systematic ordering until the given totality has been fully comprehended 'pulls' the theory to its end point.[39] After the concept of capital has been introduced in Volume I, Marx's theory proceeds through a dialectical development of that concept. The three volumes of *Capital* that have come down to us move to

---

[39] Marx 1973, pp. 100–1; see Smith 1990, Chapters I, II.

ever-greater levels of complexity and concreteness, a progression that was to
have culminated with the unwritten books on the state, foreign trade, and
the world market.[40]

Yet there is no stage in the subsequent dialectic of capital that resolves the
fundamental contradiction between capital as essence and collective social
labour as essence. Subsequent stages of the theory are developed *within* this
contradiction; the contradiction is not itself resolved within a higher-order
structure. At the beginning of the theory, it is merely implicit that abstract
labour, value, money, and capital are ultimately defined on the level of the
world market. By the end of Marx's system, which was to have culminated
with a book on the world market and crisis, this would have become explicit.
But the contradiction between the two equally necessary and yet thoroughly
incompatible notions of essence is *precisely the same* on the level of the world
market as it is on the initial levels of Marx's theory, however great the gains
in complexity and concreteness.

In an extremely important passage from the drafts later published as *The
Theories of Surplus-Value* Marx confirms this:

> If surplus labour or surplus-value were represented only in the national
> surplus product, then the increase of value for the sake of value and therefore
> the extraction of surplus labour would be restricted by the limited, narrow
> circle of use-values in which the value of the [national] labour would be
> represented. But it is foreign trade which develops its [the surplus product's]

---

[40] Marx 1973, pp. 227, 264. Marx also mentioned possible volumes on landed property,
competition and wage-labour. In my opinion, there are three good reasons to exclude
these proposed books from the systematic project begun in *Capital*. First, a considerable
portion of the material originally intended for these works was later incorporated in
the three volumes of *Capital* (Rosdolsky 1977, Chapter 2). Second, some of the remaining
material could be easily and appropriately incorporated in accounts of the state, foreign
trade, and the world market. Finally, whatever material remains probably does not
concern essential determinations of the capital form, but, rather, contingent historical
determinations (for example, examinations of particular paths taken by particular
industries, various forms taken by households and communities in the course of
capitalist development, strategies and tactics employed in specific social struggles,
and so on). Books on landed property, competition and wage-labour remained to be
written at Marx's death. But they are part of a different theoretical project than the
project begun in of *Capital*. In contrast, the proposed books on the state, foreign
exchange, and the world market would have completed this project, the systematic
reconstruction in thought of the essential determinations of capital. The classic study
of this question is Lebowitz 1992, who comes to a different conclusion.

real nature as value by developing the labour embodied in it as social labour which manifests itself in an unlimited range of different use-values, and this in fact gives meaning to abstract wealth. . . . [I]t is only foreign trade, the development of the market to a world market, which cause money to develop into world money and *abstract labour* into social labour. Abstract wealth, value, money, hence *abstract labour*, develop in the measure that concrete labour becomes a totality of different modes of labour embracing the world market. Capitalist production rests on the *value* or the transformation of the labour embodied in the product into social labour. But this is only [possible] on the basis of foreign trade and of the world market. This is at once the pre-condition and the result of capitalist production.[41]

Four closely interconnected themes are presented here, all based on the thesis that 'the increase of value for the sake of value' is the organising principle of capital on the level of the world market.

(i) Generalised commodity exchange is just that, generalised. Any and all restrictions of exchange to a particular set of use-values are thoroughly arbitrary from the standpoint of the value-form, including restrictions to use-values produced within a particular region. The value-form includes an immanent drive to break through all such arbitrary restrictions and to transgress *any* given geographical limit to the exchange of commodities. As Marx writes, 'The tendency to create the world market is directly given in the concept of capital itself. Every limit appears as a barrier to be overcome'.[42] Or, again:

The development of the product into a commodity is fundamental to capitalist production and this is intrinsically bound up with the expansion of the market, the creation of the world market, and therefore foreign trade.[43]

The notion of generalised commodity exchange thus implies that the total social capital defined at the beginning of *Capital* is implicitly the total social capital of the world market.

(ii) The system of generalised commodity exchange is, by definition, a system of generalised commodity production, that is, a historically specific way of organising social labour. This is a very peculiar system of sociality,

[41] Marx 1971, p. 253.
[42] Marx 1973, p. 408.
[43] Marx 1968, p. 423; see also Marx 1976, p. 573.

based on the *dissociation* of private producers. In this system of 'asocial sociality', the social relations among producers are mediated through the things they produce. This is a feature of national economies in the capitalist epoch. But just as geographical restrictions on the exchange of commodities are thoroughly arbitrary from the standpoint of the value-form, so too are restrictions on the social relations mediated through exchanged commodities. And, just as the former restrictions necessarily tend to be overcome as long as the value-form holds sway, so too are the latter as 'concrete labour becomes a totality of different modes of labour embracing the world market'.

(iii) If the relevant scale of commodity exchange is the world market, and the relevant scale of the social division of labour is the world market as well, then it follows at once that the socially objective measure of value must operate on this same scale. Various monies may exist with a more restricted scope. But the value-form necessarily requires world money, with particular monies ultimately defined by their relationship to this world money:

> It is in the world market that money first functions to its full extent as the commodity whose natural form is also the directly social form of realization of human labour in the abstract. Its mode of existence becomes adequate to its concept. . . . World money serves as the universal means of payment, as the universal means of purchase, and as the absolute social materialization of wealth as such (universal wealth).[44]

(iv) Finally, the references to surplus labour and surplus-value at the beginning of the passage from *Theories of Surplus-Value* imply that the capital/wage-labour antagonism at the core of capital-in-general is ultimately played out on the level of the world market.[45]

Two conclusions follow from this analysis. First, the world market, for Marx, is not an aggregate of distinct national economies bound together by external relations of trade and investment. It is a higher-level totality subsuming national economies within it.[46] On this point, Marx agrees with neoliberals,

---

[44] Marx 1976, pp. 240–2. Throughout *Capital*, Marx assumes that world money must ultimately take the form of commodity money. The point made in the main text does not depend upon this assumption.
[45] In this sense, 'proletarian internationalism' is implicit in *Capital* from its first sentence onwards.
[46] This does not imply that it is always illegitimate to consider a capitalist national economy by itself in certain restricted theoretical contexts.

defenders of the catalytic state, and cosmopolitan democrats, over against adherents of the social-state model of globalisation. For these theorists, however, the power of global markets is a relatively recent story. For Marx, in contrast, the logic of capital has necessarily tended to operate on the level of the world market since its inception.[47]

Second, the concept of capital described in the previous section forms the core of the Marxian model of capitalist globalisation. In capitalist societies, artefacts, individuals, firms, networks, markets and states are subsumed under capital, and they can only be adequately comprehended in terms of their relation to its self-reproduction on the level of the world market. Once the capital-form is in place, there is an immanent end in the world market, the 'the self-valorisation of value', accumulation on the level of total social capital. None of the positions considered in Part One take into account the manner in which capital accumulation on the level of the world market is identical to the systematic reproduction of exploitative class relations.[48]

---

[47] As noted in the Introduction, the term 'contemporary epoch' is ambiguous. For defenders of the social state, it refers to the post-World-War-Two era of the welfare state, a period which has not concluded, however much neoliberals try to convince us otherwise. For proponents of neoliberalism, the catalytic state, and democratic cosmopolitanism, the rise of Eurodollar markets and the end of the Bretton Woods agreements brought the epoch of the Keynesian welfare state to a halt and inaugurated the 'age of globalisation'. For Marx, our age continues to be the epoch of capitalism, and comprehending the continuities in the course of capitalist development is of the greatest theoretical and practical significance. These continuities include a world market that has subsumed states and national economies under it.

[48] This is not to deny that the reign of capital simultaneously brings about the most profound emancipation of humanity that has yet occurred in history. As the range of use-values widens, customary restrictions on human needs are transgressed, even if in a limited and distorted fashion. The productive capacities of collective social labour as a whole are emancipated from customary restrictions as well, even as the capacities of individual labourers are continually threatened by deskilling. And the very notion of human community is also emancipated from traditional limits, albeit in a very restricted fashion. The cosmopolitan identity that was a mere moral imperative for the stoics and Kant obtains a material basis for the first time in world history when agents throughout the world market are tied together in objective social relations. However limited and distorted the radical openness to new needs, new capacities, and new identities may be, the emancipatory dimension of the value-form is no less real than its horrific alienation and exploitation: 'In place of the old wants, satisfied by the productions of the country, we find new wants, requiring for their satisfaction the products of distant lands and climes. In place of the old local and national seclusion and self-sufficiency, we have intercourse in every direction, universal interdependence of nations. And as in material, so also in intellectual production. The international creations of individual nations become common property. National one-sidedness and narrow-mindedness become more and more impossible, and from the numerous national and local literatures, there arises a world literature'. Marx 1977, pp. 224–5.

The world market is implicit throughout the three volumes of *Capital* that have come down to us. The following section will document this, showing how a Marxian model of globalisation brings to the fore issues that other models ignore or treat as secondary. In Section 6, the category 'surplus profits through innovation' will be discussed at some length. As we shall see in Section 7, this category is absolutely crucial to the case that a Marxian model of capitalist globalisation can avoid the sort of immanent contradictions that beset the positions considered in Part One.

5. The world market and the further determinations of capital

After revealing that the secret of the capital-form is the extraction of surplus labour and its appropriation by capital in the form of surplus-value, Marx turns to the factors determining the rate of surplus-value, beginning with the social definition of the value of labour-power. Everything else being equal, the lower the value of labour-power, the less of the working day that must be devoted to producing economic value equivalent to the wages workers receive, and the more that can be devoted to the production of surplus-value. The world market plays a major role in determining the value of labour-power, since foreign trade opens the possibility of lower-cost imports substituting for commodities presently consumed by workers. When this occurs, a long-term reduction in the value of labour-power becomes possible, which, in turn, opens the possibility for a rise in the rate of surplus-value.[49] The massive flow of new crops such as sugar from the 'new' world to the 'old' illustrates how this dynamic was at work in the historical beginnings of the capitalist world market. The Corn Laws debate revealed its importance in Ricardo's day; manufacturers supported a reduction in tariffs on food imports primarily because of its anticipated effects on wages. And the manner in which cheap consumer imports have been associated with stagnate real wages in the United States provides a more recent example.

A second factor affecting the rate of surplus-value is the necessary tendency for capital to attempt to increase the rate of surplus-value through extending

---

[49] If more powerful counter-tendencies are in place in the given context, this possibility will not be actualised. The key counter-tendency – the level of organisation and strength of working men and women – will be discussed immediately below.

the workday, combined with the no less necessary counter-tendency for wage-labourers to resist this extension. When resistance is successful – and even when it is not, given that there are only so many hours in the day that can be devoted to labouring – a third factor comes into play. Capital necessarily tends to raise the rate of surplus-value through technological and organisational innovations intensifying the labour process and/or increasing labour productivity at a given level of intensity. When such innovations are introduced in sectors producing consumption goods, the rate of surplus-value is directly increased in the given period, everything else remaining equal. When such innovations are introduced in sectors producing inputs to the production of consumer goods, the rate of surplus-value increases in the subsequent period, everything else again remaining equal.

The determination of the value of labour-power is never simply a matter of the costs of commodities consumed by workers and their families. The balance of class forces at a particular place and time is the truly crucial matter.[50] When productivity advances occur, workers will tend to struggle for higher real wages, attempting to redefine the value of labour-power, so that they too benefit from these advances. This provokes a search by capital for yet further technological and organisational changes, changes designed to weaken the power of labourers in the production process, thereby restricting their ability to redefine the value of labour-power upwards.

The world market fits into this picture in two main ways. First, the productivity advances that necessarily tend to emerge due to the capital/wage-labour dynamic also affect the world market. If they bring down unit costs, for example, this can enable technically advanced units of capital to take over foreign markets: 'The cheap prices of commodities are the heavy artillery with which [the bourgeoisie] batters down all Chinese walls'.[51] The reverse dynamic holds as well; innovations introduced in order to capture foreign markets may simultaneously transform the capital/wage-labour relation, affecting the rate of surplus-value.

A second point concerns the way class struggles affect the rate of surplus-value. These struggles are an ineluctable feature of the capital-form.[52] Such

---

[50] Lebowitz 1992.
[51] Marx and Engels 1988, p. 24.
[52] 'The capitalist therefore takes his stand on the law of commodity-exchange. Like

struggles can be won by workers when 'the working class's power of attack [grows] with the number of its allies in those social layers not directly interested in the question'.[53] But, as long as capitalist property relations are in place, capital possesses weapons that tend to make these victories limited and precarious.[54] One is the power to introduce technologies into the workplace with the intention of creating unemployment and/or deskilling the most combative sectors of the work force. But such technologies are not always available, and may involve high levels of investment and risk, even when they are. In some circumstances, a second option is preferable, a capital strike throwing workers out of work, threatening their access to means of subsistence. If this threat is serious enough, workers can be forced to renounce gains in real wages that would redefine the value of labour-power upwards. During the course of a capital strike, however, the accumulation process is interrupted. From the standpoint of capital, then, there are often reasons to prefer a third option, capital flight. Accumulation can continue as investment is shifted from one region to another in the hope of shifting the balance of power between capital and wage-labour to the advantage of the former.

Cross-border capital flows in the form of foreign direct investment provide one example of capital flight; subcontracting to foreign suppliers another. Even the mere threat of capital flight may allow the owners and controllers of capital to implement an effective 'divide-and-conquer' strategy playing off one sector of the labour force against another.[55] This raises the rate of surplus-value, everything else being equal.[56] One of the key distinguishing features of a Marxian model of globalisation is this emphasis on the way 'the unavoidable antagonism between the exploiter and the raw material of exploitation' stretches across territorial boundaries.

The ability to implement divide-and-conquer strategies effectively is furthered by the fact that the workforce is not homogeneous on the level of the world

---

all other buyers, he seeks to extract the maximum possible benefit from the use-value of this commodity. *Suddenly, however, there arises the voice of the worker . . .*' Marx 1976, p. 342, emphasis added. In my reading of *Capital*, the systematic logic of the capital-form includes nothing that can ultimately silence this voice; see note 35 above.

[53] Marx 1976, p. 409.

[54] One of the most important is the state. In normal circumstances, the capitalist state can be counted on to pass legislation and impose policies designed to keep the value of labour-power within bounds acceptable to capital (see the following chapter).

[55] Bronfenbrenner 1996, and 2001.

[56] Lebowitz 1994.

market. Struggles to maintain or revise upwards the 'historical and moral' component of the value of labour-power are not equally successful everywhere. Neither are struggles against extensions of the working day, or the imposition of technological-organisational innovations shifting control of the labour process away from labour. The greater the differences in outcomes, the greater the danger that more successful and less successful groups of workers will come to believe they have fundamentally different interests. Other sorts of heterogeneity within the international working class can also be mobilised as part of capital's divide-and-conquer strategies. Divisions based on nationality, religion, ethnicity, race, and gender are obviously relevant here. They may all hinder the formation of strong cross-border alliances among wage-labourers, the only effective response in the long-term to divide-and-conquer strategies.[57]

While tendencies for divisions within the international working class must be fully acknowledged, they are not the entire story by any means. In the first volume of *Capital*, Marx notes how successful struggles in one part of the world market can inspire struggles elsewhere.[58] And the very same dynamic that produces divisions within the global workforce simultaneously creates the material conditions for new forms of collective transnational identities. Capital flight in the form of cross-border subcontracting, mergers and acquisitions, and foreign direct investment, binds geographically separated workers together in a far more observable and direct fashion than trade. A tendency for workers objectively bound to the same units of capital to unite across geographical boundaries is inherent in the capital-form no less than the tendency of capital to attempt to divide them. Which tendency dominates in a particular context is a contingent matter.

The systematic tendency towards the concentration and centralisation of capital is another dimension of the capital-form that implicitly operates on the level of the world market.[59] As the concentration and centralisation process proceeds, it is necessarily the case that the geographical scale at which leading

---

[57] Moody 1998.

[58] In this respect, 'the English factory workers were the champions, not only of the English working class, but of the modern working class in general', that is, the working class considered on the level of the world market. Marx 1976, p. 413. Hardt and Negri refer to this as 'the accumulation of struggles'. Hardt and Negri 2000, p. 263.

[59] 'Concentration' is the process whereby successful units of capital expand internally. 'Centralisation' is the process whereby successful units of capital expand by assimilating less successful units.

units of capital operate tends to expand as well. Successful local firms tend to expand regionally; successful regional firms tend to attempt to operate nationally; successful national firms tend to seek foreign markets and investment opportunities; and units of capital that already operate across borders tend to extend their 'global reach' as they grow. As the concentration and centralisation of capital proceeds, for example, there is a necessary tendency for cross-border mergers and acquisitions to increase over time. Almost all firms in almost all sectors are eventually tied to circuits of capital crossing national borders.[60]

When enterprises purchase inputs from other units of capital, the prices they pay include the profits of these other units. If they produce these inputs themselves, however, they do not have to pay out these profits to others.[61] This is an important factor underlying the tendency to concentration and centralisation. But, besides this tendency towards vertical integration, there is also a counter-tendency towards disintegration. For one thing, new units of capital are constantly arising. For another, the more sections of the production chain that are incorporated within an enterprise, the longer its turnover time, that is, the more time elapses before there is a return on investment. Vertical integration also removes the option of displacing the economic risks of implementing untested technologies and declining markets to suppliers and distributors. The ability to displace the problems that arise from managing workforces whose work conditions are exceptionally dire is also abandoned. There is a point beyond which gains from further vertical integration do not compensate for longer turnover time, increased economic risk, and greater management problems. Past this point, the drive to accumulate capital tends to result in a disintegration of production processes:

> [N]ot only are accumulation and the concentration accompanying it scattered over many points, but the increase of each functioning capital is thwarted by the formation of new capitals and the subdivision of old. Accumulation, therefore, presents itself on the one hand as increasing concentration of the

---

[60] Units of capital operating in the world market have always been at the very centre of capitalist development (see Arrighi 1994 and Arrighi and Silver 1999). What has changed in recent decades is the proportion of units of capital directly participating in cross-border networks of production and distribution.

[61] Marx 1963, pp. 140, 220.

means of production, and of the command over labour; and on the other hand as repulsion of many individual capitals from one another.[62]

In the course of capital accumulation, the geographical scale of operation of hegemonic firms necessarily tends to expand, with vertical integration taking the form of extensive foreign direct investment and cross-border mergers and acquisitions. The accompanying counter-tendency to disintegration also affects the world market. Disintegration is a matter of breaking up the production chain into various parts, and assigning different sections to different firms. Whenever core firms can accumulate capital at a faster rate through outsourcing parts of the production chain to foreign suppliers, there is a necessary tendency for such cross-border subcontracting arrangements to be implemented. Which tendency is stronger in a particular context depends on a myriad of contingent circumstances.[63]

The accumulation process involves flows of labour as well as capital flows. Massive pools of labour-power form and disperse in response to the rhythms of capital accumulation and 'the desires of the multitude'.[64] These flows are as essential to the capital/wage-labour relation as the sale of labour-power and the organisation of the labour process. In Volume I, Marx emphasises how vast reserves of unemployed wage-labourers arise in regions where capital accumulation is limited, generating pressures to emigrate to regions where the pace of accumulation is more rapid. Marx's discussion of emigration from Ireland in the nineteenth century remains a paradigmatic account of this dimension of the accumulation process.[65] These cross-border labour flows simultaneously tend to exacerbate divisions within the work force and to transcend such divisions over time. Once again, systematic theory cannot deduce which tendency will prove stronger in any given historical context.

A main theme of Volume II concerns the time spent in circulation by the various forms of capital. Circulation costs are deductions from the surplus-

---

[62] Marx 1976, pp. 776–7; see also Marx 1976, p. 591; Harvey 1999, pp. 139–50; Smith 2000a, Chapter 5.

[63] Harvey 1999.

[64] Hardt and Negri 2000.

[65] Marx 1976, pp. 854 ff. The explanatory and political importance of these flows of labour in the 'new global paradigm' is stressed by Hardt and Negri, who rightly insist that 'the mobility does carry for capital a high price, however, which is the increased desire for liberation'. Hardt and Negri 2000, p. 253.

value that could potentially be accumulated in a given period. Reductions in circulation time tend to lower these costs. And, so, reducing the turnover time of capital tends to increase the accumulation of surplus-value. The drive to introduce communications and transportation technologies in the circulation process is thus no less intrinsic to the capitalist mode of production than the tendency to introduce innovations at the point of production. These innovations allow capital to proceed through its circuits more quickly and enable the geographical reach within which overlapping circuits of capital can effectively operate to be extended. They thus necessarily tend to lead to a compression of both time and space.[66] When we turn to another main topic of Volume II, the flows of investment capital and purchases of commodities connecting 'Department I' (devoted to the production of means of production) with 'Department II' (where means of consumption are produced), the tendency to develop these technologies reinforces the thesis that the systematic reproduction of total social capital is implicitly reproduction on the level of the world market. To mention only one example, as the scale of capital production grows through the concentration and centralisation of capital, it becomes increasingly unlikely that the raw materials found in any restricted geographical region will be sufficient for production in that region. Thus, there is a necessary tendency for the reproduction of total social capital to involve cross-border purchases of raw materials.[67]

In Volume III, total social capital is disaggregated into a multiplicity of sectors with different value compositions of capital, that is, different ratios between the amount of money capital invested in the purchase of means of production ('constant capital', or 'C') and the amount invested in the purchase of labour-power ('variable capital', 'V'). Marx notes that, if commodities are exchanged at cost prices plus the surplus-value ('S') produced in the given sector (C+V+S), different industries would have wildly divergent rates of profit, assuming for the sake of the argument that the rates of exploitation

---

[66] Harvey 1999.
[67] Marx 1968, p. 437. A series of historical tragedies is associated with this systematic feature of capital: 'The cheapness of the articles produced by machinery and the revolution in the means of transportation and communication provide the weapons for the conquest of foreign markets. By ruining handicraft production of finished articles in other countries, machinery forcibly converts them into fields for the production of its raw material'. Marx 1976, p. 579.

are equal. Sectors with a relatively high value composition would have a low rate of profit, and vice-versa.[68] Capital mobility and inter-capital competition, however, generate a tendency for rates of profit to equalise across sectors.[69] As capital investment flows away from sectors with lower rates of profit, and towards sectors where profit rates are higher, competitive pressures lessen in the former and increase in the latter, generating a tendency for rates of profit to increase and decrease, respectively. On the present level of abstraction, commodities produced by industrial capitals thus tend to sell at prices of production $P=(C+V)(1+R)$, with 'R' defined as a rate of profit tending to hold equally across sectors in the given period.[70] These prices of production are conceived as centres of gravity around which market prices revolve, depending on temporary contingencies of supply and demand and other factors to be considered at more concrete levels. For Marx, prices of production are the result of a (logical) redistribution of surplus-value within the given period. Before and after the consideration of this redistribution, total profits are equal to total surplus-value.[71] While the connection of profits to the exploitation of wage-labour may be quite opaque on this level of analysis, the connection remains nonetheless. Conceptualising profits as the form in which surplus-value appears captures both the inter-class relation between capital and wage-labour (the production of surplus-value), and the intra-class relations among capitals (the redistribution of surplus-value in the form of profits). In the capitalist global order, there is a systematic tendency for commodities to be produced and traded across borders, and for investment capital to flow across borders as well. It follows at once that the prices of production

---

[68] An analogous point holds for sectors with equal rates of exploitation, but different rates of turnover (Marx 1981, p. 250).

[69] Other factors are relevant as well, including labour-power mobility, a reserve army, and the credit system. See Weeks 1981, p. 162; and Marx 1981, pp. 566, 742.

[70] 'R' is fixed on the level of aggregate social capital explored in Volume I, that is, $R=S/(C+V)$ with 'S', 'C', and 'V' defined with reference to the total social capital: '[T]aking all other circumstances as given . . . the average rate of profit depends on the level of exploitation of labour as a whole by capital as a whole'. Marx 1981, p. 299; see Moseley 1993b, p. 172. According to this formula, units of capital in sectors with a higher than average organic composition of capital tend to have prices of production that exceed C+V+S, while those in sectors with a lower than average organic composition of capital will tend to have prices of production below the sum of the cost price and the surplus-value produced in that sector.

[71] Moseley 1993b.

discussed in Volume III necessarily tend to be formed on the level of the world market:

> The industrial capitalist faces the world market; [he] therefore compares and must constantly compare his own cost-price with market prices not only at home, but also on the whole market of the world. He always produces taking this into account.[72]

On a yet more complex and concrete level of Volume III, Marx introduces merchant and financial capital. Owners of both merchant capital and financial capital typically enjoy returns on their investments. Marx insists that the profits of commercial and financial capital, and the rents enjoyed by owners of land, also derive from a (logical) redistribution of surplus-value.[73] They, too, ultimately rest on the exploitation of wage-labour in commodity production.[74] To grant scraps of paper, heaps of precious metals, or soil and rocks, the power to determine inter-class and intra-class social relations is to fall into the fetishism of granting social powers to things. This redistribution

---

[72] Marx 1971, p. 470. In particular concrete contexts, this tendency can be modified or put out of play by other tendencies that also emerge from the essential determinations of capital. In *Theories of Surplus-Value 2*, for example, Marx writes that 'In itself, the assumption that variations in the price of wages in England, for instance, would alter the [price of production] of gold in California where wages have not risen, is utterly absurd. The levelling out of *values* by labour-time and even less the levelling out of [production prices T.S.] by a general rate of profit does not take place in this direct form between different countries'. Marx 1968, p. 201. (In *Theories of Surplus-Value*, Marx uses the term 'cost prices' to refer to what he later referred to as 'prices of production' in *Capital*. I have inserted the latter term in brackets for the sake of terminological consistency.) Later in this same work, however, he states that 'where commercial speculations figure from the start and production is intended for the world market [and] the capitalist mode of production exists. . . . So long as these condition endure, nothing will stand in the way of [price of production] regulating market-value'. Marx 1968, pp. 302–3. In this passage, which clearly refers to the dominant path of capitalist development, the formation of prices of production occurs ultimately on the level of the world market. See Shaikh 1979, 1979/80.

[73] With respect to rent from land, it would be more accurate to say that it is explained by a *failure* to redistribute surplus-value. Monopoly ownership of land traps surplus-value within an agricultural circuit of capital. The part of the produced surplus-value that would otherwise flow into different circuits for redistribution is appropriated by landlords in the form of rent, with the remainder retained by capitalist agricultural producers receiving the average rate of profit.

[74] 'The whole contradiction between industrial profit and interest only has meaning as a contradiction between the rentier and the industrial capitalist, but it has not the slightest bearing on the relationship of the worker to capital, the nature of capital, or the origin of the profit capital yields'. Marx 1971, p. 359.

implicitly takes place on the level of the world market as well, given that international flows of capital include flows of merchant and financial capital, as well as various forms of rent.[75]

6. The role of surplus profits from innovation

Each of the positions considered in Part One of this work suffered from an implicit immanent contradiction between the claims to efficiency and normative attractiveness asserted of a particular model of globalisation and the systematic tendencies of the global capitalist order incorporated in that same model. The most important of these are the tendencies towards overaccumulation crises, financial crises, and uneven development. The ordering of the Marxian model of capitalist globalisation after the positions considered in Part One is justified only if it can be shown that this model explicitly takes these tendencies into account. Marx's notion of surplus profits from innovation is a decisive part of this story. Unlike 'money', 'exploitation', or 'prices of production', this category does not define a distinct theoretical level considered separately in *Capital*. Nonetheless, the notion plays such a pivotal role in Marx's account of the dynamism of the capital-form that it is worth examining separately in some detail.

In Volume I, Marx notes how innovations increasing the rate of relative surplus-value further accumulation on the level of the total social capital. While introduced by particular units of capital, they are functional for the capitalist class as a whole. But we cannot simply assume that individual units of capital automatically act in a manner furthering the interests of capital as a whole. And, so, Marx discusses how individual units of capital introducing productivity advances are able to appropriate surplus profits above the social average, *ceteris paribus*. This provides individual units of capital with the motivation to engage in behaviour furthering the collective interests of capital.[76] Innovations lessening circulation time, reducing constant capital costs, and improving productivity in the commercial capital, financial capital, and agricultural sectors also tend to further accumulation on the level of the total

---

[75] Harvey 2001.
[76] See Marx 1981, pp. 299–300.

social capital. They too are not pursued by individual units of capital for this reason, but in the hope that the individual units of capital pursing them will eventually be able to appropriate surplus profits.

Marx abstracts from the pursuit of surplus profits by individual units of capital throughout most of the three volumes of *Capital*. In most contexts, individual capitals are simply taken as 'an *aliquot* part' of either the total social capital or a particular sector. When the category 'prices of production' is considered more closely, however, matters become more complicated. On this level of abstraction, all units of capital tend to receive a share in the appropriation of surplus-value directly proportional to their size (in other words, an equal rate of profit), regardless of divergences in the value composition of capital or turnover time in different sectors.[77] This tendency is rooted in the mobility of individual units of capital in response to price signals. Whenever different sectors enjoy different rates of profit, market competition leads to a re-allocation of capital from low-profit to high-profit sectors, raising rates in the former and lowering them in the latter. The end result is a (logical) redistribution of surplus-value. The form of competition that attains this result may be termed 'weak competition', since all units of capital that were present initially remain standing, and all enjoy the same rate of profit. But Marx's account of prices of production in Volume III also invokes what may be termed 'strong competition', in which size is no guarantee of survival, let alone a proportional share of surplus-value. In strong competition, 'victory' is defined as winning surplus profits while forcing devaluation upon one's opponents: 'loss is divided very unevenly . . . one capital lies idle, another is destroyed'.[78] Innovations are powerful weapons in this war onto death.

However, 'surplus profits from innovations' remains a subordinate category in this discussion, as the notion of 'cancelling out' in the following passage suggests:

> The capitalist who employs improved but not yet universally used methods
> of production sells below the market price, but above his individual price
> of production; his profit rate thus rises, until competition cancels this out.[79]

---

[77] Marx 1981, p. 258.
[78] Marx 1981, p. 362.
[79] Marx 1981, p. 338.

'Cancelling out' implies that surplus profits from innovations are temporary, with the tendency for rates of profit to equalise across sectors of industrial capital remaining dominant. Marx's subsequent discussion of the (logical) redistribution of surplus-value to commercial capital, financial capital, and landlords reinforces this impression.[80] This is not the whole story, however.

Marx's account of the production and distribution of surplus-value in any given period takes prices of production as the long-run centres of gravity for market prices. But reflection on the dynamism of the capitalist mode of production suggests that this holds true only on relatively abstract theoretical levels. This point can be elaborated by referring to Marx's discussion of capitalist historical development.

In Volume I, there is a long discussion of the evolution from the early factory through manufacturing to machinofacture. The early factory arose when a number of wage-labourers were placed under the direct supervision of a capitalist or his representative. In manufacturing, this 'formal subsumption' of wage-labour under capital gave way to a 'real subsumption' in which control of the labour process was taken away from the worker. The labour process was fragmented whenever possible, with each distinct part assigned to a separate worker (the 'detail labourer'). This process of real subsumption was continued with the rise of machinofacture ('big industry'). Many of the routinised activities of wage-labourers were now taken over by steam-driven machines, to whose rhythms the work force had to adjust. In the present context, the main point to emphasise is that *the transition from one stage to the next in this historical progression does not occur uniformly in all industries.* New industries emerge in a given historical period, grow as that period declines,

---

[80] For Marx, there is a systematic tendency for the rate of profit to equalise between industrial and commercial capital (Marx 1981, p. 429). The cases of financial capital and rent are somewhat more complex. Interest rates, for example, are the contingent result of the particular balance of supply and demand for money capital in the given period. So the rate of return on loans of money capital may not equalise with the rate of profit holding in sectors of industrial capital (Itoh and Lapavitsas 1999, pp. 70–1). Similarly, the amount of rent appropriated by landlords is affected by a myriad of contingent matters, especially the level of demand for agricultural commodities relative to the level of agricultural productivity on different lands. Here, too, there is no systematic necessity that the rate of returns to landlords will tend to equalise with the rate of profit of sectors of industrial capital. (But as note 73 mentioned, on this level of abstraction, Marx does assume that there is a tendency for rates of return to capitalist agriculture undertaken on rented lands to equalise.)

and become hegemonic in the succeeding period, even as many of the dominant industries from the previous stage disappear and others operate on a greatly diminished scale.

Prices of production cannot be the centres of gravity for market prices throughout this extended transition. If firms in both leading and declining industries tended to enjoy the same rate of profit throughout, if they both tended to receive returns directly proportional to the size of their capital investments, then investment capital would not tend to flow towards the one and away from the other over this extended period. But that is precisely what happens in the transition from one epoch in capitalist development to the next.

A more detailed analysis of technological dynamism and its relationship to value theory reinforces this conclusion. Consider again the passage quoted earlier in which Marx refers to the process whereby 'the form of a machine becomes settled':

> It is only after a considerable development of the science of mechanics, and an accumulation of practical experience, that the form of a machine becomes settled entirely in accordance with mechanical principles, and emancipated from the traditional form of the tool from which it has emerged.[81]

The sequence of innovations in machinery introduced by various units of industrial capital thus has a basic trajectory.[82] This pattern is a function of material (use-value) considerations, including both the principles discovered in the course of scientific labour and the practical experience of workers at the point of production. These use-value considerations clearly possess a value dimension as well:

> If the productivity of labour has increased in the place where these instruments of labour are constructed (and it does develop continually, owing to the uninterrupted advance of science and technology), the old machines, tools,

---

[81] Marx 1976, p. 505.

[82] The notion of 'technological trajectories' or 'paradigms' is central to the work of contemporary neo- Schumpeterians. In this view, technologies 'develop along relatively ordered paths shaped by the technical properties, the problem-solving heuristics, and the cumulative expertise embodied in *technological paradigms*'. Dosi and Orsenigo 1988, p. 16. As the passage in the main text show, this concept is already explicit in Marx (see Smith 2004).

apparatus, etc. will be replaced by more efficient and (considering their increased efficiency), cheaper ones. . . . Like the increased exploitation of natural wealth resulting from the simple act of increasing the pressure under which labour-power has to operate, *science and technology give capital a power of expansion which is independent of the given magnitude of the capital actually functioning*. They react at the same time on that part of the original capital which has entered the stage of renewal.[83]

There is no systematic reason whatsoever to assume that innovation trajectories will tend to be the same in all sectors. There is every reason to think that they will be 'steeper' in some sectors than others, as 'science . . . and an accumulation of practical experience' uncover a wider range of possibilities for innovation in some sectors than others.[84]

The notion of 'technological systems' is also relevant to the present discussion. It refers to cases where technical advances originating in one sector can be employed to improve productivity or quality levels in a number of different sectors. The significance of this phenomenon was fully grasped by Marx. Regarding the diffusions of innovations that reduce constant capital costs he wrote:

[T]he development of the productive power of labour in *one* branch of production, e.g. of iron, coal, machines, construction, etc., which may in turn be partly connected with advances in the area of intellectual production, i.e. the natural sciences and their application, appears as the condition for a reduction in the value and hence of the costs of means of production in *other* branches of industry, e.g. textiles or agriculture. This is evident enough, for the commodity that emerges from one branch of industry as a product enters another branch as means of production. Its cheapness or otherwise depends on the productivity of labour in the branch of production from which it emerges as a product, and is at the same time a condition not only for the cheapening of the commodities into the production of which it enters as means of production, but also for the reduction in value of the constant capital whose element it now becomes, and therefore for an increase in the rate of profit.[85]

[83] Marx 1981, pp. 753–4 (emphasis added).
[84] Marx 1981, p. 505; see also p. 894.
[85] Marx 1981, pp. 174; see also pp. 175, 177, 179, 266.

No one would ever assume that innovations in all sectors have the same importance for the system of capital accumulation as a whole. Innovations arising in certain sectors will have profound positive spillover effects for units of capital dispersed throughout the economy. Innovations in other industries will lack these consequences, however successful they may be on their own terms.[86]

If we combine the notions of innovation trajectories and innovation systems, the problem considered at the beginning of this discussion can be posed once again. If prices of production were, in fact, the final long-run centres of gravity for market prices, such that all sectors tended to enjoy equal rates of profit, then there would be no systematic drive to shift investment towards sectors with steep innovation trajectories, or towards those with huge potential implications for the system of accumulation as a whole, and away from sectors with less steep trajectories and fewer foreseeable system implications. But the valorisation imperative that is the organising principle of capitalist society demands that investments flow in precisely these directions. Different industries thus have different 'warranted rates of growth'.[87] Marx's theory of the technological dynamism of capitalism implies that units of capital operating in sectors with a greater horizon of scientific-technological possibilities, and/or a greater potential to improve productivity in numerous industries, will tend to accumulate capital at a faster rate than other units of capital over an extended period of time.

This issue of time is obviously crucial here. Marx himself certainly recognised that different sectors have different warranted rates of growth, and thus different rates of profit:

> Since the development of labour productivity is far from uniform in the various branches of industry and, besides being uneven in degree, often takes place in opposite directions, it so happens that the mass of average profit (= surplus-value) is necessarily very far below the level one would expect simply from the development of productivity in the most advanced branches. . . . [T]he development of productivity in different branches of industry does not just proceed in very different proportions, but often also in opposite directions.[88]

---

[86] See Freeman et al., 1982; Rosenberg and Frischtak, 1983; Kleinknecht, 1987.
[87] Walker 1988, pp. 169–72.
[88] Marx 1981, pp. 368–9.

Marx, however, seems to have assumed here too that the different warranted rates of growth in different sectors are short-to-medium term phenomena that do not modify the medium-to-long term tendencies holding on the level of prices of production:

> Something that must also be considered here, however, is the cycle of fat and lean years that follow one another in a given branch of industry over a particular period of time, and the fluctuations in profit that these involve. This uninterrupted emigration and immigration of capitals that takes place between various spheres of production produces rising and falling movements in the profit rate which more or less balance one another out and thus tend to reduce the profit rate everywhere to the same common and general level.[89]

But, if our temporal horizon time is, say, the extended transition from the period of the early factory to the manufacturing epoch, or the transition from manufacturing to big industry, there is no reason whatsoever to posit a tendency for the profit rate to reduce 'everywhere to the same common and general level'. The leading industries of a preceding period and those associated with the succeeding one surely tend to enjoy quite different rates of profit and growth over the course of these transitions. Similarly, differences in the slope of innovation trajectories, and in the impact of innovations on the economy as a whole, are *not* necessarily short-to-medium-term phenomena. The most dynamic sectors of the economy generally enjoy advantages in these two areas that last throughout an extended historical epoch, a 'long wave'.[90]

It is perfectly legitimate to abstract from such matters when we consider the production of surplus-value and its (logical) redistribution among capitals and landlords in a given period. But, once we move to a more concrete and complex stage in the dialectic of capital, we cannot continue to abstract from

---

[89] Marx 1981, p. 310.

[90] Long-wave theory is a quite contested field. For present purposes, I do not have to take a stand on many of the issues in dispute, such as the relevant weight of 'technology push' (Schumpeter 1939), 'demand pull' (Schmookler 1966), class struggle (Mandel 1972, pp. 130 ff.), and the state (Arrighi 1994) in explanations of long waves of capital expansion and decline. It is not even necessary to assert that long-wave theory provides the best framework for comprehending capitalist economic history (see Webber and Rigby 1996, Chapter 3). It is sufficient to note that all of the contending parties in these disputes grant that new periods of expansion are associated with the rise of new industries enjoying higher than average rates of growth for an extended time.

differences in the warranted growth rates of different sectors. The emergence and persistence of such differences are essential features of capital's dynamism. They are not mere contingencies of history, mere 'inessential, accidental circumstances that cancel each other out'.[91] They are tendencies that necessarily arise from the essential determinations of the capital-form.

If this is granted, it follows that we need to introduce explicitly a theoretical level in Marxian theory that 'transforms' the tendencies regarding profits and prices holding on more abstract and simple levels. The two dominant tendencies on the level of prices of production are for rates of profit to equalise and for prices of production to serve as centres of gravity for market prices. These tendencies are not modified with the introduction of the logical redistribution of surplus-value between industrial capital and commercial capital, financial capital, and landlord rent. But, with the move to the level of surplus profits due to innovations in leading sectors, where notions such as 'innovation trajectories', 'technology systems', and 'warranted rates of growth' have their proper systematic place, rates of profit do not tend to equalise in the relevant time period. And prices of production $[P=(C+V)(1+R)]$ are *not* the centres of gravity for market prices.

On the relatively abstract level of prices of production, the flow of capital into higher-profit areas tends to equalise profit rates, and unequal profit rates reflect barriers to capital mobility. On the level of surplus profits from innovation, in contrast, capital investment unlocks the growth potential in certain industries, a growth potential that is not identical across sectors.[92] And, so, the mobility of capital investment now necessarily tends to lead to uneven rates of growth in the economy, reflected in different rates of profit across sectors.[93] This is a *transformation*, not a mere complication, of the general tendency holding on the level of prices of production and retained in Marx's subsequent discussion of the logical redistribution of surplus-value between

---

[91] Marx 1981, p. 252.

[92] Marx 1981, p. 166.

[93] This point is overlooked by Weeks: 'Competition tends to equalize returns by industry and also to generate unequal returns within industries. . . . The tendency for the rate of profit to equalize hides a fiercely competitive struggle within industries between the strong and the weak'. Weeks 1981, p. 172. Reflection on innovation trajectories and technological systems suggests that there are strong and weak *sectors*, not just strong and weak individual units of capital within sectors.

industrial capital, on the one hand, and commercial capital, financial capital, and landowners, on the other.

If the dominant tendencies regarding profits are transformed, there are implications for the theory of prices as well. Once we drop the assumption that warranted growth rates and profit rates are identical in all sectors, we must also drop the assumption that market prices revolve around prices of production $P=(C+V)(1+R)$. On a more concrete theoretical level, market prices instead revolve around a different centre of gravity, which Walker terms 'prices of expanded reproduction'. While prices of production involve a redistribution of surplus-value towards those units of capital operating in sectors with higher-than-average organic compositions of capital (or longer than average turnover times), prices of expanded reproduction redistribute surplus-value to units in sectors with above-average rates of warranted growth and above-average profit rates. For any sector i, the formula for prices of expanded reproduction will be $Pi=(Ci+Vi)(1+Ri)$; as profit rates differ, so too do these prices.[94] Walker's reasoning here is compelling:

> I suggest the term *prices of expanded reproduction* to capture the dynamic element. That is, centres of gravity are now set by long run conditions of uneven growth in different industries, which are determined by the real terms of production, but in a way that includes change. Unit costs (and behind them, labour-time) are still the foundation for price formation, but in a way that combines both levels in the present and change over time. Surplus-value is still generated from labour and reallocated among industries, not just in terms of already invested capital and its composition, but in terms of *future* build up of production in faster- and slower-growing industries.[95]

---

[94] Unlike prices of production, this formula for prices of expanded reproduction is general enough to be modified at later stages of the theory, where other factors systematically affecting prices are introduced, such as monopoly power, state taxes and subsidies, unequal exchange across national borders, and so on. None of these modifications calls into question the central claim that 'taking all other circumstances as given . . . the average rate of profit depends on the level of exploitation of labour as a whole by capital as a whole'. Marx 1981, p. 299.

[95] Walker 1988, p. 167. This perspective contrasts with the received view in Marxian theory that 'the law of value achieves its fullest development under capitalist conditions' with prices of production. Itoh and Lapavitsas 1999, p. 40.

Industries with higher growth trajectories consequently have higher prices (relative to unit costs), not so much because of their present organic composition, but because they are able to generate revenues for future expansion. Weak competition, which tends to lower prices (relative to unit costs) in higher-profit sectors, does not dominate here. In the most dynamic sectors, unit costs may fall quite rapidly, so prices can remain high relative to unit costs and yet still be falling in absolute terms. Prices may not even fall at all if the new products produced in these sectors are in sufficient demand.[96] This is generally the case for innovations that play a crucial role in technology systems, that is, innovations that have a significant impact on productivity throughout the economy. Also, the most dynamic industries in capitalism are often more concerned with creating new markets than with meeting pre-existing market demands. Price competition is secondary to new use-value considerations in such cases.

One of the main reasons for ordering the Marxian model of capitalist globalisation after the positions considered in Part One in the systematic dialectic is that this model explicitly takes into account the tendencies to overaccumulation crises, financial crises, and uneven development. The drive to appropriate surplus profits through innovation is a key premise in the argument that these tendencies are inherent features of the capitalist global order, as the following section will establish.

7. Crises and uneven development

In *Capital*, Volume III, Marx sketches a number of factors that may lead to disruptions of capital accumulation, including the need to replace fixed capital, interruptions in trade credits, foolish monetary policies, and so on. It is possible to construct at least a rough outline of a theory of short-to-medium-term economic cycles from these scattered remarks. The seeds of a different sort of theory are also found in Volume III, a theory that takes as its object more serious and extended downswings in the rhythm of capital accumulation. Raw materials for this theory are found in Marx's discussion of the tendency for the rate of profit to fall and in the chapters devoted to financial capital, both of which presuppose the category 'surplus profits from innovation'.

---

[96] Walker 1988, p. 172.

In Part Three of Volume III, Marx introduces the so-called law of the tendency of the rate of profit to fall. While various factors behind capitalist crises are explored at different points in Marx's writings, in this crucial text Marx assigns the overwhelming weight to the overaccumulation of fixed capital; the rate of profit tends to fall because C/V increases at a faster rate than the rate of exploitation, S/V.[97] While this law comes into play in short-to-medium-term cyclical downswings, I believe that Marx also meant it to apply to more long-term downturns in capital accumulation.

Critics of this tendency law have complained that Marx fails to provide a plausible explanation why rational agents would invest in ways that lower profits. As long as all units of capital within a sector are treated as homogeneous, the complaint holds. But individual units of capital necessarily tend to seek surplus profits through innovation. Geert Reuten has shown that the resulting heterogeneity and differences in fixed capital within sectors allow us to provide the microfoundations called for by Marx's critics. The importance of this topic to the study of tendencies in the global economy more than justifies returning to his argument, first introduced in Chapter 4.

In general, older production facilities in any given sector have a lower value composition of capital (that is, a smaller ratio between investment in means of production and investment in labour) and a lower level of labour productivity. With output prices assumed uniform in the sector, firms owning these facilities also appropriate lower profit rates from operating them. Suppose an existing stratification extends from plant 1 to plant n, and then assume that some new plant n+1 with a higher value composition and a higher level of labour productivity is added to the sector stratification. It will enjoy lower unit costs, and hence be able to win surplus profits. From the standpoint of this individual unit of capital, it was quite rational to enter the sector in question. As plant n+1 wins market share, this forces some of the oldest units of capital, plants 1 to h, say, to withdraw from the sector. But it is not necessarily rational for all plants to withdraw from a sector when a new, more productive, competitor enters. Nor is it necessarily rational for all the remaining plants to adopt immediately the new technical innovation introduced by plant n+1. Plants h to n have made previous investments in fixed capital that they may not wish to write off. It can be rational for them to remain in operation as

---

[97] Clarke 1994.

long as the prices they receive are sufficient to cover their operating costs, that is, as long as they receive the average rate of profit on their circulating capital. The lower unit costs of the leading plant tend to bring down the output prices of the sector as a whole, leading Reuten to conclude,

> [B]ecause investments and costs are unaffected whilst revenue decreases, the rate of profit of the capital accumulated in the remaining part of the previous stratification (1+h, . . . , n) decreases. That of the capital invested in the new plant (n+1) tends at the new price to increase, as compared with the average rate of profit (1, . . . , n) at the previous price, or with the rate of profit of the plant just below it in the stratification, n, at the previous price. Since the new plant (n+1) operates at lower production costs than the previous plant (n), then in any case the rate of profit of the new plant capital at the new price is above that of the nth and the average rate of profit. (This is in fact sufficient for the argument.) Because with the additional plant the average VCC [value composition of capital] tends to increase, the average rate of profit tends to decrease.[98]

This argument, however, only shows that, in any given sector, there is a tendency for the value composition of capital to increase (due to the entry of a plant with a high value composition and the exit of units with low value compositions) to the point where the surplus-value produced in that sector is not sufficient to valorise the total capital invested in that sector at the previous average rate of profit. There is nothing that suggests that different sectors will necessarily tend to reach this point simultaneously. There is thus nothing in this argument to suggest there is a tendency in capitalism for a general fall in the rate of profit, as opposed to random declines in particular sectors that may well be compensated by upswings in other sectors. Something more is required.

The notion of individual capitals winning surplus profits *within* sectors as a result of innovation is not sufficient. We need to introduce differences *among*

---

[98] Reuten 1991, p. 87; see Reuten and Williams 1989, pp. 135–8. This argument assumes a constant rate of surplus-value; on this level of abstraction, changes in the rate of surplus-value are due to changes in the ratio of unemployed workers to the reserve army of the unemployed, and this ratio is unaffected by the above considerations. Reuten 1991, p. 88 n. 2.

sectors based on the appropriation of surplus profits through innovation.[99] The notion of leading sectors in a particular 'long wave' of capital expansion justifies the assumption that the process described by Reuten occurs in the most important sectors of the capitalist economy more or less simultaneously, so that there is a tendency in the economy as a whole for the value composition of capital to increase to the point where the surplus-value produced in the economy is not sufficient to valorise the total social capital at the previous average rate of profit.[100]

Overaccumulation crises were introduced in Part One as an essential feature of capitalist production and property relations, undermining the claims to efficiency and normative attractiveness defended by advocates of the models considered there. This tendency is of profound importance for a systematic comprehension of the world market. Marx himself discusses the tendency to overaccumulation crises on a relatively abstract theoretical level in Volume III. But it holds on the concrete and complex level of the world market as well.[101] Robert Brenner has provided considerable empirical evidence that the

---

[99] See the attempts to integrate the dynamic of innovation in leading sectors with a long wave theory of over-investment in van Duijn 1983 and Kleinknecht 1987, pp. 208–9.

[100] This is no more than a provisional derivation of the systematic tendency to overaccumulation crises. One complicating factor is that the process described by Reuten involves a decline in output prices for fixed capital, which, in turn, implies a subsequent decline in input prices for fixed capital, thereby counteracting the increase in the value composition of capital. Reuten 1991, pp. 88–9. Does this imply that Marx's emphasis on a rising value composition as a medium-to-long-term difficulty is misplaced? The justification for a negative answer rests on the theory of the capitalist state. As the concentration and centralisation of capital proceeds, the negative effects of an extensive devaluation of previous investment in fixed capital become more and more serious to the national economy as a whole. At a certain point, the state will attempt to avoid devaluation through higher levels of direct and indirect subsidies, lower rates of effective corporate taxation, labour regulations that shift the balance of class forces in favour of capital, deficit spending to prop up growth rates, negotiations regarding currency exchange rates, and so on. These sorts of measures aim at limiting and socialising the costs of devaluation in order to buy time for established capitals to restructure. But 'restructuring' means adopting yet higher value compositions of capital themselves, that is, introducing some plant n+2. In this manner the process described above begins again on a higher level: while it is rational for plant n+2 to enter the sector, it may also be rational for plants h+y, . . . , n+1 to remain. The immediate result, once again, is a higher value composition of capital such that the surplus-value produced is not sufficient to valorise the total social capital at the previous rate of profit. The ultimate result is a need for devaluation on a yet more extensive level.

[101] '[T]he more capitalist production develops, the more it is forced to produce on a scale which has nothing to do with the immediate demand but depends on a constant

lower rates of growth afflicting the world economy beginning in the late 1960s was primarily due to excess capacity in the leading sectors of the global economy.[102] As the concentration and centralisation of capital proceeds, the overaccumulation of capital necessarily tends to occur on an ever-more massive scale. Global turbulence and generalised economic insecurity increasingly become the normal state of affairs.

Marx's remarks on financial capital in Volume III are extremely fragmentary and unpolished. One major theme has already been noted: in any given period, financial capital benefits from the (logical) redistribution of surplus-value, a process that implicitly occurs in the framework of the world market. There is also at least the broad outline of a theory (or at least a set of stylised facts) relating the financial sector to overaccumulation crises.

In the above discussion of the tendency to overaccumulation crises, the entry of new units of capital into the leading sectors of the economy is a crucial factor. The drive for surplus profits motivated this entry, and we simply presupposed that sufficient funds were available for new investments. From where do these investment funds come? We cannot rely on the retained earnings of established firms in this sector. They may not wish to devalue previous investments in fixed capital, or they may lack the resources to take full advantage of high potential 'warranted rates of growth'. Financial capital centralises a pool of investment funds that with relative ease can be shifted to fund new plants in sectors with a reasonable expectation of being able to appropriate surplus profits for an extended period of time.[103] As Marx explicitly notes, flows of financial capital from across the world market tend to be centralised in a few points at the centre of a global financial order, and then allocated across borders as well. With credit money, the extension of credit to new plants and sectors can be a multiple of the temporarily idle profits, depreciation funds, and precautionary reserves pooled in the finance sector.[104] In this manner, finance capital 'appears as the principal lever of overproduction and excessive speculation in commerce'.[105]

---

expansion of the world market'. Marx 1968, p. 468. Sooner or later, this expansion is insufficient to valorise the accumulated fixed capital.
[102] Brenner 1998, 2002; see also Smith 2000b.
[103] Marx 1981, p. 567.
[104] Mandel 1975; Bellofiore, 1989.
[105] Marx 1981, p. 572; see also Marx 1971, p. 122.

Once an overaccumulation crisis commences, the rate of investment in sectors suffering overcapacity problems slows significantly. A large pool of investment capital is formed once again, now seeking new sectors with a potential for high future rates of growth.[106] When such sectors are found, financial capital throughout the world market will tend to flow in their direction. If the flows of investment capital to these new sectors are high enough, a systematic tendency to capital asset inflation results. Expectations of future earnings eventually become a secondary matter, as financial assets are purchased in the hope of profits from later sales of these assets.[107] This tendency is then reinforced as previous (paper) gains in capital assets are used as collateral for borrowings to fund further purchases of capital assets, setting off yet more rapid capital asset inflation.[108] Throughout the course of this speculative bubble, however, it remains the case that financial assets remain in essence nothing but claims on the future production of surplus-value.[109] When it becomes overwhelmingly clear that their ever increasing prices are ever less likely to be redeemed by future profits, the speculative bubble collapses and a financial crisis ensues.

The discussion of financial capital in Volume III is one of the handful of places where Marx describes in detail how the social forms examined in *Capital* ultimately operate on the level of the world market. The financial crises he considers were not contained within the geographical borders defining England or any other particular national economy.

The intertwining of the tendencies to overaccumulation crises and financial crises implies that the impact of concentration and centralisation on the former extends to the latter as well. The devaluation of loans and fictitious capital following in the wage of financial crises necessarily tends to occur on an ever more massive scale. Units, networks, and regions of capital attempt to shift the costs of this devaluation on to other units, networks, and regions. Most of all, capital attempts to shift as much of the cost as possible onto wage-labourers and their communities. Global turbulence and generalised economic insecurity increasingly pervade the world market, justifying Marx's assertions

---

[106] de Brunhoff 1978, p. 47.
[107] Marx 1981, pp. 615–16, 742.
[108] Guttmann 1994, pp. 303–4; see also Toporowski 2000.
[109] Bonefeld and Holloway, 1995.

that, '[T]he most complicated phenomenon of capitalist production [are] the world market crises', and 'The world trade crises must be regarded as the real concentration and forcible adjustment of all the contradictions of bourgeois economy'.[110]

The Marxian account of the drive for surplus profits through innovation also provides the single best theoretical foundation for comprehending the tendency to uneven development in the capitalist global economy. Here, too, the importance of the argument to the study of globalisation justifies some repetition of points already made in Part One.

Research and development is obviously a crucial precondition for the process and product innovations that enable surplus profits to be appropriated.[111] Units of capital with access to advanced R&D are consequently best positioned to win this form of surplus profits. They are thus also best positioned to establish a virtuous circle in which surplus profits provide the funds necessary to operate at or near the scientific-technical frontier in the future, an important precondition for the appropriation of future surplus profits. In contrast, units of capital without initial access to advanced R&D tend to be trapped in a vicious circle. Their resulting inability to introduce significant innovations prevents an appropriation of surplus profits, which tends to limit their ability to participate in advanced R&D in the succeeding period, which in turn limits future innovations and future profit opportunities. The units of capital with the most access to advanced R&D, by definition, tend to be clustered in wealthy regions of the global economy, while units without such access tend to be clustered in poorer regions.[112] The former units are in a far better position

---

[110] Marx 1968, pp. 501, 510.

[111] Smith 2002.

[112] The basic data are worth repeating. At present 95% of research and development is located in the so-called 'First World'. The drive to extend the definition and enforcement of intellectual property rights obviously reinforces this inherent tendency tremendously; 97% of all patents today are held by individuals and institutions located in the first world. Friedman 2000, p. 319. It can be noted in passing that it was always a mistake for dependency theorists to associate the virtuous circle of innovation/surplus profits with industrialisation and the inverse vicious circle with agriculture. Industrialisation can be devoted to the production of ordinary commodities whose sale will not bring surplus profits. And agriculture can be devoted to the production of high 'value added' outputs (McMichael 1994). Neither the industrialisation of (parts of) the so-called 'Third World', nor the continued significance of agriculture in parts of the so-called 'First World', refute the theory of uneven development (Arrighi 2002). A survey of debates in the Marxian tradition regarding this and related themes is found in Brewer 1991 and Arrighi 2002.

to maintain the virtuous circle described above, while the latter have great difficulty avoiding the vicious circle. And so the drive to appropriate surplus profits through technological innovation tends to systematically reproduce uneven development in the world market over time.[113]

This certainly does not imply that nothing can be done to lessen inequality and remove the worst forms of material deprivation in global capitalism. As I noted in Part One, the structures and policies of the developmental state are capable of establishing effective counter-tendencies to the tendency to uneven development, at least to a certain extent in certain historical contexts. The global social investment funds called for by democratic-cosmopolitan theorists would help as well. Nonetheless, this tendency is not a subsidiary matter only loosely linked to the essential determinations of the capital-form. The tendency to uneven development is inextricably tied to the drive to appropriate surplus profits from innovation, and this drive is utterly fundamental to the capital-form.[114]

8. Conclusion

While Marx did not use the term 'globalisation', his account of the essential determinations of the capitalist mode of production in *Capital* provides a

[113] Marx 1981, pp. 344–5. Insofar as technological innovation is embodied in fixed capital a second conjunction of virtuous and vicious circles also arises here, complementing the one discussed in the main text: '[W]here much constant capital, and therefore also much fixed capital, is employed, that part of the value of the product which replaces the wear and tear of the fixed capital provides an *accumulation fund*, which can be invested by the person controlling it, as new fixed capital (or also circulating capital), without any deduction whatsoever having to be made from the surplus-value for this part of the accumulation. *This accumulation fund does not exist at levels of production and in nations where there is not much fixed capital.* This is an important point. It is a fund for the continuous introduction of improvements, expansions, etc.'. Marx 1968, p. 480, second emphasis added. See Chapter 4, note 47.

[114] It is worth recalling again the many other dimensions of the world market that reinforce the tendency to uneven development, including the remission of profits resulting from foreign direct investment in poorer regions, the ability of multinational firms to manipulate the 'prices' of commodities 'exchanged' in intra-firm transactions, the ability of units of capital in wealthy regions to play off subcontractors in poorer regions (and their work forces) against each other, capital flight undertaken by local élites desiring to escape currency risks and/or protect the fruits of corruption, the tendency for poorer regions to fall into a 'debt trap', the subsidies and protectionism of the North in precisely those sectors where producers from the South are most competitive, and so on.

starting point for constructing a Marxian model of globalisation. A number of distinguishing features of the model have already emerged:

- the emphasis on the operation of the law of value on the level of the world market;
- the identity asserted between the accumulation of total social capital and the systematic reproduction of the exploitative capital/wage-labour relation on the global level;
- the derivation of systematic tendencies to the concentration and centralisation of capital, overaccumulation and financial crises, and uneven development on the level of the world market.

A provisional assessment of the Marxian model of (capitalist) globalisation can be offered at this point. This position counts as an advance over positions considered at earlier stages in the systematic dialectic of globalisation in two main respects. The above features of the world market were merely implicit in the models of globalisation considered previously. In the Marxian model, in contrast, these essential traits of the capitalist global order are made explicit. Second, this position is not defined by claims regarding the efficiency and normative attractiveness of the contemporary global order that are inconsistent with its essential determinations. In this respect too, the Marxian model counts as an advance over the earlier positions in the systematic dialectic of globalisation.

There are other dimensions of the global order that must be taken into account in an adequate model besides those considered in this chapter. The state, the interstate system, and the régime of global governance have yet to be considered. In particular, the relationship between global markets and the state needs to be explored. This forms the topic of the following chapter.

Chapter Six

A Marxian Model of Capitalist Globalisation (2): The Dialectic of State and World Market

Any adequate Marxian model of the contemporary global order must incorporate the state, the interstate system, and the régime of global governance, while providing a way of conceptualising the essential relationships connecting these social forms and the capitalist world market. Section 1 surveys basic elements of a Marxian theory of the state. Section 2 considers whether this account needs to be modified in the light of recent developments in the global economy. A brief methodological digression on the relationship between the sort of systematic dialectics found in *Capital* and historical dialectics prepares the way for the formulation of a general claim regarding the relationship between the state and the world market in capitalism. Various dimensions of the interstate system will be introduced in the course of this discussion. Others will be considered in the following chapter, devoted to a central aspect of the so-called régime of global governance.

1. A Marxian perspective on the state

Capital can be read as an extended answer to the following question: given the systematic reproduction of capital accumulation over time, what are the necessary conditions of this reproduction?[1] Marx shows that the production of surplus-value is the most important necessary condition (Volume I). The circulation of value flows must also follow certain patterns (Volume II), and a redistribution of surplus-value among and within various sectors must occur as well (Volume III). Necessary conditions for the reproduction of capital accumulation also arise on the levels of the state, foreign trade, and the world market, although the projected volumes on these topics remained unwritten at Marx's death.

As the previous chapter showed, foreign trade and the world market are implicit throughout the three volumes of *Capital*. The same is true of the state. It, too, operates on each of the main levels of analysis in *Capital*; the state is part of the social relations of capital, not an entity outside those relations.[2] A large portion of Marx's unwritten volume on the state would presumably have made this explicit.

Capital begins by defining the capitalist mode of production as a system of generalised commodity exchange. Commodity exchanges both presuppose and generate property rights. As Hobbes and Locke well knew, and as Marx reaffirmed, the most basic manner in which the state furthers capital accumulation is through legislating and enforcing these rights. Marx's discussion of the commodity-form thus presupposes these forms of state activity from the start.

Marx then goes on to show the systematic relationship between the commodity-form and the money-form. Capitalism requires money, the only socially objective measure of the value of commodities; money is no ordinary commodity, even when it takes the form of commodity money. No capitalist state has ever had the power to control completely whether, how, or to what extent any particular form of money serves as an adequate measure of value, a means of circulation, a means of purchase, an end of accumulation, and so on. But the success of a particular form of money in performing these functions has never been determined entirely apart from the actions of political authorities either. The wide variety and contingency of state policies regarding money

---

[1] To ask this question is simultaneously to inquire into the factors tending to disrupt the reproduction of capital accumulation. *Capital* is as much concerned with the contradictions and ruptures in the accumulation process as it is with its reproduction.

[2] Burnham 1995. This implies that the standard notions of 'base' and 'superstructure' must be unequivocally rejected (see Bonefeld and Holloway 1995; de Brunhoff 1978).

in the course of the historical development of capitalism should not blind us to this element of necessity.[3]

The capital/wage-labour relation is the next major category in Marx's systematic reconstruction of the essential determinations of the capitalist mode of production. In contrast to other dimensions of the state's activities, the role of the state in the capital/wage-labour relation is explicitly and extensively discussed in Volume I. This is primarily due to the way the capital/wage-labour contract differs profoundly from other types of contractual exchange.

The purchase of labour-power grants the capitalist ownership rights to its use. But labour-power is not a fully alienable commodity; it necessarily remains tied to the body and personhood of the worker, even during the time in which its use has been sold. Capitalists have the right to use labour-power, along with all the other commodities they own, to produce as much surplus-value as possible, even if that means irreparably harming the bodies and personhood of their workers. But these workers have the right to maintain their property in their bodies and personhood, even if that means restricting the amount of surplus-value produced and appropriated by the purchaser of labour-power. Both sets of rights are equally legitimate within a capitalist framework. Conflict between them is inevitable: 'There is here therefore an antinomy, of right against right, both equally bearing the seal of the law of exchange. Between equal rights, force decides'.[4] For this reason, class struggles at the point of production will persist in one form or another as long as capitalism does.

---

[3] Marx notes in particular the inestimably profound role of public debt in the monetary flows of a capitalist economy: 'As with the strike of an enchanter's wand, it endows unproductive money with the power of creation and thus turns it into capital, without forcing it to expose itself to the troubles and risks inseparable from its employment in industry or even in usury. The state's creditors actually give nothing away, for the sum lent is transformed into public bonds, easily negotiable, which go on functioning in their hands just as so much hard cash would. But furthermore, and quite apart from the class of idle *rentiers* thus created, the improvised wealth of the financiers who play the role of middlemen between the government and the nation, and the tax-farmers, merchants and private manufacturers, for whom a good part of every national loan performs the service of a capital fallen from heaven, apart from all these people, the national debt has given rise to joint-stock companies, to dealings in negotiable effects of all kinds, and to speculation: in a word, it has given rise to stock-exchange gambling and the modern bankocracy'. Marx 1976, p. 919. On the contingency and historical variability of state policies regarding money, see Helleiner 2003. On the manner in which money is the Achilles heel of pure neoliberalism, undermining its fantasy of self-sufficient capitalist markets functioning apart from the state, see Reuten and Williams 1989, p. 243.

[4] Marx 1976, p. 344.

It is no less inevitable that these struggles will spill over to struggles in and against the state. Marx shows, for example, how struggles over the length of the working day at the point of production necessarily tend to be conjoined with struggles to formulate legislation and bureaucratic decrees favourable to one side or the other. Struggles regarding rules governing hiring and firing, labour organising, training programmes, workplace safety, the introduction of new technologies in the workplace, insurance against unemployment, sickness, disability, and old age, and so on, also necessarily tend both to arise at the point of production and to take on a political dimension.

Marx's introduces a number of general points in the course of his historical overview of legislation limiting the length of the working day:

- The 'dice are loaded'; the power of capital tends to enable its interests to dominate both in the workplace and in the realm of legislation and administrative policy.[5]
- Nonetheless, most instances of legislation and administrative policy reflect to some degree or other the organised collective power of labour, or the fear that the potential collective power of labour may become politically organised if an issue is not addressed.
- The drive for short-term profits can undermine the medium-to-long-term economic interests of capital. In some circumstances, this can lead far-sighted representatives of capital to consider legislation and policies that check that drive to a certain degreee.
- In certain conjunctures, it may be possible for labourers to forge effective political alliances with other social groups against capital.[6]

---

[5] 'Private' ownership of the means of production translates into 'public' political power in a number of familiar ways. Those who own media outlets can greatly influence political discussion. Legal and illegal lobbying, legal and illegal bribery, the implicit or explicit threat of capital strike and capital flight by industrial capitals, the ability of many firms to avoid taxation, the veto power over state policy held in effect by holders of government bonds, and so on, all play a role as well. It follows from this that, for political reforms to be successful, they generally must be compatible with the perceived self-interest of important factions of capital. As the perceived self-interest of these factions change, or as new factions arise, reforms may be rescinded. Further, reforms that seemed acceptable to capital in time of rapid growth, or that were reluctantly accepted in periods of mass mobilisations, may not seem so attractive to the class that owns and controls the means of production when profit rates decline, or when oppositional social movements lose strength. See note 15 below.

[6] In the nineteenth century, the greatest successes in the struggle to shorten the

- The resources devoted to the enforcement of legislation and administrative policies are ultimately more significant than either the legislation or administrative decrees themselves. Enforcement tends to be unfunded/underfunded in direct proportion to the degree the laws and policies go against the perceived self-interest of the leading factions of capital.

The specific forms of political regulation of wage-labour are tremendously varied and contingent. But that there is some form of political regulation of the capital/wage-labour relation at the point of production is not at all contingent.[7]

It also necessarily tends to be the case that other forms of state legislation and administrative policy politically regulate the capital/wage-labour relation outside the sphere of production. While labour-power is a commodity in capitalism, it is not itself produced and reproduced within capitalist production processes. It is produced and reproduced elsewhere, in households and communities. A capitalist state with the responsibility to ensure the reproduction of generalised commodity production cannot be indifferent to the production and reproduction of labour-power. Here, too, the specific content of legislation and administrative decrees is a matter of great historical variety and contingency. Many matters of crucial importance to households and communities can be left to benign – and not so benign – neglect for extended periods. But the general tendency for state legislation and administration to regulate households and communities is not in the least a contingent matter, as feminist theorists have correctly insisted.[8] From the dawn of capitalism the regulation

---

working day occurred when landlords were willing to support legislation to that end. In Marx's account, landlords were motivated by a desire for revenge against manufacturers, who supported the Corn Laws that drastically lowered agricultural prices.

[7] 'Factory legislation, that first conscious and methodical reaction of society against the spontaneously developed form of its production process, is, as we have seen, just as much the necessary product of large-scale industry as cotton yarn, self-actors and the electric telegraph'. Marx 1976, p. 610.

[8] 'As long as factory legislation is confined to regulating the labour done in factories, etc., it is regarded only as an interference with capital's rights of exploitation. But when it comes to regulating so-called "domestic labour", this is immediately viewed as a direct attack on the *patria potestas*, or, in modern terms, parental authority. The tender-hearted English Parliament long affected to shrink from taking this step. The power of facts, however, at last compelled it to acknowledge that large-scale industry, in overturning the economic foundation of the old family system, and the family labour corresponding to it, had also dissolved the old family relationships. The rights of children had to be proclaimed'. Marx 1976, pp. 619–20.

of wage-labour and the prison system have also been systematically intertwined.[9] For example, the necessary tendency of capital to generate a 'reserve army of the unemployed' has always been connected with the criminalisation of sections of this reserve army.

After examining the capital/wage-labour relation, Marx turns to a closer investigation of capital accumulation, deriving the tendency for the concentration and centralisation of capital. Implicit in this discussion is the need for corporate law to be revised regularly in response to (or in anticipation of) processes of concentration and centralisation. The definition of what counts as a corporate 'person', and the legally permissible and impermissible manners in which units of capital can interact with each other in mergers and acquisitions, cross-shareholding, and so on, are but two features of capitalist property relations that must be articulated and regularly revised by the juridical apparatus as accumulation proceeds.

The concluding part of Volume I also remains of great relevance to a contemporary Marxian assessment of the state. In this chapter, Marx discusses the emergence of capitalism, emphasising the necessary role played by state violence in the process of 'original accumulation'. This violence was needed to eradicate customary rights and traditions that hampered the formation of a class of wage-labourers. But the dynamic of capital accumulation requires a continuing search for new realms of society and nature to commodify, monetarise, and incorporate within circuits of capital accumulation. This project, pursued with special vigour in periods of general overaccumulation, inevitably disrupts established practices. Its success requires on-going state policies explicitly directed towards the forcible eradication of traditions and customary rights, as David Harvey has forcefully reminded us with his notion of 'accumulation through dispossession'.[10]

In Volume II of *Capital*, Marx shows how the reproduction of total social capital involves flows of commodities and investments between two Departments, one devoted to the production of means of production, the other to producing means of consumption. The reproduction of total social capital is hampered whenever the circulation of commodities and investments

---

[9] Fine et al. 1979.
[10] Harvey 2001, 2003a, 2003b.

within and between the two Departments is interrupted. The capacities of any given state are generally enhanced if the capitals operating in its jurisdiction grow in the course of the reproduction of total social capital, and diminished if they do not. It follows that there is a necessary tendency for the capitalist state to implement policies designed to foster the circulation of commodities and money within and across Departments. The specific content of such policies and their overall effectiveness depend on a myriad of contingencies, of course. But, here too, the vast range of contingencies in concrete state policies should not cover over the element of necessity: the operation of the capitalist state is implicit in both the simple and expanded reproduction of total social capital.[11]

The beginning of Volume III examines 'cost prices', a level of abstraction in which profit rates differ across sectors due to divergences in the ratio of constant capital expenditures to variable capital. Marx then introduces the category 'prices of production', a more complex and concrete determination according to which profit rates tend to equalise across sectors despite divergences in this ratio. Competitive pressures tend to lead units of capital to shift from low-profit to high-profit sectors, thereby generating the tendency for rates of profit to equalise. Inter-capital competition also generates a systematic tendency *away* from the equalisation of profit rates within any given sector. Innovations that enable surplus profits to be appropriated – that is, returns above the average rate of profit – are major weapons in competition among units of capital in the same sector. And, over the course of 'long waves' of capitalist development, sectors with steep technology trajectories, and sectors that play a central role in extensive technological systems, tend to enjoy higher rates of profit and growth than other sectors.

As I have mentioned before, the state plays a crucial role in the discovery and implementation of innovations. State support of education and training, state funding of infrastructure and research, the formation of formal and informal networks of government, business, and labour élites, and the institution of government/business partnerships for specific projects, all

---

[11] Marxists agree with defenders of the catalytic state on this point. However much economic and political élites may indulge in libertarian rhetoric, they rarely manage to move toward a minimal state when the preconditions of capital accumulation are at stake.

warrant mention in this context. The fact that all states are not equally effective in implementing such policies at all times does not lessen the systematic necessity for state policies of this sort to be pursued in the capitalist global order.

The drive for surplus profits from innovation also forms the starting point for the theories of overaccumulation and financial crises Marx sketches in Volume III. When such crises break out, neither their duration, nor the level of harm they inflict, nor the groups or regions suffering the brunt of the harm, is inevitable. While the capacity of the state to affect the unfolding of an overaccumulation or financial crises is surely limited, state policies just as surely affect how a particular crisis unfolds.[12] Marx notes, for example, how the ideological commitments of the 'currency school' led to central-bank policies that consistently exacerbated financial crises in Britain in the nineteenth century. The anti-cyclical policies of the 'banking school' could have limited the harm inflicted by those crises to a considerable degree.[13] The extent to which the costs of downswings are displaced onto working men and women, the unemployed, the elderly, and other disadvantaged groups is also a function of state policies.

Volume III of *Capital* concludes with extremely sketchy remarks on the category 'class'. The crucial role of the state in the process whereby a class 'in itself' becomes (or does not become) a class 'for itself' – that is, a class whose members are conscious of their shared interests – is implicit in this discussion. In the capitalist mode of production, states provide crucial institutional sites for the formal and informal negotiations that help articulate shared capitalist class interests, and the specific policies most likely to further those interests. Non-capitalist classes also forge a self-conscious identity in the course of political struggles to influence legislation and administrative policy, as Marx's chronicle of attempts to limit the length of the working day illustrates. Representatives of non-capitalist classes can even hold positions within the state apparatus in certain circumstances, with the state apparatus itself becoming a site of class struggle. The dominant tendency of the capitalist state, however, is to *disorganise* various factions of these other classes. To see

---

[12] Recall note 101 of the previous chapter.
[13] Marx 1981, Chapter 34.

why this is the case, we must examine the distinguishing features of a Marxian concept of the capitalist state more closely.

In most contemporary social theories, the state is conceptualised primarily as a solution to free-rider and assurance problems. For most neoliberals, an economic system dedicated to the pursuit of private self-interest necessarily tends to underproduce public goods such as the rule of law, stable money, basic research, infrastructure, education, and so on. For libertarians, the list of underproduced public goods is much shorter, while mainstream opponents of neoliberalism draw up a more extensive inventory. However long or short a particular list might be, however, the main point remains: the state is categorised as an institutional order inherently dedicated to the 'universal' interest, that is, to the provision of public goods and avoidance of public bads.[14] This is the ultimate source of its legitimation. No serious analyst believes that any state fully lives up to this categorisation, of course. State officials regularly indulge in activities ranging from fairly innocuous arbitrariness to the most extreme forms of corruption, and no one denies the need to establish institutional safeguards to minimise the harm caused by such behaviour. But mainstream social theorists still assert that, in principle at least, the state furthers the universal interests of its citizens. This claim applies to the state's essential nature, its 'actuality' as opposed to its mere 'existence', in the by now familiar Hegelian sense of the terms.

From a Marxian perspective, this manner of conceptualising the capitalist state suffers from a fundamental defect: the dichotomy between particular and universal interests does not withstand scrutiny. It is certainly not wrong to say that individuals and groups pursue their private self-interests in capitalism. But to stop there is to stay on the surface level of appearances. To stop there is to miss the 'ontological inversion' so central to Marx's theory of capital. In a capitalist society, it is the interests of *capital*, a bizarre pseudo-subject, that hold sway. While human agents do indeed purse their self-interests, these interests are inexorably shaped by the fact they live within a society whose organising principle is a non-human end, the accumulation of money capital. Similarly, it is not wrong to assert that state policies reconcile

---

[14] The democratic-cosmopolitan perspective that public goods ultimately cannot be adequately provided on the level of the state is also consistent with this view. Democratic-cosmopolitan theorists still assign the state the task of embodying the universal interest of the national political community to the greatest feasible extent.

the conflicting interests of individuals and groups. But the state is part of the social relations of capital. The manner in which the 'universal' interest is defined within the state apparatus will be inexorably shaped – inexorably distorted – by the fact that the organising principle of this society is the self-valorisation of value. The dichotomy between 'private' self-interests and the 'universal' interests of the society as a whole occludes the single most important feature of a capitalist society, the privileged place held by the interests of capital.[15]

This is only half the story. The most fundamental contradiction within the capitalist mode of production is ontological: capital is simultaneously everything and nothing, the most powerful force in society and a complete nullity. The capital whose interests hold sway is ultimately nothing but a manifestation of the powers of collective social labour; the self-valorisation of value simply is the reproduction of the exploitative capital/wage-labour relation. The capitalist state, insofar as it is a *capitalist* state, by definition necessarily tends to operate in a manner that reproduces the central social relation of capitalist society, the capital/wage-labour relation. From this perspective, too, categorising the capitalist state as an embodiment of 'universality' is completely fanciful. The capitalist state cannot even in principle eliminate the fundamental antagonisms at the heart of the exploitative capital/wage-labour relation, however much it may mitigate its worst abuses. To do so would be to cease to be a capitalist state.[16]

---

[15] As is often the case, democratic-cosmopolitan theorists recognise the force of this Marxian claim to a considerable extent. David Held, for example, grants that the capitalist state tends to systematically privilege the interests of corporate capital: '[T]he stratification of autonomy produced by modern corporate capitalism goes beyond the immediate impact of economic inequalities on the capacities of citizens to participate as equals in their collective associations. For the very capacity of governments to act in ways that interest groups may legitimately desire is, as previously noted, constrained. . . . The constraints on governments and state institutions systematically limit policy options. The system of private property and investment creates objective exigencies that must be met if economic growth and development are to be sustained. . . . A government's policies must, thereby, follow a political agenda that is at least favourable to, that is, biased towards, the development of the system of private enterprise and corporate power. . . . Democracy is embedded in a socio-economic system that grants a "privileged position" to certain interests. Accordingly, individuals and interest groups cannot be treated as necessarily equal, and the state cannot be regarded as a neutral arbiter among all interests'. Held 1995, pp. 246–7. Talk of the 'universal interest' in this context appears more than a bit hollow. For Held, however, this state of affairs is due to the contingent lack of a proper régime of global governance, rather than the state's inherent role in the social relations of capitalism.

[16] Analogous points can be made regarding capital/consumer relations, or the

This is not to deny that conflicts regarding the definition and provision of public goods must somehow be managed if the capitalist mode of production is to reproduce itself over time. The state is the primary institutional site where this management takes place. In some circumstances, those holding positions of power in the state apparatus will directly coerce other groups in this process. In other cases, explicit or implicit threats of coercion may be sufficient. In the normal case, however, some sort of reconciliation of interests beyond what can be attained at the level of immediate economic relations will be articulated and set into practice by state officials. In the Marxian tradition, Antonio Gramsci's writings have provided the most influential account of this process.[17]

The categories 'class fraction', 'ruling bloc', and 'hegemony' are central to Gramsci's reflections. 'Class fraction' refers to the heterogeneity of the various classes within the capitalist mode of production. The capitalist class, for instance, includes the owners and controllers of the largest manufacturing units of capital, as well as the owners and controllers of smaller units tied to them through various subcontracting and distributing arrangements. It also includes merchant capitalists and those who own and control units of capital devoted to credit and fictitious capital (financial capital). Each of these groups can be further subdivided into different sub-factions according to sector, geographical region of operation, growth potential, and so on. The class of wage-labourers can be divided into different factions in all these respects as well. And factions can arise within and across classes along an indefinite number of other dimensions, such as gender, race, ethnicity, and cultural traditions.

Whenever distinct factions arise, they will tend to develop divergent interests that must somehow be reconciled to some degree if the social order is to be maintained. In Gramsci's account, this reconciliation occurs when a dominant faction of capital is able to form a 'ruling bloc', a coalition uniting both other factions of capital and factions of non-capitalist classes under its leadership.

---

relations among capitals, which also are characterized by elements of irreconcilable antagonism overlooked in the positions considered in Part One. For a discussion of how these forms of antagonism persist in the so-called 'new economy', see Smith 2000a.

[17] Gramsci 1971.

This hegemonic faction will generally not be able to maintain the coalition over time if it insists on pursuing its self-interests to the maximal extent in all circumstances. For a coalition to be relatively stable, the hegemonic faction must limit its pursuit of self-interest to a certain degree in order to incorporate the interests of other members of the ruling bloc.[18] The state apparatus provides the main institutional setting in which this reconciliation of the interests of the members of the ruling bloc can be negotiated and institutionalised.[19] This is the element of truth in the claim that the state embodies a moment of 'universality' *vis-à-vis* the conflicting particularities of civil society. From a Marxian perspective, however, the state ultimately remains a 'pseudo-universal', incapable of resolving the social antagonisms lying at the heart of the capital-form.

The state is no mere epiphenomenon of capital. It is impossible in principle to deduce which factions will cohere to form a ruling bloc at a particular place and time from any map of intra- and inter-class relations holding in the economy at that place and time. Nor is it possible to deduce from the logic of capital how mutual benefits are defined, attained, and distributed within a given ruling bloc. Similarly, comprehension of the essential social forms of capitalism does not allow one to foresee how long a given coalition is likely to endure in power, or how long a given class faction is likely to maintain a position of hegemony within that coalition. All ruling blocs eventually prove unstable, as new factions of capital attempt to exert hegemony within new intra-capital and cross-class alliances. There is no systematic necessity about any of this. But there is a systematic tendency for some sort of institutional mechanism to be established that addresses crucial preconditions for continued capital accumulation. The state-form is essentially defined by the project of attaining a level of inter- and intra-class reconciliation of interests sufficient to provide the public goods required for the continuing reproduction of capital accumulation. The state-form is necessarily part of the social relations of capital; this is the reason a separate volume on the state would have been necessary to complete the systematic project Marx began in *Capital*.

---

[18] Fisk 1989.

[19] There are other sites as well, such as think tanks and other associations in civil society. In the United States, for example, the National Association of Manufacturers, the Chamber of Commerce, the Cato Institute, and the Brookings Institute have all played central roles in the formation and maintenance of ruling blocs.

Defining and enforcing property and contractual rights, regulating money and the capital/wage-labour relation, adjusting corporate law, overseeing the circuits of capital, providing education, training, infrastructure, and R&D, managing crises, and providing a site for the emergence of political self-consciousness of ruling blocs, all necessarily involve territoriality. Ideological rhetoric aside, what is of concern to any particular state apparatus is not so much the notion of rights in general, but the property rights of *these* owners *here*; not money in general, but the social force of *this* type of money in *this particular place*, and so on. Some fairly straightforward trade-offs arise in this context. If state activities were limited to local neighbourhoods, many crucial preconditions for capital accumulation would not be provided. But as the geographical range of state policies expands, it may be difficult to address the specific problems of particular regions. Effective oversight of the implementation and consequences of public policies may become increasingly difficult too. It may also be the case that cultural beliefs that help legitimate a particular régime no longer serve this function as effectively when the state is extended to areas with quite different cultural traditions.

The way these trade-offs are worked out in specific circumstances is tremendously contingent. In some cases, a particular state-form will be assigned tasks to perform on a local level, while being incorporated under a higher-level state apparatus operating on a wider geographical range. The precise relationship between these two levels of political administration is open to great variation over time. New historical developments may call for a re-negotiation of assigned tasks, leading to a new division of powers among state officials operating on different levels.[20] Systematic social theory has little to say regarding the countless ways state-forms can be organised in vertical arrangements of subordinating and subordinated formal sovereignty.

There is also tremendous indeterminacy regarding the concrete political forms that arise when a multiplicity of distinct states stand apart from each other, as opposed to being united within a single organisational structure. Each given state is defined by a limit beyond which lies its 'other', that is, another higher-order state with its own hierarchy of political apparatuses and its own independent claim to sovereignty. The thought that a general world

---

[20] The process of 'devolution' whereby certain state functions were shifted from London to the Scottish parliament provides a recent example.

government could eliminate territorially limited political forms in the contemporary epoch is ludicrous. The territoriality of any given political apparatus implies the notion of a limit, a boundary, beyond which lies another territory, governed by another political régime. In the Marxian model of globalisation, states are always already incorporated within the interstate system, a distinct level of social ontology with its own emergent properties.[21]

This list of elements of a Marxian theory of state is not intended to be comprehensive, and each of these elements warrants far more extensive consideration. As incomplete as the above survey may be, however, it should suffice to establish that Marx's framework does not systematically neglect the state. The state is not some separate thing apart from the system of capitalist social relations; it is itself a vital part of that system. Each and every moment of each and every capital circuit presupposes the state, just as each and every exercise of power by the capitalist state ultimately rests upon an appropriation of surplus-value produced in circuits of capital.

2. A Marxian critique of the 'hyperglobalisation' thesis

A number of commentators assert that globalisation vastly expands the exit options available to financial and industrial capital, creating a historically unprecedented situation. While the mere existence of these exit options may not make any particular state policy logically impossible, in practice they do effectively rule out many forms of state activity, according to defenders of what may be termed the 'hyperglobalisation thesis'.[22] These theorists argue, in effect, that the historical dialectic of capitalism has entered a new stage, characterised by a qualitative shift of power from states to global markets. Neoliberal writers applaud these developments on the grounds that they remove distortions brought about by state economic intervention; non-neoliberal defenders of the thesis lament the change.[23] But both agree that, in the age of globalisation, the state has lost much of its significance.[24]

---

[21] Barker 1997.
[22] This term was introduced in Held et al. 1999.
[23] See Wriston 1992 and Strange 1996, respectively.
[24] Guehenno 2000.

In the Marxian framework developed here, the state is conceptualised as part of the social relations of capitalism, and not as a distinct entity separate from another allegedly distinct entity, 'the economy'. The state is a necessary moment of capital accumulation, not some external force intervening in this process from the outside. No less than the world market, it too implicitly operates on each of the theoretical levels discussed in the three volumes of *Capital*. More specifically, as we have seen previously in this chapter, the reign of capital is essentially tied to states that a) enforce property and contractual rights, b) regulate money, c) regulate the capital/wage-labour relation, both inside and outside the production process, d) adjust legislation and administrative decrees as the concentration and centralisation of capital proceeds, e) oversee 'accumulation by dispossession', f) maintain flows within and between Departments required for the reproduction of total social capital, g) provide infrastructure, R&D, training, and other crucial preconditions for the appropriation of surplus profits through innovation, h) manage crises, and i) provide an institutional setting for the formation of class identities. The hyperglobalisation thesis must be unequivocally rejected from a Marxian perspective for the simple reason that the expansion of global markets does not change the fact that the reproduction of capitalist social relations requires the fulfilment of these essential functions by capitalist states, as a consideration of each of these tasks reveals.

a) Insofar as cross-border flows necessarily tend to occur on an expanding scale within generalised commodity exchange, a state's acknowledgement and enforcement of property rights cannot be restricted to indigenous property holders. The main forms of economic globalisation – foreign direct investment (FDI) and cross-border production chains, international trade, and flows of financial capital – require the enforcement of property rights, and this remains the primary responsibility of states. FDI will occur only if states extend significant protections to foreign investors in their system of jurisprudence. Extensive cross-border subcontracting arrangements also require states to maintain at least a minimally effective legal apparatus for resolving inter-capital disputes, controlling the labour force, and reducing the risk of the expropriation of foreign capital. Regarding trade, in a world of rapid technological innovation, the scope of intellectual property rights acknowledged and enforced by states becomes a matter of increasing importance, to mention only one example, of the way flows of commodities across borders are mediated by state jurisprudence. In the realm of financial capital, states retain a capacity to decree which contracts are enforceable and which are not, profoundly affecting the sorts of financial transactions that occur in the global economy. The globalisation of economic activity, and the specific paths taken in the course of globalisation, are thus, to a considerable extent, a direct function of the continuing power of states to define and enforce rights to property.

b) A system of generalised commodity exchange also necessarily requires a socially objective measure of the value of commodities, money. Insofar as generalised commodity exchange includes cross-border flows of commodities and investment, this implies that national currencies enter into relationships with each other (and with those of currency unions). These flows of money in the world market are necessarily mediated through the monetary and fiscal policies of states. The fact that these policies are not always effective does not affect this thesis. Even the most extreme neoliberals call for 'appropriate' monetary decisions by states (especially their central banks) regarding the relationship between the national currency and other currencies (especially those serving as forms of world money). It should go without saying that a decision to reduce or even eliminate state discretion (for example, the decision to let a currency float, or to create a 'hard peg' to some other currency) is itself a state policy, capable of being reversed if political circumstances change sufficiently.

c) The capital/wage-labour relation is also essentially tied to state legislation and administrative regulation. The capital/wage-labour relation is ultimately played out within the framework of the world market, and so legislation and other forms of state regulation must necessarily address this framework. State policies restricting or encouraging foreign trade, foreign investment, and immigration, for instance, play a crucial role in determining the extent to which units of capital are able to implement 'divide and conquer' strategies against labour. Two familiar features of the contemporary global economy, legislation denying workers in export processing zones legal rights granted in other sectors of the economy, and *de facto* state policies to not enforce the *de jure* labour rights that are granted in these zones, provide other examples of the general point. State decisions to allow/restrict imports also profoundly affect labour relations; 'free trade' creates vast pools of unemployed workers whenever indigenous producers are wiped out by foreign competition in substantial numbers. In brief, flows of investment in variable capital in the world market, and the balance of power in conflicts at sites of production throughout the global economy, are always mediated through *de jure* and *de facto* state labour policies. This is as true in our so-called 'age of globalisation' as it was in previous centuries.

d) Marx himself does not discuss cross-border merger and acquisitions, joint ventures and subcontracting arrangements extending production chains across borders, or intra-firm trade between parts of companies operating in different national settings. But these sorts of phenomena are manifestations of the same tendency to the concentration and centralisation of capital that he does examine extensively. If anything, they increase the need for corporate law to be revised regularly by states in response to (or in anticipation of) processes of concentration and centralisation. Activity on the level of the world market does not change the fact that the definition of what counts as a corporate 'person', and the legally permissible and impermissible manners in which units of capital can interact with each other, must be articulated and regularly revised by the juridical apparatus of states as capital accumulation proceeds.

e) No development on the level of the world market has made (or could make) the continuing search for new realms of society and nature to be commodified, monetarised, and incorporated within circuits of capital less important in the global capitalist order. And general overaccumulation in the world market increases the significance of this 'accumulation by dispossession' vis-à-vis other forms of capital accumulation. State policies explicitly directed towards the forcible eradication of traditions and customary rights remain necessary for this especially perverse form of capital accumulation.[25]

---

[25] '[A]bove all we have to look at the speculative raiding carried out by hedge funds and other major institutions of finance capital as the cutting edge of accumulation by dispossession in recent times. By creating a liquidity crisis throughout South East Asia, the hedge funds forced profitable businesses into bankruptcy. These businesses could be purchased at fire-sale prices by surplus capitals in the core countries. . . . Biopiracy is rampant and the pillaging of the world's stockpile of genetic resources is well under way, to the benefit of a few large multinational companies. The escalating depletion of the global environmental commons . . . likewise resulted from the wholesale commodification of nature in all its forms. The commodification of cultural forms, histories and intellectual creativity entrails wholesale dispossession. . . . The corporatization and privatization of hitherto public assets (like universities) to say nothing of the wave of privatization of water and other public utilities that has swept the world, constitute a new wave of "enclosing the commons". *As in the past, the power of the state is frequently used to force such processes through even against the popular will'*. Harvey 2003a, p. 75, italics added.

f) The reproduction of total social capital examined in the schemes of Volume II of *Capital* involves flows of commodities and investments connecting Department I, where means of production are produced, to Department II, devoted to means of consumption. Total social capital is ultimately defined on the level of the world market, and so the flows of commodities and investments within and between the two Departments ultimately occur on the level of the world market. But access to foreign supplies of needed raw materials, foreign labour-power and technologies, foreign markets for exported goods and services, foreign sources of capital, and so on, is never automatically guaranteed. The capitalist state necessarily tends to enter into negotiations with foreign units of capital and other states to initiate, maintain, or expand this access. States with the power to do so can also engage in military intervention, or the threat of military action, in order to attain this end.[26] There is not the least sign that the globalisation of economic activities lessens the importance of the state to either the simple or expanded reproduction of capital.

g) Given the drive for surplus profits discussed by Marx in Volume III and elsewhere, it is necessarily the case that the capitalist state will tend to attempt to foster the conditions for the success of units of capital operating in its territory through support for education and training, funding for infrastructure and research, the formation of formal and informal networks of élites, government/business partnerships for specific projects of importance to regional growth, and so on. Marxists can surely agree with advocates of the catalytic state that the extent to which particular national economies enjoy success in the global economy today is to a considerable extent a function of the state's ability to direct an effective 'national innovation system'.[27]

h) The drive for surplus profits is also the starting point for a reconstruction of the theories of overaccumulation and financial crises sketched in Volume III. As the concentration and centralisation of capital proceeds, overaccumulation crises increasingly tend to be played out at the level of the world market. Flows of financial capital necessarily tend to exceed the territorial limits set by the state-form, and so financial crises too are played out on the level

---

[26] Chomsky 1996.
[27] Nelson 1993; Kantor 1995.

of the world market. All but the most extreme neoliberals grant that when crises break out in the global economy, governments must assume special responsibilities in order to 'restore investor confidence'. For Marxists, too, this is an essential task of the capitalist state. In the continued absence of an international monetary agency with the power to create credit money, the responsibility for increasing liquidity in the global economy ultimately rests with national governments. Leading states, at least, also retain a capacity to intervene to minimise losses to particular units and networks of capital, and even to lessen the danger that the losses that do occur will threaten global markets as a whole. In his heart of hearts, Alan Greenspan may remain a disciple of the libertarian Ayn Rand. This did not prevent him from using the power of the state to flood the economy with liquidity when serious downturns threatened the US, or to organise a bailout of Long Term Capital Management, a prominent hedge fund, when its losses threatened to lead to a broad financial meltdown. When crises occur on the level of the world market, the dominant factions in ruling blocs will continue to call on states to 'socialise' the costs of global downswings to the greatest extent possible.[28]

i) Volume III of *Capital* concludes with sketchy remarks on the category 'class'. There are good reasons to hold that there is always a latent tendency for transnational class identities to arise on the level of the world market, a tendency that becomes more and more overt as globalisation proceeds. This implies that the Gramscian categories 'class fraction', 'ruling bloc', and 'hegemony' must be extended to this dynamic. On the level of the world market, there will be considerable heterogeneity within various classes, with different factions developing divergent interests that must somehow be reconciled to some degree if the global order is to be maintained. On the global level, dominant factions of capital will attempt to form a 'ruling bloc', a coalition uniting both other factions of capital and factions of non-capitalist classes under its global leadership. This hegemonic faction will generally not be able to maintain the coalition over time if it insists on pursuing its self-interests to the maximal extent in all circumstances. For a coalition to be relatively stable, the hegemonic faction must limit its pursuit of self-interest

---

[28] See note 46 below. In this context, the 'socialisation' of costs primarily means that the burdens of crises are displaced onto working men and women, the unemployed, the elderly, and other vulnerable groups.

to a certain degree in order to incorporate the interests of other members of the ruling bloc. Transnational institutions will be necessary to provide institutional settings in which this reconciliation of the interests of the members of the ruling bloc can be negotiated and institutionalised.

But this does not imply that states no longer play a crucial role in the process whereby a transnational class 'in itself' becomes (or does not become) a class 'for itself'. It is true that international agencies provide crucial institutional sites for the formal and informal negotiations that allow shared class interests across borders to be articulated, policy proposals furthering those interests to be debated, and conflicts over the selection and implementation of those policies to be addressed. These institutions for 'global governance', however, are based on interstate agreements, and only possess those powers that have been delegated to them by states. Leading states also establish and maintain interstate networks that remain 'within' particular state apparatuses even as they extend beyond them.[29] Transnational class identities do not make the state obsolete; the state is a necessary precondition for the emergence and maintenance of such identities.

The fact that the world market implicitly operates on each level of *Capital* does not force us to rescind the main claim of the previous section. The capitalist state implicitly operates always and everywhere the social forms of capital are in place, however much certain types of state activity and even certain forms of state may be disadvantaged by developments on the level of the world market. After all, if the state were as irrelevant as the hyper-globalisation thesis suggests, we would expect those who own and control capital to be increasingly indifferent to its workings as globalisation proceeds. This is not at all the case. There is no shortage of instances in which the holders of economic power employ legal, quasi-legal, and outright illegal methods to influence state policy.

At the other end of the spectrum from the hyperglobalists, we find those who insist that the sovereign state has been and remains the absolute centre

---

[29] Slaughter's concept of transgovernmental networks is useful in this context, although Slaughter herself lacks an adequate theory of either capital or class (Slaughter 2004). She also tends to overstate the newness of transgovernmental networks. Political élites within hegemonic states have always attempted to establish institutional settings within the state apparatus for on-going negotiations with state officials from regions under their geopolitical influence.

of the social world. From this perspective, the single most important fact about globalisation is that it is a state project, pursued by central banks, departments of the treasury, and other sections of the state apparatus. Political and economic élites may use the concept of globalisation as an ideological weapon to further their political projects, attempting to persuade the public that global developments have made all alternative projects infeasible. But the term does *not* describe some new stage in capitalist development in which the state is all but powerless in the face of global markets. If the political will were present to pursue alternatives, the state could, in principle, implement them just as effectively as ever.[30]

The implicit operation of the world market throughout *Capital* establishes that this claim is no less incompatible with a Marxian model of globalisation than the hyperglobalisation thesis. A convincing Marxian model of globalisation must simultaneously highlight the elements of systematic necessity associated with *both* the state and the world market. On the one hand, the state is not outside the system of social forms defining capital; it is itself a necessary moment of that system. And, so, there are good reasons to reject theories neglecting the continuing importance of the state-form. There are no flows of commodities, money, or labour in the global economy that are not overwhelmingly affected by the operation of states. On the other hand, the state cannot be adequately considered apart from its relations to the other essential determinations of capital, including the world market, the culminating category in Marx's proposed systematic reconstruction of the capitalist mode of production. And, so, there are strong systematic considerations to reject perspectives ignoring how the world market necessarily tends to subsume particular states under it in ways that restrict or erode state capacities.

There is a systematic tendency for the state to assert itself over the world market, and there is a systematic tendency for the world market to assert itself over the state. Both tendencies are essential determinations of the capital form. The 'hyperglobalisers', who speak of the fundamental erosion of state capacities, and those who affirm the supremacy of the state, both defend equally one-sided, and hence inadequate, viewpoints. And both equally fail

---

[30] Recalcitrant proponents of the social state and realist international relations theorists defend versions of this viewpoint.

to see that the tendencies they emphasise are not recent developments, but essential determinations of the capitalist mode of production from its inception.

In the Marxian model of globalisation presented here, it is not assumed that state officials are mere automata, blindly fulfilling dictates programmed into their behaviour by capital operating on the level of the world market. State officials, like entrepreneurs, scientists and technicians, line workers and consumers, continually exercise considerable ingenuity and intelligence in problem solving. The specific path of capitalist development selected from the indefinite range of possibilities in any given context depends on their choices and abilities. As Arrighi documents in detail, the pursuit of national prestige and personal self-interest by political élites results in state policies following a 'territorial logic' quite distinct from the dictates of 'capital logic'.[31] Nonetheless, as the cliché goes, the state is only 'relatively autonomous'. In the medium-to-long term, states that establish the preconditions for extended capital accumulation tend to flourish, while those that do not, do not.[32] The former, not the latter, alone have an opportunity to become the hegemonic power in the interstate system for an entire systematic cycle of accumulation. The choices of state officials – no less than those of entrepreneurs, scientists and technicians, line workers and consumers, and other categories of agents – are made within structural constraints systematically rewarding behaviour furthering the accumulation of total social capital and penalising all other modes of action. This justifies the assertion that the law of value operates in the world market over and above even the most powerful individual states.

There simply are not many 'hyperglobalisers' proclaiming the 'death of the state'. Similarly, few defenders of the continuing importance of the state deny the existence of the world market, or the challenges it presents to government officials. On these issues, at least, it may appear that Marxists simply echo the fairly familiar rejection of the two extremes. This appearance is misleading, and not solely because Marx's theory is based on a concept of capital missing in other theories of globalisation. But a digression on the methodological

---

[31] Arrighi 1994.
[32] Access to credit has been a major determining factor in determining the outcome of major wars in the history of capitalism (Rasler and Thompson 1994). For credit to be voluntarily forthcoming, creditors must believe that the 'territorial logic' of the state will eventually prove favourable to 'capital logic'.

framework of Marx's theory is required before the rest of the story can be developed.

3. Systematic and historical dialectics: tendencies, trends, and a meta-tendency

In *Capital* and elsewhere, Marx considers the essential determinations of capital in a linear ordering: commodity, value, abstract labour, money, capital, wage-labour, exploitation, accumulation, turnover time, reproduction, prices of production, merchant capital, financial capital, rent, the state, foreign trade, and the world market. We can see, at once, that this is a systematic rather than historical progression. Early categories in this systematic dialectic need not have appeared earlier in history; later ones need not map more recent developments.[33] In Marx's theoretical writings, systematic dialectics and historical dialectics are quite different projects. Nevertheless, they are interconnected in various ways.

First and foremost, the categories in the systematic progression refer to historically specific social forms, forms that distinguish the capitalist mode of production from other modes of production in history. Systematic and historical considerations are also related in that Marxian systematic theory is *revisable*. Historical developments in capitalism may reveal that something previously taken as necessary to the logic of capital does not, in fact, have this status.[34] And historical developments may lead us to discover systematic necessity in previously overlooked areas.[35] Systematic dialectics is a reconstruction of empirical results, and thus revisable when new empirical material, or new developments in history, emerge.[36] If this were all there were

---

[33] See Marx, 1973, p. 107; Smith, 1990, pp. 21–2; Arthur, 1997. As noted in the Introduction above, this form of systematic dialectics (the systematic reconstruction in thought of the essential determinations of a given social order) must be distinguished from the sort of systematic ordering of different positions attempted in the present study.

[34] Marx's acceptance of commodity money is perhaps the most striking example. See Campbell 2002.

[35] The systematic necessity of the tendency to 'disintermediation' ('securitisation') presented in Chapters 3 and 4 provides an example of an essential determination of capital that was latent in earlier historical periods.

[36] Marx's correspondence shows that he was reluctant to incorporate an account of rent in his systematic theory before appropriating the massive amount of historical information that had become available regarding landed property in Russia.

to say, however, the gap between the systematic logic of capital and historical developments in capitalism would remain immense. In themselves, the social forms examined in the systematic dialectic tell us what capital is, not what it might become.

Capital, however, provides not just a theory of social forms, but also a consideration of the structural tendencies necessarily inherent in these forms. The social forms defining the capital/wage-labour relation in Volume I, for example, generate a tendency for technological and organisational innovations at the point of production to increase the rate of surplus-value. In Volume II, Marx establishes that the drive to introduce innovations reducing circulation time is no less essential to the capital-form than the drive to transform the production process. A systematic tendency towards innovations reducing constant capital costs is derived at the beginning of Volume III, while later parts of this volume establish a drive for innovation in the commercial, financial, and agricultural sectors.[37] These sorts of tendencies are systematic, in that they are in place always and everywhere the capital-form is in place. But they simultaneously refer to historical processes extending over time. They at once further our comprehension of what capital is and what it necessarily tends to become. In this manner, they provide a bridge between systematic dialectics and concrete developments in the history of capitalism.

Nonetheless, the gulf between systematic theory and historical theory remains vast at this point. For there is no *a priori* way of determining how the various tendencies derived on different levels of the systematic ordering relate to each other in concrete historical circumstances. More specifically, there is no way to argue from the various *tendencies* that are necessarily given with the social forms of capital to the dominant *trends* in place in any particular historical context.[38] In specific cases, one set of tendencies may modify another, while itself continuing to operate in a relatively straightforward fashion. In other cases, matters may be reversed. Or each set of tendencies may modify the workings of the others to a considerable extent. One set of tendencies may even put another out of play completely in certain circumstances, while, at other times and other places, it is itself put out of play. Further, we cannot

---

[37] Smith 1997a.
[38] See Sayer 1984 and Reuten 1997.

assume that the tendencies discussed at the beginning of the systematic dialectic necessarily have more weight in a given historical conjuncture than those derived on subsequent levels. Nor can we assume that the reverse holds.[39] For all the systematic necessity of the various tendencies, there is an ineluctable element of contingency, path dependency, and human agency in the determination of the dominant trends of any concrete historical context. This gulf between (systematic) tendencies and (historical) trends cannot ever be completely bridged, even in principle. Capitalism is not a mechanistic system. Its laws are tendency laws, and the simultaneous operation of a series of tendency laws makes the course of concrete history open-ended.[40]

Despite this, it is still possible to narrow the breach between the systematic and the historical dimensions of Marx's theory of capital somewhat further. Once tendencies have been derived from the social forms defining capital, it is sometimes possible to derive a 'meta-tendency' – an overarching tendency conjoining two first-order tendencies – with a comparable claim to systematic necessity. The classic example of such a meta-tendency is found in the discussion of the rate of profit in Volume III. Alongside the systematic tendencies for the rate of profit to fall, Marx also derives countertendencies pointing in the opposite direction. These countertendencies have no less systematic necessity than the tendencies; they are no less rooted in the essential determinations of capital. In any given concrete set of circumstances, either set may modify, dominate, or be dominated by, the other in countless contingent ways. It does not follow from this, however, that Marx's systematic theory has nothing to contribute to the comprehension of historical developments regarding profit rates. A 'meta-tendency' uniting the two sets of tendencies can be derived with systematic necessity: the joint operation of the tendencies and countertendencies tends to form an alternating pattern.[41]

Suppose the set of tendencies leading to a falling rate of profit comes to dominate in a specific period and region. Once it is in place, it is necessarily the case that, at some point, the set of countertendencies tends to become of increasing importance. The inverse pattern holds as well. And, so, historical

---

[39] Smith 2000b.
[40] This aspect of Marx's framework anticipates many contemporary developments in the philosophy of science. See Bensaïd 2002, Part Three.
[41] Reuten 1997.

periods in which tendencies to higher rates of profit dominate tend to alternate with epochs in which the tendencies to a falling rate of profit come to the fore. There is no necessity for different parts of the overall pattern of alteration (or the pattern as a whole) to last any particular amount of time. But, the longer the set of tendencies to a falling (rising) rate of profit underlie the dominant trend, the greater the probability that the set of tendencies leading to a rising (falling) rate of profit will come to dominate in the future.

It is surely not the case that the simultaneous operation of any two sets of tendencies always generates a 'meta-tendency' of this sort. But, whenever two sets of tendencies with equal claims to systematic necessity are derived, such that the continued dominance of one set necessarily tends to increase the probability of a shift to the dominance of the other, a pattern of alternation necessarily tends to emerge. *This meta-tendency, derived within the systematic dialectic of capital, provides a general heuristic framework for comprehending the historical dialectic of capital.* The cyclical nature of capitalist development is thus an essential determination of the capitalist mode of production, and not a merely contingent matter.[42]

Perhaps the most important tendencies lacking 'symmetrical' counter-tendencies are the tendencies to the concentration and centralisation of capital derived in Volume I. They account for the strong element of linearity super-imposed on top of the alternating patterns of capitalist development. The return to the beginning part of a cycle never brings us precisely back to the point of departure. Each new commencement of a profit cycle tends to begin at a higher point of accumulation than the previous one, and a higher point in the concentration and centralisation of capital, an essential feature of the accumulation process.

---

[42] In the present context, 'cycle' should be taken in the broadest sense of the term, including the 'long waves' of expansion and slowdown that Arrighi terms 'systematic cycles of accumulation' as well as shorter economic cycles.

I accept Ernest Mandel's argument that long waves of decline occur due to factors 'endogenous' to the processes of capital accumulation, while more 'exogenous' factors (especially political defeats of the workers and their allies) determine when a long wave of expansion commences (Mandel 1975). This implies that the latter transition may be far more complex than the former. Nonetheless, as long as the capitalist mode of production persists, there is a tendency for long waves of decline to alternate with long waves of expansion. The longer the downswing, the more desperately political and economic élites experiment with 'exogenous' factors that might enable a new period of expansion to commence.

We must now return to the question posed at the end of the previous section with these considerations in mind. Are there any other distinctive features of the Marxian account of the relationship between the state and the world market, apart from its emphasis on the law of value and the capital/wage-labour relation?

4. A meta-tendency in the Marxian model of globalisation

I have argued that four crucial notions connect the systematic ordering of social forms developed in *Capital* with concrete historical developments in capitalism: 1) the historically specific nature of these forms; 2) the derivation of the systematic tendencies that arise from these forms, 3) the derivation of meta-tendencies of alternation, and 4) the tendency for such alternations to be played out on an ever-increasing scale of accumulation. The remainder of the chapter will be devoted to an application of the last three notions. Together, they illuminate a distinctive feature of the relationship between states and global markets in the Marxian model of globalisation.

A great advantage of systematic dialectics is that it provides a methodological framework within which one-sided and apparently inconsistent perspectives can be accommodated.[43] Marx insisted that the completion of his systematic project required further volumes on the state, foreign exchange, and the world market because there is *both* a necessary tendency for capital to operate within a territory administered by a state *and* a necessary tendency for trade, foreign direct investment, and flows of financial capital to extend beyond territorial limits. Both sets of tendencies are in place always and everywhere the capital form is in place. Both sets of tendencies are in place today. In the global order today, the state is at one and the same time increasingly significant and increasingly insignificant vis-à-vis the world market. It is increasingly significant, in that the systematically necessary tasks of the state, that is, the tasks that necessarily tend to be required for the reproduction of capital accumulation over time, are, if anything, more pressing in the so-called age of globalisation. It is increasingly insignificant, in that the law of value operating on the systematic level of the world market now operates with ever more force vis-à-vis states and national economies. An adequate account must grant equal weight to both dynamics.

---

[43] Pinkard 1988.

Here, as elsewhere, there are many ways different sets of tendencies may operate simultaneously. Tendencies arising from the state-form may modify those associated with the world market, while themselves continuing to operate in a relatively straightforward fashion. Or matters may be reversed, with tendencies associated with the state modified and those associated with the world market relatively untouched. It might be the case that each set of tendencies significantly alters the workings of the other. Or one set of tendencies may put the other out of play to a considerable extent in certain circumstances, while, at other times and in other places, it is itself put out of play to a comparable extent. Despite the systematic necessity of the various tendencies arising from the state-form and the world market, there remains an ineluctable element of contingency, path dependency, and human agency in the determination of the dominant trends of any concrete historical context.

At this point, it might seem that a Marxian model of globalisation has fairly little to say about the concrete historical nature of the relationship between the state and the world market, beyond the relative banality that extreme formulations of both the hyperglobalisation thesis and its denial are inadequate. The resources of Marxian theory, however, are not yet exhausted.

In Marx's discussion of rates of profit, he does not merely point out that there are two sets of tendencies pointing in opposite directions, each with an equally valid claim to systematic necessity. He goes on to derive a meta-tendency, a cyclical pattern in which periods dominated by tendencies to a falling rate of profit tend to alternate with periods in which countertendencies hold sway. In this manner, he derives a framework for comprehending the historical dialectic of capital from the standpoint of his systematic theory. In the previous section, the following generalisation was formulated: whenever two sets of tendencies with equal claims to systematic necessity are derived, such that the continued dominance of one set necessarily tends to increase the probability of a shift to the dominance of the other, a pattern of alternation necessarily tends to emerge. Might a similar move be made regarding the state and the world market? Arrighi's masterful study of the rise and decline of hegemonic powers in the world system over the course of capitalist history suggests that a positive answer can be given.[44]

---

[44] Arrighi 1994.

Arrighi distinguishes a number of 'systematic cycles of accumulation' in world history since the sixteenth century. While each involves numerous historically specific and contingent matters, a general pattern can nevertheless be perceived. The rapid economic expansion of an incipient hegemonic power tends to begin with expenditures far exceeding what could be justified in narrow economic calculations of profit and loss. State prestige and military strategy ('territorial logic') provide a spur to investment in military technologies and interventions, infrastructure, research and development, and so on, far beyond what could be justified in terms of 'capital logic'. Hegemonic regions in the history of capitalism thus win and retain their hegemonic status through the effective exercise of state capacities.

The more effective the state is at fulfilling the functions necessary to capital accumulation, the more units of capital operating within its borders tend to grow. The more they grow, the greater the threat of overaccumulation difficulties eventually arising. When overaccumulation difficulties do occur in a given national context, leading units of capital necessarily tend to search for favourable investment opportunities in industrial sectors elsewhere. Also, in these circumstances, profits made in the industrial sphere tend to flow into the financial sphere, where capital is far more mobile ('liquid'), seeking out profitable opportunities wherever they might arise. In this manner, the success of state projects in providing the material preconditions for effective capital accumulation leads to an extension and intensification of flows in global circuits of capital that eventually tend to undermine those very state projects. Even a hegemonic state remains in a precarious position vis-à-vis the world market. Even the most developed set of state capacities is inevitably restricted in scope, fragile in nature, and reversible in practice, however successful it might be for an extended historical period.

If a particular region happens to stumble upon a set of technologies and organisational forms that show exceptional promise, mobile financial capital in the world market will tend to flow to this region, providing the material preconditions for the development of new state capacities in that region. A new period of material expansion can then commence. As Marx writes in Volume I:

> [T]he villainies of the Venetian system of robbery formed one of the secret foundations of Holland's wealth in capital, for Venice in her years of decadence lent large sums of money to Holland. There is a similar relationship between

> Holland and England. By the beginning of the eighteenth century, Holland's manufactures had been far outstripped. It had ceased to be the nation preponderant in commerce and industry. One of its main lines of business, therefore, from 1701 to 1776, was the lending out of enormous amounts of capital, especially to its great rival England. The same thing is going on today between England and the United States. A great deal of capital, which appears today in the United States without any birth-certificate, was yesterday, in England, the capitalised blood of children.[45]

The parallel with the tendencies and countertendencies of profit rates is quite close. Here, too, the predominance of one set of tendencies in a particular context eventually increases the odds of a shift to a state of affairs in which the set of countertendencies comes to dominate.

A similar pattern can be detected in states that have not been at the centre of the world system. If a series of favourable factors are in place in the world market, variants of the developmental state can successfully nurture the growth of indigenous industrial and financial firms. But, as these units of capital grow, they will eventually extend their participation in global circuits of industrial and financial capital, hoping to appropriate surplus-value produced beyond national borders. If the state attempts to restrict this activity, these firms tend to become increasingly effective at evading state regulation. The developmental state can quickly be transformed from an apparent master of its own fate, able to direct flows in the world market as it wills, to a fairly helpless on-looker, reacting to forces far more powerful than itself. Even the most developed capacities of the developmental state, then, are inevitably restricted in scope, fragile in nature, and reversible in practice, however successfully they might be exercised for an extended historical period. In the course of adjusting to the external pressures of the world market, a particular developmental state may be fortunate enough to develop new capacities, capable of overseeing a new period of expanded growth in the territory under its jurisdiction.[46] Otherwise, it will suffer yet further losses, as domestic capitals shift investments to regions where other states have developed such capacities.

---

[45] Marx 1976, p. 920.

[46] Few techniques of state crisis management went unused following the outbreak of the East-Asian crisis in the 1990s. These include the nationalisation of bad debts (Korea, Japan), controls on short-term capital inflows (Malaysia, Hong Kong, Taiwan,

If conditions do not allow an effective developmental state to evolve in a particular region at a particular time, that country will feel the full brunt of the tendency to uneven development. Political élites, lacking other options for enrichment, will be more tempted by the joys of kleptocracy. The debt trap will be all but inescapable, for reasons explained in the following chapter. The structural adjustment programmes imposed by international agencies in response are likely to result in a further erosion of state capacities. But even many neoliberal academics and policymakers now concede that more effective state institutions must somehow be forged in these circumstances.[47] In some cases, at least, 'failed states' may be able to develop more effective capacities for a period. Here, too, however, these capacities will eventually prove to be restricted in scope, fragile in nature, and reversible in practice as conditions for accumulation on the level of the world market change over time.

It follows that the relationship between state and world market is categorised in a more complex and dynamic fashion within a Marxian framework than within any of the positions examined previously in the systematic dialectic of globalisation. Advocates of the social state and the catalytic state emphasise the capacities of the state. Proponents of neoliberalism and democratic cosmopolitanism stress the state's inadequacies in the face of the world market. Each of these positions is one-sided, highlighting certain matters while downplaying others no less fundamental to the capitalist mode of production. Within a Marxian framework, it is possible to derive a meta-tendency that both incorporates and transcends these one-sided positions: periods in which capitalist states develop effective capacities regularly tend to alternate with periods in which developments in the world market restrict those capacities and encourage a restructuring of the state.

---

with the explicit encouragement of Japan), state purchases of equity and restrictions on stock market trading (Hong Kong, Taiwan), industrial planning to reduce excess capacity (Korea), and so on (Wade and Veneroso 1998). The same sort of responses can be expected if (when) financial crises of comparable magnitude break out in the US or Europe.

[47] World Bank 1992; see also Fukuyama 2004. There are, of course, no guarantees that this project will be successful in any given region. This no more refutes the claim that tendencies associated with the state and the world market tend to alternate than the fact that not all regions enjoy high rates of profit in a period of expansion refutes the claim that periods of expansion and downturn tend to alternate in the capitalist global order.

5. Conclusion

State and world market; world market and state. From the standpoint of a Marxian model of globalisation, nationalists and globalists play a spirit-numbing con game. Each takes its turn promising a humane and just form of capitalism. Each takes its turn waiting for the promises of the other to prove illusory, as they invariably do. Neither the capitalist state nor the capitalist world market can resolve the fundamental irrationality and social antagonisms at the heart of capitalist social relations. A resurgence of nationalism will not reverse this state of affairs. But further deregulation of global capital flows, or further attempts to subject global capital flows to the precepts of cosmopolitan ethics, will not reverse this state of affairs either. Only a revolutionary rupture from the capital-form can accomplish this world historical task. This is, I believe, the main practical conclusion that follows from the systematic dialectic of globalisation traced in this work.

As we know from Chapter 4, this conclusion is deeply contested by democratic-cosmopolitan theorists. They hold that the proper political regulation of the world market can, in fact, reverse the otherwise pernicious effects of a capitalist global order. The following chapter continues the critical assessment of this position provided in Chapter 4, while simultaneously developing a facet of the Marxian model of capitalist globalisation that has been neglected thus far, the so-called 'régime of global governance'. Before turning to this topic, however, I would like to propose a speculation on the future course of the dialectic of state and world market that has been the topic of this chapter.

Let us return to Arrighi's account. Building on clues in Marx (such as the passage from *Capital* quoted above), he emphasises the crucial role of hegemonic states in the course of capitalism's historical development. These states foster the emergence of units of capital capable of attaining surplus profits through innovation for an extended historical period. The privileged place of these units of capital in the world market then reinforces the privileged place of that state in the hierarchical interstate system. Eventually, the units of capital associated with a given hegemonic state face irresolvable overaccumulation difficulties. The phase of material expansion then gives way to a phase in which the primary form of profit-seeking shifts to financial speculation. Over the course of this second period, investments flow to a different region, where a new type of state with new sorts of capacities nurtures units of capital capable of attaining surplus profits throughout the next systematic cycle of accumulation. If Arrighi is correct, this pattern has characterised the development of capitalism since its inception.

Predicting the course of history is a fool's game. Nonetheless, I believe that there are good reasons to think that the above pattern may not continue. The role of the state and the financial system in fostering innovation has become so well understood, and effective national innovation systems have become so widely institutionalised in the North, that it is unlikely that any region will again enjoy surplus profits from innovation for an extended historical epoch.

Suppose some form of scientific-technical advance shows promise of leading to commercialisable products capable of generating surplus profits. Some states will be quicker than others to support this advance, and some financial sectors will be more effective than others at mobilising credit to new units of capital dedicated to commercialisation. Certain units of capital will enjoy 'first mover' advantages, which can be considerable. But other states with effective national innovation systems and financial systems capable of allocating credit on a large scale will quickly target the sector in question. There are enough states in the North with effective national innovation systems, and enough financial sectors capable of allocating massive amounts of credit to units of capital starting up (or moving into) sectors where high future profits are anticipated, that the period in which the initial innovator enjoys surplus profits from a quasi-monopoly on an innovation necessarily tends to shrink drastically, relative to all earlier periods in the history of capitalism.

From this standpoint, the extension of intellectual property rights is more than a privatisation of types of scientific-technical knowledge previously considered public goods. It is a desperate attempt to use state law and inter-state agreements to change the rules of the game in order to appropriate surplus profits from innovation for an extended period in radically changed historical circumstances. I believe the attempt is doomed to fail. Units of capital with intellectual property rights to one part of complex technology systems will find themselves having to purchase licenses or enter into cross-licensing agreements with other units with intellectual rights to other parts of the same complex technology systems. This will most likely prevent any subset of them from enjoying surplus profits from innovations over an extended historical epoch.

I am not arguing that the dynamism of capitalism is eroding in use-value terms. Given the increased effectiveness at generating and mobilising scientific-technical knowledge, this dynamism tends to increase, everything else being equal. Nor am I suggesting that surplus profits from innovation will no longer play a role in reproducing uneven development in the world market. The relative brevity of the period in which surplus profits can be won in the North in comparison to earlier epoch will strongly motivate state officials in the wealthiest regions to increase their efforts to foster the next generation of innovations.[48] The countries of the South will, in general, have great difficulty matching these efforts, although successes in niche areas cannot be ruled out. The general convergence of the national innovation systems of the North, in other words, is completely consistent with a continued gap between the innovation systems of the North and the innovation systems of the South, and the continuing importance of this gap in reproducing uneven development.[49]

I am arguing that the dynamism of the capitalist world market may be eroding in value terms. Surplus profits from innovation has been a crucial source of that dynamism, and such profits may not be appropriated on anything approaching the scale that has held in past periods in the history of capitalism. I do not expect that non-financial sectors of the US economy will dominate the world market in the twenty-first century the way they did throughout most of the twentieth century, despite the fact that most patents in the world continue to be granted to corporations based in the United States. The horrifically low wages of China's workforce probably ensure that it will continue to receive a disproportionate share of the world's new investment fund in coming decades. But I do not foresee Chinese firms dominating the world market in the twenty-first century the way US firms did throughout most of the twentieth century either. I do not expect *any* region to take the next place in the historical chain extending from Venice to Holland to England to the United States that Marx described in the above quotation. I expect, instead, that individual firms, or networks of individual firms, based mostly

---

[48] This argument strengthens the conclusion of Chapter 3: the catalytic state necessarily tends to become a 'competition state', with the result that the revenues required to further communitarian values necessarily tend to be inadequate to fulfil the normative claims of its leading proponents.

[49] We must also recall that the more other sources of surplus profits are threatened, the more capital accumulation takes the form of 'accumulation by dispossession'. This exacerbates the tendency to uneven development, since countries of the South are far more vulnerable to the most predatory forms of capitalism. See note 25 above.

in the North, will introduce innovations, enjoy surplus profits from those innovations for relatively brief periods, and then watch their surplus profits erode as national innovation systems and financial sectors operating elsewhere funnel massive amounts of state subsidies and private credit to competitors. I am predicting, in brief, that the overaccumulation difficulties that erode surplus profits will arise in emerging sectors at an ever-faster rate.

Even if this speculation is correct, it does not imply that capitalism has at long last entered into the terminal crisis period expected by Marxists at the turn of the twentieth century. It does mean, however, that the period of global turbulence that has characterised the capitalist world market since the end of post-World-War-II 'Golden Age' may persist indefinitely.[50] If there is not a new period of material expansion setting off a new systematic cycle of accumulation in the world market, it will not be due to an erosion of state capacities in the 'age of globalisation'. It will be because numerous states in the North have established effective national innovation systems.

---

[50] See Brenner 1998, 2002.

Chapter Seven

A Marxian Model of Capitalist Globalisation (3): The 'International Financial Architecture'

Marx did not compose his projected volumes on the state, foreign trade, and the world market. But the state and the interstate system, and foreign trade and the world market, are implicit on each level of the three volumes of *Capital* that we do have, as the previous two chapters have established.

Any comprehensive Marxian model of (capitalist) globalisation must also refer to the so-called 'régime of global governance'. This requirement follows immediately from the fact that the main tasks faced by the capitalist state necessarily generate the potential for both interstate co-operation and interstate conflict. The capitalist state must define and enforce rules governing commodity exchange and money, assign rights to investors and corporate bodies, and ensure an adequate supply of wage-labour, raw materials, and so on. Commodities, money, and labour necessarily tend to flow across national borders. The regulation of commodity flows in the world market, the management of currency exchange rates, the legal rights granted to non-national investors and corporations, the rules governing cross-border flows of immigrant labour, and so on, all regularly require negotiations among states. These negotiations may lead to informal or formal agreements, or they may break down in the face of unresolved conflicts.

The persistence of interstate conflicts necessarily tends to reinforce the role of military apparatuses within the interstate system. In certain circumstances, attempts will be made to resolve interstate conflicts through military intervention. And the threat of military action persists even in periods where military force is not being employed.[1] In other cases, however, interstate agreements will be formulated to articulate, revise, and enforce the formal and informal rules holding on the global level. Today, as in the past, organisations defining and enforcing the global régime are housed within particular states (the US Department of the Treasury and the Pentagon are perhaps the central sites in the contemporary régime of global governance, just as the analogous British ministries were in an earlier age). Interstate agreements can also be negotiated to found and maintain international organisations, such as the World Bank, the International Monetary Fund, and the World Trade Organisation.

A régime of global governance with its own essential determinations emerges from the complex and contingent patterns of co-operation and conflict among states and international agencies. A great many issues of profound importance arise in this context, besides military conflicts, including global environmental problems and health crises, and criminal activity across borders.[2] The present chapter will consider only one of these issues, the 'international financial architecture' (IFA).[3]

One hardly needs to be a Marxist to recognise that there are serious structural flaws in the global financial order today. Paul Davidson, a leading post-Keynesian economist, defends a variant of the democratic-cosmopolitan model of globalisation discussed in Chapter 4. But he has developed a far more radical critique of the structural shortcomings of the contemporary IFA than David Held or any other theorist discussed in Part One. The proposals to reform the international financial architecture developed in his recent book, *Financial Markets, Money and the Real World*, are far more radical as well. If Davidson develops a viable alternative to the contemporary régime of global governance, this could call into question the systematic transition from democratic cosmopolitanism to Marxism.

---

[1] Marx 1976, pp. 915 ff.; see also Chomsky 1996; Wood 2003; Johnson 2004.
[2] Kaul et al. 1999.
[3] In future works, I hope to show that the main assertions defended in this chapter can be extended to other components of the capitalist régime of global governance.

In the present chapter, I shall not be examining Davidson's position as an end in itself, but as a means for accomplishing two goals. First, I hope to reinforce the arguments justifying the course of the systematic dialectic traced in the present study. This can be done by showing that Davidson's viewpoint is ultimately beset by the same sort of immanent contradictions as those considered in Chapter 4. Second, I hope to elucidate further essential features of a Marxian model of capitalist globalisation through discussion of Davidson's proposals.

In Section 1, I shall present Davidson's critique of the present international financial architecture. His proposals for reform will then be introduced, followed by a critical assessment of them from a Marxian standpoint. The chapter concludes with some reflections on the course of the systematic dialectic of globalisation.

1. The structural flaws of the contemporary international financial architecture

In Davidson's view, the present international financial architecture suffers from three crucial defects. They concern global currency markets, deregulated financial markets in general, and the burdens of trade imbalances.

(i) *Currency markets and the depressionary bias in the global economy*

In earlier historical periods, national and local currencies have been tied to one (or more) commodities serving as world money. This is not the case today; transactions across currency regions require the exchange of one form of national/regional currency for another.[4] At present, three currencies enjoy a special status in the world market: the dollar, the euro, and the yen. Foreign trade, foreign loans, and so on, are most often denominated in these 'strong currencies', even when the transacting parties do not originate in any of their home regions. (Well over half of the dollars in the world economy today are held outside the borders of the United States.) The contemporary international financial architecture is thus partially defined by the exchange-rate régimes

---

[4] While calls for a return to a gold exchange standard are by no means rare among neoliberal theorists, this remains very much a minority view.

in place. In Paul Davidson's judgement, all of the present options impose a very high price: excessive unemployment and an unnecessarily low level of satisfaction of human wants and needs.

Neoliberals hold, as a matter of principle, that most countries or currency unions ought to leave the determination of the relative value of their currencies to the marketplace. In their view, most governments are incapable of indefinitely maintaining a 'hard peg' between the national/regional currency and some other currency when relevant economic conditions change significantly. As circumstances change, the commitment to maintaining a hard peg becomes increasingly implausible. Betting that a revaluation will occur becomes close to a sure thing, attracting enormous speculative bets to that effect. The longer an inappropriate peg is maintained, the sharper the eventual revaluation and the more severe the resulting social disruptions, as the 1997 East-Asian crisis demonstrated.[5]

If, on the other hand, there has been an extended history of economic mismanagement in a given region, it may be better for the value of the local currency to *not* float freely in currency markets, according to most neoliberal theorists. Two alternatives are available. A currency board could be established, institutionalising a strong commitment to maintain a fixed peg between the national currency and a hard currency like the dollar. (This is done by strictly tying the amount of national currency in circulation to the country's reserves of the hard currency.) In truly exceptional cases, outright abandonment of the local currency might be preferable ('dollarisation').

These options are all flawed, in Davidson's view. When exchange rates among currencies are allowed to float freely, rates do not necessarily tend to oscillate narrowly around an equilibrium point. Instead, shifts in bearish/bullish sentiments can set off bandwagon effects, leading to wild overshooting in both directions. Re-alignments of currency values can have devastating social consequences: excessive overvaluations cause otherwise viable industries to be wiped out by cheap foreign imports; excessive undervaluations lead to higher prices for necessary imports, which also wipe out otherwise viable industries. Davidson agrees with Robert Brenner that much of the 'global turbulence' in the world economy in recent decades has been set off by the

---

[5] DeRosa 2001.

relative overvaluing or undervaluing of the yen, the dollar, and the mark/euro in relationship to each other.[6]

The instability of global currency markets implies that potential foreign investors in long-term projects face greater currency risks regarding the profits (measured in their home currency) that they can appropriate from foreign direct investment. Potential domestic investors face greater currency risks regarding the profits (measured again in their home currency) they can appropriate through exports. The mere possibility of volatility in currency markets tends to result in lower rates of long-term investment. And lower rates of long-term productive investments lead to lower rates of growth, higher unemployment, and a higher level of unmet wants and needs.

Government officials, realising the harm a speculative run on their currency can cause, tend to act in ways that reinforce this depressionary bias. Public policies accommodating 'market sentiments' are implemented in the hope of reducing exchange-rate volatility. Participants in currency markets widely believe that government deficit spending and higher wages tend to set off inflation and, eventually, flight from the national currency. These beliefs can become a self-fulfilling prophecy. With everyone betting that everyone else will flee a currency, even investors who believe that deficit spending and higher wages could have positive medium-to-long-term effects in the given context must join the stampede or be crushed. Knowing this, governments will tend to abandon such policies, or refuse to consider them in the first place. When a danger of outflows looms they will also aggressively institute high real interest rates, despite the knowledge that this tends to create unemployment and low real wages.[7]

From the post-Keynesian standpoint, other currency régimes in the present international financial architecture are even more defective. When an economic

---

[6] Brenner 1998, 2002.

[7] None of these policies removes volatility in currency markets. When are interest rates high enough? When are austerity programmes austere enough? What will currency risks be in the future? There are no certain answers to any of these questions. And so stampedes of inflows and outflows of financial capital are all but guaranteed in unregulated currency markets, no matter what governments do, as investors attempt to guess what other investors will guess the dominant view will probably be in the next year, the next month, the next day, hour, minute, second. In Keynes's famous analogy, financial markets are like beauty contests in which winners correctly predict which contestant will be selected by the most fellow judges.

crisis breaks out in a country making use of a currency board, capital flight will increase, reducing reserves of the target strong currency. Currency board rules dictate that domestic currency must then be eliminated in the same proportion as lost target currency, automatically draining liquidity from the national economy at precisely the time greater liquidity is required.[8] Similarly, with 'dollarisation' the government rules out in principle any possibility of developing the capacity to stimulate economic growth or avoid/minimise crises through monetary policy. The severity and duration of crises are thus likely to worsen.

One other sort of exchange-rate régime remains to be considered, the one selected by most countries. A commitment can be made to maintain exchange rates within a given band. This approach promises to lessen exchange-rate risks considerably relative to a pure free-floating exchange-rate régime, without committing policymakers to maintaining a particular hard peg. If the band is too wide, however, this option approaches a free-floating exchange-rate régime with its high exchange-rate risks, discouraging long-term investments and encouraging depressionary government policies to accommodate 'market sentiment'. If the band is too narrow, this option approaches a hard peg, inviting the same sort of speculative attacks whenever economic circumstances change. Given the ineluctable uncertainties of economic life, setting the band just right is a matter of brute luck, unlikely to continue indefinitely as economic circumstances change.

For Davidson, the defects of global currency markets form but one dimension of a fatally flawed financial order.

(ii) *The tyranny of the financial sector*

In Davidson's view, it is possible in principle to maintain a golden age of full employment growth in capitalism. Two necessary preconditions for this state of affairs are:

---

[8] As the crisis worsens as a consequence, the political pressure to abandon the currency board becomes stronger and stronger. Betting that it will be abandoned and the currency revalued becomes very close to a sure thing, and so massive bets to that effect are made. The longer the currency board arrangement persists, the sharper the eventual revaluation, and the more severe the harm inflicted on the society, as Argentinean experience in the late 1990s demonstrated. See Smith 2003b.

- The banking system must provide sufficient endogenously created credit money to accommodate the requirements of expanded investment.[9]
- Real interest rates must remain low.

Even if these two preconditions are given, however, a golden age will not necessarily endure. Uncertainty about the future may lead a critical mass of economic agents to prefer holding money in its most liquid ('high powered') form to investing in the securities that directly or indirectly fuel industrial development and employment opportunities. If special measures are not introduced to address this liquidity preference, a gulf will arise between what is rational from the standpoint of individual agents and what is rational from the standpoint of society as a whole. Suppose, for example, doubts arise regarding the continued creditworthiness of some firms. They may then have difficulty rolling over their loans, leading to lay-offs and bankruptcies. Enterprises that previously extended credit to these firms soon become vulnerable themselves; their own survival may be threatened if they cannot roll over *their* loans. These ripple effects may set off a general economic crisis, harming enterprises that would otherwise remain creditworthy. From the standpoint of society as a whole, it is not rational for human resources to go unemployed on such a vast scale, and for human wants and needs to remain unmet, simply due to a shift in liquidity preferences by some investors.

For Davidson, the most essential task of the state is to minimise the conflict between individual rationality and collective rationality. In the present context, this means that bankruptcy provisions must be designed to enable firms with positive medium-to-long-term prospects to restructure onerous debts. And the central bank must step in as the lender of last resort when an economic crisis threatens, providing liquidity more or less on demand. In this manner, the severity and temporal duration of a disturbance can be minimised, and a general crisis avoided altogether. Some debtors may still go under. But most fundamentally sound corporations facing temporary difficulties meeting their financial obligations should be able to attain financing to hold them over

---

[9] In mature capitalism, the main form of money is the *endogenously* created credit money arising when banks and other financial institutions extend credit to their customers. In normal times, financial institutions are generally able to provide loans to all customers considered creditworthy, through financial innovations, if need be. See Wray 1990; a superb Marxian discussion is found in Campbell 2002.

until conditions improve. If the central bank provides liquidity in sufficient quantities, the demand of those who desire to keep their wealth in liquid forms can be met without inflicting significant harm on the industrial sector.

These necessary preconditions for a golden age of full-employment growth themselves have a necessary precondition: the financial sector must be subject to effective social controls.

Davidson's second major objection to the present international financial architecture is that fulfilling this all-important task is ruled out by today's international financial architecture.

For neoliberals, financial markets gather, process, and transmit relevant information regarding the real counterparts of financial assets and the condition of borrowers in a rationally efficient manner.[10] While neoliberal theorists grant that individual traders in these markets may err, the collective wisdom of the market exceeds any possible alternative form of allocation. Market competition, after all, provides both material incentives for traders to get the relative values of financial assets right, and effective sanctions on those who consistently err. As a result, asset prices necessarily tend to reflect the true value of their real counterparts (the 'fundamentals').[11] While risks remain, probabilities can be estimated accurately, enabling traders to offer savers financial investments precisely fitting the level of risk they are willing to accept for any given level of potential reward. It follows that credit money tends to be allocated to industries with the greatest productive potential. No set of government officials is likely to be better informed than the collective wisdom of financial markets, and so government intervention in these markets necessarily tends to lower efficiency.

For post-Keynesians, this account abstracts from a number of essential features of the global economy. First of all, it abstracts from the fact that in a world of free capital flows much of the credit money created in regions with weak national currencies will be lost to capital flight. Effective demand for financial assets from wealthy regions rises, rather than levels of indigenous productive investment.[12]

---

[10] McKinnon 1973.

[11] More technically, according to this view the values of capital assets necessarily 'gravitate toward the means of normal probability distribution of the present values of their net revenue streams'. Eatwell 1996, 10.

[12] As L. Randall Wray has pointed out, the process of endogenous money creation

The neoliberal story also abstracts from the single most critical feature of financial markets, their radical uncertainty, a point stressed already in Chapter 2. Given this uncertainty, successful investment in financial assets is primarily a matter of anticipating shifts in the 'bearish' and 'bullish' sentiments of fellow traders. It follows that the motive for investing in financial assets will generally not be to hold the fixed assets they represent for the long-term, but to profit from selling the former in the short-to-medium term. As investment sentiment shifts in a 'bullish' direction, investors who anticipated this shift win high profits, attracting further 'bullish' investments. A self-reinforcing boom may then occur, leading to a speculative bubble in the given asset class. Many of those who realise the boom cannot be sustained indefinitely will join the bandwagon, expecting to find yet bigger fools to whom yet more inflated assets can be sold. When, at some contingent point, investor sentiment reverses – that is, a critical mass of investors fears the pool of bigger fools is close to being depleted – a stampede out of the asset commences, accompanied by a hunt for a new asset class where the game can begin anew.

Deregulated financial markets are thus not rationally efficient mechanisms of allocating capital for industrial development. Endogenously created credit money may never escape the financial sector. On the level of the world market, the deregulation of the financial sector has led to the emergence of a 'global casino' in which investments take the form of speculative bets on financial assets (equities, currencies, various forms of securities, real estate, etc.), rather than long-term investments in industrial development.[13] Nor do these investments fluctuate smoothly in the neighbourhood of an equilibrium point. Unregulated financial markets are prone to instability. In George Soros's striking image, they career wildly like wrecking balls, leaving havoc in their wake.[14] A deregulated financial sector also necessarily tends to lead to real

in so-called 'less developed countries' (LDCs) is distorted under the present IFA, since wealth owners there often prefer the debts of developed countries: 'That is, even at high interest rates, agents in the LDC will not be able to issue debt to finance spending because the liabilities of the DC are preferable. In this case, the money supply of the LDC cannot be endogenously increased because high "liquidity preference" (that is, preference for DC debts) prevents creation of LDC money'. Wray 1990, p. 63.

[13] Strange 1998; Duménil and Lévy 2004. Strictly speaking, the casino analogy is misleading. In casinos, the probabilities of various outcomes are known, or at least knowable. This is not the case for global markets in capital assets, where uncertainty, not risk with known probabilities, is the relevant category.

[14] Soros 1998.

interest rates being fixed at a level far higher than what is compatible with full employment. Governments that do not keep real interest rates sufficiently high are threatened with unacceptable levels of capital flight.

Finally, when financial crises break out, the present international financial architecture is either ineffectual or actually exacerbates the difficulties. On the national level, attempts to increase liquidity in periods where financial crises threaten suffer from the same difficulty as attempts to accommodate full employment growth through endogenously created credit money. If financial markets are deregulated, the increased liquidity may simply set off inflation in capital assets. On the global level, there is no effective lender of last resort to even attempt to provide the required liquidity to the global economy. There is also no international bankruptcy court with the power to enable firms that would be solvent in the medium-to-long term to free themselves from foreign debts that could destroy them in the short-term.

For Davidson, as for Rawls, Gray, Veblen, Stiglitz, Held, and other critics of neoliberalism discussed in Part One, financial capital should be a mere means to serve the proper ends of economic life, the satisfaction of human wants and needs and the provision of the material preconditions for autonomous agency. Without proper regulation, however, means illicitly usurp the place of ends.

(iii) *Trade imbalances and the burdens of adjustment*

Many nations today aggressively encourage export industries, seeking economic growth through trade surpluses. When high growth is attained through success in export markets, the currency of countries enjoying trade surpluses generally appreciates, lowering the prices of imports. This allows the living standards of workers to increase, even if real wages stagnate. Other strategies for high levels of growth are more likely to require an incomes policy, that is, a politically negotiated agreement regarding the distribution of income between investors and employees. Economic and political élites generally prefer to avoid such negotiations. The problems with the growth through exports strategy are legion, in Davidson's view. For every nation with a trade surplus, there must be one or more suffering deficits. The flip side of the tendency for the currency of surplus nations to appreciate is a tendency towards devaluation of the currency of deficit nations; the lowering of import prices in the former is matched by an increase in the latter. To the extent wages increase in response to this price increase, the price stability of surplus nations comes at the cost of inflation in deficit nations. This ability of surplus nations to shift inflationary dangers to others is reminiscent of the 'beggar thy neighbour' policies of the period immediately preceding the Great Depression.

In standard neoliberal theory, this entire set of issues falls off the radar entirely. When trade imbalances occur, flexible exchange rates supposedly allow a more or less automatic adjustment. Devaluation of the currency of the deficit nation lowers the prices of its exports and increases the prices of its imports. The increase of the former and the decrease of the latter necessarily tend to resolve the problem.

I have already noted a tendency for currency markets to 'overshoot' exchange rate adjustments. But, even if we abstract from overshooting, the neoliberal perspective on the issue is marred by a neglect of differences in the elasticities of demand of imports. Suppose a country falls into deficit, and its currency is devalued in response. It will then import less in physical terms, but pay more in terms of its own currency for each unit that is imported. It will also export more, but receive less in terms of its own currency for each unit exported. Now, suppose this country is a 'less-developed nation' with

> a comparative advantage in the exports of raw materials and other basic commodities that typically have a low income elasticity of demand, while . . . hav[ing] a high income elasticity of demand (eldc) for the manufactured products of the developed world.[15]

In such circumstances, devaluation can *exacerbate* the trade deficit. The effect of fewer imports in physical terms is swamped by the increase in their cost; the benefit of greater exports in physical terms is undermined by the decrease in their prices.[16]

In the present international financial architecture, the burden of adjusting to persistent trade imbalances between wealthy surplus countries and poorer deficit countries falls almost entirely on deficit nations. Deficits in the current account must be balanced by surpluses in the capital account; capital inflows such as loans from global capital markets must exceed capital outflows. For a variety of reasons, these loans may not be self-liquidating. First of all, to

---

[15] Davidson 2002, p. 160.
[16] These issues will be developed in greater detail below.

be self-liquidating, they would have to be used to fund projects resulting in the accumulation of hard currency, rather than the capital flight, luxury consumption, or vanity projects of local élites. Nothing in the contemporary global order ensures this result. Even if these loans are invested productively, niches have to be found that fundamentally change the relationship between the price elasticities of imports vis-à-vis exports. This is not so easy to do, especially if firms from other nations pursue the same goal simultaneously. A new form of widget with high-income elasticity in global markets can quickly become just another commodity with low-income elasticity as numerous enterprises from a variety of regions begin to produce it.

If the initial loans are not self-liquidating, additional borrowing will eventually have to take place to cover interest payments as they become due. These new loans will almost surely be placed in the 'high risk' category, with correspondingly high interest rates. To the extent these loans are devoted to meeting interest payments, they are even less likely to be self-liquidating than the initial ones. And, so, yet more borrowing will eventually be required to meet interest payments on the loans that were taken out to meet the interest payments on the initial loans. And so on and on. Once a country has fallen into this 'debt trap', a high portion of a nation's income will take the form of means of payment to international creditors, becoming incorporated within circuits of capital beginning and ending in world centres of financial capital. This income is not available to fund a golden age of full employment growth.[17]

Davidson's analysis of global currency markets, the general social consequences of deregulated financial markets, and the distribution of the burdens of trade imbalances, together constitute a fairly radical critique of the present international financial architecture. In his view, this IFA represents 'a regression toward the barbaric policies of the classical system where unemployment is the main weapon against inflation and available resources are rarely used to their full potential'.[18] From his post-Keynesian standpoint, these features of the IFA amount to a horrible inversion of the proper relationship between the financial sector and the industrial sector. Financial flows, which should serve the end of industrial development, now hamper

---

[17] See also Guttmann 1994, pp. 439–40.
[18] Davidson 2002, p. 5.

it. It should thus be no surprise that the neoliberal period is associated with a lower rate of growth, lower wages, and higher unemployment than the 'golden age' of the quarter century after World War Two:

> For almost a quarter of a century after the Second World War, governments actively pursued the types of economic policies that Keynes had advocated in the 1930s and 1940s. The result was that per capita economic growth in the capitalist world proceeded at a rate that has never been reached in the past or matched since.... By 1973 Keynes's analytical vision of how to improve the operation of a market-oriented, entrepreneurial system had been lost by politicians, their economic advisors and most academic economists. As a result, Keynes's policy prescriptions fell from grace.... [R]esurrecting Keynes's analytical vision [is] an aid for developing twenty-first century policies that will reinstate a golden age of rapid economic growth that is the prerequisite for creating a civilized society for our global community.[19]

As noted in Part One, many theorists have proposed reforms to the international financial architecture. A partial list of recommendations includes Tobin taxes, standstills on debt repayment when financial crises occur, special bankruptcy provisions kicking in when exceptional macro-economic disturbances break out, debt to equity and debt forgiveness plans, international credit guarantee schemes (with strict regulation of the banks authorised to distribute this credit), more stringent capital adequacy standards, limited government insurance, co-operation between currency blocs (for example, unlimited swap agreements between the dollar and the euro), margin requirements for all derivatives, swaps and forwards transactions, licensing of all synthetic financial instruments (similar to new issues of securities), increased reliance on domestic sources of capital (the use of pension funds in Chile is often taken as a paradigm here), reserve requirements on short-term capital inflows, co-operation among central banks to curb speculation, improved regulation of banking (for example, restrictions on speculative real estate lending), improved safety nets, social investment funds targeted to the poorest regions

---

[19] Davidson 2002, pp. 1–4. See also Eatwell 1996; Eatwell and Taylor 2002; and the text associated with note 61 in Chapter 2.

in the global economy, and so on.[20] Proposals such as these are, in effect, calls to institutionalise a priority of certain forms of money over others in the world market. Money in the form of investment capital in the industrial sector, and money in the form of a means of circulation culminating in the consumption of goods and services, are granted privileged status over money in the form of means of investment in financial speculation or means of payment to creditors.

From Davidson's post-Keynesian standpoint, however, these proposals do not go nearly far enough. They leave in place the single greatest problem afflicting the global order today, the lack of an adequate form of world money. They also fail to provide the proper social regulation of the financial sector. And the burdens of adjusting to trade imbalances would still disproportionately fall on deficit nations. Far more radical proposals are called for.

2. Davidson's proposals to reform the international financial architecture

Davidson defends a number of specific reforms of the international financial architecture. Rather than follow his order of presentation I shall group them under the headings of the previous section.

(i) A new form of world money

Davidson first calls for a new form of world money:

> First, the unit of account and ultimate reserve asset for international liquidity is the International Money Clearing Unit (IMCT). All IMCUs can be held *only* by the central banks of nations that abide by the rules of the clearing union system. . . . [T]he exchange rate between the domestic currency and the IMCU is set initially by each nation or currency union's central bank.[21]

---

[20] George Soros has suggested a 'triple 2/3 test' for implementing these sorts of global reforms. If representatives in the United Nations of two-thirds of member countries, two-thirds of the world's population, and of countries providing two-thirds of the UN's budget, all agree on a certain reform, that reform should be implemented as a matter of international law. Soros 1998.

[21] Davidson 2002, pp. 232–3.

He also insists that the long-term purchasing power of the IMCU in terms of foreign-produced goods remains stable. If inflation breaks out in a particular national economy, the exchange rate between its currency and the IMCU must be devalued. If a permanent improvement in efficiency wages occurs in a nation as a result of productivity advances, leading to declining production costs measured in the local currency, then the country could choose to revalue the exchange rate so that the IMCU buys fewer units of domestic currency without any loss of purchasing power. In this case, all the benefits from the productivity advance are captured in the national economy. Or the nominal exchange rate could be kept constant, allowing the country's export prices to be lowered, expanding its export markets. The benefits of the productivity advance are now shared with the nations importing its commodities at lower prices. The rules fixing the exchange rate between the IMCU and national currencies guarantee that firms will not suffer a competitive disadvantage due to changes in nominal exchange rates having nothing to do with alterations in the real costs of production. This proviso, in other words, removes the temptation for a nation to pursue growth through a real exchange-rate devaluation that does not reflect its relative efficiency in the world market.

With only one form of world money, the global casino of currency markets would be shut down. The horrific economic and social disruptions caused by abrupt and massive revaluations of the dollar, the mark, the yen, and other currencies linked to them directly and indirectly would be eliminated.

(ii) *The taming of global capital markets*

A second set of proposals addresses the tyranny of global financial markets over societies in general and governments in particular. This tyranny can be dismantled if and only if the relationship between national currencies and the world money is transformed along the following lines:

> [E]ach nation's central bank or, in the case of a common currency (for
> example, the euro) a currency union's central bank, is committed to guarantee
> one-way convertibility from IMCU deposits at the clearing union to domestic
> money. Each central bank will set its own rules regarding making available
> foreign monies (through IMCU clearing transactions) to its own bankers
> and private sector residents. . . . Contracts to be settled in terms of foreign
> currency will require some publicly announced commitment from the central

bank (through private sector bankers) of the availability of foreign funds to meet such private contractual obligations.[22]

One-way convertibility permits each nation to control international flows of capital funds:

> The guarantee of only one-way convertibility permits each nation to institute controls and regulations on international capital fund flows if necessary. The primary economic function of these international capital-flow controls and regulations is to prevent rapid changes in the bull-bear sentiment from . . . inducing dramatic changes in international financial market price trends that can have devastating real consequences.[23]

Prior to the outbreak of the East-Asian crisis, local banks extensively borrowed dollars from global capital markets, using much of the debt for speculative investments in capital assets such as real estate. When bubbles in these assets collapsed, the local currency was devalued, tremendously exacerbating the difficulty of repaying foreign creditors in the dollars owed. Post-Keynesians insist that governments must have the tools to avoid this state of affairs.

From the neoliberal standpoint, the above proposals amount to an especially despicable form of 'financial repression', contravening the principle that investors ought to be free to decide for themselves where they wish to invest. Even worse, these measures undermine the ability of poor regions in the global economy to acquire the funds necessary to generate economic growth and improve living standards. Restrictions – or even the mere threat of restrictions – on 'contracts to be settled in terms of a foreign currency' discourage such money flows, hampering the process of eradicating material deprivation in the global economy. Neoliberals conclude that such restrictions should be vehemently rejected on normative as well as efficiency grounds.

The empirical case for this conclusion is weak. The great success stories of economic development in the history of capitalism have not been based on neoliberal precepts, but rather on some variant of the 'developmental-state' model, with the state directing domestic savings and credit creation to local

---

[22] Davidson 2002, pp. 232–3.
[23] Davidson 2002, p. 232.

industrial enterprises while strictly regulating inflows of portfolio investment and FDI.[24] The neoliberal international financial architecture attempts to dismantle the developmental state, the single most effective means of industrial development in the history of capitalism. Turning to developed economies, full employment growth requires an accommodating banking system in which endogenously created credit money supports long-term investments, interest rates are kept low, and liquidity created by the state in response to pessimistic market sentiments is funnelled to industrial investments rather than speculation in capital assets. None of this will occur in the absence of effective social regulation of the financial sector.

Davidson's reforms of the international financial architecture are designed to allow states in both the developing and the developed regions of the globe to institute the policies required for a golden age of full-employment growth.[25] An international financial architecture guaranteeing convertibility from world money to the national currency, but not from this currency to International Money Clearing Units, is an essential element of this programme. This measure gives states the power to prevent pools of domestic savings and newly created credit money from leaking from the domestic economy to global financial markets.

(iii) *Adjustments to imbalances in the global economy*

If some nations are allowed to accumulate surpluses indefinitely, the inevitable result is a world in which the most vulnerable regions of the globe are condemned to severe and relentless austerity. Significant human wants and needs go unmet, and incalculable human potential is wasted. Insofar as this state of affairs is not inevitable, but results from specific social policies, these policies can properly be termed 'barbaric'.[26]

---

[24] Wade 1990.

[25] '[I]n recent decades, the mainstream of the economics profession has promoted this persistent unemployment flaw to a positive virtue in its concept of a non-accelerating inflation rate of unemployment (NAIRU) instead of labelling unemployment for what it is – a social waste and public disgrace. Positive actions and innovative institutions can be developed to prevent any significant, persistent unemployment from occurring in an open multinational economic system'. Davidson 2002, p. 253.

[26] Davidson 2002, p. 5.

In the short term, this situation can be alleviated by mobilising temporary surpluses for industrial development:

> [A]n overdraft system should be built into the clearing union rules. Overdrafts should make available short-term unused creditor balances at the clearing house to finance the productive international transactions of others who need short-term credit. The terms will be determined by the *pro bono publico* clearing union managers.[27]

In the medium-to-long term, no nation should be permitted to accumulate excessive surpluses:

> [A] trigger mechanism to encourage any creditor nation to spend what is deemed (in advance) by agreement of the international community to be 'excessive' credit balances accumulated by running current account surpluses [is required]. These excessive credits can be spent in three ways: (a) on the products of any other member of the clearing union, (b) on new direct foreign investment projects, and/or (c) to provide unilateral transfers (foreign aid) to deficit members.[28]

This proposal removes excessive oversavings in the global economy, providing nations suffering a payments deficit greater opportunities to sell abroad. Keynes insisted long ago that both economic efficiency and elementary normative considerations demand that surplus and deficit nations share the burdens of adjusting to a disequilibrium in payments. Nothing has occurred in the intervening decades to make the point less valid.

International payments deficits may still persist, even if no nation accumulates excessive surpluses indefinitely. Davidson's final proposal addresses this problem. If a poor country falls into deficit, rich countries must transfer some of their excess credit balances, enabling that country to develop its productive capacity and increase its exports to the point where it can maintain its standard of living.[29] If the deficit nation is relatively wealthy, it must devalue its exchange rate by gradual increments until the lowering of export prices and raising of import prices eliminate the export-import imbalance.

---

[27] Davidson 2002, pp. 233–4.
[28] Davidson 2002, p. 234.
[29] Davidson here assumes that the country is at full employment. If it is not, then presumably Keynesian public policies must be instituted in order to bring about full employment.

What if these measures succeed in attaining a positive balance of trade in goods and services, but the payment deficit is not eradicated? This suggests that the international debt service load is too high. Negotiations must then commence to consider lengthening the payments period, reducing interest charges, and forgiving previous debts.[30]

The above proposals are based on an accurate assessment of the weaknesses of the contemporary international financial architecture. Post-Keynesians like Davidson share with Marxists an outrage regarding the combination of indifference and obfuscation with which most mainstream social theorists respond to global inequalities, which deprive billions of people of the material preconditions for developing their capacities and exercising their autonomy. Rather than following Marx's path, however, post-Keynesians attempt to imagine a form of capitalism capable of fulfilling its unmet promises. Marxists who wish to argue that the flaws of the present 'régime of global governance' are structural should not contemptuously dismiss the deep utopian drive underlying this project. Its limits must be carefully specified, for they are the limits of the reign of capital.

3. A Marxian assessment of Davidson's proposals

Before proceeding to an examination of the details of Davidson's case, a general comment on his methodological framework is in order. He begins with the assumption that the régime of global governance ought to be designed to allow the greatest feasible satisfaction of human wants and needs in the world market. He then attempts to deduce what rules for world money must be established in order to achieve that goal. From a Marxian standpoint, this methodological framework is 'idealist' and, as such, fatally flawed. If the goal is to comprehend a given set of social forms, we should not simply assume that these forms are ultimately subordinate to some normative principle or other. The normative principle in question may turn out to be quite extrinsic to those social forms, or even incompatible with them. In the case at hand, a historical-materialist approach would begin instead with an examination of the basic social relations defining capitalism, tracing their implications to

---

[30] Davidson 2002, pp. 236–7.

the bitter end. In other words, the proper question here is not, 'What must the international financial architecture be, if human wants and needs are to be satisfied to the greatest feasible extent?'. The question is, instead, 'What must the international financial architecture be, given the social relations defining capitalism?'. This question will be examined in three stages, paralleling the division of the two previous sections.

(i) *World money as an end in itself*

Davidson correctly notes the depressionary bias introduced by global currency markets. His proposal to introduce a new form of world money, International Money Clearing Units, is explicitly designed to remove this bias. A brief review of the Marxian theory of money introduced in Chapter 5 provides reasons to doubt whether this proposal is consistent with the social relations of capitalism.

The simplest and most abstract way of categorising capitalism is as a system of generalised commodity production, in which privately undertaken labour may or may not prove to be socially necessary. Such a system requires a socially objective measure of value. Value-producing labour cannot appear directly and be measured according to its immanent measure, time. It can only appear in the form of an external thing with a special property distinct from whatever concrete and heterogeneous qualities it might possess as a physical entity: the abstract and homogeneous quality of universal exchangeability. Such a thing is money.

From the neoliberal standpoint, money is merely a generalised means to aid individuals and groups in the pursuit of their private goals. For post-Keynesians, in contrast, uncertainty about the future, combined with inadequate regulation of financial activities, can lead to a perverse outcome in which liquidity preferences – the desire of savers to hold 'high-powered' money, instead of less liquid instruments such as securities – systematically prevent human wants and needs from being satisfied to the greatest feasible extent. They insist, however, that this socially irrational outcome can be avoided with proper regulation of the financial sector.

From a Marxian standpoint, neither viewpoint adequately comprehends the ontological inversion introduced by the money-form. The capitalist mode of production is not some complicated form of generalised barter in which money is a mere instrument introduced for our convenience. To recognise that money is the only socially objective measure of value is to recognise that there is, in fact, an overall goal or end of social life conceptually and ontologically distinct – if inseparable – from the intentions of particular social agents and groups. The valorisation imperative – Money must beget money! – is the dominant principle of the capitalist system; monetary accumulation is the immanent end of capitalist society. The satisfaction of human wants and needs necessarily tends to occur only to the extent it is compatible with the 'self-valorisation of value', that is, the accumulation of a sum total of money at the conclusion of a given period exceeding the sum invested at the beginning of that period (M-C-M', with M' > M).

Value, abstract labour, and money are ultimately defined on the level of the world market. The generalised insecurity resulting from the danger that concrete labour may be socially wasted is an essential determination of the world market, and this is inherently tied to the need for a socially objective validation of labour as socially necessary. *The accumulation of world money, the sole socially objective measure of abstract labour on the level of the world market, is thus the immanent end of the capitalist world market.*

International Money Clearing Units, the new form of world money advocated by Davidson, are units of account and means of circulation in international transactions. But they are not ends in themselves. In Davidson's reformed international financial architecture, they are supposed to circulate in a smooth and balanced fashion across the world economy, as opposed to being the objects of a mad drive to accumulate in a competitive war to the (economic) death. Post-Keynesians thus call for a form of world money in fundamental tension with the most basic determination of world money in the global capitalist order, its perverse ontological status as an end in itself over against human ends.[31]

(ii) *The state, full employment, and the role of the financial sector in systematic cycles of accumulation*

Davidson is surely correct that a deregulated financial sector is, in principle, incompatible with instituting and maintaining a golden age of full-employment

---

[31] It should come as no surprise that attempts within the IMF to institute 'special drawing rights', a form of world money related to IMCUs, have come to so little.

growth. In response, he insists that an international financial architecture is required in which Central Banks guarantee only one-way convertibility, from IMCUs to national currencies. The ability to control capital flight by denying convertibility from the national currency to IMCUs would, indeed, discourage speculative inflows of financial capital far more effectively than Tobin taxes or the other proposed reforms of the régime of global governance considered in Part One. After the power of global financial markets has been broken in this manner, Davidson concludes, governments would then be free to implement Keynesian policies capable of maintaining a golden age similar to that following World War Two. Unfortunately, however, this conclusion fails to take either the capital/wage-labour relation or intercapital relations into account adequately.

How does money, an inert thing, beget money? Any adequate theory of capital must explain this mystery. The units of production in which concrete labour is privately undertaken are units of capital employing wage-labourers. The accumulation of money capital is not merely the social validation of privately undertaken labour. It is, simultaneously, the reproduction of the exploitative capital/wage-labour relation, for capital is not productive of anything in itself:

> Capital is productive of value only as a *relation*, in so far as it is a coercive force on wage-labour, compelling it to perform surplus-labour, or spurring on the productive power of labour to produce relative surplus-value. In both cases it only produces value as the power of labour's own material conditions over labour when these are alienated from labour; only as one of the forms of wage-labour itself, as a condition of wage-labour.[32]

Accumulation ultimately occurs on the level of the world market, and, so, world money cannot be adequately comprehended in abstraction from the systematic reproduction of the capital/wage-labour relation on the global level.

Post-Keynesians want a form of world money enabling states to pursue full employment policies in their national economy without being punished by financial markets. They rightly fear, however, that full employment may

---

[32] Marx 1963, p. 93.

set off a wage-price inflationary spiral. And, so, they call for an incomes policy. Representatives of capital and wage-labour must agree to a fair distribution of income under the helpful guidance of the state:

> Since domestic inflation is a symptom of a fight over the distribution of income, the government, in its role of the protector of the economic peace, will have to restrain the domestic combatants in this battle via an incomes policy that is compatible with the political and cultural ethics of the nation.[33]

There are two fundamental problems with this analysis. First, it fails to recognise the inflationary tendencies built into monetary régimes based on credit money. The extension of credit to the industrial sector can be seen as a 'private prevalidation' of the private and concrete labour undertaken in that sector.[34] In Marxian terms, loans are made under the assumption that surplus-value will eventually be produced and realised in the market, enabling industrial firms to repay the loans out of their profits. If surplus-value is not produced on a sufficiently broad scale within a certain time period, however, the central bank may intervene, providing liquidity to banks and other financial institutions. If the latter use this liquidity to make further loans to industrial firms, these firms can roll over previous loans by taking on more debt. Crises can be temporally displaced in this manner, at least in certain regions and at least for certain periods. The sharp and abrupt slowdowns that occurred when credit money was strictly subordinate to commodity money are then avoided. However, this 'pseudo-social validation' of private labour comes at the cost of inflationary tendencies having little to do with 'excessive' wage demands.[35]

Second, the assumption that there is a 'fair' distribution of income between capital and labour waiting to be discovered is disputable, to put it mildly.

---

[33] Davidson 2002, p. 254.

[34] de Brunhoff 1978.

[35] 'The untrammelled operations of the credit system might create quantities of credit money, willingly held at all times, that are not in harmony with real accumulation. The possibility exists of price inflation arising purely due to monetary factors, as well as of speculative bubbles involving stock exchanges and other assets. In this respect, the incomes policy proposed by post-Keynesians is not only irrelevant to inflation, but also inimical to workers' interests as it prevents the proper readjustment of nominal (hence real) wages'. Itoh and Lapavitsas 1999, p. 244. See also de Brunhoff 1978, p. 128 and Chapter 2.

From the standpoint of Marx's concept of capital, this claim is utter nonsense. Capital is nothing but a product of collective social labour that has taken an alien form over and against working men and women.[36] No level of wages consistent with the reproduction of this set of social forms could ever be 'fair', even in principle.

Talk of fairness here is dubious, even apart from the theory of exploitation. Not all 'stakeholders' are created equal in the present mode of production. The interests of investors and top managers have priority; they are the ones making the 'contributions' and bearing the 'risks' that capitalist ideology, law, and practice proclaim merit the greatest reward. Further, the generalised insecurity of capitalism means that no amount of monetary surplus is ever sufficient from the standpoint of a representative unit of capital. Funds must be on hand to expand in good times, withstand downturns in particular markets, and shift to new markets as opportunities arise. However ample the funds already accumulated, and however great the hope that credit will always be forthcoming on demand, more is always better in the competitive struggle unto death among units of capital. What is 'fair' from the standpoint of capital will thus necessarily tend to be far different from what is 'fair' from the standpoint of wage-labourers. And this is but one area of irresolvable conflict. Issues regarding the length and intensity of the work day, the appropriate level of skill and creative work for each job, the introduction and employment of new technologies, and so on, necessarily tend to generate systematic antagonisms as well.

'Between equal rights, force decides'.[37] Generally speaking, full employment shifts the balance of power in labour's favour. Whatever the role of the pre-validation and pseudo-validation of value in contemporary capitalism, the self-valorisation of value remains the overriding end of the system as a whole. The shift of the balance of power in labour's favour that would occur from lasting full employment profoundly threatens the attainment of this end. And, so, those who control money capital necessarily tend to attempt to reverse this state of affairs. Unemployment in regions of labour strength can be brought about through investments in labour-saving (and deskilling) technologies, capital flight to regions where the workforce is relatively docile/intimidated,

---

[36] Marx 1976, pp. 755–6. See Chapter 5 above.
[37] Marx 1976, p. 344.

and capital strikes, including shifts of investment from production to speculation on financial assets. To maintain full employment over time under such circumstances would demand far more than an incomes policy. It would demand a fundamental change in social forms.

There is no systematic necessity for world money to be silver, gold, sterling, dollars, or euros. But whatever shape it does take, world money in capitalism must of necessity reflect the social antagonisms of the capital/wage-labour relation. There is a tendency in post-Keynesianism to treat 'producers' as a homogenous group, failing to appreciate the immense class divide between industrial capital and wage-labour. It is true, of course, that global financial markets and international organisations like the IMF often harm the interests of industrial capitals and their workers simultaneously. But, from a Marxian perspective, the class antagonism at the heart of the capital/wage-labour relation cannot be overlooked. Whatever form of existence world money takes, it must necessarily allow investments in labour-saving technologies, capital flight to regions of the world market where wage-labourers are more easily subsumed under the imperatives of valorisation, and capital strikes, including especially a shift from money wages to funds for speculative investments in capital assets. In brief, lasting full employment throughout the global economy is simply not consistent with the systematic reproduction of the capital/ wage-labour relation.[38] It is thus incoherent for post-Keynesians to accept the social relations defining capitalism, while simultaneously advocating a new form of world money on the grounds that it allows full employment in the capitalist world market.

The defining social relations of capital also include inter-capital relations. For present purposes, it is sufficient to note the distinction between financial capital, merchant capital, and industrial capital. I have already mentioned the quite obvious point that Davidson's proposals would be decried as 'financial repression' and fiercely resisted by financial capital. Wealthy investors desire to escape the domestic financial system whenever higher rates (relative to assessed risks) are offered elsewhere. Banks wish to be free from long-term commitments to corporations when rapid rates of technological innovation threaten the latter's prospects (which is generally the case for even the most

---

[38] See de Brunhoff 1978, Chapter 1.

prosperous companies). Both groups, in short, desire the greatest possible number of 'exit options' from the domestic economy. Arguments that reforms to the international financial architecture limiting these options are in the long-term interest of the financial sector itself can be expected to have no force whatsoever to agents operating in this sector.

The largest (and most politically influential) merchant capitals throughout the capitalist world system would generally resist the proposal as well. Their access to the means of purchase for traded commodities would be far more regulated and restricted, and could even be shut off entirely. And they, too, are engaged in foreign direct investments, outsourcing, and cross-border mergers and acquisitions. This leaves industrial capital to be considered. First, however, a brief excursus on the historical context of the present discussion is in order.

Post-Keynesians like Davidson hold that the policies they advocate regarding world money are as relevant today as they were when Keynes formulated similar ideas decades ago.[39] Arrighi's contributions to the historical study of capitalism implicitly call this claim into question.[40] As noted in the previous chapter, Arrighi documents how capitalism as a world system has been characterised by a number of distinct 'systematic cycles of accumulation', each with a different geographical centre. One pattern emerging in the historical progression from one systematic cycle to the next is the ever-increasing scale of concentration and scope of economic and political power.[41] A second pattern is the division of each systematic cycle into two main parts. A period of rapid material expansion eventually reaches its limit, and is then followed by a period in which capitals in the hegemonic region increasingly turn to financial activities, enjoying a 'golden autumn' prior to the shift of the centre of global accumulation elsewhere.

From this perspective, it is possible to assert that there was a 'Keynesian moment' in the historical development of capitalism, a moment in which the interests of industrial capital could be best furthered through 'financial

---

[39] Keynes 1980; see Guttmann 1994, Chapter 15.
[40] Arrighi 1994; Arrighi and Moore 2001.
[41] 'The development of historical capitalism as a world system has been based on the formation of ever more powerful . . . blocs of governmental and business organizations endowed with the capability of widening (or deepening) the functional and spatial scope of the world capitalist system'. Arrighi and Moore 2001, pp. 69–70.

282 · Chapter Seven

repression'. This historical moment was defined by the conjuncture of two factors. First, the concentration and centralisation of industrial capital reached the point where production was organised primarily on the level of the national economy, however much national economies were incorporated within the world market by the need to import raw materials, export finished products, and so on. Second, the systematic cycle of accumulation was in its first phase, a period of material expansion. In this specific historical context, a Keynesian approach to world money, that is, so-called 'financial repression', combined with industrial development programmes that focused on job creation, would, in fact, provide industrial capitals with opportunities for a rapid rate of capital accumulation. These circumstances were more or less in place in the 'Golden Age' after World War Two. It is no coincidence that this period was the golden age of Keynesianism as well.

This moment has now passed. The concentration and centralisation of industrial capital has proceeded apace. And the period of material expansion has given way to a global overaccumulation crisis. 'Golden age' periods in capitalism come to an end for endogenous reasons; as the concentration and centralisation of capital proceeds, the overaccumulation of capital necessarily tends to occur on an ever-more massive scale. Global turbulence and generalised economic insecurity increasingly become the normal state of affairs. The period of expansion after World War Two did not conclude because policymakers and academic élites simply 'forgot' (or never properly comprehended) Keynes's message, as Davidson claims.[42] The seeds of its demise were built into its premises, that is, in the operation of money-capital in the world market. The sort of full employment policies pursued in this period became ineffectual under conditions of overaccumulation. Maintaining them necessarily tended to have inflationary consequences, which undermined the class compromise that Keynesianism both reflected and furthered.[43]

At this point, there were two fundamental options. Either the social relations reflected in the operation of world money could be transformed in a manner furthering the interests of working men and women. Or these social relations could be transformed in a manner that furthered the interests of capital. An

---

[42] Davidson 2002, p. 5.
[43] Clarke 2001.

unexplained amnesia regarding the ABCs of Keynesian doctrine cannot explain why the latter path was taken.

In the present moment of world history, it is in the interests of leading industrial firms in all regions to have easy access to world money. They need to fund the cross-border production chains, joint ventures, and mergers and acquisitions that are sure to become increasingly important in twenty-first century capitalism.[44] They need access to world money to respond to overcapacity difficulties in their home market by invading markets where they have a competitive edge. Industrial corporations also desire to be freed from the oversight that local banks are able to enjoy on their activities in bank-centred systems, as noted in Chapter 4. Last but not least, it is in the interest of industrial capitals to have easy access to world money in order to respond to overcapacity difficulties by shifting more and more of the surplus-value they have accumulated (and more of the credit money they have borrowed) into global capital markets. Returns from speculative investments in financial assets can be far more promising than expanded investments in fixed capital in industrial sectors already characterised by excess capacity. And there is always the hope that the industrial profits that have mutated into portfolio investments will eventually flow to new centres of material accumulation, siphoning off surplus-value produced there to financial circuits whose alpha and omega points lie elsewhere.

For a set of (non-revolutionary) proposals to be feasible in a capitalist order, a ruling bloc must be formed under the leadership of a dominant faction of capital.[45] For the post-Keynesian form of world money to be remotely feasible, a coalition led by industrial capital would have to be formed and attain political hegemony against the alliance led by financial capital that would surely be formed against this proposal. To understand the historical dialectic of capitalism is to understand why such a bloc will not emerge in the present historical conjuncture. The bloc that has been formed, and will surely stay in place for the foreseeable future, is a coalition of financial, merchant and industrial capitals to maintain and extend a form of world money allowing cross-border trade, joint ventures, mergers and acquisitions, production chains,

---

[44] See Held et al. 1999; Moody 1997.
[45] Gramsci 1971.

investments in financial assets, and foreign direct investment to occur with minimum hindrance. This rules out post-Keynesian proposals for world money.

(iii) *Uneven development and the interstate system*

Davidson's third complaint against the present international financial architecture is that it systematically reproduces uneven development and material deprivation in the global economy. In his account, there are two main mechanisms generating this result. The first is based on the fact that different regions specialise in the export of commodities with quite different income elasticities. The heart of the argument is formulated in terms of 'Thirlwell's Law', an equation stating the conditions that must be met for growth in a nation's demand for imports to equal the growth in the demand for its exports: $(ya/yrw) = (erw/ea)$.[46] In words:

> [I]f nation A's international payments position is not to deteriorate, then the ratio of the growth of income in nation A to the income growth rate in the rest of the world must be equal to the ratio of rest of the world's income elasticity of demand for A's exports to A's income elasticity of demand for imports.[47]

Given this equation, a mechanism underlying the systematic tendency towards uneven development can be formulated:

> [I]f less-developed nations (LDCs) of the world have a comparative advantage in the exports of raw materials and other basic commodities that typically have a low income elasticity of demand, while the LDCs have a high income elasticity of demand (eldc) for the manufactured products of the developed world, then, for these LDCs:

$$(erw/eldc) < 1.$$

> Consequently, if LDCs follow the conventional advice of classical economists and continue to develop only their comparative advantage industries and simultaneously try to maintain a position where the market value of exports

---

[46] This law is derived in Davidson 2002, pp. 158–60, based on Thirlwell 1979.
[47] Davidson 2002, p. 160.

just equals the market value of imports, then the LDCs are condemned to relative poverty, and the global inequality of income will become larger over time.[48]

Differences in the income elasticity of exports also explain why devaluations in deficit countries need not automatically restore trade balance. This brings us to the second mechanism underlying the tendencies to global inequality and material deprivation discussed by Davidson: once an imbalance has arisen in current accounts, the burdens of adjusting to it fall almost entirely on deficit nations. The most likely result of this state of affairs is a level of debt that is neither economically efficient, normatively acceptable, or easy to reverse.

In Davidson's view, the first difficulty is resolved by the social regulation of financial markets discussed in the previous section. This enables states in developing regions to implement effective industrial policies, resulting in exports whose income elasticities are roughly comparable to those of developed nations. The resolution of the second difficulty has also been presented above. The burden of adjusting to trade imbalances should fall primarily on surplus nations, who must adopt policies that automatically allow exports from impoverished deficit nations to increase. The amount of foreign direct investment, and foreign aid that they receive must increase as well. Poor nations that still find themselves in a debt trap after these adjustments have been made must have the right to demand that payment periods be lengthened, interest charges reduced, or previous debts forgiven.

I argued in the previous section that the historical moment of the Keynesian state in the developed world has passed. These same arguments can be extended to the developmental state. Here, too, the capital/wage-labour relation is ultimately incompatible with universal full employment. And, here too, in the present historical context, there is no faction of capital whose interests would lead it to form a ruling bloc dedicated to making access to world money more difficult. Even if we put all this to the side, however, there are still good reasons to think that Davidson's proposals to reform the international financial architecture would leave in place the systematic tendency to uneven development.

---

[48] Ibid.

Consider Davidson's proposed rule that exchange rates between the IMCU and local currencies are to be fixed, changing only when a permanent improvement in efficiency wages occurs in a region as a result of advances in labour productivity. The nation in which the improvement occurs can then choose to revalue its domestic currency so that the IMCU buys fewer units of it without any loss of purchasing power. Or the nominal exchange rate can be kept constant, with the advance in labour productivity lowering the unit prices of the country's exports. *Either option generates a systematic tendency for uneven development in the world market.*

Suppose the former option is taken, and the IMCU buys fewer units of the technically advanced nation's currency. The advance in labour productivity enables that country to enjoy a more rapid rate of economic growth and a higher level of material output. This implies in turn that a virtuous circle can be established in this region; high levels of growth and output can fund a high level of future R&D funding, providing important preconditions for future advances in productivity. In contrast, lower levels of growth and output in other regions limit their ability to participate in advanced R&D, limiting opportunities for productivity advances in the succeeding period.

If the second option is selected, and nominal exchange rates are kept constant in the region enjoying the productivity gain, precisely the same virtuous and vicious circles necessarily tend to emerge. The nation enjoying the advance can lower the unit prices of its exports, gaining share in export markets while increasing profits. These profits can then fund the high levels of R&D that are preconditions for future productivity advances and high levels of growth. Other regions, unable to match this level of R&D funding, are condemned to significantly fewer future opportunities. Here, too, global inequality is systematically reproduced.

As I have noted in previous chapters, the drive to appropriate surplus profits through technological innovation is an inherent feature of inter-capital competition. This drive necessarily operates on the level of the world market, generating a systematic tendency towards uneven development in the world market over time. Reversing this tendency would require that scientific-technological advance be seen as a creation of social collective labour whose benefits belong to all members of the human community. And that would demand far more than reform of the capitalist régime of global governance.

Davidson's other proposal for overcoming uneven development in the world economy is to place the burden of adjusting to imbalances in the world economy primarily on surplus nations. What are the prospects for this reform? I shall argue that they are quite bleak, given the social relations defining global capitalism. Once again, I would like to take Arrighi's account of capitalist development as my starting point.

Arrighi divides systematic cycles of accumulation into two parts. In the first, the dynamism of the world market is centred on particular units of capital able to appropriate surplus profits for an extended historical epoch. One important precondition for the success of these units is a state pursuing a 'territorial logic' that justifies expenditures whose justification in 'capital logic' terms is far from obvious.[49] Hegemony in the world market, and hegemony in the interstate system, mutually condition and reinforce each other; 'territorial logic' and 'capital logic' are two moments of a complex dynamic whole. When overaccumulation difficulties undermine the ability of units of capital in the hegemonic region to continue appropriating surplus profits through non-financial investments, investments shift to the financial sector, enabling the region to enjoy a 'Golden Autumn' in the second part of a systematic cycle of accumulation. Throughout both periods there is an enduring imbalance in the world market benefiting the hegemonic power. In the period of material expansion, the leading units of capital associated with the hegemonic state enjoy trade surpluses. These surpluses that can be re-invested in a way that enables these units of capital to take full advantage of the high 'warranted rates of growth' they enjoy (see Chapter 5). In the second stage, there is an abiding imbalance in financial flows, allowing surplus value to be appropriated through subsuming foreign circuits of production and distribution under financial circuits based in the hegemonic region. Hegemonic states are able to pursue their perceived geopolitical interests vigorously due to their ability to appropriate sufficient revenues and credits from the economic sphere. They thus have a strong and abiding interest in maintaining a global order characterised by these two forms of fundamental imbalances. Without a fundamental transformation of both 'capital logic' and the 'territorial logic' with which it is inseparably connected, proposals to avoid imbalances in the world market are thoroughly utopian, in the bad sense of the term.

---

[49] Arrighi 1994; see also Marx 1976, p. 919.

This conclusion is reinforced when we consider that the currency of the hegemonic state necessarily tends to play a privileged role in the world market; it necessarily tends to become the main *de facto* form of world money. The hegemonic state necessarily tends to enjoy additional privileges as a direct result.[50] It does not face the same limits on its ability to create credit money and borrow from global capital markets as those imposed on other nations. For extended periods of time, at least, it can fund massive trade deficits without significant declines in the value of its currency; it can, in effect, trade paper promises for goods and services. These privileges of 'seigniorage' (in the broadest sense of the term) rest on the need and desire of foreign economic agents to obtain the dominant reserve currency of the world market in order to undertake international payments and investments. As long as credit flows to the hegemonic state continue, that is, as long as loans are rolled over by new loans, these trade deficits can balloon. For extended periods of time, deep recessions can be avoided, as more and more of the world's output is consumed in the domestic markets of the hegemonic state, with the only costs of maintaining this state of affairs the fees involved in the new loans.[51] When levels of debt to foreign investors are finally judged to be excessive by relevant authorities, a devaluation of the currency can then erode the value of foreigners' claims.[52]

---

[50] A brilliant account of the US government's role in determining the operation of world money in the early and mid-twentieth century is found in Hudson 1972. The story is brought up-to-date in Gowan's equally valuable study, *The Global Gamble* (Gowan 1999). Both works, however, tend to overestimate the ability of hegemonic states to shape flows of world money to their interests, while underestimating the extent to which the irrationalities of the capitalist world market present unforeseen challenges that even hegemonic states cannot fully control. Walter gets the balance better: 'American power consists not in an ability to force the adoption of its preferred solutions, but to prevent collective reform if the costs are perceived as being too high for itself'. Walter 1991, p. 227.

[51] 'With its own currency having a monopoly status as world money, [the US] was the only country whose capacity to run external deficits was not restricted by its available foreign exchange reserves. We could therefore run much more stimulative policies and escape recessionary policy adjustments much longer than would otherwise have been possible'. Guttmann 1994, pp. 114–15. In the decade since these words were written, the processes they describe have intensified enormously. Seigniorage also intensifies the systematic tendency to overaccumulation in the world market. The expanded ability to create credit money enjoyed by the hegemonic power, combined with inflows of foreign capital, allows the build-up of excessive capacity in leading sectors of the dominant economy to proceed far beyond the point it would otherwise attain.

[52] The US government appears to be implementing this strategy today, proving the

This implies that there can be an extended period in a systematic cycle of accumulation in which the hegemonic region stands in a deficit position vis-à-vis the remainder of the world system. 'Deficit' is an odd term to use here, since the hegemonic region still appropriates a massively disproportionate share of both the world's output and the global funds for new investment year after year after year; 'excess' seems far more appropriate. Be that as it may, in this circumstance too the interests of both leading capitals in the world market and the leading state in the interstate system are thoroughly opposed to regulations preventing imbalances in money flows from arising in the world system. It is true that the greater the build-up of fictitious capital, the greater the social disruptions that may eventually follow, both for the hegemonic power in particular and for the world market as a whole. A massive flight out of the dominant world currency may even occur, threatening the international monetary system with paralysis. None of this makes the call for an international financial architecture abolishing abiding imbalances in money flows any less utopian.

The increasing importance of cross-border joint ventures, mergers and acquisitions, production chains, portfolio flows, foreign direct investment, and so on, complicate the capital/state relationship immensely. At the present moment, new transnational capitalist class identities are undoubtedly being forged.[53] Nonetheless, it remains the case that the interests of the dominant sections of the hegemonic state, and the interests of the dominant factions of capital in the world system, remain in a symbiotic relationship.[54] Insofar as it is against the interests of the dominant factions of capital to maintain a balanced flow of commodities and money in the world market, this directly challenges the interests of the dominant state as well.

Matters are even worse, perhaps, if the historical speculation offered at the end of the previous chapter should prove correct. What if the effectiveness of national innovation systems in the North prevented any particular subset

---

accuracy of Guttmann's observation that 'There is a contradiction between being the issuer of the key currency [in the world market] and at the same time also the world's largest debtor nation. The former status depends on maintaining a stable currency, whereas the latter encourages lower exchange rates'. Guttmann 1994, p. xx. Guttmann, like Davidson, his fellow post-Keynesian, 'overcomes' contradictions of this sort by simply imagining a capitalist global order without a hierarchical interstate system.

[53] Robinson and Harris 2000.

[54] Wood 2003.

of units of capital from winning surplus profits from innovations for an extended historical period? Capital would continue to be accumulated. But the series of systematic cycles of accumulation that has characterised the historical development of capitalism since its inception would conclude. No new period of material expansion would arise, no new set of non-financial units of capital would enjoy the pre-eminence in the production and distribution of commodities enjoyed by US firms in 'the long twentieth century'. In these circumstances, the 'accumulation by dispossession' David Harvey has emphasised would have increasing importance to both leading units of capital and the states most closely associated with them.[55] By definition, this form of accumulation rules out balanced flows of money in the global economy. And, so, the earlier conclusion remains in force: as long as the main objective of units of capital operating in the world market is to appropriate as much surplus-value as possible, and the main objective of states is to maintain or improve their position in the interstate hierarchy, with each both the precondition and the result of the other, the call for an international financial architecture abolishing abiding imbalances in money flows is utopian in the bad sense of the term.

Post-Keynesians understand clearly that the way world money flows in the present international financial architecture is not consistent with the claim that the capitalist global order furthers human flourishing. But, if IMCUs were to become the sole form of world money, this claim could be maintained, in their view. There would then be no space for the currency of a hegemonic state to play a special role in the world market, or for the volatility of global capital markets to undermine social life. But we cannot simply pretend that the capitalist global order does not necessarily tend to include a hegemonic state with particular interests and the power to further them effectively. To leave capitalist production relations in place is to leave in place the hierarchical interstate system. Is it really plausible to hold that a hegemonic capitalist state (or any states imagining themselves playing this role in the near future) will give up the immense benefits of seigniorage? The question answers itself.[56]

---

[55] See note 25 of the previous chapter.

[56] The privileges enjoyed by the hegemonic state (and the units of capital most closely associated with it) in the world market are so great that no such state has ever quietly accepted a basic restructuring of the system of states. Each period of transition

There is, indeed, something deeply troubling from a moral point of view about the way institutionalised austerity in the poorest regions of the world economy is systematically connected with the extensive privileges enjoyed by hegemonic states and the units of capital most closely associated with them. But the logic of capital is not a moral logic.

4. Conclusion

An adequate account of world money must be rooted in the essential determinations of the capitalist world market. Theorists such as Davidson advocate a form of world money that, while not itself an object of accumulation, allows full employment and industrial development across the world market, thereby bringing about geopolitical balance among states and economic balance among regions of the global economy. But capitalist property and production relations require a form of world money whose accumulation is an end in itself. Flows of world money must also reproduce the structural coercion that lies at the heart of the capital/wage-labour relation, ruling out the lasting full employment that would pose insuperable difficulties to capital accumulation. The passing of the historical moment of the Keynesian state, the tendency for cross-border joint ventures, mergers and acquisitions, production chains, portfolio flows, loans, and so on, to increase over time, and the tendency for periods of rapid material expansion to alternate with periods in which investments increasingly shift to circuits of financial capital, all imply that capitalism requires a form of world money that flows easily to regions and sectors where potential rates of accumulation are thought to be highest. The tendency for the interests of capitals headquartered in hegemonic regions to be intertwined with the interests of hegemonic states in the interstate system, and the compelling benefits of seigniorage enjoyed by these hegemonic powers, imply that capitalist world money is not a neutral instrument of trade, but a geopolitical weapon. And the ability of leading capitals to operate on the scientific-technical frontier implies that world money necessarily tends

---

from one hegemonic power to the next in the history of capitalism has occurred in the course of conflicts on an ever-increasing scale, conflicts made more dangerous to humanity as a result of the technological dynamism that is at once capitalism's greatest achievement and its greatest horror. See Arrighi and Silver 1999.

to flow unevenly, with capitals from privileged regions able to appropriate surplus profits from innovations, financial speculation, and other forms of 'accumulation by dispossession', while individuals and communities elsewhere languish. Neoliberal theories and policies ignore each and every one of these structural features of the world market. When all is said and done, the far more radical proposals of post-Keynesians leave these tendencies in place as well.

The ideals underlying post-Keynesian calls for a new form of world money are commendable. But no form of world money can fulfil the tasks Davidson assigns as long as the social relations of capitalism remain in place. As long as capitalist property and production relations persist, 'value' will remain an alien power, an abstract pseudo-subject imposing its imperatives on working men and women and their communities. The reproduction of the capital/wage-labour relation will remain the reproduction of class exploitation. Overaccumulation crises and financial crises will inevitably re-occur. Globalisation, in brief, will remain characterised by alienation, exploitation, crises, and uneven development.

The international financial architecture is but one dimension of the so-called régime of global governance in capitalism. I believe that, as long as capitalist property and production relations are in place, similar difficulties will arise in other areas as well. Global capitalism is certainly not the only system in which military conflicts, global environmental problems and health crises, criminal activity across borders, and so on, occur. And the régime of global governance may evolve in ways that deal with these issues far more satisfactorily than is the case today. But, as long as economic and political élites suffer from global 'bads' far less than other groups – and as long as significant cross-sections of these élites strongly benefit from them – these ills will continue to plague humanity far more than capitalism's reformers are prepared to admit. But establishing this claim can be left for another day.[57] The limits to the reform of the international financial architecture presented

---

[57] In the meantime, the following works may be consulted. On war see Wood 2004 and Johnson 2004 and the International Committee of the Red Cross 2000. Global environmental issues are examined in Burkett 1999 and Foster 1994. Important dimensions of the failures of the corporate global health system are explored in Goozner 2004. De Brie 2000 and de Maillard 2000 have made important contributions to the study of 'crime, the dark side of globalisation'.

in this chapter are sufficient to establish the distinguishing features of a Marxian perspective on the régime of global governance.

This completes the overview of a Marxian model of capitalist globalisation, and of the distinctive ways in which the household, civil society, the state, the interstate system, the régime of global governance, and the world market can be conceptualised within a Marxian framework. I have examined this model in more detail than those considered in Part One. Even so, the account provided here has been very incomplete. How much detail is enough? This question arises at each stage of the present work, and the same answer must always be given: at least as much detail must be provided to determine the place of a particular position in the systematic dialectic of globalisation. However incomplete the presentation in the last three chapters may have been, it suffices to justify the claim that the Marxian model counts as a systematic advance over those considered in Part One.

There are three main reasons for this conclusion. First, the Marxian model of globalisation avoids the immanent contradictions that plagued earlier positions. Second, this model makes explicit what remained merely implicit in all of the earlier positions: the essential determinations of capital are fundamentally in tension with a global order in which the free development of each is a precondition for the free development of all. This is the single most important fact about the contemporary global order. Finally, the Marxian model of globalisation accomplishes all this without itself falling into immanent contradictions. The contradictions lie in the global order it describes, not in its descriptions of that order.[58] More specifically, defenders of this position do not make claims regarding the efficiency and normative attractiveness of the model that are undermined by its essential features.

The method of determinate negation has pushed the systematic dialectic of globalisation forward from the beginning. The immanent contradictions of a position have forced us to 'negate' that viewpoint and move to another explicitly addressing those contradictions. The assertion that the Marxian model is not troubled by immanent contradictions at its heart implies that the systematic dialectic of globalisation begun in Chapter 1 has concluded.

---

[58] I am speaking only of the 'hard core' of the Marxian research programme here. In the programme as a whole, there are countless anomalies and unresolved issues. This is a far different matter from having contradictions at the heart of the position. See Smith 1997b.

Systematic dialectics should be understood as a form of rational reconstruction, in this case, the rational reconstruction of positions in globalisation debates. As such, it is revisable. Perhaps I have left out some crucial dimension of a position that would have forced a quite different assessment from that given here. Perhaps there is some version of a position that does not fit the account given here. Perhaps there are compelling arguments for ordering positions differently that trump the considerations I have stressed. Perhaps there are positions that do not fit neatly under any of the headings I have employed, positions that would have pushed the dialectical ordering in entirely different directions. Perhaps the Marxian model of globalisation suffers from internal contradictions no less serious than those afflicting other positions in ways I have not comprehended. Perhaps the manner in which different positions construct different objects of investigations (and are thus incommensurable) is far more profound than the way they all investigate the contemporary global order, and are thus commensurable, at least to a certain degree.

No doubt this list of possible ways the systematic dialectic of globalisation might have gone wrong could be extended. Defending a systematic-dialectical ordering is not like proclaiming a transcendental truth. It is an invitation to dialogue, and dialecticians, no less than other theorists, must be prepared to abandon their claims if convincing counter-arguments are forthcoming. All I can say at this point is that I know of no arguments refuting the contention that the Marxian model of capitalist globalisation counts as a systematic advance over competing frameworks, one that brings the systematic dialectic of globalisation to a point of closure.

In another sense, however, the systematic dialectic remains incomplete. Theorists holding a Marxian position avoid falling into an immanent contradiction between their model of capitalist globalisation and the claims they assert of it. But they avoid this only by making explicit the immanent contradictions in the model itself, most especially the immanent contradiction at the heart of the concept of capital between capital as (pseudo) essence and collective social labour as essence. What might a determinate negation of this contradiction look like? If such an alternative global framework could be built upon the positive features of capitalist globalisation – most especially, the tendency to improve labour productivity, which creates the material preconditions for human flourishing on a global scale – then it could be said

to 'sublate' capitalism, incorporating its strengths while going beyond it. This is exactly the relationship of each succeeding stage in a systematic dialectic to its predecessor. Suppose, finally, that essential clues to the construction of this alternative order were implicit in the systematic dialectic traced thus far. This, too, would provide a reason to proceed, since a systematic dialectic should continue forward as long as there is some essential implicit matter to be made explicit.

These considerations suggest that we must ask whether there is a possible form of globalisation that would institutionalise a qualitatively higher level of efficiency and normative attractiveness than any possible form of global capitalism. If a model of such an alternative form of globalisation could be constructed, there is a sense it would count as a radical break with the ordering of positions considered thus far. In an equally valid sense, however, it would count as the culmination of the systematic dialectic of globalisation.

The final chapter of this work is devoted to this alternative.

A Marxian Model of Socialist Globalisation

Part One of this work was devoted to the four most significant mainstream positions in the globalisation debate. Defenders of each position claim that the underlying 'actuality' of the contemporary global order is 'rational' in Hegel's sense of the term. They believe that a feasible and normatively attractive global framework is emerging at the heart of the contemporary global order, whatever contingencies and shortcomings continue to beset it. The various models of globalisation examined in Part One are designed to articulate this supposed rational core, providing a spur to reform existing institutions and practices. Proponents of the social state call for a renewed state commitment to social welfare and full employment. Neoliberals advocate increased free trade and capital liberalisation, along with the dismantling of 'crony capitalism'. Defenders of the catalytic state insist that public authorities must aggressively and comprehensively provide the necessary preconditions for a region's successful participation in the global economy. Democratic-cosmopolitan theorists propose a global social charter guaranteeing the material preconditions for autonomy and substantive equality of opportunity.

Many significant reforms of the capitalist global order have been instituted over the centuries, and many more are likely to follow. Global financial instability,

the environmental harm inflicted on future generations, global inequality, and so on, can all be lessened. But there are limits to what such reforms are able to attain when capitalist property and production relations are in place, just as there were limits to the reforms possible within slavery, feudalism, or Stalinism. These limits must be acknowledged.

The proposals considered in Part One leave the core structural problems of global capitalism untouched. The collective power of social labour would continue to appear as the power of capital, an alien power subjecting every nook and cranny of social life to the valorisation imperative. Structural coercion and exploitation would continue to be at the centre of the capital/wage-labour relation. The inherent tendencies to overaccumulation crises, financial crises, and uneven development would continue to plague the world market. No reform of the capitalist state, the capitalist world market, or the capitalist régime of global governance can resolve the fundamental irrationality and social antagonisms at the heart of this mode of production. Further deregulation of global capital flows will not reverse this state of affairs. A resurgence of nationalism will not reverse this state of affairs. Attempts to institute social democracy on the global scale will not reverse this state of affairs, even if it includes proposals for a reformed 'international financial architecture'. Only a revolutionary rupture from the capital-form can accomplish this world historical task.

These considerations do not absolve us from striving for reforms that alleviate human suffering. But they do suggest that we need to stretch our political imaginations to consider a world beyond the limits of global capitalism. The systematic dialectic of globalisation culminates in a call to socialise the means of production.

This practical imperative would have no force if it contravened the 'ought implies can' precept. However valid the critique of global capitalism might be in an abstract theoretical sense, it is of no political significance unless there is a feasible and normatively attractive alternative. The very idea that there might be an acceptable alternative to the global capitalist order is almost universally dismissed today. The twentieth century was a period of experimentation with alternative social frameworks, and for most observers – including many who trace their political lineage to Marx – the result of these experiments could hardly be more conclusive. The superiority of a capitalist social order over central planning based on state ownership of the means of

production appears to be one of the major lessons of the twentieth century. Familiar versions of market socialism that have been proposed as alternatives to state central planning do not appear to offer viable options either.

The main goal of the present chapter is to present and defend a model of globalisation that is both feasible and normatively attractive, while incorporating the Marxian critique of the capitalist forms of globalisation presented in previous chapters. This model does not include either a bureaucratic command economy or the standard version of market socialism. Given the level of abstraction of the present work, a complete account of this model is not required. Nor is it necessary to prove that the framework presented below is the absolutely best alternative to a capitalist global framework. To bring the systematic dialectic of globalisation to completion, it is sufficient to present a global framework that builds upon the most significant strengths of capitalism, while avoiding its most profound structural flaws.

Before turning to this task, however, it is worth taking a moment to appreciate the full force of the case against socialism. This is the topic of Section 1. After presenting the socialist model of globalisation in Section 2, Sections 3, 4 and 5 establish that the standard criticisms of socialism leave the model defended here untouched. In the final section, I shall argue that this framework deserves to be termed a 'Marxian' model of globalisation, despite the fact that it incorporates markets more than is customary in the Marxian tradition.

1. The case against bureaucratic central planning and the standard model of market socialism

A wide variety of objections have been proposed against Soviet-style bureaucratic central planning, widely taken to be either the only form of socialism or the form to which all others degenerate. I shall first list what I take to be the eight most significant criticisms of this framework. I shall then consider the extent to which these criticisms are also relevant to the influential model of market socialism developed by Lange, Lerner, and Taylor.

The case against state socialism is fairly familiar:

(i) Ownership of the means of production lies in the same hands as control of the coercive state apparatus. While this arrangement may not make the worst forms of totalitarianism inevitable, no one familiar with the

historical record could deny its close association with authoritarian régimes.[1]

(ii) Ownership by everyone in general is equivalent to a lack of ownership by anyone in particular. When private property rights to capital goods are not defined, no one has an incentive to use them efficiently.[2]

(iii) Product quality tends to be poor. It is far easier for planners to formulate, implement, and monitor plans in quantitative than qualitative terms. The lack of an effective feedback mechanism connecting producers and users/consumers also leads to a neglect of product quality.

(iv) The informational burdens placed on bureaucratic central planning are now almost universally acknowledged to result in economic inefficiency. Central planners cannot appropriate adequate information regarding all potential inputs, all potential outputs, and all potential social wants and needs, when possible inputs, outputs, and wants and needs are all changing over time.[3]

(v) If we take planners as 'principals' and managers of enterprises as their 'agents', centralised bureaucratic planning necessarily tends to generate severe principal/agent problems. Collective ownership leads managers to distort the information they pass on to central planners, underestimating the output their enterprises are capable of producing while overestimating the inputs required to produce any given level of output.[4]

(vi) Authoritarian central planning is not able to develop successfully in areas where personal initiative and creative responses to unforeseen problems are important. Ordinary workers feel dehumanised and cynical, with pernicious economic effects.[5]

(vii) State ownership of the means of production and centralised planning by a bureaucratic caste cannot match the technological dynamism of capitalism. In certain circumstances, bureaucratic central planning is able to attain considerable *extensive* growth, that is, growth resulting from the mobilisation of greater and greater inputs. And, in certain

---

[1] Stiglitz 1994, pp. 2–3.
[2] Coase 1960; see Stiglitz 1994, pp. 12, 173.
[3] Hayek 1976.
[4] Stiglitz 1994, pp. 17, 91.
[5] Stiglitz 1994, pp. 169, 266–7.

sectors where mass resources could be devoted and where success or failure was relatively easily measured (for example, space, military, heavy industry), significant accomplishments were in fact attained in the Soviet Union and elsewhere.[6] But this sort of social order is unable to generate *intensive* growth based on the more efficient use of inputs. The lack of incentives for managers to engage in risky activities like innovative behaviour is surely a significant factor. Managers appropriate few of the fruits of such activities when they are successful, and may suffer significant penalties when they are not.[7]

(viii) A lack of hard budget constraints allows inefficient firms to continue in production and even expand over time.[8]

Taking all of these factors into account, most observers conclude, it should have come as no surprise that bureaucratic central planning with state ownership of the means of production eventually generated vast material and spiritual stagnation.

Most of the structural shortcomings of bureaucratic central planning were theoretically understood long before the ultimate implosion of the Soviet model. Lange, Lerner, and Taylor proposed a model of market socialism as an alternative.[9] This model retains government ownership of the means of production, while employing the price mechanism to free central planners from impossible burdens connected with collecting and processing information. Central planners are no longer required to make endless decisions regarding what goods are produced, how they are produced, which factories do the producing, from where these factories get their inputs, and to where they ship their outputs. Consumer prices and wages are left primarily to the market. The role of central planners is limited to determining the level of accumulation in the economy as a whole (by setting the interest rate on capital), allocating investment (either directly or through differential interest rates), and setting producer prices.

---

[6] Stiglitz 1994, p. 204; see Roemer 1994, pp. 42–3.

[7] 'It is unwise to criticise upward, come out with unusual ideas, or take initiatives. It does not pay to think for oneself or take risks on one's own. . . . The character-forming and training effect, and the selection criteria of bureaucratic control, reinforce each other: servility and a head-down mentality prevail'. Kornai 1992, p. 121.

[8] Kornai 1986.

[9] Lange and Taylor 1964.

This last task is analogous to the function of the Walrasian auctioneer in general equilibrium theory. Central planners propose an initial set of prices, and then require managers to choose production techniques minimising unit costs at these prices. They must also choose the output level where marginal costs equal prices. The managers then transmit their input requests and output plans to the central planners, who subsequently adjust prices so that markets clear, raising the prices of goods in excess demand, and lowering them to avoid excess supply. Lange and his colleagues argue that supply and demand can be efficiently adjusted in this manner, while simultaneously eliminating the exploitation, crises, and neglect of social needs that inevitably accompany all variants of capitalism.

The Lange, Lerner, and Taylor model of market socialism explicitly addresses one of the structural flaws of bureaucratic central planning, its inflexibility. The introduction of a price mechanism is designed to overcome this difficulty. But markets do not actually work according to the principles of general equilibrium theory.[10] The myth of the Walrasian auctioneer fundamentally distorts our comprehension of capitalist markets. It is just as useless for understanding how markets might function in socialism.

Further, the other flaws of central planning are not addressed in the standard model of market socialism. In this model, too, control of the means of production falls in the hands of the very officials who control the coercive powers of the state, a combination that has invariably led to authoritarianism. Here, too, the state owns the means of production, which means that, in effect, no one owns them. And, so, the worry persists that no one has an adequate incentive to ensure that they are used rationally.[11] In the absence of market competition, there is no reason to think that the mere use of a price mechanism automatically ensures a proper interest in the quality of output. Further, in the market-socialist model presented by Lange, Lerner, and Taylor, it is simply assumed that managers will carry out the dictates of central planners. No concern is taken to ensure that they transmit to planners the accurate information required for a rational allocation of investment. Similarly, no institutionalised incentives are provided to make certain that individual

---

[10] See Davidson 2002, Chapter 3.
[11] This problem may not arise in traditional societies, where usage is fixed by fairly rigid conventions. That is not a solution a socialist could advocate.

workers are motivated to act in an appropriate manner. It is simply assumed that they, like their managers, behave in ways that automatically generate the desired results. In this market-socialist model, as in the general equilibrium models to which it is closely related, technologies are assumed to be exogenous, and the selection of techniques is assumed to follow automatically, given the relevant prices. The problem of innovation is simply abstracted from, not resolved, as if there were no difficulties in providing adequate incentives to engage in innovative behaviour. Finally, there is every reason to expect that, in this model of market socialism, budget constraints will be 'soft', with dire results for the efficiency of the economy over time.

These considerations appear to justify the conclusion that there is simply no feasible alternative to capitalist markets with private ownership of the means of production. Market competition appears to provide private owners with incentives to ensure a level of efficiency and dynamism unattainable in either bureaucratic socialism or market socialism. One can accept this conclusion without having to deny that capitalism brings with it profound social costs. Financial crises, environmental crises, extreme levels of economic and political inequalities, and so on, are not likely to ever be entirely eliminated. But the harms they inflict can be lessened over time. If there is no feasible and normatively attractive alternative to a capitalist framework, lessening these harms must be our goal, and the failed project of collective ownership of the means of production must be unequivocally abandoned.

In the present historical context, the burden of proof lies entirely with those who continue to call for the socialisation of the means of production. Meeting this burden requires developing an alternative model of socialism capable of avoiding the fundamental structural flaws listed above.

2. An alternative model of globalisation

Alex Callinicos is surely correct that it is far too early to propose a fully worked out alternative to the capitalist global order:

> The emergence of the anti-capitalist movement [against the present form of globalisation, T.S.] provides an opportunity. . . . The very incoherence of the movement – that is, the presence within it of a variety of ideological currents, Green, socialist, Third Worldist, anarchist – that are themselves internally complex is likely to encourage the elaboration of different, mutually

incompatible alternative models. Through attempts theoretically to articulate and practically to implement these models we are likely to develop a much clearer sense of how we can transcend capitalism.[12]

While it is premature to sketch a fully elaborated alternative, a beginning can be made, building on what is now a fairly extensive body of work.[13] I shall adopt the model of economic democracy developed by David Schweickart, adding three modifications to make it a more adequate alternative form of globalisation.

The model Schweickart defends has the following essential elements:

(i) Production and distribution are primarily undertaken within worker collectives. Workers are not hired as wage-labourers by capital; they instead join worker collectives as fellow members. There is a basic right to employment, with state enterprises providing jobs for those unable to find positions in collectives.

(ii) Managers of worker collectives are democratically accountable to those over whom they exercise authority, either through direct elections or through appointment by a workers' council that is itself directly elected. These enterprises are required to have representatives from a range of social movements (environmental groups, consumer groups, feminist groups, and so on) on their boards of directors, accountable to those movements.[14]

(iii) Worker collectives produce public goods, inputs into the production process, or final consumption goods. Funds for the first are directly allocated to collectives by the relevant planning agencies (see below). The latter two categories of products are offered for sale in producer and consumer markets. In Schweickart's view, attempts to centrally plan all inputs and outputs in a top-down fashion are simply not feasible, at least not in a complex and dynamic economy. But it does not follow that *capitalist* market societies are the only acceptable forms of economic organisation. It is possible to imagine a feasible and normatively attractive society combining markets with the socialisation of the means of production, that is, a society making use of producer and consumer markets after abolishing both capital markets and labour markets.

---

[12] Callinicos 2001, p. 119.
[13] See Elson 1988, 1999; Fisk 1989; Roemer 1994; Ollman 1998; Smith 2000a, Chapter Seven; Devine 1988, 2002a, 2002b; and, especially, Schweickart 1993, 2002.
[14] Fisk 1989; Devine 2002b, p. 77.

(iv) Workers in enterprises are granted use rights to facilities and other means of production. But ultimate ownership rights remain with the local community. Workers cannot use their enterprise as a cash cow and then walk away; they have a legal duty to maintain the value of the community's investments. If sufficient depreciation funds cannot be appropriated from revenues to maintain the value of these investments, it is the responsibility of community banks to shut down an enterprise. Once depreciated funds have been deducted, the remainder of the revenues from public allocations or sales in consumer/producer markets (apart from the taxes to be considered below) are then distributed among the members of the collective according to formulae set by the democratically accountable management.[15]

(v) The origin of funds for new investment and public goods is a flat tax on the non-labour assets of all enterprises.[16] In Schweickart's proposal, the rate of this tax is initially set by a democratically elected legislature, operating on the national level. This legislature also decides on the appropriate division of revenues between funding for national public goods and funds that are allocated to democratically elected regional and local legislative bodies. Each of these assemblies, in turn, must also decide upon the level of funding for public goods to be supplied in the relevant geographical area vis-à-vis the level of funds set aside for distribution to the level below it. These legislative bodies can also set aside a percentage of funds for investment in areas of pressing social needs.

(vi) After all decisions have been made regarding the general level of new investment and the order of social priorities, and after funds required for public goods on the national, regional, and local levels have been allocated,

---

[15] If these depreciation funds formed hoards apart from circulation, undesirable price effects might follow. One possibility is that they could be used to provide consumer credit in 'socialist savings and loan associations' that allow people to purchase high-cost items when they do not have ready cash. These associations would not be allowed to provide business credit, since 'What should *not* be done is what capitalism does: Merge the institutions that generate and distribute investment funds with the institutions that handle consumer credit. Business investment, as opposed to consumer credit, is too important to the overall health of the economy to be left to the vagaries of the market'. Schweickart 2002, p. 82.

[16] One objection to bureaucratic centrally planned economies is that they include a perverse incentive to hold excess inventories due to the lack of an interest charge for holding inventories (Stiglitz 1994, pp. 201–2). The flat tax on non-labour assets avoids this problem.

the remaining revenues are distributed to local communities on a per capita basis (at least this should be the presumption in the absence of compelling reasons to do otherwise, such as the need to temporarily favour historically disadvantaged regions). Community banks would then undertake the actual allocation of new investment funds to worker collectives. The boards of directors of these banks would include representatives of a broad range of social groups affected by the banks' decisions. New enterprises would be formed, and existing ones expanded, through allocations by community banks rather than private capital markets.

(vii) When allocating investment funds for new worker collectives and the expansion of existing ones, community banks must take three main questions into account. Is there likely to be sufficient demand for the output of the given enterprise for it to maintain the value of the community's investment and provide adequate income for its members? Will the investment provide stable employment? And is the investment consistent with the set of social priorities democratically affirmed on the national, regional and local levels? Extensive external financial and social audits can be regularly imposed on all enterprises and community banks to assess their performances in terms of these criteria. These independent social audits are a crucial component of the socialist version of the principle of transparency, institutionalising a level of accountability and transparency far beyond the limited neoliberal version of the principle.[17] Community banks can then be ranked on the basis of the results of these audits. The level of income of the staff of a particular bank, and the amount of funds allocated to this bank for distribution in the future, are determined by the bank's place in this ranking.

(viii) In Schweickart's model, there are no markets for capital assets, and so there will be no capital flight in the form of cross-border investments in capital assets. There will also be little foreign direct investment, since worker collectives are unlikely to outsource their own jobs, and community banks are assessed according to the extent they create employment in their own communities. But there will still be trade across borders. For a period of time, this may include trade with regions that have not institutionalised a version

---

[17] Elson 1999. Neoliberals call only for the disclosure of information relevant to investors. Why should not *all* transactions in the global economy be publicly disclosed, using accounting criteria designed to enable the greatest feasible transparency of those transactions?

of economic democracy. In such circumstances, regions committed to socialist globalisation should follow the principle of *fair* trade rather than 'free' trade. To ensure that this occurs, Schweickart calls for a 'social tariff'.[18] If oppressive labour practices hold down wage levels in a given region, the prices of imports from that region will be raised to what they would have been had worker income been comparable to the level prevailing in the importing country. A social tariff will also be imposed to compensate for a lack of adequate spending on the environment, worker health and safety, or social welfare in the exporting nation. The revenues collected by this tariff will then be distributed to the groups in the exporting country with the best record of effectively implementing anti-poverty programmes, whether or not they are agencies of the government.[19]

I believe that three additions to this framework should be made:

(ix) Schweickart does not investigate the monetary dimension of international trade in his model. I believe that the proposals made by Paul Davidson discussed in the last chapter are incompatible with capitalist social relations, but quite feasible if socialist production relations are established. In the latter set of circumstances, it would be possible to have something like Davidson's International Monetary Clearing Units serve as the sole form of world money. It would also be feasible to establish a set of rules that ensure that excessive trade imbalances do not persist, and that the burdens of adjusting to the imbalances that do arise are not disproportionately imposed on the most vulnerable regions of the global economy.

(x) David Held's proposals for democratic-cosmopolitan law are also incompatible with capitalist social relations, as Chapter 4 established. But they, too, would be feasible if socialist production relations were in place. More specifically, a level of global governance above the state should be established. This would include a representative assembly selected more democratically than the United Nations, a global social charter, an international court of justice, and so on.[20]

---

[18] Schweickart 2002, pp. 79–80.
[19] 'Economic Democracy is a competitive market economy, but it discriminates between socially useful kinds of competition – those fostering efficient production and satisfaction of consumer desires – and socially destructive kinds of competition – those tending to depress wages and other social welfare provisions and to encourage lax environmental controls. Social tariffs are meant to block the latter without interfering with the former'. Schweickart 2002, p. 79.
[20] Held 1995, pp. 83–9.

(xi) Schweickart holds that local communities within a nation ought to receive new investment funds on a per capita basis. In this manner, the material preconditions for both individual autonomy and flourishing communities are furthered. The force of this argument extends to the global level. There should be a democratically accountable socialist international planning agency to ensure the provision of global public goods.[21] It must also guarantee that regions across the planet have access to new investment funds in direct proportion to their population in the absence of special considerations (such as the need to temporarily favour previously disadvantaged regions of the global economy). This is an extension of Held's proposal for global social investment funds, but with these funds now replacing, rather than merely 'complementing', global capital markets. In this manner, the systematic tendency to uneven development that afflicts all possible forms of capitalism could be abolished.

This model of economic democracy undoubtedly needs to be greatly supplemented and modified, and compared and contrasted with other approaches with which it shares 'family resemblances'. Once again, however, the goal here is not to provide a fully fleshed-out blueprint of the single best form of socialism. If the model is developed enough to show that a feasible and normatively attractive socialist alternative is possible in principle, that is sufficient.

Of course, it is always open to critics of socialism to reject the feasibility and/or normative attractiveness of any proposed model of socialism, arguing that if a serious attempt were made to implement it, the results would be far different – and far worse – from what its defenders claim. In the absence of historical evidence, both sides of this dispute must rely on speculation, *a priori* reasoning, and analogies with historical examples, all of which involve matters of great controversy. There certainly is no hope of conclusively resolving

---

[21] The set of global public goods includes new scientific-technological knowledge. The equal moral worth of all individuals implies that scientific-technological knowledge should not treated as a weapon of economic warfare, monopolisable by the economically powerful (Perelman 1998). The advance of scientific-technological knowledge is a collective achievement, building upon the collective heritage of humankind's past accomplishments and essentially dependent on continuing public subsidies. As such, it should not be a means for condemning certain regions of the planet to poverty and material deprivation while other regions flourish. It must be treated as a public good, freely available to all.

disagreements through theoretical reasoning alone. Ultimately, social practice, measured in world-historical terms by centuries, not decades, must provide the answers. But, since the burden of proof today lies so clearly on the side of defenders of an alternative to capitalist globalisation, a response to the most significant criticisms must be attempted.

3. Another look at criticisms of socialism

In the first section of this chapter, eight structural flaws of state socialism (bureaucratic central planning) were formulated:

   (i) It has a structural affinity with political authoritarianism.
  (ii) It is beset by social pathologies resulting from the lack of private property rights.
 (iii) It suffers from a systematic tendency to produce products of dubious quality.
 (iv) The informational burdens placed on central planners generate profound inefficiencies.
  (v) Irresolvable principal/agent problems arise in the relationship between planners and the managers of enterprises.
 (vi) The workforce tends to suffer severe motivation deficits.
(vii) There is insufficient technological dynamism.
(viii) There is an absence of hard budget constraints.

There are plausible reasons to think that attempts to institutionalise the market-socialist model presented by Lange, Lerner, and Taylor would suffer from most of these difficulties as well. Is the alternative model of socialism sketched in the previous section susceptible to similar objections?

   (i) In Schweickart's model, central planners set the level of taxes for new investment and public goods, decide the allocation of revenues between new investment and public goods, and determine social priorities on global, regional, national, and local levels. But these planners are democratically elected legislators. Many other features of the socialist model of globalisation also operate against political authoritarianism. Final property rights to means of production remain with the local community, while use rights are granted to the collective workforce of particular enterprises. Political planners possess neither set of rights. Further, the managers of both worker co-operatives and

community banks are elected by the workforces of those bodies (or by workers' councils elected by these workforces). They are not appointed by state officials from a list of candidates selected by these same officials.[22] While the boards of directors of both worker co-operatives and community banks ought to include political officials, representatives of the workforce and of mass social movements independent from the state should also serve on these boards. This, too, subjects the power of the state over economic life to effective checks. Finally, workplace democracy greatly furthers the capacity for autonomous action of working men and women, rather than subservience to state dictates.

Taking the institutional framework of socialist democracy as a whole, there does not seem to be any reason to think that this form of socialism would have a structural affinity with political authoritarianism, despite the lack of private ownership of the means of production. It is difficult to overstate the importance of this issue. Janos Kornai is perhaps the world's leading economist on the topic of 'actually existing socialism'.[23] In *The Socialist System*, he argues that structural problems of forced growth, investment hunger, soft budget constraints, and the socially irresponsible behaviour of managers, consumers, and planners, all stem from an organic system with a single root, the undivided power of a Communist Party:

> The Communist party must gain undivided possession of political power for the process to get under way. This historical configuration bears the 'genetic program' that transmits the main characteristics of the system to every cell within it. This is the seed of the new society from which the whole organism grows.[24]

Kornai insists that this authoritarian power 'forms the deepest layer in the causal chain explaining the system'; it is 'necessary and sufficient for the system to emerge and consolidate'.[25] He does not appear to appreciate how this thesis implies that the 'genetic program', the 'seed', the 'deepest layer in the causal chain' of the inherent structural flaws of 'actually existing socialism'

---

[22] In the old Yugoslavia, the workers' assemblies could, in principle, fire managers. But appointment rights were held by political authorities, who also interfered extensively with the day-to-day running of firms (Lydall 1988; Roemer 1994, pp. 86 ff.). The fact that worker oversight failed to work in *this* setting is neither a surprise nor proof that it would fail to operate properly in *any* possible setting.
[23] This discussion of Kornai is based on Lebowitz 2000.
[24] Kornai 1992, p. 368.
[25] Kornai 1992, pp. 375, 409.

is *not* found in the socialisation of the means of production *per se*. According to his own argument, socialising the means of production in the absence of a 'power elite, hierarchically structured and sharing power with no other group, [with] the exclusive right of disposal over the state-owned means of production' would be an entirely different matter from undertaking this project with such a power élite in place.[26] If 'the characteristics of the power structure are precisely the source from which the chief regularities of the system can be deduced', a form of socialism whose power structure has quite different characteristics would possess a quite different set of 'chief regularities'.[27]

(ii) What of the lack of private property rights in (large-scale) means of production?[28] Defenders of the socialisation of the means of production must address what has come to be called 'Coase's theorem'. Ronald Coase has argued that, if private property rights are assigned throughout the economy, markets can be relied upon to automatically optimise welfare levels. His argument is straightforward and familiar. Private owners only freely agree to trade if they believe they will benefit from the exchanges, so difficulties primarily concern third parties externally affected by market transactions. In an effective private-property rights régime, however, any third party suffering negative effects can simply sue those who have harmed her property. Models in which private-property rights are not clearly assigned and enforced, in contrast, lack this mechanism, and so cannot be expected to optimise welfare levels.[29] From this perspective, any and all attempts to socialise the means of production are doomed to result in social nightmares.

Stiglitz has presented three compelling arguments against Coase's theorem. First, the clear assignment of property rights does not necessarily lead to efficiency. For that conclusion to follow, we need to abstract from public goods, transaction costs, and imperfect information, each of which generates inefficient outcomes in even the most extensive and rigorously enforced private-property rights régime.[30] In any actual market economy, the need to provide public goods will be pervasive, almost all market transactions will involve transactions

---

[26] Kornai 1992, p. 98.

[27] Kornai 1992, p. 33; see also p. xxii.

[28] The model of socialism described in Section 2 does not rule out private-property rights in either small-scale means of production or individual consumption goods.

[29] Coase 1960.

[30] Stiglitz 1994, pp. 12, 174.

costs, and perfect information will be impossible to obtain, even in principle. This makes Coase's theorem all but completely irrelevant to a comparative assessment of capitalist markets and alternative forms of organising production and distribution.

Stiglitz's second remark rests on the fact that almost all members of large organisations in capitalism are managers and employees of firms owned by others. There is no *a priori* reason to assume that it makes a tremendous difference whether managers, for example, work for a disparate set of shareholders or for the community. Principal-agent problems could well be comparable in the two cases (I shall return to this issue).

Third, Stiglitz notes that there is extensive empirical evidence that public ownership can function as efficiently as private ownership. In the oil industry, publicly-owned British Petroleum did not operate qualitatively worse than privately-owned Amoco. The economic success of communally owned co-operatives in China also strongly suggests that if there are fundamental problems with form of socialism making use of markets, they do not lie in the lack of private property rights *per se*.[31]

Given the compelling force of these three points, it can be concluded that the claim that the socialist model of globalisation presented in the previous section is both feasible and normatively attractive is entirely untouched by Coase's theorem.[32]

(iii) Regarding quality concerns, in the model of socialism under discussion, consumer and producer markets provide effective feedback mechanisms connecting users and collectives. Such mechanisms are lacking when rewards

---

[31] Stiglitz 1994, pp. 175–6; see also Roemer 1994, p. 128.

[32] Roemer writes, 'It used to be thought that if LMF's [labor managed firms] acted to maximize net revenues per worker, Pareto-inefficiency would result at equilibrium. Such a scheme . . . does not lead to Pareto-inefficiency when there are capital suppliers who must be paid'. Roemer 1994, p. 48. The presence of producer input markets (combined with the flat tax on non-market assets) in the above model fulfils this condition. But the problem may not even arise in the first place: 'It is also noteworthy that LMF's might not maximize revenue per worker. For example, they might maximize the number of workers employed subject to a minimum income for workers – at least this might be the objective during hard times. There has been no study of the efficiency properties of the equilibrium if all LMF's maximize employment subject to a floor on income'. Roemer 1994, p. 48. (And, of course, the assumptions of general equilibrium theory are ultimately irrelevant to an assessment of either capitalism or socialist alternatives, for reasons compellingly developed in Davidson 2002, Chapter 3.)

and sanctions are assigned to managers by central planners based on success in meeting quotas.[33] But, when producer and consumer markets are in place, workers and managers have a clear incentive to produce high-quality consumer and producer goods and services at a reasonable cost. The more they do so, the higher the revenues of their enterprise, and the higher these revenues, the higher their own income.

The price mechanism is not the only mechanism at work in the model of socialism defended here. The reputation mechanism is also in play.[34] A worker co-operative with a reputation for high-quality products would likely be able to attract consumers and new investment from community banks, even if its prices were somewhat higher than another worker collective producing a substitute product. Worker collectives that develop and maintain a reputation for quality products will tend to thrive over time relative to their competitors.[35]

(iv) There are no capital markets and no labour markets in this model. But there are consumer markets and markets for producer inputs. The informational burdens of trying to plan millions of inputs and outputs simultaneously are thus not placed on central planners.

(v) Two principal-agent relations define the role of managers in the democratic model of socialism sketched in the previous section. Managers are both the direct agents of the workforce that has selected them, and the indirect agents of the community that owns existing assets and provides new investment funds. The broad-based representation of community interests on boards of directors helps ensure that managers will tend to act in a manner compatible with the latter.[36] Regarding the former, workers clearly have an incentive to elect effective managers who are concerned with both the efficiency of production and the well-being of the workforce to whom they are accountable. Since the self-esteem, social status, and income of those who

---

[33] Stiglitz 1994, p. 199.

[34] See Stiglitz 1994, p. 196.

[35] The reputation mechanism would likely be even more pervasive in democratic socialism than it is in capitalism. In the former, the relevant matters for reputation would encompass other dimensions than just the trade-off between quality and price in the final product. The oversight of representatives from social movements on the boards of directors of both worker co-operatives and community banks would result in widespread information regarding environmental practices, consumer safety, and so on, much more effectively than information about such matters is conveyed today (Wainwright 1994).

[36] Devine 1988 and 2002b stress the importance of this point.

wish to become or remain managers is furthered by being elected by the workforce or its representatives, it is clearly in the self-interest of managers to dedicate themselves to these ends.[37]

There are good reasons to think that the above model of socialist globalisation would address principal/agent issues far more effectively than market capitalism. In capitalism, there are serious principal/agent problems regarding the relationship between the owners of firms and their managers. The latter are legally the agents of the former, and the former have sufficient social power to ensure that their interests are not neglected by managers indefinitely. But investors generally do not have access to sufficient information to be able to prevent managers from pursuing their own interests in ways that may diverge from the interests of shareholders to a considerable extent for extended periods of time.[38] This problem is much less likely to arise in the analogous principal/agent relation in democratic socialism. Workers (or their representatives) will not suffer from a systematic lack of relevant information regarding the performance of managers. Participation in the day-to-day decision-making of the enterprise provides the workforce and workers' councils with much more accurate information regarding the performance of managers than that provided to investors in capitalism by stock-market analysts and company public-relations departments.

(vi) A sixth objection concerns incentives for workers. One major problem with motivating workers to work hard in centrally planned economies was the lack of available consumer goods.[39] A model of economic democracy with consumer markets holding a central place would not be afflicted with this structural difficulty.

Other considerations suggest that a democratic form of socialism could solve the motivation problem in a far superior fashion to capitalism. In socialist

---

[37] In the version of socialism advocated here, there is a carrot as well as a stick for managers. Worker co-operatives will compete to attract competent managers. It is likely that they will offer effective managers shares in the revenues of the enterprise that exceed the average workers' share. Historical evidence from West Germany, Japan, earlier periods in the history of the United States, and elsewhere, strongly suggests that effective management can be encouraged when the ratio of management reward to average worker return is fairly narrow compared with the present state of affairs in the US. There is every reason to think that a ratio providing the requisite incentive is consistent with the egalitarian values of socialism.

[38] Stiglitz 1994.

[39] Roemer 1994, p. 39.

democracy, the net profits of firms are returned to workers directly, according to a formula decided by a management democratically accountable to the workforce. Under such an arrangement, workers have a clear incentive to contribute to gains in labour productivity in the enterprise as a whole. Eliminating the capital/wage-labour antagonism also tends to encourage higher levels of co-operation, honesty, and trust, all of which contribute to productivity gains, and all of which are inevitably constricted in capitalist enterprises.[40] Democratic control over the introduction of innovations in the labour process will also tend to make work more creative and enjoyable, considerably lessening the problem of motivation.

Unfortunately, we cannot simply assume that free-rider problems will never arise in socialism. There will always be those who attempt to maximise their benefits from the contributions of others, while minimising their own efforts. But free riding is much easier for co-workers to monitor than for supervisors, let alone distant personnel departments. In lean production systems, peer pressure has proven very effective at mobilising worker effort for the sake of capital accumulation.[41] This mechanism is likely to encourage a fair distribution of worker effort far more effectively when the resulting gains are shared among the workforce.[42]

With an ethos of solidarity, individual self-interest, and peer pressure all pointing in the same direction, there will be much less need for supervision in the model of socialism defended here. With fewer unproductive expenditures required, productivity in worker co-operatives is automatically heightened.

---

[40] '[E]conomic incentives, narrowly construed, seem to provide an insufficient explanation for why many individuals work as hard and as effectively as they do. I have stressed the importance of cooperation, honesty, and trust, virtues that make *economic* relations run more smoothly but that themselves frequently (and thankfully) lead to behavior that goes well beyond that called for by self-interestedness'. Stiglitz 1994, p. 273; see also Lester 1998. Proponents of lean production argue that it raises levels of 'cooperation, honesty, and trust'. See Smith 2000a for a critical assessment of this claim, and defence of the thesis that these virtues are far more likely to be developed within socialist democracy. I shall return to this issue below.

[41] Smith 2000a, Chapter Three.

[42] 'Peers often have more information, simply as a by-product of their other activities; just as learning can be a relatively costless joint product with production, so too can monitoring be. But for peer monitoring to be effective, peers must have an incentive to monitor'. Stiglitz 1994, p. 78. In worker collectives, where 'workers get all that remains, once nonlabor costs . . . have been paid', this incentive is clearly present. Schweickart 2002, p. 49.

There is a well-established body of literature corroborating the thesis that higher levels of participation in itself tends to lead to higher levels of productivity.[43] Since participation in worker co-operatives is greatly increased relative to the pseudo-participation that characterises employee 'empowerment' schemes in capitalism, efficiency can be expected to increase greatly throughout the production and distribution process.

A set of troubling questions remains. Should managers of worker co-operatives have the power to fire members for absenteeism, idleness on the job, or other forms of free riding? What if managers decided that staffing levels are too high, given shifts in producer input and consumer markets? If they lack a right to fire, overstaffing in the face of low levels of demand might eventually force enterprises to go under that could thrive with fewer hands. Also, the *de facto* job rights workers enjoyed in the Soviet Union and other instances of 'actually existing socialism' limited the ability of enterprises to replace workers with machines, which would seem to be a requirement for a transition from extensive to intensive growth.[44] Would not the democratic model of socialism advocated here face similar difficulties?

I fear that this set of issues cannot be wished away on the micro-level of individual enterprises. A general right to employment is not the same as a right to any particular job; solidarity does not necessarily imply that there can never be legitimate reasons to think that a particular worker is not a good fit with a particular workplace at a particular time. But one of socialism's world-historical goals is to overcome the generalised economic insecurity that pervades capitalism. This surely implies a profound lessening of insecurity regarding employment, that is, *de facto* job rights. If community banks operate properly, however, intensive growth need not be undermined on the macro-level.

If community banks fund new enterprises making use of more advanced machinery, these enterprises will tend to bring prices down, forcing older firms in the given sector to pay lower shares to their workers. Workers in

---

[43] Schweickart 1993, Chapter 3. See also Florida and Kenney 1990; Dosi, et al. 1988, Part IV; and Smith 2000a, Chapter 3, all of which stress how the collective knowledge of the workforce is a tremendous source of insights for improving the production process.
[44] Lebowitz 2000.

these firms would then have to decide for themselves how to bear the costs of economic restructuring. They could stay in older enterprises, accepting lower income. Or they could leave for one of the stream of promising start-ups formed by local community investments, and not be replaced. Depreciation funds could then be devoted to replacing old technologies with more advanced, less labour-intensive, production systems. Requests could be made to community banks for additional funds for this purpose. The older enterprises would only have to be shut down if they could no longer pay at least the minimum level of income to their workers, while maintaining the value of the community's fixed investments. In this manner, a middle path could be forged between the brutal adjustments of capitalism – which sacrifice individuals and communities whenever technological change furthers capital accumulation – and the failure to adjust satisfactorily to new technological possibilities that characterises 'state socialism'.

I began by addressing worker motivation, the sixth in the list of eight crucial issues regarding the feasibility and normative attractiveness of socialism introduced in Section 1. This has led to a consideration of the seventh topic, technological dynamism. The relative lack of this dynamism in bureaucratic command economies is one of the major reasons for the widespread dismissal of the socialist project today. The standard market-socialist model not only does not address this problem adequately; it abstracts from technological change altogether. The central importance of this question justifies considering it much further.

4. Democratic socialism and technological dynamism

Technological change, in itself, does not necessarily further the social good. As the precautionary principle states, at any given time, there will be a variety of possible paths of innovation that ought not to be pursued aggressively on a massive scale, given the limits of scientific-technical understanding at that time. And, in societies characterised by class exploitation and gender, racial, and ethnic, and other forms of oppression, many forms of technological change will have serious pernicious social consequences. Nonetheless, technological stagnation does not further the social good either. If an otherwise acceptable form of socialism would inevitably suffer from a lack of technological dynamism, that alone would provide reasonable grounds for rejecting it.

According to John Roemer, 'the weaknesses [of labour managed firms] are that, without profit-maximization, it is less clear that the economy would remain on the cutting technological edge'.[45] Is this a justified worry?

On the organisational level, enterprises have a clear incentive to undertake risks associated with innovation for one simple and familiar reason. Since the model being discussed includes producer and consumer markets, worker collectives that succeed in product innovations and process innovations will tend to prosper. Those that do not, will not.[46]

On the individual level, workers in enterprises have every incentive to institute innovations to help their firm prosper, since they directly benefit from positive results. They also have every incentive to approve innovations that promise to make the labour process more creative, less stressful, or less time-consuming. The elected managers of worker collectives have a clear incentive to search for innovations as well. They, too, benefit directly from innovations that help the firm prosper. And, if searches for innovations improving the creativity, and so forth, of the work process are not undertaken, they can be replaced. Managers are also accountable to boards of directors that include representatives of consumer groups, environmental groups, and other social movements. This provides a spur to seek innovations improving consumer safety, avoid environmental harms, and so on. External social audits can regularly assess the enterprise's record in these areas of innovations, providing managers with further incentives to pursue them.[47] The constitutional protection against interference from state officials also encourages managerial initiative in the search for innovations.[48]

There is considerable evidence that as a result of the 'learning by doing' process, the labour force on the shop floor or in the office can be as important to the innovation process as the scientific-technical staff. Their suggestions to

[45] Roemer 1994, p. 51.

[46] The flat tax on non-labour assets that funds new investments and public goods might be thought to push in the opposite direction, discouraging investments in the facilities and machinery that improve labour productivity. But, as Schweickart argues, 'The capital access tax is, in fact, a *cost of production*, and hence covered by the market price of the goods being produced. That is to say, firms in a given industry are all subject to the same tax burden, and so they can (and will) set their prices to cover these taxes'. Schweickart 2002, p. 53.

[47] Elson 1999.

[48] Contrast this arrangement with Kornai's description of management psychology in 'actually existing socialism', quoted in footnote 7 above.

improve productivity, new product design, and so on, can lead to incremental innovations that are often more economically significant than revolutionary innovations. One of the proclaimed goals of the recent changes in technology and the forms of social organisation in capitalism grouped under the term 'lean production' is to tap the creative insights of workers.[49] But, under lean production, there are no effective guarantees that the result of sharing insights will not lead to lay-offs for some and horrific work intensification for others. Management literature talks endlessly of the need to create and maintain trust in order to elicit sharing of the 'tacit knowledge' possessed by line workers. But the private ownership and control of the means of production results in such an asymmetry of power that enduring relationships of trust are all but impossible.[50] In worker collectives, in stark contrast, most of the benefits to the enterprise from productivity advances and new product possibilities flow directly to workers themselves. With democratically accountable managers, the ability to forge stable relationships of trust is tremendously enhanced. If the 'tacit knowledge' of the workforce is as important as recent research suggests, this provides another reason to assert that socialising the means of production is compatible with a high degree of technological dynamism.[51]

At this point in the discussion, critics of socialism are likely to refer to two features of socialism widely thought to pervert the innovation process. First, managers use other people's money. Would this not often lead them to undertake excessively risky paths in the search for innovations? The historical record of government-funded innovation projects is not encouraging:

> When a government department attempts to evaluate an Airbus, or a proposal for a supersonic transport, it is not the bureaucrats' own money that is at stake. These projects are so long-lived and there are so many uncertainties associated with their success that there is no way that those approving projects can be punished for bad mistakes (or rewarded for good decisions). . . . [T]he fact that it is the corporation's future that is at stake alters how projects are evaluated: When everyone pays for a project through tax dollars, it often is as if no one is bearing the cost.[52]

---

[49] Kenney and Florida, 1993.
[50] Smith 2000a, Chapter 3.
[51] Devine 2002b.
[52] Stiglitz 1994, p. 152.

On the other hand, other factors suggest that the level of innovative activity and risk-taking would often be far too low, given how strongly the income of workers is tied to the fate of their collectives. The absence of a market for capital assets means that workers are not able to diversify their risks through pension plans investing in a broad range of enterprises across the economy. Would this not lead to an excessive aversion to risk?

> [L]abor management may make firms too risk-adverse. . . . It may, for instance, be socially optimal for firms to take a degree of risk that results in the likelihood that each worker will have to change jobs, say, three of four times in her working life, because of a layoff or bankruptcy. But individuals might well wish to avoid even this degree of risk.[53]

Regarding the first concern, exactly the same tension holds in capitalism whenever managers allocate capital that is not their own personal property. *And, in the course of capitalist development, this becomes the typical case*, as Marx correctly anticipated in his discussion of joint stock companies in Volume III.[54] If the threat of failure is generally sufficient to discourage excessive risk taking despite this arrangement in capitalism, there would appear to be no good reason to assume that excessive risks would be undertaken in socialism, as long as a similar threat is present (see the discussion of budget constraints below).

The second worry can be answered in an analogous manner. The pressure of competition in producer input and consumer markets tends to force firms to accept risks associated with innovation, whatever the psychological dispositions of their members might be. But adequately funded re-training programmes, a constitutionally recognised right to employment with public-sector firms serving as employers of last resort, and a guarantee that the local community receives its equal per capita share of new investment funds, would surely lead to quite different psychological dispositions from those formed in the absence of such measures. These policies would make the members of worker co-operatives far less risk-adverse than they would otherwise be, and certainly far less risk-adverse than employees are under capitalist institutions, where the social costs of unemployment are almost always extremely severe.

---

[53] Roemer 1994, p. 123.
[54] See also Duménil and Lévy 2004.

If we wish to assess the likely technological dynamism of the socialist model of globalisation, we must also take into account that research and development is treated as a public good in this model, funded with public monies. How would the absence of privately-held intellectual property rights affect the innovation process? In previous chapters, I have referred to the many ways the extensive intellectual property-rights system of contemporary capitalism hampers innovation. Firms regularly take out patents they have no intentions of using, simply in order to harm their competitors. In these and other cases, significant resources are devoted towards the socially wasteful goal of end runs around existing patents. Patent races can also result in immense resources being expended for relatively small social gains, for instance, when a non-essential product becomes available marginally earlier than would otherwise have been the case.[55]

Despite these widely accepted facts, however, it is almost universally assumed that an extensive intellectual property-rights system is a necessary precondition for a technologically dynamic society. If, it is argued, firms cannot appropriate at least a significant portion of the fruits of innovation they will not have sufficient incentives to engage in an appropriate level of innovative activity. Monopoly profits resulting from claims to intellectual property ('technological rents') are thus required. If these profits are absent in socialism, could it still attain a high level of technological dynamism, even in principle?

The force of this objection rests entirely on the claim that people will engage in an activity in direct proportion to their ability to appropriate privately the social benefits resulting from that activity. This behaviour is, indeed, an expression of capitalist 'rationality'. But it is not an expression of human nature in general. Even under capitalism, people often choose to engage in activities in which they are able to appropriate a relatively small portion of the resulting benefits. The vast majority of actions in the innovation process illustrate this thesis. In the history of innovation, high private reward has not been the main motivation for those undertaking important R&D. Most of the central innovations of our day (micro-electronics, biotechnology, and so on) can be traced to academic researchers who did not have private claims to intellectual property in their discoveries. In the corporate sector, most of those

---

[55] *The Economist* 2002; Goozner 2004.

engaged in innovative activity are forced to sign away patent rights as a condition of employment. Other sorts of reward are clearly more important motivating factors, such as the ability to engage in a form of creative and intrinsically rewarding labour, the greater likelihood of future funding if present research is successful, the status and prestige enjoyed within the scientific-technical community, the hope to contribute to a better future, and so on. Of course, in capitalism, the owners of capital and their representatives will typically not fund a search for innovations unless *they* are confident they will be able to appropriate a significant proportion of any resulting benefits. But that is a quite different matter.

The failure of the *a priori* argument for intellectual property rights does not conclude the discussion. It could still be the case that a socialist global order would necessarily tend to enjoy a significantly lower level of technological dynamism than a system with extensive intellectual property rights, even if the latter hampers innovation in a number of respects. The following considerations, however, show that there are no good reasons to think this would be the case.

In the model of socialism under discussion, there are a variety of research and development facilities competing for available funding. A reputation mechanism operates, such that documented past successes are a crucial factor in this competition. In these circumstances, R&D labs have ample incentive to succeed. If they do not, future grants will not be forthcoming, and the lab will be dismantled.

Second, those working in worker collectives, once again, have clear incentives to undertake innovative activity. This holds true even in the absence of patent rights. If searches for innovations are successful, the workforce prospers. If searches are not undertaken, the workforce suffers in producer and consumer markets.

Third, even if intellectual property rights were abolished, there would still be a gap between scientific-technical knowledge and the implementation of that knowledge in concrete processes of production and distribution. In order to take advantage of newly available knowledge, particular enterprises must themselves develop workers with the skills required to follow developments in publicly funded research labs, reflect on how these developments could be concretely applied to the products and processes of the particular firm in question, and then carry out these applications. Collectives that are successful in developing such skills in the workforce will tend to prosper far more than others, even if they cannot claim private intellectual property rights. In other words, under the form of socialism being discussed, there would continue to be significant first-mover advantages. Enterprises developing new products first could establish customer relations that might be difficult for later innovators to replicate. And a worker co-operative with a documented record for successful innovations would be in a superior position when requests were made to community banks for new investment funds.

Under capitalism, such possible advantages for early innovators are typically combined with a very high level of risk. If a proposed innovation is not successful, or if other firms are able to copy it quickly and effectively, early innovators may suffer significant losses, discouraging innovation. These losses are minimised in a system in which R&D is treated as a public good and funded accordingly. Now, many of the risks associated with early innovation are socialised, encouraging a higher degree of innovative activity than might otherwise be the case. This provides us with another good reason to suppose that this version of socialism would be technologically dynamic.

Finally, firms able to co-ordinate their innovative activity with their suppliers and distributors, R&D labs, and academic research communities have significant advantages, even in the absence of an extensive system of intellectual property rights.[56] A body of work in organisational theory has arisen emphasising the importance of trust in the formation and reproduction of networks of innovation.[57] But, enduring trust in inter-capital relations is no more likely than in capital/wage-labour relations. Perhaps the most significant inter-firm relations in contemporary capitalism are core-ring networks, in which firms with concentrated economic power are surrounded by a ring of smaller subcontractors and distributors.[58] There is a sense in which the network as a whole can be seen as the unit of capital accumulation. But core firms are still forced by the law of value (in the form of inter-capital competition in the given sector) to squeeze their suppliers and distributors, while retaining the sections of the value chain with the highest 'value added' activities. In Marxian terminology, core firms are forced by the law of value to attempt to appropriate

---

[56] Storper and Walker 1989.
[57] Granovetter 1985.
[58] Kenney and Florida 1993.

the greatest amount of surplus-value produced in the chain as a whole. And, when overaccumulation difficulties and financial crises arise, as they inevitably do under capitalist production relations, core firms necessarily tend to shift the burden of these downswings to their suppliers and distributors (who, in turn, attempt to subject their work force to 'superexploitation' relative to prevailing standards).[59]

There is no form of socialism that will attain a magic equilibrium point and reproduce it indefinitely. In socialism, too, there will be disruptions in production and distribution due to innovations, shifts in wants and needs, changes in demography and emigration patterns, and so on. In any foreseeable form of socialism, economic agents will no doubt attempt to shift the burden of adjusting to these disruptions to others, no matter how much more a general ethos of solidarity permeates everyday life than in capitalism. But three counteracting factors come into play. First, the rhythms of production and distribution would not fluctuate as wildly as they do in capitalism.[60] Second, one is more willing to make sacrifices the more limited and temporary those sacrifices are. In capitalism, the costs of economic adjustment can be serious and long-lasting to both investors and their employees, giving both groups a strong incentive to shift these burdens to others as much as possible. In democratic socialism, in contrast, the right to employment, and the right of each community to its per capita share of new investment funds, lessen the costs of these adjustments. These measures also shorten the duration in which these costs are imposed. Third, the boards of directors of the various enterprises do not represent the interests of private investors seeking to

---

[59] See Smith 2000a, Chapter 5. The most vulnerable sectors of the workforce tend to be employed by small-scale suppliers and distributors. The class relations of capitalism that generate 'superexploitation' thus systematically reproduce the marginalisation of these sectors, a crucial component of the reproduction of, gender, racial, and ethnic oppression in capitalist society. (The impressionistic term 'superexploitation' refers to factors such as work conditions, wage levels, employment security, and so on. It is not a species of the Marxian category notion of exploitation, which refers to the ratio of surplus labour to necessary labour. A high degree of 'superexploitation' is compatible with a low rate of exploitation in Marx's technical sense of the term. Indeed, the two usually go together. Workplaces with the exceptionally bad work conditions, wage levels, employment security, etc., typically do not have high investments in the state of the art technology systems that enable the most relative surplus-value to be produced.)
[60] See footnote 84 below.

maximise their return. Community representatives on these boards would surely realise that any gains won by one collective that comes at the cost of serious harm to others in the region would not improve the position of the community as a whole.

To summarise, the formal and informal communication across enterprise boundaries within inter-capital networks can be a great spur to innovation. These inter-firm networks are an important source of capitalism's technological dynamism. But capitalist social relations also undermine cross-firm communication and co-operation. The law of value makes it difficult for trust to arise in inter-capital relations, and ensures that the trust that does arise will be extremely precarious. The structural factors underlying these tendencies would not operate in a democratic form of socialism. And, so, the cross-enterprise formal and informal communication that contributes so much to innovation would be far more likely to occur.[61]

One last topic must be addressed before concluding this discussion of socialism and technological dynamism. I have given some reasons for thinking that the innovative potential of a socialist global order can in principle be comparable to that of capitalism. But, in the former, the level of innovation in society as a whole is partially a function of the revenues set aside for the public good of research and development and new investments. Democratically elected officials determine how extensive these revenues will be. When all is said and done, the representatives delegated to make these decisions could choose a course of action that results in a lower level of innovation than what could be attained within a capitalist order, even if no structural factors preordain this result.

This possibility must be granted. But a slower rate of innovation is not necessarily a bad thing in itself. There is no 'natural' rate of technical change to serve as a benchmark, and it would be foolish to assume that more is always better. When contrasting the technological paths selected under capitalism with those that would result from socialist democracy, it is not enough to contrast respective rates of innovation. The *direction* of the paths that tend to be taken is at least as relevant. If the paths of technical change

---

[61] The manner in which all forms of scientific and technological knowledge are categorised as public goods rather than private property obviously would also greatly further formal and informal communication across enterprise boundaries.

selected under socialist democracy would be far superior to those taken under capitalism, the former way of organising innovation could be far superior to the latter, even if the latter boasted a somewhat faster rate of innovation.

Within the institutional framework of socialist democracy, the development of technology would not be associated with exploitation. Every advance in labour productivity presents a choice. A higher level of output could be produced in the same time. Or the same level of output could be produced with less time devoted to work. In a capitalist society, the former is the default setting. Capital accumulation is the name of the game, and if more commodities are produced and sold, more capital can be accumulated. From a normative standpoint, one of the worst features of capitalism is the way men and women are forced to devote such a significant portion of their brief life span to capital accumulation, even as labour productivity advances.[62] One of the great advantages of socialist democracy is that it allows the members of society to decide democratically whether they would rather enjoy the benefits of these advances in the form of greater output or increased leisure, and to shift the rate of new investment accordingly.

There is absolutely compelling empirical evidence that greater and greater consumption is *not* correlated with greater and greater happiness. This correlation holds only up until a certain level of material consumption has been reached. Past that point, other factors – the quality of social relationships (family, friends, and so on) and the level of work satisfaction – are far more important to one's sense of well-being.[63] The socialist model of globalisation sketched in Section 2 reflects this profound human truth in a way that no possible form of global capitalism can.

Technological development in socialism would also not be associated with the domination of money and capital as alien social forms. It would not be an essential mechanism reproducing uneven development in the global economy. It would not be associated with high levels of inequality or environmental harms the way it is in capitalism.[64] We may conclude that the

---

[62] See Schor 1993; Fraser 2001.

[63] Lane 1991, Layard 2005.

[64] Improvments in labour productivity in principle could lead to a reduction of the working week at the same level of output, or to a greater level of output and the same work week. The 'grow or die' imperative of capitalism implies that the latter is the 'default setting'. A systematic tendency to the depletion of natural resources and the excessive generation of wastes necessarily results. See Foster 1994; Foster and Clark 2003.

direction of technological change in a socialist global order would be far preferable, more than enough to compensate for a somewhat lower rate of change, should that in fact occur.

Another sort of difficulty needs to be considered in this context. For all the obvious short-termism infecting capitalism, considerable funds are still devoted to long-term investments. Wealthy individuals hope to provide an ample legacy for their children and grandchildren, and most managers of pension funds devote at least a certain portion of their holdings to relatively safe long-term investments. In an economy without capital markets, such activities are ruled out. Might it be the case that the very institutional mechanisms set up to prevent a small group of economic élites from pursuing their private interests enables present members of society to pursue *their* good at great cost to future generations? It is one thing for a present generation to decide democratically how to make a trade-off between its leisure and its consumption. It is a quite different matter for a present generation to decide the trade-off between its present consumption and that of future generations.

There are limits to procedural democracy. A normatively acceptable form of socialism must include a number of socially acknowledged rights that are not up for majority vote, including rights to employment, adequate living standards, political participation, and so on. While non-existent future generations cannot literally make rights-claims, present generations ought to grant anticipatory force to the fundamental interests that future generations can be reasonably expected to have. No present generation ought to be able to set the level of new investment funds so low that present consumption is maximised at serious cost to the life prospects of future generations.[65] In Schweickart's model of economic democracy, all enterprises must set aside sufficient depreciation funds to maintain the value of the community's investment over time. This ensures that there are no endogenous factors tending to lower the opportunities of future generations below what the present generation enjoys. To this we should add a constitutional mandate that sufficient revenues be raised each generation to allow a level of new investment funds sufficient to ensure that subsequent generations enjoy comparable opportunities to pursue their life plans as those enjoyed by the present generation.

---

[65] Blackburn 2002. See also the discussion of the just savings principle in Rawls 1971.

While technological change in itself does not necessarily further the social good, neither does technological stagnation. If an otherwise acceptable form of socialism systematically discourages innovations, that, in itself, would be sufficient grounds for rejecting it. But this is not at all the case for the form of socialism defended here.

The eighth and final objection to the socialisation of the means of production introduced in Section 1 remains to be considered, the alleged tendency for budget constraints to be 'soft'. For Kornai and many other theorists of socialism, this is the most serious objection of all.[66]

5. Socialism and budget constraints

It is one thing to say that, if worker collectives do not perform effectively, they will be dissolved by community banks, thereby providing a 'stick' encouraging efficiency and innovation to complement the 'carrot' of success in consumer and producer markets. But, if a firm fails to maintain the value of the community's investment over time, what ensures that community banks will in fact shut it down? Four considerations suggest that this may not occur with sufficient regularity.

The ability to co-ordinate production and distribution is a major advantage of socialism. It should be far easier to establish the networks of co-operating enterprises so crucial to innovation than it is in capitalism. Funds for start-ups and for expansion can be allocated to worker co-operatives up and down production and distribution chains in a synchronised fashion. This state of affairs has many advantages. But shutting down any one link in the chains connecting suppliers, producers, and distributors might have profoundly negative consequences on other enterprises in these networks. Would this not discourage community banks from dissolving even insolvent enterprises in many circumstances?

A second problem in implementing hard-budget constraints consistently over time stems from the mandate placed on community banks to maintain full employment in their region. The greater the institutional commitment to full employment, the less inclined community banks will be to eliminate

---

[66] Kornai 1986, 1992.

positions. Suppose a worker collective provides a significant proportion of employment in a given region. Might not local community banks regard this enterprise as 'too big to fail'?

Third, suppose we grant that, in obvious cases of utter financial collapse, community banks will be willing to restructure enterprises. What of cases that are not so clear, cases in which judgment calls are involved? Would not these judgements most likely be biased against shutting down a troubled co-operative? If, for example, a short-term deficit were due to extraneous and temporary factors, the extreme step of shutting an enterprise down would not be justified. When can we know with certainty that extraneous and temporary factors are not the cause of the problems? And how short is the short term? What would prevent community banks from allowing troubled enterprises to operate years or even decades before a drastic restructuring was considered? If this problem were to occur on a system-wide scale, would it not undermine the efficiency of the system?

Finally, in many cases the financial problems of an enterprise may be due to social demands placed on enterprises. In such cases, economic restructuring is not necessarily the appropriate response. Community banks may not be in a position to distinguish these cases from cases of straightforward economic inefficiency, where forced restructuring would be in the interest of society as a whole. As Stiglitz writes in a related context:

> State enterprises may be under pressure to pursue noneconomic goals, such as regional employment. State enterprises may be subjected to civil service constraints in their employment policies. All of these may adversely affect the efficiency of state enterprises. It may be hard for the government to commit itself to allow state-owned enterprises to act as if they were private; that is, it may be hard to commit itself to allowing competition, to hardening budget constraints, not to subjecting it to civil service requirements. These commitment problems – which may be viewed as 'political economy problems' or 'public sector incentive problems' – appear to be closer to the core of the distinction between markets and market socialism than do differences in managerial incentives.[67]

---

[67] Stiglitz 1994, p. 81; see also p. 238.

Two preliminary responses can be introduced at this stage of the argument. First, the systematic tendency to overaccumulation crises shows that the problem of hard-budget constraints is not solved in capitalism in the automatic and relatively painless manner assumed by neoliberal theory, as Stiglitz himself admits. Second, it is worth recalling that Stiglitz also grants that, in principle, this problem can be addressed adequately in the absence of capitalist property relations:

> Government can create government enterprises that are given hard budget constraints; it can set up a set of procedures that can at least increase the transaction costs associated with softening the budget constraint.[68]

Matters cannot be left here, however. Proponents of a version of socialism incorporating markets must acknowledge that penalties for failure must be present alongside rewards for success if these markets are to function effectively. Both are required to provide the proper incentives for boards, managers, and individual workers to act in a manner furthering efficiency and dynamism. If, for example, there are no penalties for excessive risk-taking, or for insufficient risk-taking, then there would be no institutional mechanisms ensuring that the actual amount of risk-taking was appropriate. In my view, the following considerations provide adequate grounds for holding that a feasible form of socialism need not generate insuperable difficulties in this regard.

In centrally planned economies, firms that otherwise would have failed were kept afloat by loans, 'soft' prices, and 'soft' taxes.[69] None of these practices would play a comparable role in the model of socialist globalisation sketched in this chapter. The provision of new investment funds by community banks is the functional equivalent of loans. If banks consistently provide these funds to failing firms, the income of the bank's managers and workers would be negatively affected as a direct result. Also, these banks would receive significantly fewer funds to allocate in the future, as more funds were shifted to other, more successful, community banks in the region. The functioning of producer input and consumer markets undermines the ability of state officials to set 'soft' prices. And, if taxes are set at a flat rate on all non-labour assets, there is no scope for the state to impose 'soft' taxes on worker collectives.

---

[68] Stiglitz 1994, p. 239.
[69] Roemer 1994, pp. 32–3; see also Kornai 1992.

Second, in bureaucratic-command economies, firms were not exposed to competition, making it very difficult to know whether a particular enterprise failed to attain an adequate level of efficiency. The model of socialism defended here includes competition in producer and consumer markets. While the presence of competition may not make the relative efficiency level of a given firm immediately obvious, in most cases it will make this clear sooner rather than later. Competition in producer and consumer markets is sufficient for this purpose; capital markets and labour markets are not required.

Third, the fact that the selection, promotion, and dismissal of managers in both worker collectives and community banks depend on worker democracy – rather than political loyalty to party bosses – also works against merely soft budget constraints. Hard budget constraints are undermined by cronyism between managers and politicians. Socialist democracy eliminates this cronyism.

That, at least, is the claim. But would cronyism in fact be eliminated? Or would it just take a different form? Would not bonds form between officials from community banks and the enterprises in a given region? Would that not lead these banks to refrain from funding new enterprises that might compete against existing ones in the region? Would this not in effect free the established enterprises from having to worry about budget constraints, undermining the competitive pressure to innovate?[70] As long as a variety of community banks operate in the given region, the danger of competition-limiting collusion should be kept in check. Continuing competition in producer and consumer markets from enterprises outside the given region provides an additional corrective.[71]

Fifth, in capitalism, banks often hesitate to force firms to restructure for the simple reason that they do not wish to write off previous loans or equity investments. For an extended period, at least, they will continue to make further loans to and investments in corporations experiencing great difficulties, hoping that things will eventually turn around. This phenomenon is referred to as 'hooking' onto a lender; once a lender has made an initial loan, it is often more or less forced to provide additional credit.[72] In the model of socialism presented above, in contrast, community banks allocate public funds.

---

[70] Stiglitz 1994, p. 135.
[71] See Stiglitz 1994, p. 256.
[72] See Stiglitz and Weiss 1990.

While those working in the banks enjoy benefits from good decisions and suffer sanctions from bad ones, the costs of bad investments are borne predominantly by the community as a whole. Most mainstream theorists see this as a major flaw of socialism, and it is certainly true that proper incentives and oversight must be in place for this arrangement to work. But there are important advantages to socialising the costs of misallocations. Managers of community banks will be far more prone to push for restructurings when the banks themselves do not directly or indirectly have to bear a major burden of these costs.

Sixth, community banks can be placed under a mandate to not provide funds for expanded investments to firms with poor records of innovation. Since the resources distributed to these community banks (and thus the income of their workers and managers) are a function of independent social audits, these banks have a strong incentive to monitor and encourage innovation to improve the efficiency of local enterprises, thereby preventing the need for restructurings in the first place.

Seventh, however much bankers in capitalism proclaim that capital flows should not be distorted by anything as trivial as worker resistance, the reality is that workers are never completely depoliticised in capitalism, and never without some means of expressing their interests. Restructurings tend to provoke social unrest if they involve massive lay-offs in a society where there are no rights to employment, next-to-no effective re-training programmes, and few mechanisms to ensure that new jobs are created in a region as old ones are displaced. In some circumstances, at least, the potential for sizeable social disturbances results in a softening of budget constraints. In the model of socialism advocated here, there are rights to employment, extensive re-training programmes, and an institutional mechanism that ensures that new jobs will be created in the region as old ones are displaced (the *prima facie* right of each region to the same per capita share of new investment funds). Shutting down inefficient enterprises would not come at the same catastrophic cost to workers as in capitalism. Further, community banks that imposed hard budget constraints when publicly available information showed it was called for would have a social legitimacy banks imposing hard budget constraints in capitalism lack.

These considerations all suggest that community banks can be expected to impose the hard-budget constraints on failing enterprises required for the

332 • Chapter Eight

efficiency of the socialist model of globalisation. A last point suggests that community banks may actively welcome imposing these constraints in many circumstances. Both enterprises and community banks have representatives from various social movements on their boards of directors, representatives accountable to the rank and file of these movements. In the present context, the representatives from consumer movements are most relevant. It is part of their responsibility to monitor issues regarding consumer safety, consumer cost, product quality, product need, and so on. A firm that failed in consumer markets would most likely have seriously failed in one or more of these dimensions. The boards of directors of the enterprise and the relevant community bank(s), including representatives accountable to consumer movements, would have a far different attitude towards a firm in these circumstances than a board concerned first and foremost with the interests of private shareholders. Both boards would generally be more open to arguments for dissolving the enterprise, since doing so would send a powerful message to other firms that consumer interests are to be taken seriously.

The weakest conclusion to be drawn from this discussion is that any problems regarding 'hard'-budget constraints in socialist democracy are unlikely to be significantly worse than those found in capitalism. As Stiglitz constantly reminds us, capitalist markets do not function in the manner described by general equilibrium theory. There are countless instances where banks have continued lending to doomed corporations, and numerous others where private losses have been made good by governments.[73] Such 'moral hazard' problems are inevitable in the global capitalist economy. Further, multiple objectives are often placed on contemporary capitalist firms, making it difficult for those with the power to force restructurings to judge whether such a drastic course of action is warranted.[74] Given the myriad advantages of a socialist global order presented in this chapter, if this order were not significantly worse than capitalism in dealing with the problem of budget constraints, that would be good enough.

In the first section of this chapter, I introduced the eight most significant criticisms of socialism proposed by mainstream social theorists. In Section 2,

---

[73] Stiglitz 1994, p. 184.
[74] Stiglitz 1994, pp. 234–5, 283.

I presented a model of socialist globalisation, and then in Sections 3–5, I showed that the eight criticisms do not apply to this model. I conclude that the claim that the alternative global framework sketched in Section 2 is both feasible and normatively attractive can be asserted without falling into an immanent contradiction.

One final question must be raised before asserting that the model defended in this chapter brings the systematic dialectic of globalisation to a fitting conclusion. Does this alternative framework incorporate ('sublate') the Marxian model of capitalist globalisation presented in Chapters 5–7? In other words, does it adequately take into account the Marxian critique of the commodity-form, the money-form, and the capital-form?

6. A Marxian model?

I have described the alternative to capitalist globalisation presented above as a 'Marxian' framework. There are many who would insist that this is a horrible misuse of terms, despite the fact that capital and labour markets play no role in the model. In this final section, I shall attempt to respond to the most important arguments raised by Bertell Ollman in his critique of so-called 'market socialists', a group that in his view includes David Schweickart, upon whose work the present chapter is based.[75]

The underlying insight behind many of Ollman's criticisms is both profound and correct. Marx's critique is a critique of capital, not capitalists. The latter are relevant to his theory only insofar as they function as personifications of the former. In principle, it is possible for a society without capitalists to still be subject to the alien logic of capital. A society of nationalised firms subject to the valorisation imperative would remain under the alien logic of capital, even if there were no capitalists owners of those firms. Inter-firm competition,

---

[75] Ollman is surely correct that Marx himself would most likely have decried a vision of socialism including extensive use of commodity markets, opting instead for far more extensive democratic central planning. But as he recognises, in itself this does not decide any substantive issue. Ollman's position echoes the powerful criticisms of market socialism found in Mandel 1986 and McNally 1993. Neither of these theorists, however, refers to Schweickart's writings. Given the importance of these writings to the present chapter, I shall concentrate on Ollman's critical assessment of them here. I would like to thank Patrick Murray for forcefully raising many questions regarding Schweickart's model in private correspondence.

and the treatment of individual workers as mere means to further success in that competition, would characterise this society no less than more familiar forms of capitalism. The crucial matters from a Marxian standpoint are production relations, not property relations.

In the model of socialist globalisation under discussion, the production of commodities for sale in the market remains the dominant form of production. There are still prices and profits. And inter-firm competition continues to penalise less successful enterprises and workers. From a Marxian standpoint, what are prices but the form in which the value produced by abstract labour appears? What are profits but a disguised form of surplus-value from exploitation? What does inter-firm market competition impose if not the valorisation imperative? And so, Ollman concludes, worker co-operatives in this system become, in effect, collective capitalists:

> The fundamental error in their [market socialists'] analysis is to identity capital with capitalists, the current embodiment of capital, and not see that capital, as a relations of production, can also be embodied in the state (as in state capitalism) or even in workers' cooperatives (as in market socialism).[76]

While wage-labour may be abolished, workers would still be subsumed under the alien power of capital, including real subsumption at the point of production:

> The collective, after all, will only hire new people if it believes their work will increase its profit, or secure or improve its market share (ultimately reducible to profit). With this approach, the collective is unlikely to show more concern for the human needs, including the need for a job, of the unemployed and others in the community than businesses do under capitalism. Even on the job, the interests of the individual worker and the interests of the collective do not coincide, for while he may wish to work shorter hours at a reduced pace the collective may force him to work longer and faster so that it can keep up with the competition, which will still be viewed as an impersonal power beyond human control.[77]

Money fetishism would also not be abolished. Individuals 'will constantly desire more money so that they can buy more, or have the power and status

---

[76] Ollman 1998, p. 106.
[77] Ollman 1998, pp. 99–100.

of someone who could. As now, they will worship money as something that gives them this power'.[78] All in all, the project of socialising markets is quite similar to the attempt by social democrats to humanise market societies through the so-called 'mixed economy'. And we know how this attempt ends: 'it doesn't take long before maintaining the health of the private sector gets interpreted as the most important social need'.[79] The public sector becomes increasingly squeezed as the private accumulation of capital becomes increasingly prioritised.

Three other criticisms involve issues of social agency. Ollman insists that the extensive use of markets in Schweickart's model of economic democracy is incompatible with the class solidarity required for socialism to work:

> Expanding a worker's sense of self to include others in his enterprise is a
> poor substitute for perceiving one's identity in an entire class, especially in
> light of the no-holds-barred competition between enterprises (and therefore
> between groups of workers) that would mark this arrangement.[80]

In Ollman's view, socialists willing to concede a role for markets also fail to appreciate the transformation of subjectivity that would occur in the course of a successful transition to socialism. For such a transition to occur, the majority of workers will have to understand their common interests, develop a very high level of mutual concern, and accept personal responsibility for how political affairs turn out. 'But these are the same qualities that make building socialism after the revolution, including democratic central planning, possible'.[81] With these new qualities – and with input into both plans and the selection of the planners – workers would give planners the accurate information they needed, be able to make compromises among themselves, and do their best to ensure that the plan succeeded.

Finally, socialists who advocate an extensive use of markets are too focused on the failure of the Soviet Union, a historical catastrophe that has weighed heavily on the present chapter. A socialism following the most advanced forms of capitalism would be able to institute a form of socialist planning based on a plentiful supply of goods, extensive scientific knowledge, skilled

---

[78] Ollman 1998, p. 100.
[79] Ollman 1998, p. 104.
[80] Ollman 1998, p. 101.
[81] Ollman 1998, p. 108.

labour, and democratic traditions. Most planning would consist of revisions to capitalist priorities, rather than preparations for building entire sectors from scratch. Effective communications technologies would allow any needed adjustments to be implemented reasonably quickly in a process of trial and error. Planning could also take place on appropriate levels, in contrast to the excessive centralisation in the USSR.[82] If these points are recognised, the implosion of the Soviet system justifies neither hasty generalisations about supposedly inevitable shortcomings of central planning, nor a desperate embrace of markets in response to these alleged flaws.

Before considering these objections, I would first like to make a general point: the social forms analysed by Marx in *Capital* are historically specific. Commodities, money, profits, and so on, can all be found in precapitalist societies. One of Marx's fundamental insights is that *these were not the same social forms as commodities, money, and profits in capitalism*, although we use the same words. In *Capital*, Marx examines these social forms insofar as they are moments of a social order whose organising principle is the self-valorisation of value (or, equivalently, the systematic reproduction of the exploitative capital/wage-labour relation). This was not the organising principle of precapitalist societies, nor is it the organising principle of democratic socialism. Commodities, money, and 'profits' (in one sense of the term, at least) may be found in the latter. But *these are not the same as the commodities, money, and profits of capitalism*, although, here too, we use the same words.

In capitalism, the collective social powers of labour appear in the alien form of value, a power standing over and above working men and women. In the above model of socialism, a high proportion of production is still undertaken for the market. But decisions regarding the overall level of new social investment, the provision of public goods, and the social priorities for new investment, are all determined in a democratic planning process, prior to private decisions in the market. The self-valorisation of value is *not* the organising principle of the social order when these measures are in place; they are sufficient to overcome the tyranny of the law of value. This democratic co-ordination of production *ex ante* through these measures may not be as extensive as the central planning of all (most) inputs, outputs, and distribution.

---

[82] Ollman 1998, p. 107.

But it still counts as a qualitative break from any and all variants of capitalism, a break sufficient to undermine the power of commodity and money fetishism.[83]

It is not the mere presence of markets *per se* that establishes the alien power of the value, but the institutionalisation of the drive to accumulate surplus-value to the greatest extent possible, whatever the cost to social life. When decisions regarding the overall level of new investment and the provision of public goods determined in a democratic planning process, prior to private decisions in the market, the 'grow or die' imperative of capitalism is eliminated. Funds for new investment on the level of society as a whole can be increasingly shifted to public goods. Or a collective decision could be made to enjoy the fruits of productivity advances in the form of increased leisure rather than increased output.[84] In brief, the accumulation of capital as an end in itself is no longer the immanent end of social life. This overcoming of the valorisation imperative on the level of society as a whole is reinforced by the fact that successful worker co-operatives tend to expand only as long as taking on new workers leads to greater shares for existing workers. There is no reward for growth for its own sake, as there is in capitalism.[85]

What of the role of money in this framework? The output of collectives will be sold for money, and workers will purchase personal consumption goods with money. But holders of money will not have the social power of determining the level of new investment or the overall direction of investment in the economy. Money will not be used to hire the labour-power of another person as a commodity. Money will not grant its holders the ability to determine which regions of the globe will flourish, and which will be trapped in material deprivation. Money will not be desperately sought as a store of value providing security in the face of an uncertain future; security in the face of an uncertain future is found instead in the institutionalisation of the basic precepts of

---

[83] McNally makes an important distinction between 'the use of market mechanisms within the framework of socialist planning' and the market as the regulator of economic relations. McNally 1993, p. 172. Schweickart's model of economic democracy illustrates the former, not the latter. In McNally's sense of the terms, then, Ollman is mistaken to refer to it as 'market socialism', which illustrates the latter, not the former.
[84] These measures also allow overaccumulation difficulties to be held in check. And, with the abolition of financial markets, the systematic tendency to financial crises would be completely eliminated. I therefore cannot accept Ollman's repeated claims that crises would be as prevalent in a global order based on worker collectives as in global capitalism.
[85] Schweickart 1993, p. 169.

socialism, including especially the right of employment and the right of all communities to receive their per capita share of new investment funds. Finally, there will be no M-M' circuits, and so no material basis for the most extreme form of money fetishism. For Ollman, none of this makes any substantive difference. In his view, the role of money remains essentially the same as in capitalism. Is this really plausible?

Is it any more plausible to hold that the capital/labour relation is not fundamentally transformed either? The answer must be no, for reasons that can be seen after a quick review of the theory of exploitation. 'Exploitation', in Marx's sense of the term, is not merely a matter of workers not receiving back in wages the equivalent of what they have produced. In any plausible form of socialism, there must be a surplus product, that is, economic wealth that does not return to the workers who produced it.[86] For the category of exploitation to be applicable, the surplus product (a) must be produced within a social framework characterised by structural coercion, and (b) must not be under the control of workers or their representatives.[87]

Regarding (a), the framework of structural coercion that is the basis of surplus-value production in capitalism rests upon wage-labourers' alienation from the means of production and subsistence. With guaranteed employment rights, this coercion is absent in the model of socialism under discussion. This does not mean that all workers will always be able to work in any collective they choose. I see nothing wrong in principle with letting the members of a given worker community decide for themselves which applicants are likely to be best suited to a particular workplace (assuming, of course, that no pattern of systematic discrimination emerges from their choices). This arrangement is not the Garden of Eden. But neither is it equivalent to the structural coercion characterising labour markets in capitalism.

Regarding (b), the surplus product produced by worker collectives is divided into two parts. The first returns directly to the members of the workforce for their personal consumption, following principles either directly determined by the workers themselves or by representatives directly accountable to them.[88]

---

[86] Resources are required to insure and expand the means of production, provide for public goods, fund the young, sick and elderly, and so on. See *Critique of the Gotha Programme*, Marx 1977, p. 567.

[87] See Smith 2000a, Chapter 3.

[88] Strictly speaking, then, there are no 'profits' in this framework, in the sense of the term in capitalism.

The second is appropriated by taxes and devoted to the provision of public goods and new investment funds. The level of taxation, the ratio of investment in public goods to new investment funds, the specific public goods funded, and the priorities for new investment, are all determined by democratically accountable bodies. The community banks responsible for the final allocations of new investment funds must respect the democratically determined priorities, with boards of directors charged to ensure that they do precisely that, and a system of social audits to aid these boards in carrying out their duties. In my view, these arrangements justify the assertion that the disposal of the surplus product is in the hands of collective social labour.[89]

Even if the socialist model of globalisation presented above is not based on the exploitation of wage-labour, it could still be characterised by a level of alienation in the labour process making it unacceptable from a Marxian standpoint. This is Ollman's view. He insists that the need to remain competitive in producer or consumer markets will influence the pace of the labour process perniciously.

The most important point to note in response is the range of choice granted to collectives. The option to increase the pace of work to keep up with competitors is indeed one possibility. But a collective could democratically decide to work slower, or for fewer hours. This would come at the cost of a lower market share for the enterprise, and lower income for its members. The right to make this decision would be taken out of their hands only if the collective were no longer able to maintain depreciation funds and a minimally adequate level of income for its members. Of course, an individual worker could find herself working in a collective in which the normal pace was more intense than she wished. In many cases, workers can be reasonably expected to allow some workers to work less intensely than others in return for a lower share of the collective's earnings. If technical considerations or a sense of

---

[89] These arrangements also reveal why Ollman's analogy between Schweickart's model and the so-called 'mixed economy' breaks down. Attempts to establish a 'mixed economy' in capitalism have indeed failed to attain their objectives, with the public sector increasingly squeezed and the private accumulation of capital increasingly prioritised (see Chapter 1 above). This result is inevitable, given the social power granted to those who privately control investment capital. The mere threat of a capital strike or capital flight is usually sufficient to subordinate the public sector to the needs of capital accumulation. *This threat is entirely absent in the socialist model of globalisation.*

fairness ruled out such arrangements, a person who did not want to labour at the normal pace in a particular collective would be free to seek to join a different one.

These sorts of decisions are indeed forced upon people because individual collectives must compete against each other in producer and consumer markets. Is Ollman correct to conclude that this would inevitably erode the solidarity required to maintain socialism over time? It is certainly not the case that all forms of competition always and everywhere undermine solidarity. Even in capitalist society, family, friends, acquaintances, and even strangers vigorously compete against each other in a host of activities – from the most trivial board game to the most exalted theoretical and aesthetic challenges – without loss of mutual respect and good will. The social alienation we see in capitalist markets does not come from competition *per se*, but from the all-encompassing and vicious nature of the competition that characterises capitalist markets.

In economic democracy, competition is far less encompassing than in capitalism. Democracy in the workplace, and the democratic central planning of new investment, the provision of public goods, and social priorities, is no less central to the model than competition in producer and consumer markets. The region of social life where social agents relate to each other as citizens rather than as competitors is vastly greater than in any possible form of capitalism. In economic democracy, the right to employment, the right of all regions to its per capita share of new investment funds, the priority given to the provision of public goods, and so on, also implies that the competition between workers in different collectives would lack the viciousness of inter-capital competition. It would be fair in a way that no possible form of capitalism can be. And it would be without either the devastating consequences inflicted on 'losers' or the obscene gains appropriated by 'winners' in the capitalist mode of production. Ollman's assertion that competition among worker collectives would undermine the solidarity that is a necessary condition of socialism rests on the assumption that the social-psychological effects of all-encompassing and vicious competition are identical to those of a competition that is neither all-encompassing nor vicious. Why should we accept this assumption?[90]

---

[90] In Devine's model of democratic planning, technological change is implemented through a negotiated co-ordination involving all social groups significantly affected

Two issues remain. Would the transformations of subjectivity that would occur in any successful transition to socialism eliminate the free-rider and principal/agent problems that motivate versions of socialism making use of markets? And are the historical failures of the USSR of little-to-no relevance to socialists attempting to construct a form of socialism incorporating the most advanced developments of contemporary capitalism?

I myself am sceptical of the idea that the tension between altruism and self-interest, universality and particularity, will be forever eradicated from world history in the course of a transition to socialism. I am also sceptical of the idea that capitalism will lead us to the very threshold of a society of abundance, and, in my view, anything short of that makes the historical lessons of the Soviet model extremely relevant to the socialist project.[91] As

---

by the change, including horizontal negotiations with other enterprises in the sector and negotiations to determine the prices that enterprises can charge. Devine 1988. He correctly stresses that that extended negotiation can have a transformative effect, encouraging economic agents to internalise the perspective of other agents, furthering solidarity in a manner that Ollman would surely approve of. Negotiated co-ordination is a feature of Schweickart's model, insofar as the allocation of funds for new investment is made by community banks with a broad representation of affected social groups on their board of directors, and insofar as requests for funds for new investments are made by worker collectives that also have broad representation of affected social groups on their boards. Devine, however, goes much further. Devine himself admits, however, that, in his model, when negotiations break down, widespread social paralysis can result. He asserts that the desire to not be blamed for causing such paralysis should be sufficient to ensure that the relevant agents will reach agreements in the required time frame. Perhaps. But this sort of paralysis could horribly erode solidarity were it to occur. The danger does not arise to the same degree in Schweickart's model, since only the general direction of technological change is a matter of negotiation, with particular details of implementation (like pricing) decentralised to the enterprise level. Devine's model is like a collective composition of a musical score, in which the musicians decide ahead of time every note they will play. Agents in Schweickart's model are more like jazz musicians who agree of the general framework of the music beforehand but then improvise within that framework, adjusting to unexpected developments as they arise. It is not obvious to me why the former is necessarily a better metaphor for solidarity in socialism than the latter.

[91] There is a tendency in capitalism for technologies to be developed that allow certain types of use-values to be distributed to unlimited numbers of individuals at marginal costs approaching zero. In contemporary capitalism, tremendous resources are being devoted to technologies and legal decrees creating artificial scarcity so that these goods can be treated as regular commodities to be sold for private profit (Perelman 1998). In any form of socialism worthy of the name, the costs of the infrastructure and social labour required to produce products such as these would be socialised, and the products would then be directly distributed as free public goods to any and all who wanted them, a point rightly emphasised in Mandel 1986 and McNally 1993. If the course of capitalist development led to a state of affairs in which the production

interesting and important as these questions are, however, I do not believe that the way in which they are answered affects the results of this book.

The course of the systematic dialectic of globalisation has shown that all the major forms of capitalist globalisation are implicitly beset by immanent contradictions, contradictions made explicit in the Marxian model of capitalist globalisation. The main conclusion of the systematic dialectic is that these contradictions can only be resolved in a socialist model of globalisation. In this chapter, I have presented a model that can be affirmed as feasible and normatively attractive in face of the strongest criticisms that have been proposed against the socialist project. I have also given reasons why this framework deserves to be called 'Marxian', even if it makes more extensive use of markets than most theorists in the Marxian tradition have accepted.

Systematic dialectics are revisable. If it should turn out that there were some other socialist model of globalisation with a better claim to feasibility and normative attractiveness, that model would form the proper culmination of a systematic dialectic of globalisation. But this would not change the main thesis of this book: the immanent contradictions of capitalism can only be overcome in a socialist model of globalisation.

7. Conclusion

I have presented the main objections proposed against the socialist project. These objections have considerable force when applied to either bureaucratic-command models or models of market socialism in the tradition of Lange, Lerner, and Taylor. But these objections do not provide compelling reasons to reject a democratic model of socialist globalisation. This model, which explicitly transcends the immanent contradictions of all variants of global capitalism, has a legitimate claim to be termed 'Marxian'.

Can such a model claim to be 'actual' in Hegel's sense of the term? Does it capture what Rawls called 'the deep tendencies and inclinations of the

---

of additional units in all the major sectors of the economy had a marginal cost approaching zero, there would be no reason to include extensive producer and consumer markets in a model of socialism designed to replace it. The Soviet experience, plagued by scarcity issues, would indeed be completely irrelevant to the socialist project. However, for the foreseeable future, at least, it is doubtful this will be the case in most sectors of the economy.

social world'? No. The deep tendencies and inclinations of the contemporary social world continue to be defined by the social forms of global capitalism, best formulated in the Marxian model of capitalist globalisation considered in Chapters 5–7. But contingent existence and mere logical possibility are not the only alternatives to 'actuality'.

The restriction of the creative energies of collective social labour to forms compatible with the valorisation imperative will inevitably be experienced as arbitrary and harmful. The not-to-be underestimated force of ideologies, the distractions of consumption, and the dull compulsion of daily routine can never fully erode this experience. It follows that *resistance to capital is part of the concept of capital*.[92] The form this resistance takes profoundly depends on the forms of organisation in place in a given historical setting, and the strategy and tactics that can be developed and implemented within them. These issues must ultimately be considered on far more concrete levels of analysis than a systematic dialectic of globalisation.[93] But, on this level, we may affirm that cross-border flows of trade, money, capital investments, production chains, and so on, are likely to spur the development of organisations, strategies, and tactics of resistance to capital that increasingly take on an internationalist form. Insofar as this is the case, a model providing a feasible and normatively attractive alternative to capitalist globalisation can be far more than a mere logical possibility. It may have material force in the extended historical process whereby a transnational class 'in itself' is transformed into a transnational class 'for itself', to resort to Hegelian jargon one final time.[94]

Perhaps the greatest of capital's many powers is the power to constrict political imagination. Of all its powers, this is probably the most difficult to resist. Today, an increasing number of progressive individuals and groups

---

[92] 'As the number of co-operating workers increases, so too does their resistance to the domination of capital, and, necessarily, the pressure put on by capital to overcome this resistance. The control exercised by the capitalist is not only a special function arising from the nature of the social labour process, and peculiar to that process, but it is at the same time a function of the exploitation of a social labour process, and is consequently conditioned by *the unavoidable antagonism* between the exploiter and the raw material of exploitation'. Marx 1976, p. 449, emphasis added; see also pp. 635, 793, and Chapter 5 above.
[93] McCarney 1990.
[94] Robinson and Harris 2000.

accept the 'common-sense' view that the means of production must be predominantly privately owned and controlled for an efficient and normatively acceptable global system. The long view of world history does not support this surmise. The flaws of capitalism, and the creative capacities of humanity, are both far too great for us to abandon the search for a feasible alternative to global capitalism. The model of socialism presented in this chapter is certainly not anything like a full vision of a future society. As inadequate as it is, however, it suffices to establish the possibility of a future beyond the private ownership of the means of production. At this point, systematic dialectics concludes, and must give way to the vastly more important dialectic of theory and practice.

References

Alesina, Alberto and Edward Glaeser 2004, *Fighting Poverty in the US and Europe: A World of Difference*, Oxford: Oxford University Press.

Anderson, Terry and Donald Leal 1991, *Free Market Environmentalism*, Boulder: Westview Press.

Archibugi, Daniele, David Held, and Martin Koehler (eds.) 1998, *Re-Imagining Political Community: Studies in Cosmopolitan Democracy*, Cambridge: Polity Press.

Arrighi, Giovanni 1994, *The Long Twentieth Century*, London: Verso.

Arrighi, Giovanni 2002, 'Global Inequalities and the Legacy of Dependency Theory', *Radical Philosophy Review*, 5, 1–2: 75–85.

Arrighi, Giovanni and Jason Moore 2001, 'Capitalist Development in World Historical Perspective', in *Phases of Capitalist Development: Booms, Crises and Globalizations*, edited by Robert Albritton, Makoto Itoh, Richard Westra, and Alan Zuege, Basingstoke: Palgrave/Macmillan.

Arrighi, Giovanni and Beverly Silver 1999, *Chaos and Governance in the Modern World System*, Minneapolis: University of Minnesota Press.

Arthur, Chris 1993, 'Hegel's *Logic* and Marx's *Capital*', in *Marx's Method in 'Capital'*, edited by Fred Moseley, Atlantic Highlands, NJ.: Humanities Press.

Arthur, Chris 1997, 'Against the Logical-Historical Method: Dialectical Derivation versus Linear Logic', in *New Investigations of Marx's Method*, edited by Fred Moseley and Martha Campbell, Atlantic Highlands, NJ.: Humanities Press.

Arthur, Chris 2003, 'On Enrique Dussel's *Towards an Unknown Marx*', *Historical Materialism*, 11, 2: 247–63.

Barker, Colin 1997, 'Some Reflections on Two Books by Ellen Wood', *Historical Materialism*, 1: 22–65.

Barry, Brian 1998, 'International Society from a Cosmopolitan Perspective', in *International Society: Diverse Ethical Perspectives*, edited by David Mapel and Terry Nardin, Princeton: Princeton University Press.

Becker, Gary 1981, *A Treatise on the Family*, Cambridge, MA. Harvard University Press.

Beitz, Charles 1979, *Political Theory and International Relations*, Princeton: Princeton University Press.

Beitz, Charles 1985, 'Justice and International Relations', in *International Ethics*, edited by Charles Beitz, Marshall Cohen, Thomas Scanlon, and A. John Simmons, Princeton: Princeton University Press.

Bellofiore, Riccardo 1985, 'Marx After Schumpeter', *Capital & Class*, 24: 60–74.

Bellofiore, Riccardo 1989, 'A Monetary Labour Theory of Value', *Review of Radical Political Economics*, 21, 1–2: 1–25.

Bensaïd, Daniel 2002, *Marx for Our Times: Adventures and Misadventures of a Critique*, London: Verso.

Bhagwati, Jagdish 2004, *In Defense of Globalization*, Oxford: Oxford University Press.

Blackburn, Robin 2002, *Banking on Death – Or, Investing in Life: The History and Future of Pensions*, London: Verso.

Bonefeld, Werner 2004, 'On Postone's Courageous but Unsuccessful Attempt to Banish the Class Antagonism from the Critique of Political Economy', *Historical Materialism*, 12, 3: 103–24.

Bonefeld, Werner and John Holloway (eds.) 1995, *Global Capital, National State and the Politics of Money*, Basingstoke: Macmillan.

Borsook, Paulina 2000, *Cyberselfish*, New York: Public Affairs.

Boyer, Robert 1996, 'State and Market: A New Engagement for the Twenty-First Century?', in *States Against Markets: The Limits of Globalisation*, edited by Robert Boyer and Daniel Drache, London: Routledge.

Brenner, Johanna 2000, *Women and the Politics of Class*, New York: New York University Press.

Brenner, Robert 1998, 'The Economics of Global Turbulence', *New Left Review*, I, 229: 1–264.

Brenner, Robert 2002, *The Boom and the Bust: The US in the World Economy*, London: Verso.

Brewer, Anthony 1991, *Marxist Theories of Imperialism: A Critical Survey*. London: Routledge.

Bronfenbrenner, Kate 1996, 'The Effects of Plant Closing or Threat of Plant Closing on the Right of Workers to Organize', North American Commission for Labor Cooperation, September 30.

Bronfenbrenner, Kate 2001, *Uneasy Terrain: The Impact of Capital Mobility on Workers, Wages and Union Organizing*, Washington: Report to US Trade Deficit Review Commission.

Buchanan, Alan 2004, *Justice, Legitimacy, and Self-Determination*, Oxford: Oxford University Press.

Burkett, Paul 1999, *Marx and Nature: A Red and Green Perspective*, New York: St. Martin's Press.

Burkett, Paul and Martin Hart-Landsberg 2000, *Development, Crises and Class Struggle: Learning from Japan and East Asia*, New York: St. Martin's Press.

Burkett, Paul and Martin Hart-Landsberg 2001, 'Crisis and Recovery in East Asia: The Limits of Capitalist Development', *Historical Materialism*, 8: 3–47.

Burnham, Peter 1995, 'Capital, Crisis and the International State System', in *Global Capital, National State and the Politics of Money*, edited by Werner Bonefeld and John Holloway, Basingstoke: Macmillan.

Burtless, Gary, Robert Lawrence, Robert Litan, and Robert Shapiro 1998, *Globaphobia: Confronting Fears About Open Trade*, Washington: Brookings Institution.

Callinicos, Alex 2000, *Equality*, Cambridge: Polity Press.

Callinicos, Alex 2001, *Against the Third Way: An Anti-Capitalist Critique*, Cambridge: Polity Press.

Campbell, Martha 1993, 'Marx's Concept of Economic Relations and the Method of *Capital*', in *Marx's Method in 'Capital'*, edited by Fred Moseley, Atlantic Highlands, NJ.: Humanities Press.

Campbell, Martha 2002, 'The Credit System', in *The Culmination of Capital: Essays on Volume III of Marx's Capital*, edited by Martha Campbell and Geert Reuten, New York: Palgrave/Macmillan: 212–27.

Chang, Ha-Joong 2002, *Pulling Up the Ladder? Policies and Institutions for Development in Historical Perspective*, London: Anthem.

Chomsky, Noam 1996, *World Orders Old and New*, New York: Columbia University Press.

Christensen, Clayton 1997, *The Innovator's Dilemma*, Cambridge, MA. Harvard Business School Press.

Cigler, Allan and Burdett Loomis 1998, *Interest Group Politics*, Washington: CQ Press.

Clarke, Simon 1994, *Marx's Theory of Crisis*, Basingstoke: Macmillan Press.

Clarke, Simon 2001, 'Class Struggle and the Global Overaccumulation of Capital', in *Phases of Capitalist Development: Booms, Crises and Globalizations*, edited by Robert Albritton, Makoto Itoh, Richard Westra, and Alan Zuege, Basingstoke: Palgrave/ Macmillan.

Coase, Ronald 1960, 'On the Problem of Social Costs', *Journal of Law and Economics*, 3: 1–44.

Cobb, John and Herman Daly 1997, *For the Common Good*, Boston: Beacon Press.

Colas, Alejandro 2001, *International Civil Society: Social Movements in World Politics*, Oxford: Blackwell.

Council of Foreign Relations Task Force 1999, *Safeguarding Prosperity in a Global Financial System: The Future International Financial Architecture*, Washington: The Institute for International Economics.

Dam, Kenneth 2001, *The Rules of the Global Game: A New Look at US International Economic Policymaking*, Chicago: The University of Chicago Press.

Davidson, Paul 2002, *Financial Markets, Money and the Real World*, Chettenham, Edward Elgar.

de Brie, Christian 2000, 'Crime – The World's Biggest Free Enterprise: Thick as Thieves', *Le Monde Diplomatique*, April: 7.

de Brunhoff, Suzanne 1978, *The State, Capital, and Economic Theory*, London: Pluto Press.

de Maillard, Jean 2000, 'Crime – The World's Biggest Free Enterprise: The Dark Side of Globalisation', *Le Monde Diplomatique*, April: 6.

DeRosa, David 2001, *In Defense of Free Capital Markets: The Case Against a New International Financial Architecture*, Princeton: Bloomberg Press.

Devine, Pat 1988, *Democracy and Economic Planning: The Political Economy of a Self-Governing Society*, Boulder: Westview Press.

Devine, Pat (ed.) 2002a, *Building Socialism Theoretically: Alternatives to Capitalism and the Invisible Hand*, Science and Society, special issue, 66/1.

Devine, Pat 2002b, 'Participatory Planning Through Negotiated Coordination', in *Building Socialism Theoretically: Alternatives to Capitalism and the Invisible Hand*, edited by Pat Devine, Science and Society, special issue, 66/1: 72–85.

Dosi, Giovanni and Luigi Orsenigo 1988, 'Coordination and Transformation: An Overview of Structures, Behaviours and Changes in Evolutionary Environments', in *Technical Change and Economic Theory*, edited by Giovanni Dosi, Christopher Freedman, Richard Nelson, Gerald Silverberg, and Luc Soete, New York: Pinter Publishers.

Dosi, Giovanni and Luigi Orsenigo, Christopher Freedman, Richard Nelson, Gerald Silverberg, and Luc Soete (eds.) 1988, *Technical Change and Economic Theory*, New York: Pinter Publishers.

Drache, Daniel 1996, 'From Keynes to K-Mart: Competitiveness in a Corporate Age', in *States Against Markets: The Limits of Globalisation*, edited by Robert Boyer and Daniel Drache, London: Routledge.

Duménil, Gérard, and Dominique Lévy 2004, *Capital Resurgent: Roots of the Neoliberal Revolution*, Cambridge, MA. Harvard University Press.

Dussel, Enrique 1997, 'Hegel, Marx, and Schelling', presented at the 1997 conference of the International Working Group on Value Theory, available at www.greenwich.ac.uk/-fa03/iwgvt.

Eatwell, John 1996, *International Financial Liberalization: The Impact on World Development*, New York: United Nations Development Programme Discussion Paper Series.

Eatwell, John and Lance Taylor 2000, *Global Finance at Risk: The Case for International Regulation*, New York: The New Press.

The Economist 2000, 'Debt in Japan and America', January 22: 21–2.

The Economist 2002, 'Patently Absurd', June 23: 40–2.

The Economist 2003, 'Guiding the Pack: Regulators Should Worry Less About Individual Banks and More About Systems', July 26: 72.

The Economist 2004a, 'Corporate Tax: A Taxing Battle', January 31: 71–2.

The Economist 2004b, 'A Survey of International Banking', April 17: 1–24.

Elson, Diane 1988, 'Market Socialism or Socialisation of the Market', *New Left Review*, I, 172: 3–44.

Elson, Diane 1999, 'Socialised Markets, not Market Socialism', in *Socialist Register 2000: Necessary and Unnecessary Utopias*, edited by Colin Leys and Leo Panitch, London: Merlin Press.

Etro, Federico 2004, 'Innovation by Leaders', *Economic Journal*, April: 281–303.

Ewing, Jack 2004, 'Is Siemens Still German?', *Business Week*, May 17: 50–1.

Fine, Bob, Richard Kinsey, John Lea, Sol Picciotto, and Jock Young 1979, *Capitalism and the Rule of Law: From Deviancy Theory to Marxism*, London: Hutchinson.

Fisk, Milton 1989, *The State and Justice: An Essay in Political Theory*, Cambridge: Cambridge University Press.

Florida, Richard and Martin Kenney 1990, *The Breakthrough Illusion: Corporate America's Failure to Move from Innovation to Mass Production*, New York, Basic Books.

Foley, Duncan 1986, *Understanding Capital*, Cambridge, MA.: Harvard University Press.

Foster, John Bellamy 1994, *The Vulnerable Planet: A Short Economic History of the Environment*, New York: Monthly Review Press.

Foster, John Bellamy and Brett Clark 2003, 'Ecological Imperialism: The Curse of Capitalism', in *The New Imperial Challenge: Socialist Register 2004*, edited by Leo Panitch and Colin Leys, New York: Monthly Review Press.

Fraser, Jill 2001, *White-Collar Sweatshop: The Deterioration of Work and Its Rewards in Corporate America*, New York: Norton Press.

Freeman, Christopher, John Clark, and Luc Soete 1982, *Unemployment and Technical Innovation: A Study of Long Waves and Economic Development*, London, Francis Pinter.

Friedman, Milton 1953, 'The Case for Flexible Exchange Rates', in *Essays in Positive Economics*, Chicago: Chicago University Press.

Friedman, Thomas 2000, *The Lexus and the Olive Tree: Understanding Globalization*, New York: Random House.

Fukuyama, Francis 2004, *State-Building: Governance and World Order in the 21st Century*, Ithaca: Cornell University Press.

Ganssmann, Heiner 2004, 'Germany: Capital Flees', *Le Monde Diplomatique*, February: 13.

Goozner, Merill 2004, *The $800 Million Pill: The Truth Behind the Costs of New Drugs*, Berkeley: The University of California Press.

Gowan, Peter 1999, *The Global Gamble: Washington's Faustian Bid for World Dominance*, London: Verso.

Graaf, Jan de Villiers 1957, *Theoretical Welfare Economics*, Cambridge: Cambridge University Press.

Gramsci, Antonio 1971, *Selections from the Prison Notebooks*, New York: International Publishers.

Granovetter, Mark 1985, 'Economic Action and Social Structure: The Problem of Embeddedness', *American Journal of Sociology*, 913: 481–510.

Gray, John 1998, *False Dawn: The Delusions of Global Capitalism*, London: Granta.

Guehenno Jean-Mobarie 2000, *The End of the Nation-State*, Minneapolis: University of Minnesota Press.

Guttmann, Robert 1994, *How Credit-Money Shapes the Economy: The United States in a Global System*, Armonk: Sharpe.

Habermas, Jürgen 1979, *Communication and the Evolution of Society*, Boston: Beacon Press.

Hacker, Jacob 2004, 'Call It the Family Risk Factor', *New York Times*, January 11 'Week in Review': 15.

Hale, David 1998, 'The IMF, Now More than Ever', *Foreign Affairs*, 77, 6: 7–13.

Hardt, Michael, and Antonio Negri 2000, *Empire*, Cambridge, MA. Harvard University Press.

Harvey, David 1996, *Justice, Nature & the Geography of Difference*, Oxford: Blackwell.

Harvey, David 1999, *The Limits to Capital*, Second Edition, London: Verso.

Harvey, David 2001, 'The Art of Rent: Globalization, Monopoly and the Commodification of Culture', in *A World of Contradictions: Socialist Register 2002*, edited by Leo Panitch and Colin Leys, New York: Monthly Review Press.

Harvey, David 2003a, 'The "New" Imperialism: Accumulation by Dispossession', in *The New Imperial Challenge: Socialist Register 2004*, edited by Leo Panitch and Colin Leys, New York: Monthly Review Press.

Harvey, David 2003b, *The New Imperialism*, Oxford: Oxford University Press.

Hayek, Friedrich 1976, *Law, Legislation, and Liberty, Volume 2: The Mirage of Social Justice*, Chicago: University of Chicago Press.

Hegel, G.W.F. 1956, *The Philosophy of History*, New York: Dover.

Hegel, G.W.F. 1967 [1821], *Hegel's Philosophy of Right*, Oxford: Oxford University Press.

Hegel, G.W.F. 1971 [1830], *Hegel's Philosophy of Mind: Being Part Three of the Encyclopaedia of The Philosophical Sciences*, Oxford: Oxford University Press.

Hegel, G.W.F. 1975 [1830], *Hegel's Logic: Being Part One of the Encyclopaedia of The Philosophical Sciences*, Oxford: Oxford University Press.

Hegel, G.W.F. 1977 [1807], *Hegel's Phenomenology of Spirit*, Oxford: Oxford University Press.

Hegel, G.W.F. 1988, *Hegel's Lectures on the Philosophy of Religion: One-Volume Edition, The Lectures of 1827*, edited by Peter Hodgson, Berkeley: University of California Press.

Held, David 1995, *Democracy and the Global Order: From the Modern State to Cosmopolitan Governance*, Stanford: Stanford University Press.

Held, David 2004, *Global Covenant: The Social Democratic Alternative to the Washington Consensus*, Cambridge: Polity Press.

Held and David, Anthony McGrew, David Goldblatt, and Jonathan Perraton, (eds.) 1999, *Global Transformations: Politics, Economics and Culture*. Stanford: Stanford University Press.

Helleiner, Eric 1996, 'International Capital Mobility and the Scope for National Economic Management', in *States Against Markets: The Limits of Globalisation*, edited by Robert Boyer and Daniel Drache, London: Routledge.

Helleiner, Eric 2002, 'The Politics of Global Financial Regulation: Lessons from the Fight Against Money Laundering', in *International Capital Markets: Systems in Transition*, edited by John Eatwell and Lance Taylor, Oxford: Oxford University Press.

Helleiner, Eric 2003, *The Making of National Money: Territorial Currencies in Historical Perspective*, Ithaca: Cornell University Press.

Hirst, Paul and Grahame Thompson 1996, *Globalisation in Question: The International Economy and the Possibilities of Governance*, Cambridge: Polity.

Hoogvelt, Ankie 2001, *Globalization and the Postcolonial World: The New Political Economy of Development*, Second Edition, Baltimore: Johns Hopkins University Press.

Hudson, Michael 2003, *Super Imperialism: The Origin and Fundamentals of U.S. World Dominance*, Second Edition, London: Pluto Press.

Hutton, Will and Anthony Giddens (eds.) 2000, *On The Edge: Living With Global Capitalism*, London: Jonathan Cape.

International Committee of the Red Cross 2000, *Forum: War, Money and Survival*, Geneva: International Committee of the Red Cross.

International Monetary Fund 1997, *World Economic Outlook: May 1997*, Washington: International Monetary Fund.

Irwin, Douglas 2002, *Free Trade Under Fire*, Princeton: Princeton University Press.

Itoh, Makoto and Costas Lapavitsas 1999, *Political Economy of Money and Finance*, Basingstoke: Macmillan Press.

Jagger, Alison 1988, *Feminist Politics and Human Nature*, Lanham: Rowman and Littlefield.

Jagger, Alison 2002, 'A Feminist Critique of the Alleged Southern Debt', *Hypatia*, 174: 119–41.

Jameson, Fredric 2000, 'Globalization and Strategy', *New Left Review*, II, 4: 49–68.

Jessop, Bob 1997, 'Capitalism and the Future: Remarks on Regulation, Government and Governance', *Review of International Political Economy*, 4, 3: 561–81.

Johnson, Chalmers 2004, *The Sorrows of Empire: Militarism, Secrecy, and the End of the Republic*, New York: Metropolitan Books.

Johnson, Harry 1976, 'Money and the Balance of Payments', *Banca Nazionale Del Lavoro Quarterly Review*, March: 3–16.

Jones, Charles 1999, *Global Justice: Defending Cosmopolitanism*, Oxford: Oxford University Press.

Kantor, Rosemary 1995, *World Class: Thriving Locally in the Global Economy*, New York: Touchstone.

Kapstein, Ethan 1999, *Sharing the Wealth: Workers and the World Economy*, New York: W.W. Norton.

Kaul, Inge, Isabelle Grunberg, and Marc Stern (eds.) 1999, *Global Public Goods: International Cooperation in the 21st Century*, Oxford: Oxford University Press.

Kenen, Peter 1994, *The International Economy*, Third Edition, Cambridge: Cambridge University Press.

Kenney, Martin, and Richard Florida 1993, *Beyond Mass Production: The Japanese System and its Transfer to the U.S.*, Oxford: Oxford University Press.

Kessler-Harris, Alice 2002, *In Pursuit of Equality: Women, Men, and the Quest for Economic Citizenship*, Oxford: Oxford University Press.

Keynes, John Maynard 1980, *Activities 1940–1944: Shaping the Post-War World, The Clearing Union, The Collected Writings of John Maynard Keynes, Vol. 25*, Basingstoke: Macmillan.

Kindleberger, Charles 1989, *Manias, Panics, and Crashes: A History of Financial Crises*, New York: Basic Books.

Kindleberger, Charles 1993, *A Financial History of Western Europe*, Second Edition, Oxford: Oxford University Press.

Klein, Naomi 2000, *No Logo: Taking Aim at the Brand Bullies*, New York: Harper Collins.

Kleinknecht, Alfred 1987, *Innovation Patterns in Crisis and Prosperity: Schumpeter's Long Cycle Reconsidered*, New York: St. Martin's Press.

Kornai, János 1986, 'The Soft Budget Constraint', *Kyklos*, 39, 1: 3–30.

Kornai, János 1992, *The Socialist System: The Political Economy of Communism*, Princeton: Princeton University Press.

Kotz, David 2001, 'The State, Globalization and Phases of Capitalist Development', in *Phases of Capitalist Development: Booms, Crises and Globalizations*, edited by Robert Albritton, Makoto Itoh, Richard Westra, and Alan Zuege, Basingstoke: Palgrave/ Macmillan.

Kuttner, Robert 1997, *Everything for Sale: The Virtues and Limits of Markets*, Chicago: University of Chicago Press.

Layard, Richard 2005, *Happiness: Lessons from a New Science*, New York, Penguin Press.

Landreth, Harry 1976, *History of Economic Theory: Scope, Method, and Content*, Boston: Houghton Mifflin.

Lane, Robert 1991, *The Market Experience*, Cambridge: Cambridge University Press.

Lange, Oskar and Fred Taylor 1964, *On the Economic Theory of Socialism*, New York: McGraw-Hill.

Lebowitz, Michael 1992, *Beyond Capital: Marx's Political Economy of the Working Class*, Basingstoke: Macmillan.

Lebowitz, Michael 2000, 'Kornai and the Vanguard Mode of Production', *Cambridge Journal of Economics*, 24: 377–92.

Lester, Richard 1998, *The Productive Edge: How U.S. Industries are Pointing the Way to a New Era of Economic Growth*, New York: Norton.

Levine, Andrew and Erik Olin Wright 1980, 'Rationality and Class Struggle', *New Left Review*, I, 123: 47–68.

Levins, Richard and Richard Lewontin 1985, *The Dialectical Biologist*, Cambridge, MA: Harvard University Press.

Lindert, Peter 2004, *Growing Public: Social Spending and Economic Growth Since the Eighteenth Century*, Cambridge: Cambridge University Press.

Löwy, Michael 1981, *The Politics of Combined and Uneven Development*, London: Verso.

Luttwak, Edward 1999, *Turbo-Capitalism: Winners and Losers in the Global Economy*, New York: Harper Collins.

Lydall, Harold 1988, *Yugoslav Socialism*, Oxford: Oxford University Press.

Mandel, Ernest 1975, *Late Capitalism*, London: Verso.

Mandel, Ernest 1986, 'In Defence of Socialist Planning, *New Left Review*, I, 159: 5–37.

Mansfield, Edward, John Rapoport, Anthony Romeo, Samuel Wagner, and George Beardsley 1967, 'Social and Private Rates of Return from Industrial Innovations', *Quarterly Journal of Economics*, 41: 221–40.

Markusen, Ann and Joel Yudken 1992, *Dismantling the Cold War Economy*, New York: Basic Books.

Marx, Karl 1963 [1862–3], *Theories of Surplus-Value, Volume I*, Moscow: Progress.

Marx, Karl 1968 [1862–3], *Theories of Surplus-Value, Volume II*, Moscow: Progress.

Marx, Karl 1971 [1862–3], *Theories of Surplus-Value, Volume III*, Moscow: Progress.
Marx, Karl 1973 [1857–58], *Grundrisse*, New York: Vintage Press.
Marx, Karl 1976 [1867], *Capital, Volume I*, New York: Penguin Books.
Marx, Karl 1977, *Selected Writings*, David McLellan, editor, New York: Oxford University Press.
Marx, Karl 1981 [1894], *Capital, Volume 3*, New York: Penguin Books.
Mattick, Paul 1991–2, 'Some Aspects of the Value-Price Problem', *International Journal of Political Economy* 214: 9–66.
Mattick, Paul 2002, 'Class, Capital and Crisis', in *The Culmination of Capital: Essays on Volume III of Marx's 'Capital'*, edited by Martha Campbell and Geert Reuten, Basingstoke: Palgrave/Macmillan.
McCarney, Joseph 1990, *Social Theory and the Crisis of Marxism*, London: Verso.
McCarney, Joseph 2000, *Hegel on History*, London: Routledge.
McKinnon, Ronald 1973, *Money and Capital in Economic Development*, Washington: Brookings Institute.
McLellan, David (ed.) 1988, *Marxism: Essential Writings*, Oxford: Oxford University Press.
McMichael, Philip (ed.) 1994, *The Global Restructuring of Agro-Food Systems*, Ithaca: Cornell University Press.
McNally, David 1993, *Against the Market: Political Economy, Market Socialism and the Marxist Critique*, London: Verso.
Melamed, Leo (ed.) 1988, *The Merits of Flexible Exchange Rates*, Fairfax: George Mason University Press.
Miller, David 2000 *Citizenship and National Identity*, Cambridge: Polity Press.
Moody, Kim 1998, *Workers in a Lean World*, London: Verso.
Moseley, Fred 1991, *The Falling Rate of Profit in the Postwar United States Economy*, Basingstoke: Macmillan.
Moseley, Fred 1993, 'Marx's Logical Method and the "Transformation Problem"', in *Marx's Method in 'Capital'*, edited by Fred Moseley, Atlantic Highlands, NJ.: Humanities Press.
Mulford, Charles and Eugene Comiskey 2002, *The Financial Numbers Game: Detecting Creative Accounting Practices* New York: John Wiley & Sons.
Murray, Patrick 1993, 'The Necessity of Money: How Hegel Helped Marx Surpass Ricardo's Theory of Value', in *Marx's Method in 'Capital'*, edited by Fred Moseley, Atlantic Highlands, NJ.: Humanities Press.
Murray, Patrick 1998, 'Beyond the "Commerce and Industry" Picture of Capital', in *The Circulation of Capital: Essays on Volume Two of Marx's 'Capital'*, edited by Chris Arthur and Geert Reuten, Basingstoke: Macmillan.
Neftci, Salih 2002, 'Synthetic Assets, Risk Management, and Imperfections', in *International Capital Markets: Systems in Transition*, edited by John Eatwell, John, and Lance Taylor, Oxford: Oxford University Press.
Nelson, Richard (ed.) 1993, *National Innovation Systems*, Oxford: Oxford University Press.
Nozick, Robert 1974, *Anarchy, State, and Utopia*, New York: Basic Books.
Nussbaum, Martha 2001, *Women and Human Development*, Cambridge: Cambridge University Press.
OECD 2000, *A New Economy? The Changing Role of Innovation and Information Technology in Growth*, Paris: Organisation for Economic Co-operation and Development.
Okin, Susan Moller 1989, *Justice, Gender, and the Family*, New York: Basic Books.
Ollman, Bertell 1976, *Alienation: Marx's Conception of Man in Capitalist Society*, Cambridge: Cambridge University Press.
Ollman, Bertell 1993, *Dialectical Investigations*, Cambridge: Cambridge University Press.
Ollman, Bertell (ed.) 1998, *Market Socialism: The Debate Among Socialists*, London: Routledge.
Ollman, Bertell and Tony Smith (eds.) 1998, *Dialectics: The New Frontier*, special issue, *Science and Society*, 62, 3.

O'Rourke, Kevin and Jeffrey Williamson 2000, *Globalization and History: The Evolution of a Nineteenth-Century Atlantic Economy*, Cambridge, MA. MIT Press.

Palley, Thomas 1998, *Plenty of Nothing: The Downsizing of the American Dream and the Case for Structural Keynesianism*, Princeton: Princeton University Press.

Perelman, Michael 1998, *Class Warfare in the Information Age*, New York: St. Martin's Press.

Phillips, Kevin 2002, *Wealth and Democracy: A Political History of the American Rich*, New York: Broadway Books.

Pinkard, Terry 1988, *Hegel's Dialectic: The Explanation of Possibility*, Philadelphia: Temple University Press.

Plender, John 2000, 'Froth Blown Away as the Bull is Caged', *Financial Times*, April 18: 20.

Pogge, Thomas 1989, *Realizing Rawls*, Ithaca: Cornell University Press.

Pogge, Thomas 2002, *World Poverty and Human Rights*, Oxford: Blackwell.

Pogge, Thomas (ed.) 2001, *Global Justice*, Oxford: Blackwell Publishing.

Pogge, Thomas and Sanjay Reddy 2002, 'Unknown: The Extent, Distribution and Trend of Global Income Poverty', <www.socialanalysis.org>.

Polanyi, Karl 1944, *The Great Transformation*, Boston: Beacon Press.

Popper, Karl 1950, *The Open Society and Its Enemies*, Princeton: Princeton University Press.

Postone, Moishe 1993, *Time, Labor, and Social Domination: A Reinterpretation of Marx's Critical Theory*, Cambridge: Cambridge University Press.

Rai, Shirin 2002, *Gender and the Politics of Development*, Cambridge: Polity Press.

Rasler, Karen and William Thompson 1994, *The Great Powers and Global Struggle: 1490–1990*, Lexington: University Press of Kentucky.

Rawls, John 1971, *A Theory of Justice*, Cambridge, MA.: Harvard University Press.

Rawls, John 1985, 'Justice as Fairness: Political not Metaphysical', in *Collected Papers*, edited by Samuel Freeman, Cambridge, MA.: Harvard University Press 1999.

Rawls, John 1993, 'The Law of Peoples', in *Collected Papers*, edited by Samuel Freeman, Cambridge, MA.: Harvard University Press 1999.

Rawls, John 1997, 'The Idea of Public Reason Revisited', in *Collected Papers*, edited by Samuel Freeman, Cambridge: Harvard University Press 1999: 573–615.

Rawls, John 1999, *The Law of Peoples*, Cambridge, MA. Harvard University Press.

Reinecke, Wolfgang 1998, *Global Public Policy: Governing without Government?*, Washington, DC.: The Brookings Institution.

Reuten, Geert 1991, 'Accumulation of Capital and the Foundation of the Tendency of the Rate of Profit to Fall', *Cambridge Journal of Economics*, 15 1: 79–93.

Reuten, Geert 1997, 'The Notion of Tendency in Marx's 1894 Law of Profit', in *New Investigations of Marx's Method*, edited by Fred Moseley and Martha Campbell, Atlantic Highlands, NJ.: Humanities Press.

Reuten, Geert and Michael Williams 1989, *Value-Form and the State*, London: Routledge.

Ricardo, David 1970, *On the Principles of Political Economy and Taxation, The Work and Correspondence of David Ricardo, Volume 1*, edited by P. Sraffa, Cambridge: Cambridge University Press.

Robin, Corey 2001, 'The Ex-Cons: Right-Wing Thinkers Go Left!', *Linguafranca*, February: 24–33.

Robinson, William and Jerry Harris 2000, 'Towards a Global Ruling Class: Globalization and the Transnational Capitalist Class', *Science and Society*, 64, 1: 11–54.

Rodrik, Dani 2001, 'Trading in Illusions', *Foreign Policy*, March/April: 55–62.

Roemer, John 1994, *A Future for Socialism*, Cambridge, MA. Harvard University Press.

Rohter, John 2003, 'Once Secure, Argentines See Jobs, Food and Hope Shrivel', *New York Times*, March 2, A 1: 6.

Rosdolsky, Roman 1977, *The Making of Marx's 'Capital'*, London: Pluto Press.

Rosenberg, Nathan, and Claudio Frischtak 1983, 'Long Waves and Economic Growth: A Critical Appraisal', *American Economic Association, Papers and Proceedings*, 73, 2: 146–51.

Rubin, Issac Ilich 1972, *Essays on Marx's Theory of Value* <translated from third [1928] edition>, Detroit: Black and Red.

Sandel, Michael (ed.) 1984, *Liberalism and Its Critics*, New York: New York University Press.

Sassen, Saskia 1998, *Globalization and Its Discontents: Essays on the New Mobility of People and Money*, New York: The New Press.

Sayer, Andrew 1984, *Method in Social Science: A Realist Approach*, London: Hutchinson.

Schmookler, Jacob 1966, *Invention and Economic Growth*, Cambridge, Harvard University Press.

Schor, Juliet 1993, *The Overworked American: The Unexpected Decline of Leisure*, New York: Basic Books.

Schumpeter, Joseph 1934, *The Theory of Economic Development*, Cambridge, MA. Harvard University Press.

Schumpeter, Joseph 1939, *Business Cycles: A Theoretical, Historical, and Statistical Analysis of the Capitalist Process*, New York, Harper and Row.

Schumpeter, Joseph 1947, *Capitalism, Socialism, and Democracy*, London: George Allen and Unwin.

Schweickart, David 1993, *Against Capitalism*, Cambridge: Cambridge University Press.

Schweickart, David 2002, *After Capitalism*, Lanham: Rowman & Littlefield.

Sennett, Richard 1998, *The Corrosion of Character: The Personal Consequences of Work in the New Capitalism*, New York: W.W. Norton.

Shaikh, Anwar 1979, 'Foreign Trade and the Law of Value – Part One', *Science and Society*, 43: 281–302.

Shaikh, Anwar 1979/80, 'Foreign Trade and the Law of Value – Part Two', *Science and Society*, 44: 27–57.

Shiller, Robert 2000, *Irrational Exuberance*, Princeton: Princeton University Press.

Slaughter, Anne-Marie 2004, *A New World Order*, Princeton: Princeton University Press.

Smith Adam 1976 [1776], *An Inquiry into the Nature and Causes of the Wealth of Nations, Vol. 2*, Oxford: Clarendon Press.

Smith, Tony 1990, *The Logic of Marx's 'Capital'*, Albany: State University of New York Press.

Smith, Tony 1991, *The Role of Ethics in Social Theory*, Albany: State University of New York Press.

Smith, Tony 1993, *Dialectical Social Theory and Its Critics: From Hegel to Analytical Marxism and Postmodernism*, Albany State University of New York Press.

Smith, Tony 1995, 'The Case Against Free Market Environmentalism', *Journal of Agricultural and Environmental Ethics*, 8, 2: 126–45.

Smith, Tony 1997a, 'A Critical Comparison of the Neoclassical and Marxian Theories of Technical Change', *Historical Materialism*, 1: 113–33.

Smith, Tony 1997b, 'Marx's Theory of Social Forms and Lakatos's Methodology of Scientific Research Programs', in *New Investigations of Marx's Method*, edited by Fred Moseley and Martha Campbell, Atlantic Highlands, NJ.: Humanities Press.

Smith, Tony 1999, 'The Relevance of Systematic Dialectics to Marxian Thought: A Reply to Rosenthal', *Historical Materialism*, 4: 215–40.

Smith, Tony 2000a, *Technology and Capital in the Age of Lean Production: A Marxian Critique of the New Economy*, Albany: State University of New York Press.

Smith, Tony 2000b, 'Brenner and Crisis Theory: Issues in Systematic and Historical Dialectics', *Historical Materialism*, 5: 145–78.

Smith, Tony 2002, 'Surplus Profits from Innovation: A Missing Level in *Capital III*?', in *The Culmination of Capital: Essays on Volume III*, edited by Geert Reuten and Martha Campbell, Basingstoke: Macmillan.

Smith, Tony 2003a, 'Systematic and Historical Dialectics: Towards a Marxian Theory of Globalization', in *New Dialectics and Political Economy*, edited by Robert Albritton and John Simoulidis, Basingstoke: Palgrave/Macmillan.

Smith, Tony 2003b, 'Why Madonna Should Cry for Argentina', in *Readings in American*

Government, Fourth Edition, edited by Mack Shelley, Jamie Swift, and Steffen Schmidt, New York: Thompson/Wadsworth.

Smith, Tony 2004, 'Technology and History in Capitalism: Marxian and Neo-Schumpeterian Perspectives', in *The Constitution of Capital: Essays on Volume One of Marx's 'Capital'*, edited by Riccardo Bellofiore and Nicola Taylor, Basingstoke: Palgrave/Macmillan.

Soros, George 1998, *The Crisis of Global Capitalism*, New York: Public Affairs.

Stiglitz, Joseph 1994, *Whither Socialism?*, Cambridge, MA. MIT Press.

Stiglitz, Joseph 2002, *Globalization and Its Discontents*, New York: W&W Norton.

Stiglitz, Joseph and A. Weis 1990, 'Banks as Social Accountants and Screening Devices and the General Theory of Credit Rationing', *Greek Economic Review Supplement*, 12: 85–118.

Storper, Michael, and Richard Walker 1989, *The Capitalist Imperative: Territory, Technology, and Industrial Growth*, Cambridge: Blackwell.

Strange, Susan 1996, *The Retreat of the State: The Diffusion of Power in the World Economy*, Cambridge: Cambridge University Press.

Strange, Susan 1998, *Mad Money: When Markets Outgrow Governments*, Ann Arbor: Michigan.

Therborn, Goran 1995, *European Modernity and Beyond: The Trajectory of European Society 1945–2000*, London: Sage.

Thirlwall, Anthony 1979, 'The Balance of Payments Constraint as an Explanation of International Growth Rate Differences', *Banca Nazionale del Lavoro Quarterly Review*, 128: 43–53.

Tirole, Jean 2002, *Financial Crises, Liquidity, and the International Monetary System*, Princeton: Princeton University Press.

Toporowski, Jan 2000, *The End of Finance: The Theory of Capital Market Inflation, Financial Derivatives and Pension Fund Capitalism*, London: Routledge.

Toussaint, Eric 1999, *Your Money or Your Life! The Tyranny of Global Finance*, London: Pluto.

UNCTAD 2002, *World Investment Report*, Geneva: United Nations Conference on Trade and Development.

van Duijn, J.J. 1983, *The Long Wave in Economic Life*, London: George Allen and Unwin.

Wade, Robert 1990, *Governing the Market: Economic Theory and the Role of Government in East Asian Industrialization*, Princeton: Princeton University Press.

Wade, Robert and Frank Veneroso 1998, 'The Gathering World Slump and the Battle Over Capital Controls', *New Left Review*, I, 231: 13–42.

Wainwright, Hilary 1994, *Arguments for a New Left: Answering the Free Market Right*, Oxford: Blackwell.

Walker, Richard 1988, 'The Dynamics of Value, Price and Profit', *Capital and Class*, 35: 146–81.

Wallerstein, Immanuel 1979, *The Capitalist World Economy*, Cambridge: Cambridge University Press.

Walter, Andrew 1991, *World Power and World Money: The Role of Hegemony and International Monetary Order*, New York: Harvester Wheatsheaf.

Webber, Michael, and David Rigby 1996, *The Golden Age Illusion: Rethinking Postwar Capitalism*, New York: Guilford Press.

Weeks, John 1981, *Capital and Exploitation*, Princeton: Princeton University Press.

Weisbrot, Mark, Dean Baker, Robert Naiman, Gila Neta 2002, 'Growth May be Good for the Poor – But are the IMF and World Bank Policies Good for Growth?', Center for Economic and Policy Research, <www.cepr.net>.

Weiss, Linda 1998, *The Myth of the Powerless State*, Ithaca: Cornell University Press.

Went, Robert 2000, *Globalisation: Neoliberal Challenge, Radical Responses*, London: Pluto Press.

Went, Robert 2002, *Enigma of Globalization: A Journey to a New State of Capitalism*, London: Routledge.

Wessner, Charles available at 2001, 'The Advanced Technology Program', *Issues in Science and Technology*, Fall, <www.issues.org/issues/18.1/p_wessner.html>

Wolf, Martin 2004, *Why Globalization Works*, New Haven: Yale University Press.

Wood, Ellen Meiksins 1986, *The Retreat From Class*, London: Verso.

Wood, Ellen Meiksins 2003, *Empire of Capital*, London: Verso.

World Bank 1992, *Good Governance and Development*, Washington: World Bank.

Wray, L. Randall 1990, *Money and Credit in Capitalist Economies*, Cheltenham: Edward Elgar.

Wriston, Walter 1992, *The Twilight of Sovereignty* 1992, New York: Charles Scribners Sons.

Wood, Ellen 1996, 'The Future of Money', interview with Thomas Bass, *Wired*, October, available at <www.wired.com/wired/archives/4.10/wriston.html>

Index

HISTORICAL MATERIALISM BOOK SERIES

ISSN 1570–1522

1. ARTHUR, C.J. The New Dialectic and Marx's *Capital*. ISBN 90 04 12798 4 (2002, hardcover), 90 04 13643 6 (2004, paperback)
2. LÖWY, M. The Theory of Revolution in the Young Marx. 2003. ISBN 90 04 12901 4
3. CALLINICOS, A. Making History. Agency, Structure, and Change in Social Theory. 2004. ISBN 90 04 13627 4
4. DAY, R.B. Pavel V. Maksakovsky: The Capitalist Cycle. An Essay on the Marxist Theory of the Cycle. Translated with Introduction and Commentary. 2004. ISBN 90 04 13824 2
5. BROUÉ, P. The German Revolution, 1917-1923. 2005. ISBN 90 04 13940 0
6. MIÉVILLE, C. Between Equal Rights. A Marxist Theory of International Law. 2005. ISBN 90 04 13134 5
7. BEAUMONT, M. Utopia Ltd. Ideologies of Social Dreaming in England 1870-1900. 2005. ISBN 90 04 14296 7
8. KIELY, R. The Clash of Globalisations. Neo-Liberalism, the Third Way and Anti-Globalisation. 2005. ISBN 90 04 14318 1
9. LIH, L.T. Lenin Rediscovered: *What Is to Be Done?* in Context. 2006. ISBN 90 04 13120 5
10. SMITH, T. Globalisation. A Systematic Marxian Account. 2006. ISBN 90 04 14727 6
11. BURKETT, P. Marxism and Ecological Economics. Toward a Red and Green Political Economy. 2006. ISBN 90 04 14810 8

.

www.ingramcontent.com/pod-product-compliance
Lightning Source LLC
Chambersburg PA
CBHW022133020426
42334CB00015B/881